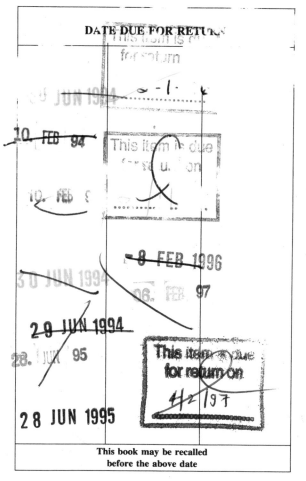

Consciousness

B

READINGS IN MIND AND LANGUAGE

Consciousness

Psychological and Philosophical Essays

Edited by
Martin Davies and
Glyn W. Humphreys

BLACKWELL
Oxford UK & Cambridge USA

Copyright © Basil Blackwell Ltd 1993

First published 1993

Blackwell Publishers
108 Cowley Road
Oxford OX4 1JF
UK

238 Main Street, Suite 501
Cambridge, Massachusetts 02142
USA

British Library Cataloguing in Publication Data

A CIP catalogue record for this book is available from the British Library.

Library of Congress Cataloging-in-Publication Data

Consciousness : psychological and philosophical essays / edited by
  Martin Davies and Glyn W. Humphreys.
    p.   cm. – (Readings in mind and language; 2)
  Includes bibliographical references and index.
  ISBN 0–631–18563–1 (alk. paper). – ISBN 0–631–18564–X (pbk. :
alk. paper)
    1. Consciousness. I. Davies, Martin, 1950– . II. Humphreys,
Glyn W.   III. Series.
BF311.C656 1993
126 – dc20

92–25223
CIP

Typeset in 9$^{1}/_{2}$ on 11 pt Palatino
by Graphicraft Typesetters Ltd, Hong Kong
Printed in Great Britain by TJ Press Ltd., Padstow, Cornwall

This book is printed on acid-free paper

Contents

vi *Contents*

List of Contributors

KATHLEEN A. AKINS   Xerox PARC, 3333 Coyote Hill Road, Palo Alto, CA 94304

JOHN I. BIRO   Department of Philosophy, University of Florida, Gainesville, FL 32611

MARTIN DAVIES   Department of Experimental Psychology, South Parks Road, Oxford OX1 3UD

EDWARD H. F. DE HAAN   Department of Psychonomics, Utrecht University, P.O. Box 80.140, 3508 TC Utrecht, The Netherlands

ANTHONY DICKINSON   Department of Experimental Psychology, University of Cambridge, Downing Street, Cambridge CB2 3EB

CECILIA HEYES   Department of Psychology, University College London, Gower Street, London WC1E 6BT

GLYN W. HUMPHREYS   Cognitive Science Research Centre, School of Psychology, University of Birmingham, Edgbaston, Birmingham B15 2TT

COLLEEN M. KELLEY   Department of Psychology, Macalesler College, 1600 Grand Avenue, St. Paul, MN 55105

LARRY L. JACOBY   Department of Psychology, McMaster University, Hamilton, Ontario L8S 4K1, Canada

JOSEPH LEVINE   Department of Philosophy and Religion, School of Humanities and Social Sciences, North Carolina State University, Box 8103 Raleigh, NC 27695-8103

COLIN McGINN   Philosophy Department, Davison Hall, Douglass Campus, Rutgers University, New Brunswick, NJ 08903

PHILIP M. MERIKLE   Department of Psychology, University of Waterloo, Waterloo, Ontario N2L 3G1, Canada

NORTON NELKIN   Department of Philosophy, University of New Orleans, New Orleans, LA 70148

KEITH OATLEY   Centre for Applied Cognitive Science, Ontario Institute for Studies in Education, 252 Bloor Street West, Toronto M5S 1V6, Canada

EYAL M. REINGOLD   Department of Psychology, Erindale College, University of Toronto, Mississauga, Ontario L5L 1C6, Canada

GEORGES REY   Department of Philosophy, University of Maryland, College Park, MD 20742

DAVID M. ROSENTHAL   PhD Program in Philosophy, CUNY Graduate Center, 33 West 42nd Street, New York, NY 10036-8099

ROBERT VAN GULICK   Department of Philosophy, Syracuse University, Syracuse, NY 13244-1170

ANDREW W. YOUNG   Department of Psychology, Science Laboratories, Durham University, Durham DH1 3LE

Acknowledgements

This book, the second in the series of Mind and Language Readers, grew out of a Special Issue of *Mind and Language* (volume 5, number 1, spring 1990) on Approaches to Consciousness and Intention. The five psychological essays here are reprinted from that Special Issue, sometimes with modest revisions. The eight philosophical essays are all new for this book. We are grateful, as always, to Rosalind Barrs for her secretarial assistance.

Introduction

MARTIN DAVIES AND GLYN W. HUMPHREYS

Consciousness is, perhaps, the aspect of our mental lives that is the most perplexing, for both psychologists and philosophers. The *Macmillan Dictionary of Psychology* contains as its entry for *consciousness*: 'the having of perceptions, thoughts, and feelings; awareness. The term is impossible to define except in terms that are unintelligible without a grasp of what consciousness means' (Sutherland, 1989, p. 90). On the side of philosophy, Daniel Dennett notes in *The Oxford Companion to the Mind* that consciousness 'is both the most obvious and the most mysterious feature of our minds' (Gregory, 1987, p. 160); and Thomas Nagel famously remarks (1974, p. 166), 'Without consciousness the mind–body problem would be much less interesting. With consciousness it seems hopeless.'

These remarks might suggest that consciousness – indefinable and mysterious – falls outside the scope of rational enquiry, defying both scientific and philosophical investigation. But, in fact, the topic spans the history of psychology from William James until the present; and the past fifteen or twenty years have also seen an upsurge of philosophical interest in the place of consciousness in the natural order.

Consciousness in Psychology

The classic view of James (1890) was of consciousness as an organ, necessary to prevent 'buzzing chaos', given the plethora of stimuli in the environment and the multitude of different behaviours that may be addressed to them. Freud (1953b) – *contra* the dictionary definition of intention as 'having a conscious aim' – proposed that behaviour could be determined by both conscious and unconscious intentions, but that incompatible intentions need to be conscious in order to be resolved.

During the reign of the behaviourists, mention of either consciousness or intention was deeply unpopular. However, with the resurgence of the New Look in psychology (see Bruner and Postman, 1949), experimental work on the topic became respectable again, with much research focused on the issue of whether stimuli that subjects were not aware of could nevertheless be 'perceived'. That is, the research focused on whether responses could be differentially affected by the category or nature of stimuli presented below some measured threshold of conscious perception (e.g. the minimal exposure needed for subjects to report that the stimulus was present).

Yet more recently still, attempts have been made to account for consciousness in information-processing terms. For example, Shallice (1972) proposed that consciousness corresponds to the input that determines the currently dominant thought, or alternatively that it reflects the operation of a central 'supervisory system' that has access to the outputs of perceptual systems but cannot penetrate the perceptual systems themselves (Norman and Shallice, 1986; Shallice, 1988).

The Need for a Psychological Theory of Consciousness and Intention

Why should consciousness and intention attract such long-standing and continuing interest? One reason is that consciousness is, as Dennett remarked, such an obvious feature of our minds: consciousness exists as an intrinsic characteristic of our everyday experience. The interplay between intended and (apparently) unintended behaviour is also part of common experience – as in well-known cases of 'slips of action'. For example, William James noted the occasion of going upstairs to change and finding that he had climbed into bed instead – an example of intended behaviour being overridden by some environmental signal (see Reason, 1979). In lay terms, our behaviour in such instances is typically described in terms of consciousness and intention. On occasions when people find themselves doing an action other than that they intended they may speak of 'something catching their attention' and of it 'taking what they meant to do from their mind'. Theories devoted to explaining such incidents need to concern themselves with issues of consciousness and intention.

Again, consider the theory of the control of action put forward by Shallice and his colleagues (Norman and Shallice, 1986; Shallice, 1988). In this theory, stimuli – particular external or even internal events, like thoughts – activate so-called 'contention schedules'. These schedules comprise learned stimulus–action routines. There is competition between the many contention schedules that could be activated at any one time, with one being dominant. (Quite why just one should be dominant is an issue we return to shortly.) The outcome of this competition is determined not just by stimulus-driven activation, but also by top-down activation from a separate supervisory system. The supervisory system acts to maintain goal-states, and does so by respectively activating and inhibiting appropriate and inappropriate contention schedules. It follows that the control of action is dependent on a fine balance between separate processing systems and between stimulus-based and goal-based events. A goal may be overridden if there is a strong stimulus–action link, even if the action is inappropriate in the context. Similarly, inappropriate actions may be inhibited when there is a well-maintained goal.

A theory such as this can readily be applied to explaining phenomena such as action slips. It predicts, correctly (Reason, 1979), that action slips are likely when a subject is confronted by a stimulus that routinely evokes a given action, and when a goal is poorly maintained (e.g. when the subject is tired or distracted). Given its applicability to everyday situations, where notions such as consciousness (being aware that an inappropriate object 'grabbed our attention') and intention ('I hadn't intended to do it!') are used descriptively, such a theory can be conceived as being concerned with consciousness and intentional behaviour. Indeed, it starts to flesh out an account of consciousness in terms of processing mechanisms, and, once armed with this, distinctions between different kinds of consciousness become possible. There may be a difference between consciousness of a stimulus that determines a dominant contention schedule, and consciousness of the intended behaviour. These two forms of consciousness may respectively be linked to the stimulus driving the dominant contention schedule and to the contents of the supervisory system. In the theory, contention schedules and the supervisory system are separate; they can be influenced by different variables, show different developmental rates, be differentially localized within the brain and so forth. An animal, or even a machine, with one mechanism but not the other may achieve consciousness of just one particular kind. Psychological theories of everyday events that are described using the language of consciousness and intention provide a means for clarifying the different processes involved. We shall see that it is also useful to distinguish different forms of consciousness to elucidate different philosophical treatments of the subject. In that context we begin by distinguishing *phenomenal* consciousness from *access* consciousness (see p. 10 below). We leave open the question of the relation between these philosophical distinctions and psychological distinctions such as that between a dominant contention schedule and a supervisory system.

Psychological Theory as the Glove that Fits

A second, and perhaps more important, reason for continued psychological interest in the topic of consciousness is that psychological theory may provide the appropriate level of description for explanations of conscious thought and intentional behaviour. In particular, it may be that information-processing accounts, couched in terms of a functional architecture of knowledge representations and transcoding algorithms, can be linked to conscious and intentional thought in a way that accounts couched at a physiological or perhaps even a microcognitive level cannot (see Shallice, 1988, for this argument). That is, information-processing accounts may provide the appropriate descriptors to explain moves among beliefs, goals and intentions, states which are intuitively *about* the world. This may be so, even if this kind of psychological account cannot fully explain the 'what it is like' aspect of conscious experience that prompted Nagel's remark about the hopelessness of the mind–body problem.

This argument, that psychological theory is the glove that fits for questions of consciousness and intentional behaviour, is not accepted universally. Crick and Koch (1990), for instance, have suggested a neurobiological account of visual awareness in which such awareness is based on semi-synchronous temporal oscillation patterns between neurons in the neocortex. Cells within the cortex respond to different properties of visual patterns – to colour, shape, depth, motion and so forth. If the cells that are activated by a particular object have a synchronized firing rate, then the different properties of the object can be bound together, even though different cell populations are involved. This notion has several attractive properties. For instance, if only a few oscillation patterns can be maintained without interference, a limitation naturally emerges on the number of objects that we can be aware of at one time (see above). The notion of synchronized oscillations also provides one solution to the difficult question of how the different properties of visual objects are bound together.

But is this a general account of consciousness? This seems unlikely. The momentary binding together of visual features, characteristic of visual awareness, seems quite different from the long-term maintenance of an intended goal-state, or the verbal description of a set of events. There is, for example, no neurobiological reason to think that verbal descriptions are linked to synchronized temporal oscillations in the visual cortex, even should good evidence for such oscillations exist. In addition, the limitations on human performance do not solely reflect the number of objects that may be present in a scene but also the number of actions possible and the relations between the actions (e.g. Allport, 1987). Again, we are drawn to a distinction between different aspects of consciousness. Transitory visual awareness may be one thing; intentioned, conscious choice of action another. Psychological theories, if they are valid, need to make appropriate distinctions between these different states. The special explanatory status of psychological theories, however, may apply only to some aspects of conscious behaviour.

But Does It Do Anything?

Psychologists are concerned – some may say preoccupied – with measurement. For any concept to be useful to psychological theory, the concept must do something: it must lead to predictions with behavioural consequences. Thus one, if not the, major issue faced by psychologists interested in these topics is this: if consciousness is to play an operational role within an information-processing theory (and not simply to be 'epiphenomenal'), then consciousness needs to have some functional effect on processing. Processes that are conscious need to differ in some way from those that are unconscious. Were this not the case, psychological theory need not be concerned with the topic.

This brings us to a third reason for the recent resurgence of interest in the topic: the existence of new means of making empirical distinctions between conscious and unconscious processes, and thus new means for assessing whether these processes do lead to differing behavioural consequences. The work of Marcel (e.g. 1983a) was influential here. Marcel conducted experiments using a technique called visual masking. In this technique a visual target stimulus, presented for a short period, is followed by a second, masking stimulus. The effect of the mask is to disrupt the identification of the target stimulus. Under some circumstances, masking can be so severe that people perform at chance level when asked to decide whether *any* target stimulus was presented. Marcel used a level of masking such that people were close to chance at deciding whether any target was present. He then followed the mask by another word, which was clearly presented, and subjects made a response to this word. This second word could be related or unrelated in meaning to the first. Surprisingly, responses to the second word were faster when the first, masked word was related than when it was unrelated. The first word 'primed' the second on the basis of their having related meanings, even though subjects failed to report that the first word was present. Apparently, information about the meaning of the first word could be extracted unconsciously. By examining the effects of masked items on responses to other stimuli, experimenters are provided with a new technique for probing the kinds of stimulus coding that take place unconsciously. Comparisons can also be made between priming from stimuli masked so that they cannot be detected and priming from clearly presented stimuli that can be consciously reported. Hence the question of whether consciousness has some functional purpose can begin to be assessed.

The Psychological Essays

The five psychological essays in this book have in common a concern with functional effects of consciousness on behaviour. The first essay (chapter 1), by Reingold and Merikle, focuses on the issue of perception without awareness. Despite the burst of research on this question fostered by Marcel's (1983a) experiments – and, predating that, work on the so-called New Look in psychology – the area remains controversial. Claims for perception without awareness typically depend on the demonstration that behaviour can be influenced by the categorical nature of a stimulus presented below some objectively measured threshold of conscious awareness (e.g. Dixon, 1981; Marcel, 1983a). However, such demonstrations have been subject to strong criticism (Eriksen, 1960; Merikle, 1982; Purcell et al., 1983). For instance, were sufficient trials used to establish that the threshold for awareness was validly set? Alternative approaches are needed.

Reingold and Merikle discuss two such alternatives. One stresses the contrast between direct measures of stimulus detection and indirect measures of stimulus processing (that reflect the effects of the stimulus on another task that does not make reference to stimulus detection). For instance, an investigator might be interested in the contrast between the ability to judge whether a brief stimulus has been presented (a direct measure of conscious perception), and that item's effect on responses to a subsequent supra-threshold stimulus (an indirect measure of the processing carried out on the sub-threshold stimulus). Priming represents one example of this.

The second alternative is concerned with *qualitative* differences in processing according to whether a subject is consciously aware of a stimulus. Such qualitative differences reflect a functional change in processing when stimuli are consciously perceived. An experiment reported by Marcel (1980) illustrates this point (cf. Swinney, 1979). When subjects in an experiment are given related pairs of words (such as *bank* and *money*), responses to the second word can be facilitated relative to when the words are unrelated. However, the beneficial effect of the first word can be eliminated if the word is polysemous, and if its other (inappropriate) meaning is biased by a pre-ceding context (e.g. *river, bank, money*). The context seems to inhibit one of the meanings of the polysemous word. Marcel (1980) showed that this is not true when the polysemous word is presented sub-threshold. Under sub-threshold conditions, the polysemous word facilitates responses to the second word irrespective of the preceding context. Thus the contextually inappropriate meaning of a polysemous word may only be inhibited when subjects are conscious that the word has been presented. The search for qualitative differences between the processing of stimuli that subjects are or are not aware of provides one approach towards defining a functional role for consciousness in behaviour.

A somewhat different approach is outlined in chapter 2 by Young and de Haan, who are concerned with neuropsychological disturbances of conscious processing. In rare cases, neurological damage can impair the ability of people to be conscious of certain types of information. Perhaps the best known ex-ample of this is *blindsight* (e.g. Weiskrantz, 1986), where people with damage to the primary visual cortex show discriminatory responses to visual stimuli that they claim no conscious awareness of. This is sometimes spoken of in broad terms as demonstrating that visual perception can occur unconsciously. However, this misses some of the subtlety of the syndrome. Patients with blind-sight show the ability to discriminate some visual properties (e.g. for stimu-lus location, motion and orientation), but by no means all the properties that the same patients can discriminate in sighted parts of their visual fields (and, in particular, there seems to be no discrimination of form). That is, there appears to be a qualitative difference between the properties discriminated in the 'blind' and sighted parts of the field. Another example of a qualitative difference between conscious and unconscious processing seems apparent.

Yet again, though, it is wise to be prudent in our conclusions concerning such patients. It is possible to claim that the qualitative processing differences exhibited by blindsight patients may be best explained in terms of selective impairments of processes specialized for handling different types of visual information (e.g. for form but not, say, motion); the qualitative differences need not reflect functional properties endowed by virtue of processes being conscious, it is simply the case that consciousness is tied to form perception (this may say something interesting about conscious perception, or it may be a mere epiphenomenon; at this stage the question is unresolved).

Blindsight is by no means the only example where neurological damage can alter a patient's conscious knowledge of the world, while that knowledge would still appear to exist (unconsciously) providing it is tested *covertly* (e.g. using tasks that do not require the patient knowingly to draw on the knowledge). Covert knowledge may exist in patients demonstrating neglect of stimuli on the side of space contralateral to the site of the lesion, in patients who experience no familiarity for familiar faces, in patients with amnesia, and so forth. The evidence on covert knowledge following neurological damage is covered by Young and de Haan. They argue that, at least in some patients, there is specific damage to the mechanisms dealing with conscious awareness for particular types of information, although the *processing* of that same information can be intact. Since such patients are typically very impaired in everyday life, we can conclude that the mechanisms responsible for conscious awareness do play an important, indeed vital, functional role in behaviour. From the evidence reviewed by Young and de Haan, it is possible to suggest that there is no single mechanism responsible for conscious awareness (cf. Norman and Shallice, 1986; Schacter et al., 1988), but rather separate mechanisms tied to particular stimulus characteristics (e.g. for face recognition, for language, for autobiographical memory, and so on).

One way in which the behaviour of patients with covert knowledge is abnormal is that they act in a overly 'data-driven' way. An amnesic patient will gradually become more fluent at playing a piano piece from a written manuscript (in the classic example, this improvement would take place alongside a complete lack of awareness that the piece had even been encountered before). However, what if the manuscript had a misprint, so that the patient became more fluent at playing a sequence of wrong notes? On hearing the piece played correctly, and being told that this is indeed the piece that she had learned, such a patient would be most unlikely to make the connection between the piece played correctly and their own incorrect rendition. Given the manuscript again, she would likely continue to play the piece incorrectly. In contrast, normal subjects who have conscious recognition that the piece they heard is the same as the piece they have learned to play (incorrectly) may be able to make the adjustment to their own future performances. In such an instance, having conscious recollection would enable a new connection to be made between the piece as heard and the piece as seen: consciousness would be instrumental in the adaptation of the organism to its environment.

This last point is taken up here by Kelley and Jacoby (chapter 3). However, they propose that conscious recollection *per se* is not instrumental in determining a person's behaviour. Indeed, they hold that conscious recollection itself emerges from inferences made on the basis of data-driven 'cues', such as the ease with which a piece is played following practice, or the perceived quality of the same piece when heard again. However, the experience of conscious recollection is thought to be a prerequisite for intentional action, and it is intentional action that enables people not to operate in an overly data-driven way (unintended actions being stimulus-driven phenomena, as in the example of William James's action slip discussed earlier). Kelley and Jacoby's argument concerning the construction of conscious memories is given support by clever experiments where normal subjects are tricked into illusory recollections by manipulating the ease with which they perceive stimuli.

Kelley and Jacoby's chapter illustrates some of the ways in which experimental psychologists are attempting to operationalize the notion of intention in order to provide a wider, and in many ways more realistic, account of memory than found within static, 'boxes and arrows' models of information processing. Oatley (in chapter 4) proposes that the first attempt to develop a psychology of intention dates back to Freud, and Freud's interest in the role of unconscious intentions in behaviour. It almost goes without saying that much of Freud's work has proved unpalatable for many cognitive psychologists, interested as they are in establishing models of the mind based on replicable experimentation (though see Wegman, 1985). Oatley's chapter tries to redress the balance. One interesting point concerns the relations between psychoanalysis and the interpretation of narratives given by current computational models; such models may provide an explicit account of the putative processing mechanisms involved in interpreting the behaviour of a client from the narrative they give when undergoing psychotherapy. They may also provide an explicit account of the role of intention in behaviour.

One question that may be asked at this juncture concerns the relation between consciousness as discussed by Freud, pertaining to a kind of personal consciousness that each person has of his or her own autobiographical history, conscious intentions, and so forth, and the kind of perceptual consciousness (awareness) of perceived stimuli discussed in the chapters by Reingold and Merikle, and Young and de Haan. Are we dealing with two very different beasts, which bear no relation to each other? One possible answer to this question is that perceptual consciousness of events is itself a prerequisite for the incorporation of those events into an accurate conscious autobiographical history. Indeed, this is suggested by some of the work discussed by Kelley and Jacoby. For instance, subjects can be duped into forming illusory memories when the identification of visual stimuli is primed by the earlier presentation of the stimuli below the subjective threshold for conscious perception. When subjects do not have perceptual consciousness of the earlier occurrence of a stimulus, they are unable to make an accurate inference concerning the ease of perceptual identification they then experience. Hence they infer (incorrectly) that the stimulus must have been consciously seen earlier, and form an inaccurate autobiographical (personal) memory.

One final question concerns the extent to which intentional thought and action are particular to humans. If conscious intentional thought allows people to make new connections between pieces of previously learned knowledge (see above), then it may constitute a crucial component in our problem-solving ability, marking a qualitative advance on non-human animals. Linked to this proposal is the argument that conscious intentional thought is associated with activity in the frontal lobes, the evolutionarily youngest part of the brain (e.g. Shallice, 1988). The last of the psychological chapters, by Heyes and Dickinson, discusses the problems involved in inferring intentional action in non-human primates. They present a convincing argument that proof of intentional action cannot be gained from observational studies alone; rather, experimental intervention is required. They go on to argue that the presence of intention has been established by experimentation, though there are a minimal number of relevant studies. The experiments they discuss illustrate one way in which empirical research can address the issues of consciousness and intention, and are thus relevant to human as well as animal research.

These five chapters show that psychological interest in consciousness continues unabated, and that new experimental techniques are enabling issues to be uncovered in exciting ways. Future work using these techniques will provide an increasingly accurate understanding of the role of consciousness in behaviour.

Consciousness in Philosophy

One idea about consciousness that has captured the philosophical imagination is that, while there is nothing that it is like to be a brick, or an ink-jet printer, there is, presumably, something that it is like to be a bat, or a dolphin; and there is certainly something that it is like to be a human being. A system – whether creature or artefact – is conscious just in case there is something that it is like to be that system (Nagel, 1974, p. 166): 'an organism has conscious mental states if and only if there is something that it is like to *be* that organism – something it is like *for* the organism.' Likewise, we can say that a state of a system is a conscious state if and only if there is something that it is like, for the system, to be in that state. In our own mental lives, perceptual and sensational states seem to be the clearest candidates – seeing a bottle of red wine on a white tablecloth, feeling an itch, a pain, or a tickle. Such experiences have an intrinsic subjective, or phenomenal, character.

This subjective character of experience is, intuitively, something that is accessible in a privileged way 'from the inside'. The subject of perceptual and sensational experiences is in a peculiarly authoritative position to make judgements about those experiences. But, privileged first-person introspective access does not seem to be restricted to experiences. Many philosophers hold that we are also in an especially authoritative position to pronounce upon our own thoughts – our beliefs and intentions, for example. Consequently, it is tempting to group experiences and thoughts together as conscious states. Certainly, it is natural to describe both seeings and tickles, on the one hand, and beliefs and intentions, on the other, as components in our conscious mental lives.

However, this tempting assimilation has an unattractive consequence; namely, that the idea of an unconscious belief or intention becomes just as problematic as the idea of an unconscious pain or tickle. It may be that, at the end of the day, we shall be obliged to recognize the existence of unfelt sensations. But, it is not an obviously contradictory or incoherent idea that we might want to reject the category of unconscious pains or tickles, without also placing the whole Freudian strand of empirical psychology under a cloud.

Arguably, the classification of experiences and thoughts together is, in any case, too simple. Our privileged access to thoughts is, to a first approximation, a matter of the contents of our beliefs and intentions being available for verbal report (Fodor, 1983, p. 56). Beliefs and intentions are states with semantic content, or aboutness; and a normal adult human being can express the contents of those states in a public language. The case of sensations – pains or tickles – seems to be rather different, since it is not clear that they have any semantic content at all. And, while perceptual experiences do have semantic content – they present the world to the subject as being a certain way – it is far from obvious that they have the same kind of content, or have content in the same way, as thoughts.

Some Distinctions: Phenomenal Consciousness and Access Consciousness

We shall have more room for theoretical manoeuvre if we make some distinctions. As a first step, we can distinguish between *phenomenal* consciousness and *access* consciousness (cf. Block, 1991, forthcoming). Phenomenal consciousness – the 'something that it is like' notion to which Nagel draws attention – applies most directly to sensations and other experiences. Access consciousness – the idea, roughly, of availability of content for verbal report – applies most directly to thoughts. On the face of it, these two notions seem to be relatively independent of each other. On the one hand, it is natural to suppose that there can be sensations without thoughts; there can be phenomenal consciousness without access consciousness. On the other hand, it is very plausible that a system may be capable of information processing and of language production, although there is nothing that it is like to be that system. Such a system would exhibit nothing of phenomenal consciousness, but a good part of what is involved in the idea of access consciousness.

Then, second, we can make some distinctions within the cluster of notions that are included in the initial rough idea of access consciousness. As a preliminary, however, we need to clarify the notion of access itself.

As we have already noted, access consciousness applies most straightforwardly to states that have semantic content; as we have sketched the idea so far, it consists in the availability of that content for verbal report. So, suppose that a subject is in some state with the semantic content that *p*. Imagine, perhaps, that this is an information-processing state; the information processing might be going on within the subject's visual system, or language-processing system, for example. Now, the question whether the subject is herself capable of verbally reporting that *p*, or of reporting that one or another system is registering the information that *p*, is clearly not what is crucial for access consciousness. For the subject might be able to say those things even though the state with the content that *p* is intuitively not one to which access consciousness applies; she might be able to say those things in virtue of being a theorist of vision, or of language processing, for example. We need to tighten up the notion of availability for report. What matters for access consciousness is whether, *simply in virtue of being in the state* with the semantic content that *p*, the subject is able to report that *p*, or to report that she is in a state with that content.

So construed, availability of content for report is plausibly a sufficient condition for access consciousness. But it is not so plausibly a necessary condition. For, when a verbal report actually occurs, it is intuitively a contingent effect of something more fundamental; namely, the subject's *judging* that *p* (or, more generally, thinking or entertaining the thought that *p*), or judging that she is in a state with the content that *p*. So, we are led to the following idea. A state with the semantic content that *p* is an access-conscious state of the subject if and only if the subject is capable, simply in virtue of being in that state, (a) of judging (or otherwise thinking) that *p*, or (b) of judging that she is in that state.

Given that preliminary clarification of the notion of access, we now need to separate out the two candidates – (a) and (b) – for the judgement that the subject is supposed to be able to make, yielding two different branches along which to pursue the initial idea of access consciousness.

Consider, on the one hand, the notion of a state with the semantic content that *p*, which is such that if the subject is in that state, then she is *ipso facto* capable of judging, or otherwise thinking, that *p*. Since thinking involves the deployment of concepts, what we have here is not very far away from the notion of a state whose semantic content is already conceptualized by the subject of that state (in contrast to a state with non-conceptual content). A subject who, being a theoretical linguist, *believes* that anaphors are bound in their governing category deploys – and therefore must possess – the concept of anaphor and of governing category. In contrast, a subject who, being an ordinary speaker, tacitly knows or *cognizes* (Chomsky, 1980, p. 69) that anaphors are bound in their governing category does not need to possess those concepts.

Thus, along this first branch, case (a), the idea of access consciousness leads us quite rapidly to the distinction between conceptualized and non-conceptual content; that is, roughly speaking, the distinction between beliefs and subdoxastic states (Stich, 1978), or between the special kind of intentionality that is characteristic of propositional attitude states and the varieties of aboutness or semanticity that are appropriate to other content-bearing states.

Consider now, on the other hand, the notion of a state with the semantic content that p, which is such that if the subject is in that state, then she is *ipso facto* capable of judging that she is in that state. Since judging involves the use of concepts, if a state is to meet this condition just as it stands then it must be impossible for a subject to be in a state of this type – say, a belief – without having the concept of this type of mental state: the concept of belief. Rather than pursue the question whether there are any types of mental state that meet this strict requirement, we can consider a slightly weaker notion. This is the notion of a state with the semantic content that p, which is such that if the subject possesses the concept of that type of state then she is capable of judging that she is in that state.

If we focus on the idea of first-person authority, then it is surely very plausible that if a subject possesses the concept of belief (a type of state) and is in the state of believing that p (a particular state of that type), then the subject is capable of judging that she is in the state of believing that p. (At least, this seems right for what we would intuitively regard as conscious beliefs.) In contrast, a subject could very well have the concept of a state of tacit knowledge embodied in the language faculty (a type of state), and be in the state of tacitly knowing that anaphors are bound in their governing category (a particular state of that type), without thereby being in a position to judge that she is in the state of tacitly knowing that anaphors are bound in their governing category.

Pursuing the idea of access consciousness along this second branch, case (b), we thus have another distinction that classifies (conscious) belief states on one side and states of tacit knowledge, for example, on the other. But two further cases deserve mention: the case of sensations and the case of perceptual experiences.

Suppose that a subject is in a state that does not have any semantic content at all: say, a state of pain. Then, if the subject possesses the concept of the type of mental state – in this case, the concept of pain – then she is in a position to judge that she is in that state, to judge, that is, that she is in pain. This is a kind of limiting case of the notion of access consciousness that we are considering.

The case of perceptual experiences is rather more complicated. Suppose that a subject is in a visual perceptual state which presents the world as containing a red cube 4 ft in front of her, and that the subject possesses the concept of a visual experience. Is this state access conscious on the present criterion? The answer depends upon whether we accept that perceptual states have a kind of non-conceptual semantic content. If we insist that the semantic content of an experience is always conceptualized content – so that we do not accept the idea of non-conceptual representational content for experiences – then perceptual states will be classified as access-conscious states, just as beliefs are. If, on the other hand, we do accept this distinct category of content, then we shall say that the subject who has the experience will not *ipso facto* be in a position to judge that she is having a visual experience that represents a red cube 4 ft in front of her; for she might not possess the concept of a cube, or the concept of being red, for example. In that case, perceptual experiences will not be classified as access-conscious states, given the criterion as we have stated it so far.

The viability of the notion of non-conceptual content is not our concern here, but it is worth briefly noting that we might be able to modify the notion of access consciousness so as to include even perceptual experiences with non-conceptual content. The idea would be to say something like this. A state with the semantic content that *p* is an access-conscious state of the subject if and only if, provided that the subject possesses the concept of that type of state (say, a visual perceptual experience) *and possesses the concepts used in specifying the content of the state* (the concept of a cube and the concept of being red, for example) then the subject is able, in virtue of being in that state, to judge that she is in that state. This is a more inclusive notion of access consciousness, but it still excludes states of tacit knowledge, for example. A theoretical linguist is no more able to make judgements about her states of tacit knowledge simply in virtue of being in those states than is an ordinary speaker.

Leaving aside these possible adjustments, we can say that, along this second branch, the idea of access consciousness leads to a distinction that has belief states and (by extension to a limiting case) sensations on one side, and subdoxastic information-processing states on the other side. The distinction concerns the subject's ability to make a judgement about the state – to the effect that she is in the state – provided only that she possesses the concept of the type of state in question. The status, with respect to this distinction, of perceptual states depends upon further issues.

When we first introduced the distinction between phenomenal consciousness and access consciousness, we said that phenomenal consciousness applies most directly to sensations and other experiences, while access consciousness applies most directly to thoughts or beliefs. We have now allowed the extension of the notion of access consciousness to sensations; but this is not to obliterate the difference between the two notions. On the contrary, they still seem to be relatively independent of each other. Even though, in the normal case, both notions may apply to sensations – and perhaps to other states, too – it would be a substantial and controversial piece of philosophical theory to claim that the 'something that it is like' to have a sensation is nothing other than a kind of access consciousness. We shall return to this kind of claim below (see p. 23).

Elusiveness and Demystification

Having made the initial distinction between phenomenal consciousness and access consciousness, and having pursued the idea of access consciousness along two different branches, we now have *three* theoretical notions in play. There is (a) the notion of phenomenal consciousness; there is (b) the notion of a state with conceptualized semantic content (that is, the notion of a state with the kind of intentionality that is characteristic of propositional attitudes like belief); and there is (c) the notion of a state which is such that, provided only that the subject possesses the concept of that type of state, she is in a position to judge that she is in that state. The notions (b) and (c) both arose from an initial idea of access consciousness, contrasted with phenomenal consciousness; but since we have the term 'intentionality' available as a label for the notion (b), we can now use 'access consciousness' as a label just for the notion (c).

It is the notion (a) of phenomenal consciousness that is the focus of attention for those philosophers who stress the theoretical elusiveness of consciousness. To the extent that the other two notions carry an air of mystery about them, it is largely inherited from phenomenal consciousness.

Thus, consider the notion (b) of a state with conceptualized semantic content – with intentionality, in the fullest sense of that term. There certainly are philosophical puzzles about the intentionality of beliefs. Despite the availability of various theories of aboutness – causal theories, teleological theories, functional role theories – there is no accepted analysis of this notion. In part, these puzzles about the intentionality of beliefs concern the place of normativity in the natural order. How are we to understand the idea that something may be the *right* thing to believe – what one *ought* to believe – in certain circumstances? But, in large part also, puzzles are produced by the connection between the conceptualized contents of beliefs and our perceptual experience. For the ways in which we think about objects and properties in the world – the modes of presentation of objects and properties – are fundamentally furnished by our perceptual contact with those items. Such mystery as attaches to the notion of perceptual experience is thus inherited by the intentionality of beliefs. Consequently, that latter notion partly defies a fully satisfying theoretical account (McGinn, 1988; Searle, 1989, 1990b).

The flow of mystery then continues on to the third notion (c). To be sure, there is nothing especially elusive about the idea of states of a system that contain information about other states of the same system; this is just the idea of a self-monitoring system. But, the third notion involves, not merely the idea of second-order information, but the idea of judgement, and with it the ideas of thought, and belief. So, to the extent that these latter notions are mysterious, so also is the third notion: the notion of an access-conscious state. Elusiveness trickles down from phenomenal consciousness to access consciousness, via the notion of intentionality.

But, where some philosophers see a trickle-down of elusiveness, there are others who see the opportunity for a bold project of demystification. Give or take the problem of normativity, the notions of intentionality (b) and of thoughts about mental states (c) are unmysterious apart from what they inherit of the mystery of phenomenal consciousness (a). So, perhaps the tables can be turned, and a demystified reconstruction of phenomenal consciousness can be offered in terms of those relatively better understood notions. Philosophers whose project is to demystify consciousness in this way could agree that such a reconstruction is liable to be only partial; for the demystification project could include arguments to the effect that the unreconstructed residue of the notion of phenomenal consciousness is shot through with confusion, and even incoherence.

Arguments for the theoretical elusiveness of phenomenal consciousness, on the one hand, and arguments for demystification, on the other, constitute two major strands in recent philosophical work on the topic of consciousness. For most of the remainder of this section we shall be concerned with arguments about phenomenal consciousness that culminate in an announcement of mystery. But later – and against that background – we shall return to the prospects for programmes of demystification.

The Elusiveness of Phenomenal Consciousness

Nagel (1974) not only set the notion of phenomenal consciousness in the forefront of philosophical attention; he advanced an argument for its elusiveness. In particular, he argued that the subjective, or phenomenal, properties of experience elude a physicalist view of the world:

> If physicalism is to be defended, the phenomenological features must themselves be given a physical account. But when we examine their subjective character it seems that such a result is impossible. The reason is that every subjective phenomenon is essentially connected with a single point of view, and it seems inevitable that an objective, physical theory will abandon that point of view. (Nagel, 1974, p. 176)

Clearly, the idea of a point of view is crucial to Nagel's argument; and intuitively the idea could be construed in more than one way. We might, for example, take a point of view to be something that is private to an individual; but this is not the notion that Nagel uses. He is concerned with a type: something that is shared by many individuals in virtue of their having similar perceptual systems.

A point of view constitutes a kind of limitation upon what is conceivable for an individual. Since experience furnishes the raw materials for imagination, there may be some aspects of the world that are beyond the imaginative reach of creatures with one point of view, but within the imaginative reach of creatures with a different point of view. As a plausible example – '[t]he most widely cited and influential thought experiment about consciousness' (Dennett, 1991, p. 441) – Nagel offers the suggestion that the 'specific subjective character' of a bat's experience might be 'beyond our ability to conceive' (1974, p. 170). On the other hand, we can, of course, conceive of, think about and talk about the character of our own, and each other's, experience.

The accessibility of facts about the subjective character of experience is, then, quite sensitive to our point of view. And this basic point is untouched by the suggestion that some human beings may be better placed than others to achieve an adequate conception of bat phenomenology. The contrast that is crucial for Nagel's argument is between facts about the subjective character of experience, on the one hand, and facts about physics or neurophysiology, on the other hand. In order to grasp the concepts deployed in physical or neurophysiological theory, a creature does not need to possess the same perceptual systems that we have: 'intelligent bats or Martians might learn more about the human brain than we ever will' (Nagel, 1974, p. 172). In short, the accessibility of physical or neurophysiological facts is not especially sensitive to our point of view.

That is the dialectically relevant difference between phenomenological facts and physical or neurophysiological facts. The difference may be one of degree; and, of course, we are able to grasp both kinds of facts about ourselves. But, in the one case and not in the other, that ability depends upon the nature of our perceptual systems and the character of the experiences that they furnish. If there is this difference between phenomenological facts and physical facts then it seems to follow straightforwardly that phenomenological facts are not physical facts: the subjective character of experience eludes a physicalist theory of the world.

However, in order to be clear about just what has been established by this argument, we have to pay attention to a potential ambiguity in the idea of a fact. Consider a very familiar example. The thought that Hesperus is a planet is arguably a different thought from the thought that Phosphorus is a planet. The former thought involves a conception that is grounded in the ability to recognize Hesperus in the evening sky; while the latter thought involves a conception that is grounded in the ability to recognize Phosphorus in the morning sky. We might even say that the former thought is inaccessible for someone who goes to bed sufficiently early, while the latter thought is inaccessible for someone who sleeps in sufficiently late. But is the fact that Hesperus is a planet a different fact from the fact that Phosphorus is a planet? It depends whether, in Fregean terminology, facts belong at the level of sense or the level of reference.

The answer will be 'Yes', if facts belong at the level of sense and are equated with correct thoughts. But if a fact is a state of affairs that obtains in the world – built directly from constituents of the world and so belonging at the level of reference – then the answer is 'No'. For what in the world makes the former thought correct is just the same as what in the world makes the latter thought correct; namely, the object Venus exemplifying the property of being a planet. One and the same state of affairs can be thought about in two different ways, because one and the same object can be thought about in two different ways.

A late sleeper, for whom Phosphorus thoughts are inaccessible, might build up a body of knowledge – a theory – about Hesperus: Hesperus is a planet; Hesperus appears in the evening; Hesperus also appears in the morning; Hesperus is called 'Hesperus'; Hesperus is also called 'Phosphorus'; and so on. The late sleeper might know all this and more, and yet not be able even to apprehend the thought that Phosphorus is a planet, since he lacks a certain cognitive skill – the ability to think of the planet in a particular way. But it does not follow that the late sleeper's theory provides an incomplete account of the planet Hesperus (that is, of Phosphorus; that is, of Venus).

So, in a similar way, it is open to someone to say that Nagel's argument does not show that physicalism provides an incomplete account of the world. Nagel's argument merely shows that certain physical states can be thought about in very different ways; rather as the planet Venus can be thought about in different ways. A Fregean might put the point by saying that Nagel demonstrates a difference between the physical and the phenomenal at the level of sense, but does not demonstrate a difference at the level of reference.

Nagel actually anticipates this line of response to his argument, and draws a distinction between typical cases where we can separate the level of reference from the level of sense, on the one hand, and the case of conscious experience, on the other. In the case of a planet, there is a clear separation between the object that is thought about, and the mode of presentation of that object – between the object as it is, and the way that the object appears. In the case of an experience, in contrast, there is no separation between the way that the experience is and the way that it appears. Consequently, Nagel claims, the ambiguity in the idea of a fact does not open up; and his anti-reductionist argument stands (1974, pp. 173–4).

Now, there are certainly further responses that can be made to Nagel at this point. First, it may seem that the denial of a separation between appearance and reality in the case of experience simply begs the question against the physicalist. Second, it may seem that Nagel has made the mistake of regarding experiences, including perceptual experiences of material objects, as themselves the objects of perception. But, however the ensuing turns in the dialectic may play out, Nagel poses a problem that remains even if we allow that conscious experiences are to be identified with physical events or processes:

> If we acknowledge that a physical theory of mind must account for the subjective character of experience, we must admit that no presently available conception gives us a clue how this could be done. The problem is unique. If mental processes are indeed physical processes, then there is something that it is like, intrinsically, to undergo certain physical processes. What it is for such a thing to be the case remains a mystery. (Nagel, 1974, p. 175)

Leaving aside other themes in Nagel's paper, it is this announcement of mystery that we shall focus upon.

Two Comparisons

Nagel's argument, leading up to his announcement of mystery, can be compared with two other arguments: Ned Block's (1978) *absent qualia argument*, and Frank Jackson's (1982, 1986) *knowledge argument*.

The absent qualia argument is specifically directed against functionalism: the idea that mental states are individuated by the causal roles that they play in the total mental economy, rather than by the particular neurophysiological ways in which the roles are realized. According to functionalism, a human being and a computer could be in mental states of just the same type, despite the vast differences in physical constitution. But this liberalism poses a problem for functionalism. For we can imagine the various functional roles being played by states that are very different from the states of human brains; and for at least some of these imagined systems there is a powerful intuition that there would be nothing that it is like to be the system in question. For example, there are imaginable systems such that, despite the fact that there is some realizer of the pain functional role in the system, the intuition is that the system does not experience pain. More generally, the position for which Block argues is that a system may have internal states playing each of the causal roles specified by some common-sense or scientific psychological theory, and yet lack states with phenomenal character. This is to say that qualia may be absent from such a system.

Block reveals some sympathy for Nagel's perception of a mystery at the heart of the mind–body problem:

> *No* physical mechanism seems very intuitively plausible as a seat of qualia, least of all a *brain*. Since we know that *we are brain-headed systems*, and that we have qualia, we know that brain-headed systems can have qualia. [But] we have no theory of qualia which explains how this is *possible* . . . . (Block, 1978, p. 293)

But, his actual argument seeks to demonstrate, not that phenomenal consciousness eludes physicalism, but that it eludes functionalism. The absent qualia argument would not work against a different physicalist philosophy of mind (central state materialism) that exchanges liberalism for chauvinism, and individuates mental states by the neurophysiological realizers of causal roles, rather than by the roles themselves. In short, Block's argument is importantly different from Nagel's. Block's argument is not intended for use against a physicalist who (however implausibly) identifies being in pain with having C-fibres firing, whereas such a physicalist is very much included among the targets of Nagel's argument.

In this respect, Jackson's knowledge argument is like Nagel's argument, and unlike Block's. Thus:

> I am what is sometimes known as a 'qualia freak'. I think that there are certain features of the bodily sensations especially, but also of certain perceptual experiences, which no amount of purely physical information includes. Tell me everything physical there is to tell about what is going on in a living brain, the kind of states, their functional role, their relation to what goes on at other times and in other brains, and so on and so forth, and be I as clever as can be in fitting it all together, you won't have told me about the hurtfulness of pains, the itchiness of itches, pangs of jealousy, or about the characteristic experience of tasting a lemon, smelling a rose, hearing a loud noise or seeing the sky. (Jackson, 1982, p. 127)

Jackson's argument depends upon an imaginary scientist – indeed, a neurophysiologist – Mary, who knows everything there is to know about the physics and neurophysiology of visual experience, but whose own visual experience has hitherto been exclusively monochrome. When Mary first sees in colour, she learns something 'about the world and our visual experience of it' (1982, p. 130). But, *ex hypothesi*, Mary has nothing to learn about the physics or physiology of visual experience. Consequently, what she learns is something that eludes physicalism.

Now, Jackson (1982) claims that his argument is quite different from Nagel's, for two reasons. First, Jackson says that Nagel is concerned with something essentially first-personal: what it is like to be a particular individual experiencing subject. Second, Jackson says that Nagel is concerned with the actual limits of our 'imaginative or extrapolative powers' (Jackson, 1982, p. 132). But, it is not really obvious that these concerns loom so large in Nagel's argument. On the first point, Nagel says (1974, p. 171): 'I am not adverting here to the alleged privacy of experience to its possessor. The point of view in question is not one accessible only to a single individual. Rather it is a *type*.' And on the second point, Nagel says:

> It may be easier than I suppose to transcend inter-species barriers with the aid of the imagination. For example, blind people are able to detect objects near them by a form of sonar, using vocal clicks or taps of a cane. Perhaps if one knew what that was like, one could by extension imagine roughly what it was like to possess the much more refined sonar of a bat. (Nagel, 1974, p. 172, n. 8)

So, perhaps we can agree to group Jackson's knowledge argument together with at least one important strand in Nagel's influential paper (cf. Jackson, 1986); namely, the strand, described above, which leads up to the announcement of mystery.

Epistemic Boundedness and the Prospects for Explanation

Jackson joins Nagel in acknowledging a sense of mystery surrounding the phenomenon of consciousness; and he suggests an explanation of why it is that just how consciousness fits into the great scheme of things might 'fall quite outside our comprehension' (1982, p. 135). We human beings are the products of evolution; and evolution has fitted us to understand many things, especially things that matter for our survival. But it would be absurdly optimistic to suppose that evolution has so equipped us intellectually that there is nothing about the world that lies beyond our ken.

Lest we slip into this unwarranted optimism, Jackson invites us to imagine some modestly intelligent sea slugs. The intelligence of these sea slugs is geared to the particular environment in which they have to survive; and, as we humans can see, there is much about the world that lies beyond the understanding of these limited creatures. But, it is just as imaginable that there should be intelligent beings that stand to us as we stand to the sea slugs. So, it should be perfectly intelligible to us that there may be much about the way that the world works that lies beyond our human understanding.

This idea is one that Nagel himself adopts (1986, p. 90): 'I shall defend a form of realism according to which our grasp on the world is limited not only in respect of what we can know but also in respect of what we can conceive. In a very strong sense, the world extends beyond the reach of our minds.' And a measure of modesty about our conceptual and epistemic prowess is also urged by Fodor (1983, pp. 120–6: the thesis that the mind is 'epistemically bounded'), by Chomsky (1988, pp. 147–51) and by Colin McGinn (1989), who takes it up in the service of an argument that understanding how physical processes give rise to consciousness – how it is that 'there is something that it is like, intrinsically, to undergo certain physical processes' (Nagel, 1974, p. 175) – is beyond us.

McGinn aims to steer a course between two views about the explanation of consciousness. On the one hand, there are accounts that are frankly not naturalistic: the real seat of consciousness lies in spooky, other-worldly stuff. On the other hand, there are accounts that are both naturalistic and constructive: some naturalistic property that brains instantiate is supposed to make plain to us how it is that the material brain is the seat of phenomenal consciousness.

Cartesian dualism is the canonical example of the first kind of account; and it is precisely because of its departure from naturalism that McGinn finds it unattractive:

> Resolutely shunning the supernatural, I think it is undeniable that it must be in virtue of *some* natural property of the brain that organisms are conscious. There just *has* to be some explanation for how brains subserve minds . . . . Consciousness, in short, must be a natural phenomenon, naturally arising from certain organizations of matter. (McGinn, 1989, p. 353)

Functionalism and central state materialism, on the other hand, are naturalistic; but are inadequate if offered as constructive accounts of consciousness. Thus, functional properties are as naturalistic as can be; but, as the absent qualia argument shows, the mere fact of the brain's instantiation of functional properties does not make it plain to us why we have conscious experiences. Similarly, having one's C-fibres firing is a perfectly naturalistic state to be in; but – as the absent qualia argument does not show, but as Nagel, Block and Jackson all agree – central state materialism would fail as an explanatory story since it remains unobvious to us just why there should be something that it is like to be in that neurophysiological state.

The middle way is, of course, non-constructive naturalism ('existential' rather than 'effective' naturalism: McGinn, 1991, p. 87). The brain is the seat of consciousness in virtue of certain of its properties; but what those properties are, and how they give rise to phenomenal consciousness, is beyond our cognitive grasp. Metaphysically, there is nothing miraculous going on; but epistemologically, the mystery remains. McGinn argues for this prospect by considering the ways in which we might hope to achieve a conception of what it is about the brain that gives rise to consciousness.

Essentially, the putative routes to a grasp of the neural basis of consciousness are just two. We can rely upon consciousness itself, and hope for an introspective fix upon the explanatory basis of phenomenal consciousness; or we can turn to the scientific study of the brain. Of the two, the first seems utterly hopeless, since (McGinn, 1989, p. 354): 'Introspection does not present conscious states *as* depending upon the brain in some intelligible way.' So, the argument primarily devolves upon the explanatory prospects for neuroscience.

Can we attain any conception of a neuroscientific property of the brain adequate to explain consciousness? Here, McGinn's argument proceeds in two steps. First, ordinary perception of the brain does not bring us up against any such property. Second, nor is any such property going to be introduced by inference to the best explanation from those perceptible properties.

As to the first step, it is surely right that when we casually observe a human brain – greyish-pink, clammy and somewhat granular in texture, weighing in at just over 2 lbs – we do not come upon anything that makes it intelligible that the brain is the seat of phenomenal consciousness. The colour, texture and mass of the brain, being properties that the brain shares with other organic and inorganic chunks of matter, do not carry any hint of the gaudy flow of conscious experience.

These gross observable properties of the brain, and other, smaller-scale properties too, stand in need of explanation. But, according to the second step of the argument, whatever explanatory theory may be invoked here, it will not advert to any property of the brain that explains consciousness:

> To explain the observed physical data we need only such theoretical properties as bear upon those data, not the property that explains consciousness, which does not occur in the data. Since we do not need consciousness to explain those data, we do not need the property that explains consciousness. (McGinn, 1989, p. 359)

Consequently, neither experience nor theory yields us any conception of a natural property of the brain that can explain consciousness, despite the fact that (existential) naturalism assures us that there must be some such property. Furthermore, if this argument of McGinn's works to show that the natural neural underpinnings of consciousness are beyond our conceptual grasp, then the argument can be generalized to show that the substrate of consciousness will be beyond the ken of any being whose primary modes of concept formation are introspection, perception and inference to the best explanation. Whether the argument really does work is not, of course, something over which all philosophers agree. We shall introduce some dissenting voices towards the end of this section.

Explanatory Elusiveness and Theoretical Options

We have taken some time, first, to distinguish between several notions of consciousness and, then, to spell out a line of thought – beginning with Nagel (1974) and culminating in McGinn (1989) – that stresses the explanatory elusiveness of phenomenal consciousness. In Nagel, Block, Jackson and McGinn we find the idea that it is presently mysterious, and perhaps forever beyond our grasp, how it is that physical stuff gives rise to phenomenal consciousness. Once their announcement of mystery is accepted, the logical space of possible accounts of the relationship between physical matter and phenomenal consciousness is quite closely circumscribed.

To accept that there is a mystery here is to forgo the options of an eliminativist, or of a reductionist, account of phenomenal consciousness. Eliminativism about phenomenal consciousness is not an option, for if phenomenal consciousness does not exist then it is presumably not mysterious. Reductionism about phenomenal consciousness is not an option, for the mystery is predicated upon the idea that phenomenal consciousness cannot be adequately explained in terms of the properties of the brain that figure in current neuroscience.

The *prima facie* inhabitable area of logical space then seems to divide into three regions. First, we might accept that it is simply a brute and inexplicable fact that putting certain kinds of physical stuff together in certain ways gives rise to phenomenal consciousness. This is the thesis of radical, or metaphysical, emergence (rejected by Nagel, 1979a, p. 182). Second, we might reject the metaphysical mystery of emergence, but maintain that no properties of the material brain will quite turn the explanatory trick – that properties that are to be adequately explanatory of phenomenal consciousness will require a non-physical vehicle. In short, we might opt for some kind of substance dualism.

Finally, third, we might hold that there are properties of the physical brain that account adequately for what it is like to be one of us, but that these properties are different from those that figure in current neuroscience. Panpsychism (Nagel, 1979a) belongs in this third region, as does Nagel's own recently expressed view:

> The strange truth seems to be that certain complex, biologically generated physical systems, of which each of us is an example, have rich nonphysical properties. An integrated theory of reality must account for this, and I believe that if and when it arrives, probably not for centuries, it will alter our conception of the universe as radically as anything has to date. (Nagel, 1986, p. 51)

Putting this rather pessimistic vision of the immediate future together with the thesis of epistemic boundedness, we might suggest – with McGinn – that the requisite explanatory properties of the brain have their place in an 'integrated theory of reality' that lies beyond our conceptual grasp. (Thus, given just the present tripartite classification, McGinn's position ends up in the same region as panpsychism, but in a very different tract of that region, of course.)

Demystifying Consciousness: The Higher-order Thought Account

The announcement of mystery is not, however, universally accepted. Earlier, we noted one possible strategy for demystifying the notion of phenomenal consciousness. This involves the claim that phenomenal consciousness is not really a distinct and *sui generis* category, but can be constructed out of the notion of thoughts about mental states.

One philosopher who favours this strategy is David Rosenthal, who begins (1986, p. 332) from the idea that mental states have either intentional (or semantic) properties or phenomenal (or sensory) properties. Furthermore, it is plausible that mental states are the only things that have these properties non-derivatively. (Linguistic objects have semantic properties, to be sure; but they inherit their intentionality from the mental states of language users.) Consequently, we can use the disjunction of phenomenal and (non-derived) intentional properties to mark out the class of mental states, and then hope to use some further criterion to distinguish conscious states as a sub-class of mental states. Since this starting point is supposed to stand in contrast to taking consciousness as the defining mark of mental states, it is, of course, important that the notion of phenomenal property used by Rosenthal must not already involve the idea of consciousness.

Given this starting point, the basic idea in the construction of the notion of consciousness is as follows:

> Conscious states are simply mental states we are conscious of being in. And, in general, our being conscious of something is just a matter of our having a thought of some sort about it. Accordingly, it is natural to identify a mental state's being conscious with one's having a roughly contemporaneous thought that one is in that mental state. (Rosenthal, 1986, p. 335)

Consciousness as a property of mental states is analysed in terms of the relation *x* is conscious of *y*; then this in turn is analysed as the relation *x* has a thought *about y*. Since *y* is a mental state – perhaps itself a thought – the thought about *y* is said to be a second-order, or higher-order, thought. If this is a correct account of what consciousness is, then the occurrence of consciousness in the natural order need not be especially mysterious: 'Since a mental state is conscious if it is accompanied by a suitable higher-order thought, we can explain a mental state's being conscious by hypothesizing that the mental state itself causes that higher-order thought to occur' (Rosenthal, 1986, p. 336). We can briefly consider some of the strengths and weaknesses of Rosenthal's proposal for demystification.

An initial objection to this kind of account can be set aside quickly. Someone might say that, while she certainly enjoys conscious mental states, she is largely unaware of the constellation of higher-order thoughts that seem to be required if Rosenthal's account of conscious mental states is correct. But this is not a problem for the account, since to say that the subject is unaware of (or is not conscious of) the higher-order thoughts is just to say that those higher-order thoughts are not themselves conscious mental states; and the analysis does not say that for a mental state to be conscious the subject must have a conscious thought about it – just that the subject must have a thought about it. A *conscious* higher-order thought would, of course, be one accompanied by a yet higher-order thought about *it*.

The notion of consciousness yielded by this kind of account clearly has some affinities with the notion of access consciousness (the notion (c) on p. 14 above) that we distinguished earlier. This was the notion of a state such that, if the subject is in that state, then she is *ipso facto* capable of judging that she is in that state, provided only that she possesses the concept of the type of state in question. But the affinities do not add up to identity: there are important differences between access consciousness as we described it and Rosenthal's account of consciousness in terms of higher-order thoughts. One striking difference is that access consciousness is a dispositional notion: the subject is able to judge, or is in a position to judge, that she is in the state. So, an access-conscious state might not actually be accompanied by a higher-order thought. (This is faithful to the original idea of access consciousness, cast in terms of the availability of content for verbal report. A content can be available for report without actually being reported.)

However, more important than differences between the higher-order thought account of consciousness and our earlier notion of access consciousness is the question whether the higher-order thought account provides a plausible demystifying reconstruction of phenomenal consciousness. Rosenthal certainly offers the account in the spirit of denying the Nagelian gap between the physical and the phenomenal:

> To understand how consciousness can occur in physical things, we must dissolve the intuitive force of [the unbridgeable gulf that seems to divide the conscious from the merely physical]. And we can do so only by explaining the consciousness of mental states in terms of mental states that are not conscious. For the stark discontinuity between conscious mental states and physical reality does not also arise when we consider only nonconscious mental states. And once we have explained consciousness by reference to nonconscious mental states, we may well be able also to explain nonconscious mental states in terms of phenomena that are not mental at all. (Rosenthal, 1986, p. 353)

But, equally, the account faces stern challenges when it is offered as a demystification of phenomenal consciousness.

One challenge arises from the fact that, since there is a distinction between a mental state with phenomenal properties and a thought about such a state, consciousness is not revealed as a necessary or essential property of mental states with phenomenal properties. In short, the account appears to allow for the coherence of the idea of unconscious sensations; and, at least initially, this may seem quite counter-intuitive.

However, it is not obvious that there is a really decisive objection here. The role of unconscious sensations might be underwritten both by everyday experience – the persistent headache from which one is nevertheless distracted, or which one forgets about for a while – and by the needs of philosophical theory. For example, in a series of papers (e.g. 1986, 1987a, 1989b, 1990) Norton Nelkin has argued for distinctions among three notions of consciousness: intentionality (our notion (b), roughly), introspectibility (similar to our notion (c) – access consciousness), and phenomenologicality. This last notion is not to be identified with phenomenal consciousness; rather, on Nelkin's way of carving up the territory, phenomenologicality is a property of all 'image-like' or non-sentential mental representations (1989b, 1990), and phenomenal consciousness is a composite of phenomenologicality and introspectibility. The result is a view that is much like Rosenthal's in that phenomenal consciousness is treated as a matter of the subject's introspection of a state with phenomenal properties. But Nelkin is also able to offer a principled reason for admitting unconscious sensations. For, if we appropriate the term 'sensation' for mental states with phenomenologicality and this includes all image-like representations, then it becomes more or less uncontroversial that there are many sensations of which we are not conscious.

There is, however, another challenge – which Rosenthal reckons to be '[p]erhaps the strongest objection' (1986, p. 350) – to the higher-order thought account of consciousness. This is that we intuitively ascribe phenomenal consciousness to the states of at least some creatures that we would not credit with the power of thought.

To this challenge, Rosenthal offers a response in two stages. First, he stresses that the thought that is required if a phenomenal (rather than intentional) mental state is to be conscious is not a very sophisticated thought – so the potential for such thoughts imposes relatively modest demands upon a creature. Second, he suggests that, where a creature does not even measure up to those modest demands, an intuition that the creature is nevertheless conscious can still be salvaged. For, in one sense of the term, 'For an organism to be conscious means only that it is awake, and mentally responsive to sensory stimuli' (1986, p. 351). Since, *ex hypothesi*, the creatures under consideration in this second stage lack the power of thought, this mental responsiveness to external states, or to the states of the creature's own body, cannot require having thoughts about those states. But we might well allow that a creature with some states which both contain information about external or bodily states, and are used in the direction of behaviour, counts as conscious – in this thin sense – when it is awake.

However, it is clear that someone who thinks of phenomenal consciousness in the way that Nagel, Block, Jackson and McGinn do is liable to be less than fully satisfied with this two-stage response. These friends of phenomenal consciousness may point out, for example, that everything turns upon the first stage of the response, since the second stage simply does not address the original challenging intuition that phenomenal consciousness does not require thought. What that second stage offers is not phenomenal consciousness without thought, but only a much thinner kind of consciousness without thought. But, it can be agreed on all sides that there can be sensory processing without phenomenal consciousness, and that where there is that kind of sensory processing we can – at least sometimes – draw a distinction between the creature being awake and being asleep.

As to the first stage, whereas the original challenge was that higher-order thought is not necessary for phenomenal consciousness, it is possible now to wonder whether higher-order thought as described in the first stage of the response is sufficient for phenomenal consciousness. According to the first stage, rudimentary thoughts about sensory states require little more than the ability to discriminate among such states. But, on pain of circularity in the account, neither the notion of sensory state nor the notion of discrimination can be allowed to build in the idea of phenomenal consciousness. Perhaps, then, some kind of non-sentential representation is enough for a sensory state (as Nelkin 1989b, 1990 suggests), and some kind of distinctive response is enough for a discriminatory capacity. But, in that case, it seems all too clear that rudimentary thoughts about sensory states could be present where phenomenal consciousness as conceived by Nagel is totally absent.

The defender of the higher-order thought account might take the argument a step further by insisting that thought really does require more than a mere ability to discriminate; that it requires the deployment of a network of concepts including spatial concepts and other concepts that apply to external objects, for example. Whether or not this move meets the worry about sufficiency, it makes the original question whether higher-order thought is necessary for phenomenal consciousness more pressing. The intuition behind the necessity question is that, if a subject possesses the concept of a certain type of mental state – say, the concept of pain – then, certainly, the subject is able to deploy that concept to judge that she is in a state of that type when she is. Thus, a subject who possesses the concept of pain is able to judge that she is in pain when she is in pain, provided that the pain is conscious. (Much the same goes for the concept of belief: if a subject possesses the concept of belief then she can judge that she believes that *p* when she does believe that *p*, provided that the belief is conscious: Peacocke, 1992, p. 151.) But, according to this intuition, the consciousness of the mental state – the pain's phenomenal consciousness – is not constituted by the subject's judgement that she is in pain; it is, rather, the ground of the subject's disposition so to judge given that she possesses the concept of pain – a ground that may be present when the subject does not exercise, or even does not possess, the concept of pain.

In fact, those theorists who stress the elusiveness of phenomenal consciousness may well see the higher-order thought account as confronting a dilemma. According as the account opts for a spartan or a rich conception of thought, what it says is either not sufficient or not necessary for phenomenal consciousness. The second option – invoking a rich conception of thought –

runs the risk that phenomenal consciousness will be simply imported into the account rather than reconstructed by it; and, to that extent, the first option – with a spartan conception of thought – seems preferable in the interests of non-circularity. But then, the champions of elusiveness may say, the higher-order thought account is revealed as a form of eliminativism about phenomenal consciousness. For consciousness, as the advocate of the higher-order thought account constructs it (without circularity, using only the spartan conception of thought), palpably falls short of phenomenal consciousness as the champions of elusiveness conceive it. So, it must be part of the advocate's overall picture that phenomenal consciousness (the elusive, mysterious kind) does not really exist. In short, it seems to the champions of elusiveness that nothing admitted by the higher-order thought account is sufficiently mysterious to add up to phenomenal consciousness.

Demystifying Consciousness: The Challenge to Qualia and the Appeal to Neuroscience

If this is the shape that the debate takes, then it is plainly to the advantage of the advocate of the higher-order thought account – and indeed, to the advantage of any demystifier – to call in question the coherence of the notion of phenomenal consciousness, when that notion is presumed to function as the locus of elusiveness.

An example of this kind of attack upon the very idea of phenomenal consciousness is provided by Daniel Dennett, who recommends nothing less than the view that 'there are no such properties as qualia' – and that the same goes for 'raw feels', 'phenomenal properties', 'qualitative character', and the rest (1988, p. 43; cf. 1991, p. 369). This may seem an extraordinary claim given the way that the term 'qualia' is introduced (1988, p. 42): ' "Qualia" is an unfamiliar term for something that could not be more familiar to each of us: the *ways things seem to us.*' But, as Dennett sees it, qualia – aspects of the phenomenal character of experience – have been assumed to be special in a number of ways. Qualia are supposed, in philosophical discussion, to be ineffable or incommunicable, to be intrinsic, atomic and unanalysable, to be private, and to be introspectible or 'directly and immediately apprehensible in consciousness' (1988, p. 47). But, Dennett argues, 'conscious experience has *no* properties that are special in *any* of the ways qualia have been supposed to be special' (p. 43).

These are large claims, and they invite the response that, although there might well be errors and even incoherence in some of the philosophical theories that have been erected upon the notion of phenomenal consciousness, the core idea of ways things seem to us may still be in perfectly good standing. But Dennett emphatically rejects this compromise:

> My claim, then, is not just that the various technical or theoretical concepts of qualia are vague or equivocal, but that the source concept, the 'pre-theoretical' notion of which the former are presumed to be

refinements, is so thoroughly confused that, even if we undertook to salvage some 'lowest common denominator' from the theoreticians' proposals, any acceptable version would have to be so radically unlike the ill-formed notions that are commonly appealed to that it would be tactically obtuse – not to say Pickwickian – to cling to the term. Far better, tactically, to declare that there simply are no qualia at all. (Dennett, 1988, p. 44)

Dennett bases his critique of even the core notion of qualia upon a rich diet of examples ('intuition pumps').

One example illustrates the following idea. Suppose that this morning I had woken up and gone to my computer to discover that the mouse pad no longer – as I should probably have expressed it – looked red to me. On reflection, I could recognize that, if experiences have an intrinsic phenomenal character, then there are really two distinct hypotheses to entertain. On the one hand, it may be that the experience produced by the mouse pad today is intrinsically different from the type of experience produced hitherto. On the other hand, it may be that the experience is intrinsically just the same, but that I am newly misremembering the intrinsic character of my earlier experiences of the mouse pad. As between these two hypotheses there is – if present introspection is all that I have to go on – nothing to choose (Dennett, 1988, p. 51).

Another example (of the two coffee tasters Mr Chase and Mr Sanborn, p. 52) involves a different pair of hypotheses. If I discover that I no longer enjoy the taste of Maxwell House coffee then, on the one hand, it may be that the intrinsic character of my taste experience produced by the coffee is different from the way that it used to be, while my taste preferences are the same. But, on the other hand, it may be that my taste experience is intrinsically just the same, while my preferences are different. By adding in assumptions about memory, these hypotheses can be elaborated in such a way that, once again, there is no way to decide between them on the basis of present introspection alone.

Now, one way to respond to these examples is to abandon the idea that there are determinate ways things seem to us, which are accessible to introspection. But, the question is whether that abandonment is forced upon us. To be sure, the claim that the hypotheses in each pair are empirically distinct would have to be rejected by someone who held a very strong verificationist view about qualia; the view, namely, that the content of a thesis about qualia is exhausted by what can be verified by present introspection. But, even someone who reckons that there is no more true about qualia than is immediately evident to introspection – that there is no 'is'/ 'seems' distinction for qualia – can give that view a realist, rather than a verificationist, rendition.

Thus, someone might say that there is no more true about the intrinsic character of my experience of the mouse pad yesterday than was accessible to introspection yesterday; and that there is no more true about the intrinsic character of my experience today than is accessible to introspection today. Since memory is fallible, there is no way for me to decide finally whether yesterday's experience was qualitatively the same as today's. But still, according to this imagined view, there is a fact of the matter as to whether the qualia are the same or different; and so there is a fact of the matter as to which hypothesis in the pair is correct.

This is an extreme view, and not an especially appealing one. Someone who holds this view may well be shaken by others of Dennett's examples (see also Dennett, 1991; Dennett and Kinsbourne, 1992). But, this realist view is distinct from the verificationist view about qualia and present introspection; and as such, it is at least an intelligible response to the two examples that we have just considered (cf. Block, 1992).

However, a more likely response from someone seeking to defend the core notion of qualia is to urge that it is possible to gather evidence in favour of one or the other of the hypotheses in each pair from sources other than introspection, and, in particular, from neuroscience. Owen Flanagan, who recommends the view that '[p]henomenology, psychology, and brain science are credible partners in the effort to penetrate qualia' (Flanagan, 1992, p. 85), offers this response to Dennett's challenge:

> [Dennett's] belief that it is time to discard the concept of qualia comes from the idea that qualia have further alleged features: they are atomic, nonrelational, ineffable, incomparable, and incorrigibly accessible from the first-person point of view. It is this extended list that makes the concept of qualia problematic, for its effect is to put qualia in the class of things about which nothing can be said from the third-person point of view. On this analysis, qualia are things about which the science of mind can offer no illumination. But it is a contentious list. It pins on the friend of qualia the implausible view that qualia are essentially and exclusively qualitative, that is, that they have no other properties than those implicated in their subjectively available aspects. (Flanagan, 1992, p. 61)

Once it is acknowledged that: 'The qualitative "ways things seem to us" aspect of certain mental states can be the most salient feature of these states, and the only feature available first personally, without being the only features of these states' (Flanagan, 1992, p. 61) we can readily imagine psychological or neuroscientific evidence that would count in favour of one hypothesis and against another. Thus, for example, we can imagine evidence from the neuroscientific study of perception and memory that would favour the hypothesis that the experience produced by the mouse pad today is different from that produced yesterday, and count against the hypothesis that I am mis-remembering the quality of yesterday's experience. Similarly, neuroscientific evidence could be brought to bear upon the case of the coffee tasters, Chase and Sanborn.

Dennett himself does not deny that we might accumulate psychological or neuroscientific evidence of this kind. But he is less optimistic than Flanagan about the power of such evidence to resolve the choice between hypotheses that present introspection cannot tell apart. There are at least two grounds offered for doubting 'the resolving power of such empirical testing' (Dennett, 1988, p. 56).

The first reason for pessimism is that we are not really confronted with a simple choice between two hypotheses. Rather, the two hypotheses in each pair lie at the ends of a spectrum. In between, there are hypotheses that say, for example, that today's experience of the mouse pad is a little different from the way yesterday's really was, and that, in addition, I am somewhat misremembering yesterday's experience; these two effects are adding together to produce my present impression that the mouse pad looks very different from the way it looked yesterday. The idea is, then, that there will be pairs of hypotheses which exhibit the following two properties. On the one hand, the two hypotheses will lie sufficiently close together on the spectrum so that the prospects for an empirical (particularly, neuroscientific) resolution of the question which one is correct will be bleak indeed. On the other hand, the two hypotheses will be such that the friend of qualia (the 'qualia freak', in Jackson's, 1982, p. 127 phrase) will say that there must be a fact of the matter as to which hypothesis is correct.

To this first reason for pessimism about the resolving power of neuroscience, the friend of qualia might essay two lines of response. Along the first line, he might say, with Flanagan:

> There is no doubt that it will be hard to decide between hypotheses such as these. But it is difficult to see why one would have confidence that rival hypotheses could be sorted out by indirect behavioral and neurophysiological evidence up to a point, but doubt that such evidence could ever provide us with evidence for favoring one of two subtly different rivals. (1992, p. 76)

Along the second line, he might protest that he is being saddled with a commitment to determinacy for qualia that is far greater than anything that he is genuinely obliged to take on. There is, perhaps, a conception of phenomenal consciousness according to which experiences (particularly, visual experiences) are like pictures that are determinate in every particular and lie open to the view of the experiencing subject, their details simply awaiting her attention. On this conception, perhaps, there must be an empirical fact of the matter whether the experienced colour of the mouse pad was just exactly this shade or that. Consequently, this conception of phenomenal consciousness is put under pressure by the worry that, where introspection draws a blank, neuroscience may likewise fail to yield evidence supporting one hypothesis over the other. But, however that may be, this pictorialist conception is flawed, since it postulates an inner observer. The careful friend of qualia will join Dennett in insisting that (1991, p. 106), 'In short, there is no observer inside the brain.'

The second reason for pessimism about the resolving power of neuro-scientific investigation is a little more complex to explain. The examples that Dennett favours here concern 'gradual post-operative recovery' (1988, p. 57; cf. 1991, pp. 391–5). We can illustrate the basic idea in the following two stages. For the first stage, suppose that the reason that my mouse pad seems to look different to me this morning is that overnight I have undergone surgery specifically to tamper with my colour perception; and suppose that the site of the surgical interference is at quite an early stage of the perceptual process. Given this neurophysiological fact, we shall agree that my visual experiences really are different from the way they were before the operation. Now, for the second stage, imagine that I recover from this tampering in the sense that my reactions to coloured objects become indistinguishable from the way they were before the operation. We could imagine that some adaptations occur naturally in the brain, or that the adaptations are produced by a second operation (cf. 1991, p. 392). Either way, the neural location of these changes is further in from the sensory surfaces than the site of the original operation.

The question for consideration is whether this adaptation is 'pre-experiential' or 'post-experiential'. After the adaptation, are my colour experiences just the way that they were at the outset, or are they still the way that they were after the initial tampering? There seem to be two distinct hypotheses about my qualia here, although *ex hypothesi* there is no behavioural test that you can administer to me in order to choose between them. But, Dennett's main claim about these examples is that it is far from clear that neuroscience can provide us with evidence for one hypothesis over the other. For, even if we know the exact site of the neural adaptation – of the second operation, say – neuroscience might not tell us whether to classify this site as pre-experiential or as post-experiential. Even if we know, for example, that the site of the second operation lies within the memory-accessing system, that does not settle the matter since we also need to know what role memory has in the production of the qualia, both before and after the adaptation (1988, p. 58).

In fact, Dennett claims:

> [T]he physiological facts will not in themselves shed any light on where in the stream of physiological process ... to draw the line at which the putative qualia appear as properties of that phase of the process. The qualia are the 'immediate or phenomenal' properties, of course, but this description will not serve to locate the right phase in the physiological stream .... (1988, p. 57)

And, if the friend of qualia still insists that there *must* be a fact of the matter as to which hypothesis is correct, then, Dennett argues, the qualia freak is in the grip of a major conceptual error; namely, the idea that there is a 'Cartesian Theatre': 'a place where "it all comes together" and consciousness happens' (1991, p. 39). Thus, he says (1991, pp. 394–5, 397):

[Y]ou may now think, it has to be one way or the other. There couldn't be a case where it wasn't perfectly obvious which sort of adjustment you had made! The unexamined assumption that grounds *this* conviction is that all adaptations can be categorized as either pre-experiential or post-experiential . . . .

[I]t may *still* seem just plain obvious that 'the subjective colors you would be seeing things to be' would *have* to be 'one way or the other.' This just shows the powerful gravitational force that the Cartesian Theater exerts on our imaginations.

To all this, just as in the case of the first reason to be pessimistic about the resolving power of empirical investigation of the brain, the friend of qualia may respond along two lines. On the one hand, he may suggest that Dennett is being unduly pessimistic about the deliverances of future neuroscientific theory (cf. Flanagan, 1992, pp. 78–9). On the other hand, he may reject the idea that every friend of qualia must think that there is always a fact of the matter as between these pairs of hypotheses. Indeed, he may protest that it is only by being in the grip of the image of the Cartesian Theatre – or some other observer–object model – that someone could come to insist on this total determinacy about qualia, and that Dennett is overestimating the gravitational force that this image exerts on the philosophical imaginations of the friends of qualia.

A Spectrum of Positions: Explanation or Residual Mystery

Given a response along either of the lines that we have just indicated, the debate would, no doubt, continue. On one side of this particular debate, Flanagan urges that we can usually expect to achieve a resolution as between the hypotheses in these introspectively undecidable pairs if we '[seek] co-ordination, some sort of reflective equilibrium, among evidence coming from first-person phenomenology and our best psychological and neuro-scientific theories' (Flanagan, 1992, p. 79). Furthermore, Flanagan judges that the notion of phenomenal consciousness remains in good standing provided only that it is shorn of certain excesses of philosophical theory. On the other side, as we have seen, Dennett is much less sanguine about the prospects for re-deeming phenomenal consciousness. Indeed, Dennett urges the credentials of (1991, p. 397): 'the "reductionist" path of *identifying* "the way it is with me" with the sum total of all the idiosyncratic reactive dispositions inherent in my nervous system as a result of my being confronted by a certain pattern of stimulation'. We can now – and finally in this section – locate these two positions with respect to some others along a spectrum. We do not, of course, seek to adjudicate between these various theoretical options.

Dennett is certainly a demystifier; and his aim is to explain consciousness (1991), not to eliminate it. The 'reductionist' account of consciousness that he gives (very roughly, a functionalist account: 1991, pp. 31, 460) provides only a partial reconstruction of consciousness as it is conceived of by Nagel, Block,

Jackson and McGinn. Consequently, the attack on their notion of qualia or phenomenal consciousness – whether or not it is ultimately successful – is an important component in the total account.

Further along the spectrum from Dennett are those theorists who are frankly eliminativist about consciousness. In particular, we would there locate those theorists who suspect that, once the lessons of neuroscience have been learned, we shall need to make much more radical conceptual changes than merely jettisoning the philosophical excesses of certain (real or imaginary) qualia freaks. According to the occupants of this position, we shall need to carve up the conceptual territory in a wholly different way (e.g. Churchland, 1983). We shall treat this position as marking one end of our spectrum.

At the other end of the spectrum we can locate the theorists who combine realism about qualia with the claim that there is no more true about qualia than is immediately evident to introspection (see above, pp. 28–9). Then, as we work our way back along the spectrum towards Dennett, we have the possible position that permits neuroscience to provide evidence for one rather than the other of a pair of introspectively undecidable hypotheses, but does not allow that neuroscience can provide genuine explanations of the features of experience that are accessible to consciousness. According to the occupants of this position, there are bare *de facto* correlations between facts that can be discovered by neuroscience and facts that can (generally) be discovered by introspection; and we can make use of these correlations in cases where introspection yields no answer.

The next position along the spectrum is occupied by those theorists who accept that neuroscience can, in principle, furnish explanations of specific phenomenal features of experience, but only against the background of the one great unexplained fact that we have experiences with phenomenal features at all. Thus, for example, these theorists allow that neuroscience might explain why the experience of seeing red is phenomenally more similar to the experience of seeing orange than it is to the experience of seeing blue. But they insist that neuroscience cannot explain why there is something, rather than nothing at all, that it is like to see red. They say, with Nagel (1974, p. 175): 'If mental processes are indeed physical processes, then there is something [rather than nothing] that it is like, intrinsically, to undergo certain physical processes. What it is for such a thing to be the case remains a mystery.' At just this point – something rather than nothing – they proclaim residual mystery.

Flanagan is better disposed to qualia and to first-person phenomenology than Dennett is; but, like Dennett, he is a demystifier. Indeed, he dubs Nagel and McGinn (and, by implication, Block and Jackson, too) 'the New Mysterians' (Flanagan, 1989, p. 313; cf. Dennett, 1991, p. 273), and goes on to describe them as 'mischievous reactionaries' who set 'impossibly high standards on explanation and intelligibility' (1989, p. 365). Flanagan does not call in question the coherence of the notion of phenomenal consciousness; but he does reject the idea that it functions as a locus of elusiveness.

To this end, he examines McGinn's (1989) argument (summarized above,

p. 21) which proceeds by considering the ways in which we might hope to achieve a conception of what it is about the brain that gives rise to consciousness (cf. Dennett, 1991, pp. 433–5). The first phase of McGinn's argument is to say that introspection does not reveal to us the explanatory basis of phenomenal consciousness. The second phase then goes in two steps. First, perception of the brain does not show us any neuroscientific property of the brain adequate to explain consciousness; and, second, no property that can explain consciousness can be reached by inference to the best explanation from the perceptible properties.

The aspect of this argument upon which Flanagan fixes is that inference to the best explanation is only introduced in the phase of the argument concerned with perceptible properties of the brain, not in the phase of the argument that considers introspection (Flanagan, 1992, 113–14; cf. 1989, pp. 338–9):

> McGinn's misstep comes from forgetting that consciousness has already been introduced. We are not looking for an explanation of 'physical phenomena alone', at least not physical phenomena narrowly understood. There is a prior commitment to the existence of consciousness. Thus both brain facts and facts about consciousness are on the table to be explained ....
>
> We do not *see* consciousness when we look into the brain. Our access to the surface features of consciousness is not mediated by our senses. Consciousness is experienced in an intimate first-person way. But given a prior commitment to the existence of consciousness and a naturalistic view of the world, certain observations of brain properties, especially those reliably linked to certain kinds of first-person reports and behavior, can easily warrant the claim that such and such processes subserve sensory awareness in domain *d*.

We can anticipate the response, on behalf of the mysterian, that merely showing that certain neural processes 'subserve' particular aspects of phenomenal consciousness does not really make it *intelligible* – in the desired sense – *how it is* that there is something that it is like to have those processes going on in one's brain. Equally, we can anticipate that the demystifier will reply that this imposes an 'impossibly high standard on intelligibility' (Flanagan, 1992, p. 115); and a standard that we do not insist upon in the natural sciences.

Flanagan thus occupies a position that is intermediate between, say, McGinn's and Dennett's. But along this graded spectrum, as we have seen, there is one clear divide between the optimists about explanation – particularly, though not exclusively, neuroscientific explanation – and the proclaimers of terminal residual mystery. In *Newsweek* magazine, Dennett gives his current assessment of this debate:

> One side says, 'You can't explain this,' the other says, 'I can explain it a little bit.' 'Yes, but you can't explain the rest.' 'OK, I'll explain a little bit more.' The question is, is there always a residue left over that the

other side is right about, that is simply unreachable by objective science? They say yes, I say no, and in a way it's a point of faith. (Gelman et al., 1992, p. 72)

Whether we really have reached 'a point of faith' – whether there is bound to be a permanent stand-off between the mysterians and the demystifiers – remains to be seen.

The Philosophical Essays

What we have been sketching is a background of discussion that has taken place over nearly twenty years: roughly speaking, from the publication of Nagel's paper (1974) until the present. The eight philosophical essays in this book pick up many of the different threads in this discussion.

Chapter 6, by Levine, is concerned with the anti-physicalist charge that physicalism 'leaves out' the phenomenal aspect of our mental lives. He argues that, taken as a metaphysical claim, this charge cannot be sustained. The anti-physicalist arguments that he considers – Jackson's (1982) knowledge argument and an argument due to Saul Kripke (1980) – fail to show that conscious mental states and processes are anything other than physical states and processes. Furthermore, Levine maintains, although we need to allow for different modes of presentation – or ways of thinking – of one and the same physical state, the properties that the physical state must have in order to be accessible in these different ways do not themselves pose a problem for physicalism.

While conceivability arguments, being essentially epistemological in character, cannot establish metaphysical conclusions, they can, Levine argues, demonstrate the existence of an *explanatory gap* (see also Levine, 1983) between physicalist theories and facts about the phenomenal character of experience. The idea here is that, if it is so much as conceivable that a creature should be in a particular physical or functional state without being in a state with a certain phenomenal character, then appeal to that physical or functional state cannot provide a fully satisfying explanation of why the creature's experience has that phenomenal character.

Van Gulick's chapter takes its title from a remark by McGinn (1989, p. 15): 'armadillo minds cannot solve problems of elementary arithmetic but human minds can.' Are we in the same position with respect to phenomenal consciousness that armadillos are with respect to elementary arithmetic? Van Gulick argues that neither Jackson's knowledge argument nor Levine's explanatory gap argument gives us adequate reason to think that phenomenal consciousness defies physical or functional explanation. In the case of the explanatory gap argument, he points out that there is an organized structure in the domain of, for example, colour qualia (e.g. Hardin, 1988); and this structure offers neuroscientific explanation some purchase.

This is not yet to say that there is no unexplained residue; and the thought that there will always be something about phenomenal experience that eludes physical or, particularly, functional explanation can be rendered vivid by considering Block's (1978) absent qualia argument. But Van Gulick offers two replies to this argument. On the one hand, the argument may set unreasonably high standards for adequate explanation. On the other hand, the premise of the argument that says: 'Any functional model of mental organization will be capable of being realized by systems lacking qualia (or phenomenal properties)' may simply be untrue (see p. 146). As a bare logical possibility, this does not carry much conviction. But Van Gulick explores some candidates for the distinctive functional role of phenomenal states, and urges the importance of a Kantian conception of phenomenal experience as fundamentally experience *of* a world of objects.

As we have seen, above, McGinn's view is a naturalist one (1989, p. 353): 'Consciousness, in short, must be a natural phenomenon, naturally arising from certain organizations of matter.' His is a thesis of 'emergence', though not, of course, of brute inexplicable emergence. In his contribution here (chapter 8), he gives a dramatic presentation of what he considers to be the strongest alternative to his naturalist position; namely, a thesis of cosmological dualism.

McGinn's imagined dualist interlocutor objects against naturalist theories of consciousness that they are committed to something that is flatly impossible: having consciousness 'emerge' from matter. This is a particularly telling objection to deploy against a mysterian like McGinn: if the emergence of consciousness from matter is impossible, then it is no wonder that we cannot give a satisfying explanation of it. Dualism does, of course, have well-known problems of its own; particularly, it faces the question of the nature of the interaction between the material and the mental worlds. But, from the point of view of McGinn's dualist opponent, a theory that has to explain something very difficult is to be preferred over a theory that postulates an impossibility.

Biro (chapter 9) provides a close analysis of some of the arguments that have led some philosophers to think that there can be no objective account – and therefore no scientific account – of consciousness. The focus of this analysis is the notion of objectivity, and the contrasting idea of subjectivity, about which Nagel says (1974, p. 176): '[E]very subjective phenomenon is essentially connected with a single point of view, and it seems inevitable that an objective, physical theory will abandon that point of view.' Is it possible to wring any metaphysical consequences from claims such as this about objectivity, subjectivity and points of view?

On a weak construal of Nagel's argument, what he is out to stress is just the crucial role of empathy. But, Biro claims, no substantial metaphysical conclusions are forced upon us by a recognition of the importance of empathy. On the other hand, there are strands in Nagel's work (see especially 1979b, 1986) that fit with a much more ambitious project. Biro evaluates these strands by asking whether there is a notion of objectivity for which it is the case both that scientific theories are supposed to be objective and that there are facts that are not objective.

The notion of objectivity that might seem to be the most promising for a Nagelian argument would have it that a fact is objective just in case it can be stated in a language that is accessible from any point of view at all. But Biro rejects the idea that this kind of objectivity is a requirement upon scientific theories. Given a more liberal notion of objectivity, the argument is liable to run into trouble at a different point. For the argument will turn upon the idea that there are radical differences between the languages accessible from one point of view and those accessible from another, in virtue of the radical differences between the experiences enjoyed by creatures with one kind of perceptual apparatus and those enjoyed by creatures with another. But, Biro objects that reasoning from a physiological difference to an experiential difference comes dangerously close to espousing the very reductionism against which the argument is directed.

Earlier we noted some of the features of the higher-order thought account of consciousness, favoured by Rosenthal (see especially 1986) and also by Nelkin. The basic idea is that mental states have intentional or phenomenal properties, and a mental state is conscious if the subject of the state is conscious *of* the state. This consciousness of the state is then analysed as the subject having a thought about the state.

In his essay here (chapter 10), Rosenthal offers a new argument for this account, based upon the linguistic distinction between expressing and reporting. The basic idea of the argument is this. If I think that, say, Vegemite is tastier than Marmite, then there are two ways that I can convey that thought. On the one hand, I can say that Vegemite is tastier than Marmite. On the other hand, I can say that I think that Vegemite is tastier than Marmite. In the first case, I express the thought; in the second case, I report it. Now, if I sincerely report that I have the thought that Vegemite is tastier than Marmite, then I also express a thought; namely, the thought that I am in a particular mental state – thinking that Vegemite is tastier than Marmite. In short, sincerely reporting a thought involves expressing a higher-order thought to the effect that one has the original thought.

But now – given only that I have the requisite linguistic abilities – the thoughts, and more generally the mental states, that I can report being in are my conscious mental states. (And to report a mental state is to express a higher-order thought about it.) So we have a parallel: when and only when a mental state is conscious, I can express a higher-order thought about it. This parallel stands in need of an explanation; and the explanation that suggests itself is that conscious mental states just are those that are accompanied by a higher-order thought to the effect that the subject is in that state. Rosenthal goes on from this argument to consider a range of objections to the higher-order thought account of consciousness, including the objection that there is a preferable (dispositional alternative to the idea that conscious mental states are always actually accompanied by a higher-order thought.)

Nelkin also defends the higher-order thought account, and we have noted above that this kind of account is offered as a way of demystifying the notion of consciousness. But, if the demystification is to be convincing, then the defender of the account must avoid a certain kind of circularity. He must show that the intentionality of thoughts does not simply reimport the original notion of phenomenal consciousness. In his essay here (chapter 11), Nelkin argues that there is no essential link between intentionality and consciousness. Given Nelkin's distinction between three different notions of consciousness – intentionality, introspectibility and phenomenologicality (see above) – there is a trivial sense in which there is an essential connection between intentionality and consciousness. But, the claim for a connection that Searle (1989, 1990b), for example, makes and Nelkin denies is the claim that intentionality is tied to introspectibility and phenomenologicality.

In the case of introspectibility, for example, Nelkin presents examples, such as blindsight, which it is natural to describe in terms of intentional mental states – states that are about something – even though those states are intuitively unconscious and so not introspectible. While it is open to someone to respond that, in some sense of 'could', these states could be introspected – they are not inaccessible 'in principle' – Nelkin judges that whether this is so is an empirical question in each case. Consequently, the claim that there is a philosophically essential, or *a priori*, connection between intentionality and introspectibility is undermined.

Nelkin's view is that phenomenologicality is a property of non-sentential mental representations, and that phenomenal consciousness is a composite of phenomenologicality and introspectibility. In contrast, Rey argues the case for bringing phenomenal mental states within the scope of the language of thought hypothesis: sensations are just more sentences in the head. According to the language of thought hypothesis, sentence-like representations are the brain's vehicles of intentionality. The familiar propositional attitudes – judging, believing, hoping, and the rest – are computational relations to sentences in the language of thought. Judging that Vegemite is tastier than Marmite, for example, is a matter of standing in a particular computational relation to an inner sentence that means that Vegemite is tastier than Marmite.

The distinctive cognitive roles of certain concepts are then captured in terms of the distinctive causes and effects of the occurrence of the corresponding syntactic item in tokened sentences. Rey's proposal (chapter 12) is that we can include sensations within this picture in two steps. First, we suppose that the language of thought contains certain predications (meaning roughly: it's looking red, for example) to which a subject stands in the computational relation corresponding to judging only when (or normally only when) the predication is tokened as a direct result of output from sensory systems. Second, we suppose that tokens of these predications cause characteristic subsequent processing, and we identify sensory experiences (of something looking red, for example) with instances of this processing. Rey then goes on to show how the various features of phenomenal consciousness can be reconstructed within this theoretical framework.

In the final chapter, Akins returns us to the alleged elusiveness of phenomenal consciousness and argues – as against Nagel – that there is no way of telling ahead of time just what science will reveal to us. If we start from the thought that science can shed some light upon an alien point of view, we may well find ourselves with the intuition, nevertheless, that there is something that science must leave out. Perhaps science can reveal the shape or structure of experience, but it leaves out the tone or shading. Perhaps science can make plain to us the representational properties of experience, but it is silent about the phenomenal feel.

Akins argues that this intuition, engaging as it is, is to be resisted because it rests upon the flawed idea that we can separate the qualitative from the representational aspects of experience: the idea that it makes sense to try to imagine an experience that is qualitatively just like the visual experience that I am having now, but represents quite different objects and properties in the world. Thus, Akins shares the Kantian sentiments of Van Gulick: conscious experience is constitutively representational.

If this is right, then we should pursue the empirical investigation – particularly, the neuroscientific investigation – of other creatures and of ourselves, confident in the expectation that we shall learn a great deal about their and our points of view. And we can take it, not as a point of faith, but as an open question, whether this investigation will leave us with a terminally residual mystery about consciousness.

1
Theory and Measurement in the Study of Unconscious Processes

EYAL M. REINGOLD AND PHILIP M. MERIKLE

The idea that cognitive processes can be meaningfully classified as conscious or unconscious has a long history in philosophy and psychology (see Ellenberger, 1970; Erdelyi, 1985, for reviews). However, even though many experimental reports during the past 100 years claim to demonstrate perception, learning or memory without conscious awareness, the distinction between conscious and unconscious processes remains highly controversial. For example, the same empirical findings that Holender (1986) concludes provide little or no evidence for unconscious perception are considered by other reviewers (e.g. Dixon, 1981) as conclusive and overwhelming documentation of the validity of perception without awareness.

In an attempt to explain this puzzling state of affairs, Dixon (1981, p. 200) states that 'research on closed mindedness and related traits suggests the possibility that those people with rigid belief systems, who feel threatened by the loss of control implied by subliminal perception, might be just the sort to create a milieu in which it fails to occur.' Dixon's critical evaluation of his theoretical rivals' personalities instead of their arguments represents a dangerous trend because it promotes a futile debate between 'believers' and 'non-believers' that has very little to do with empirical evidence. We do not deny that belief systems and private epistemological and existential theories held by investigators contribute both to the controversy and to the fascination surrounding this area of research (see Crowder, 1986, for candid and humorous autobiographical comments). However, while such issues may constitute an intriguing case study in the sociology of science, they should not be used as weapons in a meaningful scientific exchange. Indeed, the highly personal and emotional aspect of the study of the unconscious only highlights the need for conceptual and methodological clarity.

The purpose of this chapter is to identify the *a priori* assumptions underlying the major experimental approaches employed by researchers of the unconscious. These assumptions are rarely made explicit. We argue that much of the long-standing controversy in this area revolves around differences in the implicit assumptions adopted by different investigators. More specifically, there is no general consensus as to what constitutes an adequate operational definition of conscious awareness. Accordingly, we begin by discussing the general issues that have obscured the relationship between the theoretical construct of conscious awareness and the behavioural indicators used to measure this construct. In the second part of the chapter, we review two major approaches to the measurement of consciousness adopted in studies of perception without awareness. We conclude that the assumptions logically required by these approaches cannot be justified on an *a priori* basis. Consequently, in the third and final part of the chapter, we discuss two alternative approaches: one approach requires a considerably less stringent *a priori* assumption, while the second approach requires converging evidence to support the adequacy of the behavioural measures used to index conscious awareness.

Conscious Awareness: Theoretical Constructs versus Empirical Measures

The nonscientific nature of current conceptions of the unconscious is attested by the vagueness of definitions of what constitutes conscious and unconscious behavior. Not only are the definitions vague and operationally inadequate but there are several different terms that are used, sometimes to designate the same phenomena, other times in a partially overlapping way. (Eriksen, 1960, p. 279)

The basic definitional problems identified by Eriksen almost thirty years ago are still surprisingly relevant. In this section, we focus on two major factors that contribute to the lack of definitional and conceptual clarity in the study of the unconscious. The first problem, which becomes immediately apparent to anyone attempting to review the relevant psychological literature, is the proliferation of terminology associated with the conscious/unconscious distinction. Terms such as conscious, aware, intentional, explicit, controlled and attentional are not sufficiently differentiated and are sometimes used as synonyms. The same can be said for the terms unconscious, unaware, incidental, implicit, subliminal, pre-attentive, inaccessible and covert (see Erdelyi, 1985). The second, and even more serious problem, is the confusion between the underlying theoretical constructs and the empirical behavioural measures of these constructs.

These general issues can be illustrated through an examination of the definitional criteria currently used in the study of unconscious memory. Until recently, questions regarding the relationship between memory and consciousness attracted very little attention in mainstream cognitive psychology.

Tulving (1985, p. 1) went so far as to state that 'nowhere is the benign neglect of consciousness more conspicuous than in the study of human memory.' However, during the past several years, a growing number of studies has been directed at demonstrating memory without awareness in both amnesic patients and normal adults. This recent trend has also been accompanied by a change in terminology. In an important review, Schacter (1987) advocates a distinction between explicit and implicit memory as opposed to possible distinctions between either conscious and unconscious memory or aware and unaware memory. He states that 'the main reason for adopting implicit memory in favour of either unconscious memory or unaware memory has to do with the conceptual ambiguity of the latter two terms' (1987, pp. 501–2). However, even though Schacter attempts to avoid using ambiguous terms such as consciousness and awareness, he defines explicit and implicit memory in terms of subjective phenomenal awareness at the time of retrieval. According to Schacter, 'implicit memory is revealed when previous experiences facilitate performance on a task that does not require conscious or intentional recollection of those experiences; explicit memory is revealed when performance on a task requires conscious recollection of previous experiences' (1987, p. 501).

If the distinction between explicit and implicit memory is defined with reference 'to the key feature of implicit memory phenomena: the absence of conscious recollection of a prior experience at the time of test' (Schacter, 1987, p. 512), then nothing is gained by this new terminology. Indeed, explicit memory can be considered a synonym for conscious memory, and implicit memory can be considered a synonym for unconscious memory. The substantial difficulty introduced by the implicit/explicit terminology is that it acquires different meanings in different contexts (see Richardson-Klavehn and Bjork, 1988). More specifically, the terms explicit and implicit are employed as predicates in at least two different meanings:

1   As described above, explicit and implicit memory are used to refer to conscious and unconscious memory, respectively.
2   In addition, the terms explicit and implicit memory are used to refer to experimental tasks. Schacter (1987) defines memory tasks in which subjects are instructed to refer to a specific processing episode as explicit memory tasks or tests. For example, subjects may be instructed to recall or recognize words from a list that was presented in an earlier part of the experiment. In contrast, a variety of tasks that do not require reference to a prior study episode but which nevertheless document memory for that episode are defined as implicit memory tasks. A prototypic example of an implicit memory tasks is word-stem completion. In this task, subjects are given word stems (e.g. *tra* – for *travel*) and are instructed to complete them with the first word that comes to mind. Memory for previously presented words is reflected by an increased tendency to produce these words as responses to the stems.

Using the implicit/explicit terminology to refer both to subject characteristics (i.e. phenomenal awareness) and to task characteristics (i.e. reference to
a previous study episode) illustrates the blurring of the distinction between
theoretical constructs and empirical measures. A short allegory from *Alice's
Adventures in Wonderland* might help demonstrate what is at stake here. After
Alice and the creatures swam in the pool of Alice's tears, the problem was
how to get dry, and they had a consultation:

> ... said the Dodo ... 'the best thing to get us dry would be a Caucus-
> race.' 'What is a Caucus-race?' said Alice. ... the Dodo had paused as
> if it thought that somebody ought to speak, and no one else seemed
> inclined to say anything. 'Why,' said the Dodo, 'the best way to explain
> it is to do it.' ... First it marked out a race-course, in a sort of circle,
> ('the exact shape doesn't matter,' it said), and then all the party were
> placed along the course, here and there. There was no 'One, two, three,
> and away!' but they began running when they liked, and left off when
> they liked, so that it was not easy to know when the race was over.
> However, when they had been running half an hour or so, and were
> quite dry again, the Dodo suddenly called out 'The race is over!' and
> they all crowded round it, panting, and asking, 'but who has won?' This
> question the Dodo could not answer without a great deal of thought.
> ... At last he said 'Everybody has won, and all must have prizes.' ...
> and the whole party at once crowded around, calling out, in a confused
> way, 'Prizes! Prizes!'

The amusing, but rather chaotic, consequences of the caucus-race illustrate that without clear definitions of the rules of the game (i.e. the
best way to explain it is to do it), deciding the outcome (i.e. winners or
losers) is quite an arbitrary process. Note also, that in the midst of the
confusion, the original goal which the caucus-race 'task' was designed to
achieve (i.e. getting dry) was quickly forgotten. Likewise, the lack of
definitional and conceptual clarity in the study of the unconscious often
results in arbitrary and contradictory interpretations of empirical findings. In
addition, theoretical goals are often confused with the tasks designed to
achieve them. For example, as noted by Erdelyi (1985, pp. 58–9), the general
consensus in the late 1950s was that 'the failure of experimental methodology
to corroborate the existence of unconscious processes was taken, as a matter
of course, to reflect a failure of the concept rather than a failure of the extant
methodology.'

To date, the most extensive treatments of definitional issues related to the
distinction between conscious and unconscious processes have evolved within
the context of the study of perception without awareness. Consequently, in
the next section, we examine in some detail several of the major approaches
to the measurement of consciousness employed in studies of unconscious
perception.

Indicators of Conscious Awareness in the Study of Unconscious Perception

The vast majority of studies directed at demonstrating perception without awareness have relied on the dissociation paradigm (see Erdelyi, 1985, 1986). The basic logic underlying this paradigm is that perception without awareness can be demonstrated by a dissociation between two indices of perceptual processing: one index is assumed to indicate the availability of stimulus information to awareness or consciousness, while the second index is assumed to indicate the availability of stimulus information, independent of whether or not this information is available to consciousness. In the frequently employed version of the dissociation paradigm, such as the one advocated by Holender (1986), a demonstration of perception without awareness requires unequivocal evidence that stimulus information which is completely unavailable to awareness is nevertheless perceived and capable of influencing higher-level decision processes.

This version of the dissociation paradigm has three requirements or criteria that must be satisfied before perception without awareness is demonstrated. First, an adequate measure of the perceptual information available to consciousness or awareness must be selected. Second, this measure of conscious perceptual experience must be shown to indicate null sensitivity. Finally, given that the measure of conscious awareness indicates null sensitivity, the second measure of perceptual processing must be shown to have greater than zero sensitivity.

Obviously, the success of any approach based on this experimental strategy depends critically upon the adequacy of the behavioural measure used to index conscious awareness. If the measure is inadequate, then any dissociation between this measure and another measure of perceptual experience provides no definitive evidence either for or against unconscious perception. Thus, before any approach based on this version of the dissociation paradigm can be evaluated, it is necessary to have a clearly articulated definition of exactly what is meant by an adequate measure of conscious awareness.

Previously, we argued that the implicit assumption underlying most of the applications of the dissociation paradigm to the study of unconscious perception is that a particular behavioural measure exhaustively and/or exclusively indexes conscious perceptual information (Reingold and Merikle, 1988). The exhaustiveness and the exclusiveness assumptions define possible relations between the empirical finding of greater than zero perceptual sensitivity indexed by a particular behavioural measure and the occurrence of conscious perceptual processing. If conscious perception is assumed necessarily to result in better than zero perceptual sensitivity on a given measure, then this measure is defined as an exhaustive measure of conscious awareness. Conversely, if an exhaustive measure indicates null sensitivity, then no stimulus information is available to conscious awareness. It is important to note that an exhaustive measure of awareness is potentially sensitive to conscious, unconscious, or both conscious and unconscious information. Thus, although greater than zero sensitivity on an exhaustive measure is a necessary condition for conscious perception, it is not a sufficient condition for demonstrating perception with awareness. In contrast to an exhaustive measure, an exclusive measure of conscious awareness is defined as any measure that is influenced only by conscious perceptual experience. However, an exclusive measure is not necessarily an exhaustive measure of consciousness. For this reason, with an exclusive measure of awareness, greater than zero sensitivity is a sufficient but not a necessary condition for demonstrating perception with awareness.

To illustrate the exhaustiveness and the exclusiveness assumptions, consider the five hypothetical measures shown in figure 1. The shaded area inside each circle represents the perceptual information resulting in above-zero sensitivity on each measure. In contrast, the unshaded areas represent the perceptual information leading to zero sensitivity on the measures. As can be seen in figure 1, exclusiveness and exhaustiveness are independent assumptions: a measure can be exclusive, but not exhaustive (measure A); exhaustive, but not exclusive (measures D and E); both exclusive and exhaustive (measure C); or neither exclusive nor exhaustive (measure B).

Investigators applying the dissociation paradigm have assumed, either implicitly or explicitly, that null awareness is demonstrated whenever the behavioural measure used as an indicator of awareness shows null sensitivity. However, this assumption can only be true if this behavioural measure is an exhaustive measure of conscious perceptual processes. If the exhaustiveness assumption is not made, then it is entirely possible that stimulus information is available to consciousness despite the finding of zero sensitivity on the designated measure of awareness. Consequently, evidence for perceptual sensitivity indexed by a different perceptual measure (i.e. dissociation) may simply reflect the fact that the two measures are sensitive to different aspects of consciously available information (see Duncan, 1985; Navon, 1986). For example, consider measure A in figure 1. This measure is not sensitive to all consciously available information. Consequently, it is not an exhaustive measure of conscious perception. If measure A is designated as the measure of awareness and null sensitivity is established, then a dissociation between measure A and another measure, such a measure C in figure 1 (i.e. A = 0 and C > 0), would be interpreted erroneously as evidence for unconscious perception. However, this interpretation would be incorrect because neither measure A nor measure C indexes unconscious perceptual information. Indeed, according to the logic of the dissociation paradigm, an adequate indicator of awareness must be an exhaustive measure of conscious perceptual processing.

The importance of the exclusiveness assumption is critical if one attempts to reject the validity of perception without awareness on the basis of experimental evidence. When a designated measure of awareness indicates null sensitivity and all other measures of perception also indicate null sensitivity (i.e. no dissociation), one possible conclusion is that perception without awareness does not exist. Such a conclusion is only warranted, however, if

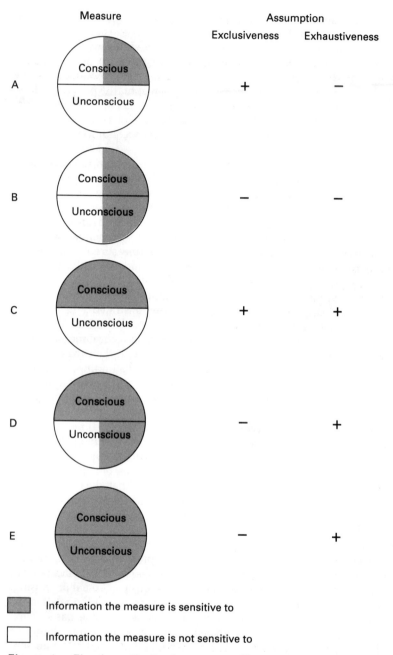

Figure 1   *Five hypothetical measures illustrating the exhaustiveness and the exclusiveness assumptions.*

the behavioral measure is an exclusive measure of conscious perceptual processing. If the exclusiveness assumption is not made, then it is entirely possible that the absence of a dissociation between measures reflects the fact that these measures index conscious, unconscious or both conscious and unconscious perceptual experiences. For example, selecting measure E in figure 1 as the measure of awareness would inevitably lead to finding no dissociations between this measure and all the other perceptual measures irrespective of whether or not these measures index unconscious perception.

In summary, both the exhaustiveness and the exclusiveness assumptions are relevant to interpretations of findings obtained within the framework of the dissociation paradigm. When one perceptual measure is shown to be dissociable from another perceptual measure, perception without awareness is indicated only if the first measure is assumed to be an exhaustive indicator of conscious perception. At the same time, the absence of dissociations between measures can only be used as an argument against perception without awareness if it can be assumed that the behavioural measure designated as an indicator of awareness is an exclusive measure of conscious perception. In attempting to satisfy the exhaustiveness assumption, it is tempting to select the most sensitive measure of perception as an indicator of awareness (i.e. measure E in figure 1). However, unless this measure is also an exclusive measure of consciousness, such a research strategy may preclude the demonstration of perception without awareness.

The controversy and polarization concerning the validity of unconscious perception is a direct consequence of the relative emphasis assigned to the exhaustiveness and the exclusiveness assumptions by different investigators. Unfortunately, such differences in the theoretical starting points are rarely made explicit. The resulting interpretive problems are illustrated by reviews of two major experimental approaches to the measurement of conscious awareness. Neither approach has provided definitive evidence for or against perception without awareness. The problematic aspect of the first approach is related primarily to a failure to satisfy the exhaustiveness assumption, while a failure to satisfy the exclusiveness assumption underlies the interpretive problems associated with the second approach.

Studies Based on Subjective Confidence

In the earliest studies of unconscious perception, the behavioural measure used to index conscious awareness was based simply on an individual's subjective confidence that the perceived stimulus information was useful for the experimental task. Many of these early studies were reviewed by Adams (1957), and the experiments reported by Sidis (1898) provide an excellent illustration of this general approach. Sidis showed observers cards containing a single printed digit or letter. The interesting aspect of these experiments is that 'the subject was placed at such a distance from the card that the character shown was far out of his range of vision. He saw nothing but a dim, blurred spot or dot' (Sidis, 1898, p. 170). In fact, 'the subjects often complained that they could not see anything at all; that even the black, blurred, dim spot often disappeared from their field of vision' (p. 171). However, when Sidis asked the subjects to name the character on a card, their responses were correct considerably more often than would be expected on the basis of pure random guessing, even though many subjects expressed the belief 'that they might as well shut their eyes and guess' (p. 171). On the basis of these and similar findings, Sidis concluded that his experiments indicated 'the presence within us of a secondary subwaking self that perceives things which the primary waking self is unable to get at' (p. 171).

Many other investigators (e.g. Stroh et al., 1908; Williams, 1938; Miller, 1939) have reported findings quite similar to those originally reported by Sidis. In fact, perception in the absence of subjective confidence is a relatively easy phenomenon to demonstrate, and the phenomenon is so robust that Adams (1957) suggested its use as a classroom demonstration. Thus, the experimental evidence clearly indicates that subjects can make accurate perceptual discriminations even when they believe that their perceptual experiences are inadequate to guide their choices.

Even more dramatic demonstrations of perception, learning and memory without subjective confidence are based on observations of cortically blind and amnesic patients (see chapter 2). Blindsight patients who exhibit absolutely no confidence as to the presence of objects in their blind field nevertheless demonstrate knowledge of the size, shape and orientation of such objects when required to guess (see Campion et al., 1983; Weiskrantz, 1986, for reviews). Similarly, amnesic patients demonstrate robust learning of skills such as reading mirror-inverted script and puzzle-solving despite their claims that they cannot remember ever performing these tasks before (see Shimamura, 1986; Schacter, 1987, for reviews).

Many investigators, however, feel uncomfortable measuring conscious awareness solely in terms of subjective reports. A major reason for caution is that it is difficult to know what criteria individuals use to decide that they are guessing (Merikle, 1984). Statements expressing no subjective confidence may simply reflect biases introduced by either the experimental instructions (i.e. demand characteristics, in psychological jargon) or an individual's preconceived ideas concerning the value of particular types of perceptual experiences for making decisions. For example, from the subjects' statements in Sidis' experiments, it is clear that, on at least some occasions, they saw both the cards and also 'dim, blurred spots or dots' on these cards. Thus, statements indicating an absence of subjective confidence may only reflect an individual's own theories of how perceptual experience guides behaviour rather than a true absence of conscious perceptual experience. As pointed out by Merikle (1984), the fundamental problem with the subjective confidence approach 'is that it transfers the responsibility for operationally defining awareness from the investigator to the observer' (p. 450).

The above considerations raise serious doubts as to whether subjective reports constitute an adequate exhaustive indicator of conscious awareness. The primary problem with this approach is that a lack of subjective confidence does not necessarily indicate an absence of conscious perceptual experience. For this reason, most investigators, with a few notable exceptions (e.g. Dixon, 1981; Henley, 1984), reject any approach for distinguishing conscious from unconscious perceptual processes that is based solely on subjective reports indicating whether or not sufficient information was perceived to perform the required task.

Studies Based on Perceptual Discriminations

Given the problems associated with subjective confidence as an exhaustive measure of awareness, many investigators prefer to define awareness on the basis of tasks that measure perceptual discriminative capacity. Typical measures used in recent studies are forced-choice, present-absent decisions, which require subjects to distinguish between the presence of a stimulus and a null stimulus condition, and forced-choice discriminations among a small, known, set of stimulus alternatives. Methodologically, measures of discriminative responding have an important advantage over measures based on subjective reports; measures of discriminative capacity allow the assessment of perceptual sensitivity with considerable precision, and independent of any possible influence of preconceived biases. Thus, the methodological rigour offered by an approach based on measures of discriminative responding is superior to any approach based on measures of subjective confidence. For this reason, operational definitions of awareness based on measures of perceptual discriminative capacity are preferred by many investigators. Implicitly, these measures seem more likely to satisfy the exhaustiveness assumption than measures based on subjective reports.

However, in early studies, this definitional change appeared to have completely eliminated the phenomenon! In retrospect, this consequence is perhaps the most plausible outcome. By defining awareness in terms of discriminative responding, the very same measures that investigators such as Sidis (1898) used to indicate the availability of perceptual information independent of consciousness were now used as indicators of awareness. For example, Sidis used forced-choice discriminations to demonstrate perception in the absence of subjective confidence. If, as implicitly assumed by Sidis, forced-choice discriminations are influenced by both conscious and unconscious processes, then using forced-choice discriminations to measure perceptual awareness violates the exclusiveness assumption. As a consequence, null sensitivity on a measure of discriminative responding may indicate an absence of both conscious and unconscious perceptual processes. In other words, discriminative responding may be an exhaustive measure of unconscious as well as conscious processes. Given these considerations, it is not surprising that Eriksen, in his classic critique of research using this approach, reached the following conclusion:

At present there is no convincing evidence that the human organism can discriminate or differentially respond to external stimuli that are at an intensity level too low to elicit a discriminated verbal report. In other words, a verbal report is as sensitive an indicator of perception as any other response that has been studied. (Eriksen, 1960, p. 298)

Eriksen's conclusions were accepted for many years by the majority of psychologists. However, they were seriously challenged in 1974 when Marcel presented a preliminary report describing a series of studies which appeared to demonstrate that visual stimuli are perceived even when observers cannot detect their presence. Although Marcel used a somewhat different methodology than had been used in previous experiments (see Marcel, 1983a), for present purposes the exact details of his methodology are unimportant. Rather, the critically important aspect of Marcel's experiments is that they appeared to demonstrate that a stimulus can be perceived even when subjects cannot discriminate between its presence or absence. Additional support for Marcel's findings came from subsequent experiments by other investigators who used similar methodologies and found comparable results (e.g. Fowler et al., 1981; Balota, 1983). These findings, taken as a whole, led to considerable excitement. They convinced many former sceptics that perception without awareness was indeed a valid phenomenon. If stimulus detection does provide an adequate exhaustive measure of perceptual awareness, then perception in the absence of stimulus detection would provide strong support for unconscious perception.

Given the potential importance of these findings reported by Marcel and subsequent investigators, these studies were carefully scrutinized by a number of critics (e.g. Merikle, 1982; Nolan and Caramazza, 1982; Cheesman and Merikle, 1985). It is interesting to note that these critics did not question the adequacy of stimulus detection as a measure of awareness. Instead, they directed their attention solely to the methodology used to establish null stimulus detection. On the basis of these critiques, it now appears that the methodology used in these experiments was probably inadequate for establishing null stimulus detection. Consequently, these studies are inconclusive as to the validity of perception without awareness. For this reason, Holender (1986), following a detailed review of these studies, concluded that there is little or no evidence for the concept of perception without awareness.

We seem to have come full circle from Eriksen (1960) to Marcel (1974) to Holender (1986) as opinion has swung from scepticism to enthusiasm and back to scepticism. If the absence of an ability to respond discriminatively to a stimulus is adequately established, then at the present time there is no evidence for any other perceptual processing. However, this absence of positive findings is only relevant to the study of perception without awareness if discriminative responding is assumed to provide an adequate exclusive measure of awareness. If discriminative responding does not measure conscious processes exclusively and actually measures the influence of both conscious and unconscious processes, then equating awareness with the capacity for discriminative responding may be tantamount to defining unconscious perception out of existence (see Bowers, 1984).

Some investigators implicitly assume that measures of discriminative responding are exclusive indicators of awareness. For these investigators, the failure to demonstrate perception in the absence of discriminative responding provides evidence against the existence of perception without awareness. For example, Holender (1986, p. 51) reviewed a number of measures of discriminative responding used in studies of perception without awareness and emphasized that 'one property common to all these indicators of awareness is that subjects make their responses intentionally. It is fundamental that an indicator of awareness must be intentional.' Thus, Holender's position implies that whenever subjects are required by task demands to discriminate between alternative stimulus states, their responses are intentional and therefore, by definition, reflect conscious processes. However, as pointed out by Marcel, it is entirely possible that:

> In attempting to make deliberate judgements based on information of whose external source one is unaware, it would seem that one makes use of the relevant nonconscious information, if it is available, by relying passively on its effects (e.g. upon attention) rather than being able selectively to retrieve it or be sensitive to it such that it can be the basis of an intentional choice. (Marcel, 1983a, p. 211)

The obvious fact emphasized by Marcel is that subjects' attempts to comply with task demands and to provide discriminative responses do not necessarily imply that their responses are informed and influenced by conscious processing exclusively. The real problem with Holender's (1986) position is that the intentions of a subject cannot be directly observed or measured. Intentionality, like awareness, is a theoretical construct that should not be confused with the characteristics of empirical tasks.

To summarize, the logic of the dissociation paradigm requires an adequate measure of awareness. To interpret any dissociation between two measures of perception as evidence for perception without awareness, one measure must be assumed to provide an exhaustive measure of awareness. In addition, to interpret the absence of a dissociation as evidence against perception without awareness, one measure must be assumed to provide an exclusive measure of awareness. Unfortunately, neither assumption can be justified on an *a priori* basis when awareness is measured in terms of either discriminative responding or reports of subjective confidence.

Alternative Approaches to the Measurement of Conscious Awareness

The lack of definitional and conceptual clarity in the study of the unconscious stems from the implicit or explicit association of certain tasks with characteristics of observers or rememberers such as intentionality or phenomenal awareness. Given that the assumed associations between tasks and observer characteristics are difficult to justify, the empirical findings have led primarily to controversy rather than to clarification. In this section, we describe two alternative approaches which appear to have some promise for resolving the conceptual/empirical confusions that characterize the study of the unconscious.

Relative Sensitivity of Direct and Indirect Measures

In the absence of a valid measure of awareness, we have suggested previously that comparisons of the relative sensitivity of different types of tasks used to assess perception and memory have the potential to provide considerable information concerning the relation between consciousness and cognition (Reingold and Merikle, 1988). The important distinction between tasks concerns whether a task provides a direct or an indirect index of a particular stimulus discrimination (see also Johnson and Hasher, 1987; Richardson-Klavehn and Bjork, 1988). Tasks in which subjects are explicitly instructed to perform the memory or perceptual discrimination of interest are defined as direct measures of memory or perception. In contrast, if the instructions given to subjects do not make any reference to the discrimination of interest, then such tasks are defined as indirect measures.

Examples of direct memory tasks are stimulus recognition and recall. In these tasks, subjects are explicitly instructed to discriminate old or previously presented stimuli from new stimuli that have not been presented within the experimental context. In contrast, a task such as word-stem completion constitutes indirect measure of memory in that no explicit reference is made in the task instructions to the distinction between old and new stimuli. For this reason, if the word stems are completed more often with old than with new words, then this task provides a sensitive indirect measure of memory.

As an illustration of direct and indirect measures of perception, consider the following variant of the Stroop colour–word interference task (e.g. Cheesman and Merikle, 1984). In this task, the presentation of a colour patch is immediately preceded by a brief presentation of a word naming either a congruent or an incongruent colour. Instructing subjects to report the identity of the word constitutes a direct measure of word identification. In contrast, if the subjects are instructed to name the colour patch, any influence of the preceding word on their colour naming performance constitutes an indirect measure of word identification. Typically, incongruence between a word and a colour patch inhibits colour naming performance, while congruence between a word and a colour patch facilitates performance. Thus, colour naming performance can provide a sensitive indirect measure of word recognition.

A critically important aspect of this distinction between direct and indirect measures of memory and perception is that it is based solely on a consideration of the instructions given to subjects. As such, it is completely neutral with respect to the nature of processing which may underlie performance on these two types of tasks. Thus, direct and indirect tasks may reflect conscious, unconscious or both conscious and unconscious processing. In other words, neither direct nor indirect measures are assumed to provide either exhaustive or exclusive indicators of conscious processing.

We believe that comparisons of the relative sensitivity of comparable direct and indirect measures have the potential to provide definitive evidence for unconscious perception and memory. The approach we advocate is based on the following minimal *a priori* working assumption: 'The sensitivity of a direct discrimination is assumed to be greater than or equal to the sensitivity of a comparable indirect discrimination to conscious, task relevant information' Reingold and Merikle, 1988, p. 556). The rationale underlying this assumption is that relevant conscious information, if it exists, would be used equally or more efficiently when subjects are instructed to make a particular discrimination (i.e. a direct task) than when subjects are not so instructed (i.e. an indirect task). Conversely, it is difficult to imagine circumstances in which conscious task-relevant information would enhance performance more when subjects are not instructed to make the discrimination, than when subjects are explicitly instructed to make the discrimination. Although any *a priori* assumption can be criticized, the proposed working assumption has two advantages. First, it is explicitly stated and thus open to evaluation. Second, it is a much more minimal assumption than either the exhaustiveness or the exclusiveness assumptions which are often made implicitly and which may, in fact, be impossible ever to justify.

The important consequence of this minimal assumption is that unconscious processes are implicated whenever an indirect measure shows greater absolute sensitivity than a comparable direct measure to a particular stimulus discrimination. This is the case because the assumption rules out the possibility that superior performance on the indirect task is attributable to conscious task-relevant information. Therefore, by default, whenever an indirect measure indicates greater sensitivity than a comparable direct measure, it must reflect a greater sensitivity of the indirect measure to unconscious task-relevant information. It is important to emphasize that this interpretation is warranted only if the direct and the indirect measures are truly comparable except for the instructions given to the subjects (see Reingold and Merikle, 1988). Otherwise, the greater sensitivity of an indirect measure may reflect a methodological artefact rather than unconscious processes.

Empirical support for the possible value of this approach to the study of unconscious processes comes from studies of unconscious memory. The results of a number of studies indicate that, at least under certain conditions, indirect measures do, in fact, exhibit greater sensitivity than comparable direct measures. In an important study, Kunst-Wilson and Zajonc (1980) initially showed subjects ten irregular geometric shapes, with each shape being presented five times for a very brief (1 ms) period. Following these initial exposures, the subjects were shown ten pairs of shapes, one old and one new, and they were instructed either to indicate which member of each pair had been presented previously (a direct measure) or to choose the shape they preferred (an indirect measure). With the indirect measure based on preference, the subjects chose the old stimulus in 60 per cent of the pairs. However, with the direct recognition test, old stimuli were selected in only 48 per cent of the pairs, which approximates a chance level of performance in this task. These basic findings have been replicated by other investigators (e.g. Seamon et al., 1984; Bonnano and Stillings, 1986; Mandler et al., 1987) and they have also been extended by Mandler et al. (1987) to other tasks requiring indirect discriminations (i.e. brightness, darkness). In addition, we have found that an indirect task requiring subjects to judge the discriminability of a visually degraded word can be a more sensitive indicator of memory for a previous presentation of this word than a comparable direct measure of stimulus recognition (Merikle and Reingold, 1991). According to the logic underlying comparisons between comparable direct and indirect measures, all of these demonstrations of greater sensitivity for the indirect measure constitute strong evidence for unconscious memory.

An approach to the study of unconscious processes based on comparisons of the relative sensitivity of comparable direct and indirect measures has distinct conceptual and methodological advantages relative to many previous approaches. Conceptually, the approach bypasses much of the controversy over the measurement of awareness. No strong *a priori* assumptions are required concerning the possible exhaustiveness or exclusiveness of any particular behavioural indicator as a measure of awareness. Rather, given that all behavioural measures are potentially sensitive to both conscious and unconscious processes, the approach only requires the much more minimal *a priori* assumption that the sensitivity of direct measures to conscious task-relevant information is equal or greater to the sensitivity of comparable indirect measures to the same information. This emphasis on the relative sensitivity of different measures also leads to an important methodological advantage. The extremely difficult methodological requirement of establishing null absolute sensitivity for assumed measure of awareness (see Macmillan, 1986) is no longer a prerequisite for demonstrating unconscious processing. Given these advantages and the suggestive findings indicating that certain indirect measures of memory are more sensitive than comparable direct measures, approaches based on the relative sensitivity of direct and indirect measures may be instrumental in documenting unconscious processes.

Converging Evidence for Measures of Awareness.

> I suggest that consciousness is no clearer a construct than, say, intelligence and that any given indicator of awareness is no more incontrovertible than a particular IQ index of intelligence. (Erdelyi, 1986, p. 31)

The preceding sections of this paper emphasize that the study of the unconscious is plagued by a lack of definitional and conceptual clarity. In general, the experimental approaches are based on implicit or explicit assumptions that cannot be justified on an *a priori* basis. Thus, the absence of definitional and conceptual clarity has led to experimental approaches to the measurement of conscious awareness that, in retrospect, appear quite arbitrary. It is now clear that any successful approach to the measurement of conscious awareness requires an operational definition of consciousness that can be validated by converging empirical evidence. In other words, empirical evidence is needed to justify any assumption that a particular measure provides an adequate index of conscious awareness. This fundamental goal cannot be achieved entirely by any amount of methodological precision in measurement or definitional precision in specifying theoretical constructs. Rather, a different experimental approach based on a somewhat different perspective is required.

The question guiding most psychological research into the unconscious concerns the issue of whether or not unconscious processing exists. We suggest that this question does not provide the most fruitful perspective for investigating the unconscious. Many investigators, in their preoccupation with trying to prove or disprove the existence of the unconscious, have neglected to consider the potential theoretical importance of the distinction between conscious and unconscious processes. Clearly, this distinction is of considerable importance if conscious and unconscious processes lead to qualitatively different behavioural consequences. However, if conscious and unconscious processes lead only to quantitative differences in behaviour, then the value of the distinction is not as obvious. We suggest that the perspective guiding research into the unconscious should be based on a search for the qualitatively different behavioural consequences that may distinguish conscious from unconscious processes. In fact, it is quite conceivable that the only way to find the necessary convergent evidence to validate a measure of awareness is to establish qualitative differences between conscious and unconscious processes.

As an illustration of this general approach based on establishing qualitative differences, consider a study reported by Marcel (1980). In this experiment, subjects were presented with a series of three successive letter strings. On critical trials, the second letter string was a polysemous word (e.g. *palm*). In the congruent condition, the first and the third letter strings were words related to the same meaning of the polysemous word (e.g. *hand, palm, wrist*), while in the incongruent condition, these words were related to different meanings of the polysemous word (e.g. *tree, palm, wrist*). The task for the subjects was to decide whether the third or final letter string was a word or a non-word (i.e. a nonsense string of letters). When the polysemous words were clearly visible, Marcel found that the decisions concerning the third letter string were only facilitated (i.e. faster) on congruent trials. In contrast, when the visibility of the polysemous word was severely degraded, the results indicated facilitation on both congruent and incongruent trials. Marcel suggested that these results indicate that conscious perception involves selection of the one meaning consistent with the context (i.e. the first word), whereas unconscious perception is not constrained by context. Interestingly, Marcel's findings are reminiscent of Freud's conceptualization of the primary processing which characterizes the unconscious id. According to Freud, primary processing allows mutually exclusive or contradictory thoughts and impulses to coexist (see Erdelyi, 1985).

Although the importance of demonstrating qualitative differences between conscious and unconscious processes has been emphasized previously (e.g. Dixon, 1971, 1981; Shevrin and Dickman, 1980; Cheesman and Merikle, 1985, 1986; Jacoby and Whitehouse, 1989; Jacoby et al., 1989b; Merikle and Reingold, 1990), this criterion has received surprisingly little empirical or theoretical attention. If it can be shown that qualitative differences can be predicted consistently on the basis of a particular behavioural measure, then this measure may constitute a valid indicator of awareness. Potentially, such measures could be based on either subjective reports or objective indicators of discriminative capacity. Thus, identification of a large number of qualitative differences provides a method for defining and, perhaps, even for discovering non-arbitrary measures of awareness. Furthermore, discovering predictable qualitative differences may constitute the ultimate empirical criteria for evaluating the value of the conceptual distinction between conscious and unconscious processes.

Conclusion

In this chapter, we have identified some of the issues that underlie the controversial status of the concept of the unconscious in psychology. In addition, possible directions for resolving this controversy have been outlined. We have argued that the confusion of constructs with tasks and the confusion of theoretical goals with methodological tools represent major obstacles in the study of the unconscious. What appears on the surface to be a debate over empirical findings is more often a reflection of differences in implicit theoretical starting points or assumptions. Thus, key players are actually playing in different courts, according to different rules, very much like the creatures in the caucus-race described in *Alice's Adventures in Wonderland*. Previous approaches based on attempts to provide indicators of awareness cannot be justified on an *a priori* basis. In the absence of a valid measure of awareness, the approach proposed by Reingold and Merikle (1988) represents a conservative methodological framework, with a minimal *a priori* assumption, for studying unconscious processing. In addition, identifying qualitative differences between conscious and unconscious processing may prove invaluable both in converging on a non-arbitrary indicator of awareness and in establishing the importance of the conscious–unconscious distinction. Given the complexity of this area of research, it is likely that different paradigms will be necessary if true progress is to be made. At the same time, the need for definitional and conceptual clarity should not be forgotten.

Acknowledgements

We thank Elizabeth Bosman and Mary Merikle for their many helpful comments on earlier drafts of this chapter.

2
Impairments of Visual Awareness

ANDREW W. YOUNG AND
EDWARD H. F. DE HAAN

Extensive areas of cerebral tissue are devoted to achieving our rich experience of the visual world. Anatomical and neurophysiological studies show clearly that multiple pathways are involved in the processing of visual information, and that each of these pathways contains a number of identifiable subcomponents (Ungerleider and Mishkin, 1982; Cowey, 1985). It seems that vision is achieved through the interaction of many processing 'modules', each of which is dedicated to a particular purpose.

Such modular organization has probably developed in response to a number of constraints, including the need for 'tidy wiring' of the nervous system, and because it confers the advantage that it becomes possible for experience to modify part of the visual system without detrimental 'knock-on' effects on our other visual abilities (Marr, 1982; Cowey, 1985).

Occasionally, the modular organization of visual abilities is revealed by the effects of brain injury. Of course, most strokes or head injuries will affect several processing modules, leaving the patient with a fairly general type of impairment. But in rare cases it is found that a single processing module is primarily involved, allowing a privileged insight into the underlying 'functional architecture'.

These highly selective visual impairments can affect what we might consider to be quite basic visual abilities, such as the ability to see colour (Damasio et al., 1980) or movement (Zihl et al., 1983). In other cases, however, specific impairments are found for 'higher' visual abilities, such as the ability to read words (Damasio and Damasio, 1983) or to recognize familiar faces (Meadows, 1974; De Renzi, 1986). Hence, it is clear that modular organization is probably characteristic of all levels of visual information processing.

Studies of the type we have been describing are essential to understanding how vision is achieved but, if anything, they leave us even more puzzled as to the nature of visual *experience*. When we look about us we see an orderly arrangement of things in three-dimensional space, and have no sense that colour might be determined independently of form, and so on. Such puzzles have, of course, been with us for a long time. One of the most exciting developments arising from recent neuropsychological studies, however, is that they are beginning to offer insights into how visual awareness is achieved. It turns out that certain types of visual impairment can be usefully construed as involving impairments of visual awareness, rather than impaired visual perceptual mechanisms *per se*.

In this chapter we will outline some of these impairments of visual awareness, and explore their implications for understanding the nature of conscious experience. We will not attempt an exhaustive review of what is already a rapidly expanding literature, but will instead concentrate on discussing representative studies that illustrate points of interest. Topics to be considered will include 'blindsight', recognition impairments, disorders of visual attention, amnesia and unawareness of impairment. We claim no special expertise in approaching the philosophical or psychological problems associated with the study of consciousness and awareness. The truth is that we had no more than a general acquaintance with such issues until they were forced upon us by research findings. We hope only that these findings are of sufficiently widespread interest to make it worth discussing what lessons and conclusions can as yet be drawn.

Blindsight

Observations of 'blindsight' derive from investigations of visual functioning in areas of the visual field that are unresponsive on standard perimetric testing. Weiskrantz's term 'blindsight' neatly encompasses the paradoxical nature of the condition; responses to visual stimuli can be demonstrated (with certain methods of testing), yet the patient denies being able to 'see' them.

A substantial number of studies of this type have now been reported; we will concentrate here on the very thorough investigation of patient DB carried out by Weiskrantz and his colleagues (Weiskrantz et al., 1974; Weiskrantz, 1980, 1986, 1987), introducing details from some of the other patients investigated as necessary.

DB underwent an operation in 1973 to remove an arteriovenous malformation from his right occipital lobe. This necessitated removal of the striate cortex of the right cerebral hemisphere. Since the optic nerves project to striate cortex the operation, predictably, left DB with a substantial blind area in his field of vision. Initially, this blind area occupied almost the entire left half of his field of vision, but over the next few years it gradually contracted until only the lower left quadrant was involved.

An area of blindness of this type is known as a *scotoma*. To test for a scotoma the patient is asked to report what s/he sees when stimuli are presented at different points in the visual field. Thus, DB did not report seeing stimuli falling anywhere in the region to the lower left of the point he was fixating, and for some time he also did not report seeing stimuli in most of the area to the upper left of fixation.

Weiskrantz et al. (1974) began by replicating a finding made by Pöppel et al. (1973). They presented brief (3 s) flashes of light at different horizontal positions within the scotoma, and asked DB to indicate the location of each flash by moving his eyes to where he 'guessed' it had occurred. There was a weak correspondence between DB's 'guesses' and the actual target position for targets presented up to 25 degrees from fixation.

This result showed that DB was getting some information about the location of the light flashes, but it was not particularly impressive. More accurate responses, however, were obtained across a wide range of stimulus eccentricities when Weiskrantz et al. (1974) asked DB to *point* to where he guessed each flash had occurred. Even at his most accurate, though, performance for DB's 'blind' field was somewhat below what he could achieve using the part of his field that still had normal vision.

Weiskrantz et al. (1974) also showed that DB could discriminate the orientation of stimuli presented within his scotoma and, by asking him to 'guess' whether a presented stimulus was a sine-wave grating of vertical dark and light bars, they were able to determine his visual acuity (in terms of the narrowest grating that could be detected). It turned out that gratings with bar widths of 1.5' could be detected in the sighted part of his field of vision, and a rather less fine but still impressive 1.9' in the 'blind' field.

What is so striking about these observations is, of course, that DB maintained that he had no experience of seeing the stimuli presented in the scotoma. Because the scotoma itself gradually contracted during the first few years after his operation, later studies have been confined to the (still scotomous) lower left quadrant. Weiskrantz (1980, 1986) has reported several studies that have confirmed and extended the original findings. In particular, DB could detect the presence or absence of a light stimulus even when it was introduced or extinguished quite slowly, he could readily distinguish static from moving stimuli, and more detailed testing of acuity in the scotoma showed that (unlike normal vision) it increased as the stimuli were moved to positions further away from fixation.

Studies of blindsight raise a number of issues. Foremost among these is, as Pöppel (1983) neatly puts it, whether blindsight is a phenomenon that has to be explained by mechanisms inside or outside the brain. In other words, is there an explanation for the observations that does not demand the existence of some form of preserved or residual visual capacity in the apparently blind area? Any inadvertent cueing of the correct responses would, of course, render blindsight no more remarkable than the abilities of 'Clever Hans', a horse that was once widely believed to be able to do mental arithmetic, but who turned out on more careful investigation to be responding to slight signals inadvertently given by his trainer (see Miller, 1966).

The most widely acknowledged hypothesis of this type is that the performances of blindsight patients might be mediated through light scattered onto portions of the retina unrelated to the scotoma, as a result of reflection off structures external or internal to the eye. Campion et al. (1983) criticized many of the early studies for failure completely to eliminate this hypothesis. However, we find this implausible as an explanation of *all* blindsight phenomena. If light scattering were responsible then one might expect all patients with scotomas to show blindsight. But it is quite clear that they do not. Weiskrantz, (1980) for instance, could find no evidence of residual visual function for 8 out of 22 cases he was able to examine under satisfactory conditions. Moreover, Weiskrantz (1986) reports that DB did not show blindsight for stimuli presented onto the ophthalmological blindspot, where the optic nerve leaves the retina. Performance based on cuing from scattered light would have been unaffected by the absence of receptor cells in this area. Finally, studies have reported blindsight phenomena under conditions in which light scattering could not provide any useful cues (Barbur et al., 1980, 1988).

As Weiskrantz (1986) observes, one can never entirely exclude the possibility that what appears to be a genuine visual capacity may be based on unintentional cues of which both subject and experimenter are unaware, but only accumulate evidence that makes such a possibility extremely unlikely. The controls that have been used in blindsight studies carried out in a number of different laboratories have been sufficient to allow us to conclude that unintentional cueing is a very unlikely explanation indeed. Thus we can turn with some confidence to the more interesting (and more generally accepted) view that blindsight has to be explained by mechanisms inside the brain.

Much of the discussion of the brain mechanisms responsible for blindsight has centred around whether they involve spared areas of striate cortex, or midbrain structures. This issue of localization is not really relevant to present concerns, except that localization to non-cortical brain structures seems to reassure those who want to argue that cortical equals conscious. Of more direct interest here is that discussions of the brain mechanisms involved have often focused on the question as to whether blindsight can be considered a form of degraded but essentially 'normal' vision, or whether it is qualitatively different. This question is central to understanding the implications of blindsight.

Since the nineteenth century psychophysical studies have shown that we cannot simply see *any* visual stimulus; there is a threshold for effective vision that is itself dependent on a number of factors. Moreover, it is known that in 'near-threshold' conditions normal people are sometimes able to make accurate decisions about stimuli that they do not always report 'seeing' (Campion et al., 1983; Cheesman and Merikle, 1985). An obvious initial hypothesis might thus be that the phenomena found in blindsight studies are those all of us would experience under near-threshold visual conditions.

To discuss this idea properly would require much more space than we have here. All we can say at present is that it seems to us unlikely to be able to provide more than a partial account. There is no evidence that the performance of a patient like DB would be greatly affected by variations in stimulus intensity within the range to which he is responsive. This makes the comparison to near-threshold conditions in normal vision at best an analogy. But there are also findings, such as the greater acuity to relatively peripheral stimuli, that can have no explanation in these terms, and instead imply a qualitative difference between blindsight and normal vision. The idea of a qualitative difference is supported by the fact that there is as yet no published evidence of true form perception in DB's scotoma (Weiskrantz, 1987), or those of other blindsight patients (Perenin and Jeannerod, 1975). The residual abilities are thus confined to the processing of relatively basic visual properties (detection, location, orientation etc.).

This brings us to the question we have been deferring; what is blindsight like? Is there really *no* visual experience?

The immediate answer is that blindsight patients *can* produce accurate responses under conditions in which they insist that they see *nothing at all*. But matters are actually rather more complicated. Usually, some degree of practice is needed before blindsight phenomena can be demonstrated, though this practice does not necessarily involve the patient's receiving any immediate feedback concerning his or her performance (Weiskrantz, 1980; Zihl, 1980; Zihl and Werth, 1984). Patients seem to be able to learn to attend to something, yet that something is seldom described as being like a visual experience. Soon after surgery, DB was not aware of stimuli in his blind field at all, except that in some regions moving stimuli could produce peculiar radiating lines. Later, though, he gradually came to say that he 'knew something was there', and roughly where it was, but that he did not in any sense 'see' it (Weiskrantz, 1980, p. 374).

Not all patients produce such unequivocal subjective reports, however. Barbur et al. (1980) state that their patient, G, perceived as dark shadows light flashes presented in the blind area at an illumination level just above threshold (a quite abnormal response; in his 'sighted' field they were perceived as brightening), but that more intense stimulation could give the sensation of a well-localized bright flash. There may thus be differences between individual patients in the degree to which all forms of visual experience are lost in the blind area.

A further complication is that in some cases practice can actually lead to the restitution of visual experience (Zihl and von Cramon, 1979, 1985; Zihl, 1981). In DB's case, we have already alluded to the shrinkage of the scotoma in the years immediately following his operation, but he continued to say that he was not aware of stimuli presented well inside the reduced scotoma (Weiskrantz, 1980, 1986).

Ought we to be so willing to rely on patients' subjective reports? There is a sense in which they are trying to describe the indescribable. But we must always face this problem when we rely on *anyone's* subjective reports; visual experience is intrinsically private. A more insidious difficulty, though, is that blindsight patients might actually be aware of the stimuli to which they respond, but that this awareness is no longer accessible to the language system used in answering questions about what was seen. This is at present difficult to rule out unequivocally. However, Weiskrantz (1988) points out that the responses of 'split-brain' patients to visual stimuli projected to the right cerebral hemisphere, which has been surgically disconnected from the left hemisphere's language centres, are unlike those of blindsight patients. This demonstrates that the explanation of blindsight is not *merely* loss of access to verbal capacities.

Studies of blindsight, then, teach us that certain types of visual response can be made in the absence of acknowledged awareness. These responses do not cover the complete range of normal, conscious, visual abilities, and may well come from parts of the visual system that operate without awareness in the intact brain.

Recognition Impairments

Brain injury can sometimes compromise ability to *recognize* visual stimuli, even though the patient remains able to 'see'. These recognition impairments may differentially affect certain types of visual stimuli. We will consider here impairments of face and of word recognition, which have produced evidence of the breakdown of awareness of recognition.

Shallice and Saffran (1986) studied the word-recognition abilities of ML, a patient who had become a letter-by-letter reader after a stroke. In letter-by-letter reading the normal mechanisms that allow words to be read 'at a glance' are apparently damaged. As a result, the patient reads slowly, one letter at a time. For ML to read a word aloud, he needed around 1 s per letter, so that brief presentation of words severely compromised his performance.

Although brief presentation prevented ML from recognizing words overtly, Shallice and Saffran (1986) showed that he performed at above-chance levels in categorization tasks (e.g. in deciding whether or not a letter string was a word, and in deciding whether a written name was that of an author or a politician).

Shallice and Saffran's (1986) study demonstrates that some degree of semantic processing of a seen word can occur in the absence of explicit identification. Although ML could not say what word had been shown when brief presentation was employed, his performance of forced-choice tasks showed that at least some aspects of its meaning were available. The case forms an interesting parallel to one described by Landis et al. (1980), who reported that a patient with inability to read words on overt tests (i.e. tests that involved asking him to read the words) could point to the objects corresponding to words presented very briefly. As his ability to read the words improved, however, ability to derive the meaning of 'unread' words was apparently lost.

Most of the work on the breakdown of awareness in recognition impairments has been concerned with prosopagnosia. Prosopagnosic patients are no longer able to recognize familiar people from their faces. The deficit can extend to even the most well-known faces, including friends, family, famous people and the patient's own face when seen in a mirror (Hécaen and Angelergues, 1962). Such patients know when they are looking at a face, and can often describe and identify facial features, or even use facial information to determine age, sex and expression, but appear not to experience any sense of recognizing who the face might belong to. In order to recognize familiar people, prosopagnosic patients must thus rely on non-facial cues, such as voice or clothing. The condition was first convincingly described by Bodamer (1947), and reviews of the underlying neurology are given by Meadows (1974) and Damasio et al. (1982).

The breakdown of overt face recognition ability experienced by prosopagnosic patients can be complete, with not even a vague feeling of familiarity remaining. This can be demonstrated by chance-level performance of forced-choice tasks in which a highly familiar face and an unfamiliar face are simultaneously presented, and the patient is asked to choose the familiar face (Young and de Haan, 1988). It thus surprised many of us when Bauer (1984) demonstrated a degree of preserved recognition in the form of autonomic responses to familiar faces.

Bauer (1984) made use of the Guilty Knowledge Test, a technique sometimes used in criminal investigations which is based on the view that a guilty person will show some involuntary physiological response to stimuli related to the crime. He showed a prosopagnosic patient photographs of familiar faces which were presented for 90 s, accompanied by five different names, one of which was the correct name. Maximal skin conductance responses to the correct name were found for some 61 per cent of trials, a figure well above the chance level of 20 per cent. Yet when the patient was asked to *choose* which name was correct for each face, he performed at chance level (22 per cent correct). Comparable findings of larger and more frequent skin conductance responses to familiar than to unfamiliar faces were reported by Tranel and Damasio (1985, 1988). Additional evidence comes from studies by Rizzo et al. (1987), who showed a difference in eye movement scanpaths when patients with impaired overt face recognition ability viewed familiar and unfamiliar faces, and Renault et al. (1989), who found differences in evoked potentials.

Such findings profoundly alter our conception of the nature of prosopagnosia, since they show that it is inadequate to think of it as simply involving loss of recognition mechanisms. Instead, at least some degree of recognition does take place; what the patient has lost is *awareness of recognition*. Although Bauer's (1984) adaptation of the Guilty Knowledge Test is a neat way of demonstrating this, no one is suggesting that the patients are lying!

Bauer (1984, 1986) offers an intriguing hypothesis concerning the neuroanatomical pathways involved in this phenomenon. He suggests that overt recognition depends on the intactness of a 'ventral' visual system–limbic system pathway, whereas a more 'dorsal' visual–limbic pathway subserves processes of emotional arousal. In prosopagnosia, the ventral pathway is impaired, whereas the dorsal pathway may remain intact, leading to 'covert' recognition of familiar faces that cannot be recognized overtly.

We have used behavioural measures to explore covert recognition in more detail, especially with the prosopagnosic patient PH (de Haan et al., 1987a, b; Young and de Haan, 1988; Young et al., 1988). The focus of interest in this investigation has been to determine which tasks will and will not produce evidence of covert recognition of familiar faces, and to compare the phenomena revealed to those that we think reflect automatic aspects of the operation of the normal recognition system.

As a result of this work, it now seems clear to us that the principal (though by no means the only) requirement for demonstrating preserved ('covert') recognition is that recognition is tested *implicitly*, that is, in terms of its effect on some other ability. In contrast, PH has so far performed at chance level on all of the *explicit* tests of familiar face recognition we have used (i.e. tests that overtly demand recognition as part of the instructions).

The implicit tasks we have used to date with PH involve variants of *matching, interference, associative priming* and *learning* paradigms. In matching tasks, he showed faster matching (as same or different) of pairs of photographs of familiar faces than unfamiliar faces, which indicates that some information about known faces as familiar visual patterns is preserved, even if he is unaware of it. By using interference tasks, however, de Haan et al. (1987a, b) also demonstrated that information about the semantic category to which a face belonged was covertly accessed by PH. In these tasks PH was asked to classify printed *names* as those of politicians or non-politicians. His reaction times for name classification were longer when the names were accompanied by distractor faces drawn from the opposite semantic category than when a distractor face was not present, or came from the same semantic category. The same pattern of interference of faces on name classification is found for normal subjects (Young et al., 1986) but, unlike normal subjects, PH could not achieve accurate overt classification as politicians or non-politicians of the distractor faces used.

Perhaps the most interesting results of all have been obtained with associative priming (Young et al., 1988). Associative priming tasks examine the influence of one stimulus on the recognition of a related stimulus; for instance, the effect of seeing Raisa Gorbachev's face on recognition of Mikhail Gorbachev's name. Typically, recognition of a target stimulus is facilitated by an immediately preceding prime stimulus which is a close associate of the target. PH shows associative priming from faces he does not recognize. Moreover, it is possible to compare the size of the priming effect onto name targets across face primes (which PH does not recognize overtly) and printed name primes (which he recognizes without difficulty). It turns out that these are exactly equivalent; the possibility of overt recognition of name primes makes no additional contribution to the associative priming effect.

Of course, many aspects of recognition operate automatically in everyday life. We cannot look at a familiar face and decide not to recognize it; the mechanisms responsible for visual recognition are simply not open to conscious control in this way. We are impressed by the parallel between PH's preserved abilities on implicit tests and those aspects of recognition that seem to operate automatically for normal people. Hence we have argued that his condition can be seen as involving disconnection of the *output* of an otherwise adequately functioning face-recognition system from whatever processes are needed to support awareness of recognition. The result is a curious disorder of awareness, in which there is no global alteration of consciousness, but one specific aspect (awareness of recognition of familiar faces) is lost.

An alternative conception would be that covert recognition is produced by a *degraded* recognition system. This seems to us unlikely because PH showed equivalent priming effects from stimuli he could not recognize (faces) and those he could recognize (names). A degraded system might be expected to produce reduced priming effects. In addition, PH performed at chance level for even the simplest explicit tests, such as choosing which of two simultaneously presented faces is familiar (Young and de Haan, 1988). Weak or degraded overt recognition should have led to above-chance performance of such tasks.

As was the case for blindsight, it must be emphasized that not all prosopagnosic patients show covert recognition. Bauer (1986), Newcombe et al. (1989) and Young and Ellis (1989) have all described patients who respond at chance level on both explicit *and* implicit tests of familiar face recognition. Thus, in some cases there seems to be a genuine breakdown of all levels of recognition, because the recognition process is itself compromised, whereas in others it is only awareness of recognition that is lost.

A second point worth emphasizing is that not all implicit tests produce evidence of covert recognition, even for patients like PH (Young and de Haan, 1988). Learning tasks are particularly useful in this respect. Bruyer et al. (1983) found that their prosopagnosic patient learnt 'true' pairings of faces and names more readily than he learnt 'untrue' combinations. That is, when shown a particular face, he could learn to associate the correct name to it more easily than someone else's name. This was also true for PH (de Haan et al., 1987b; Young and de Haan, 1988), even though he considered his responses 'just guesses'.

The particular advantage of this learning paradigm is that it is easy to vary the type of material to be learnt. When this was done with PH, better learning of true pairings was found for full names ('Norman Tebbit', 'Terry Wogan' etc.) and for occupational categories ('politician', 'actor' etc.), but was not found for first names ('Norman', 'Terry' etc.) or for relatively 'precise' semantic information (such as the political parties and backgrounds associated with a group of politicians, or the specific sports associated with a group of sportsmen). Our interpretation of these findings is that PH's covert recognition effects arise at a particular stage of the recognition process (Young and de Haan, 1988). Implicit recognition tasks requiring information that is only accessed beyond this stage will be performed at chance level.

A further variant of the learning paradigm was to use faces of people that PH had only met since his accident. For this purpose, we used our own faces, and those of colleagues. Covert recognition was still found, demonstrating that PH's recognition system had continued to build up representations of faces of the people he meets, even though he has never recognized them overtly. A similar finding with other patients was made by Tranel and Damasio (1988), using electrodermal responses.

Disorders of Visual Attention

Often, we need to attend to particular stimuli to cut down the amount of information we would otherwise have to deal with. Attentional selection can probably take place at several different levels of analysis, any of which may become impaired after brain injury.

One such disorder is known as visual extinction. Patients with visual extinction can identify a *single* stimulus falling anywhere in their field of vision, but when *two* stimuli are presented simultaneously in the left and right visual fields, they fail to report the stimulus falling in the visual field opposite to the side of the brain affected by the cerebral injury. The preserved ability to identify a single stimulus rules out blindness as a cause of their problems, and shows that the difficulties experienced when more than one stimulus is present must have an 'attentional' origin.

Volpe et al. (1979) present data for four patients with extinction following tumours affecting the right parietal lobe. All were able to identify a picture of a single object presented either in the left or in the right visual field, but all four patients only reported the right visual field object when pictures of different objects were simultaneously presented with one falling in the left visual field and one in the right visual field. If asked whether or not the two stimuli were 'same' or 'different', however, highly accurate responses were obtained even when patients denied the presence of the 'extinguished' right visual field stimulus. This finding demonstrates that considerable processing of the extinguished stimulus must have taken place, even though the results of this processing mostly did not enter awareness. As Volpe et al. (1979, p. 724) put it, extinction involves 'a breakdown in the flow of information between conscious and non-conscious mental systems'.

Extinction is generally considered to be closely related to another form of disorder observed after brain injury: unilateral neglect (Heilman, 1979). Like extinction, neglect is usually encountered in patients with right cerebral injuries, for whom it affects the left side of space. Patients with left-sided neglect ignore the left side of space in many everyday tasks, including when they are looking for things, moving around (bumping into obstacles on their left), reading, dressing (putting on clothes only on the right side of the body), and eating (leaving food on the left side of a plate).

For neglect patients with fully or largely intact visual fields, Karnath and Hartje (1987) and Karnath (1988) reported findings that were analogous to those made in Volpe et al.'s (1979) study of extinction, using a technique involving brief stimulus presentation. Most patients with left-sided neglect, however, also show blindness in the left visual field (left hemianopia), and would be unsuited to this procedure because they would fail overtly to recognize left visual field stimuli on single as well as on simultaneous presentations. Marshall and Halligan (1988), though, were able to demonstrate covert processing of a neglected stimulus presented in free vision.

Marshall and Halligan's (1988) patient, PS, showed severe left-sided neglect following a subarachnoid haemorrhage. She failed to report that bright red flames were emerging from the left-hand side of a drawing of a house, and asserted that this drawing was the same as another drawing that had no flames. Yet when asked which house she would prefer to live in, PS consistently tended to choose the non-burning picture, even though she considered the question silly ('because they're the same'). The information that the house was on fire was apparently registered at a non-conscious level.

In later trials, PS was shown a drawing in which flames emerged from the right-hand side of the house, which she immediately commented upon. Subsequently, she finally 'noticed' the fire in the house with the left-sided flames, exclaiming 'Oh my God, this one's on fire!' Thus the failure of conscious recognition of the left-sided flames was not absolute, but could be overcome by appropriate cueing.

An interesting difference between Marshall and Halligan's (1988) observations and those reported by Volpe et al. (1979), Karnath and Hartje (1987), and Karnath (1988) is that PS did *not* initially respond correctly when she was asked to make same *v.* different judgements, whereas it was precisely these same *v.* different judgements that *were* preserved for the other patients. It is thus clear that failures of awareness caused by attentional disorders can arise at different levels; with some patients having more potential information than others concerning the 'unattended' stimulus. These differences will need to be carefully explored.

Amnesia

Amnesia is not a disorder of vision as such, but we thought it necessary to mention it for completeness, since many of the demonstrations of implicit memory in amnesia relate to *visual* memory.

Most of these demonstrations were inspired by the paradigm used by Warrington and Weiskrantz (1968, 1970), who asked amnesic patients to identify fragmented pictures or words, and showed that subsequent identification of the same stimuli was facilitated. This type of finding can be obtained for amnesic patients even when they fail to remember having taken part in any previous testing sessions. The key point seems to be that the amnesics' memories are tested *implicitly*, in terms of the facilitation of subsequent recognition of the same stimuli (Schacter, 1987). *Explicit* tests, such as asking whether or not items were among those previously shown, lead to very poor performance. Hence amnesics show a form of 'memory without awareness', in which their performance can be affected by previous experiences they completely fail to remember overtly.

Unawareness of Impairment

One of the most striking forms of neuropsychological phenomena involves patients who are *unaware of their impairments* and thus may fail to comprehend, or even actively deny, their problems. The condition is called anosognosia (see McGlynn and Schacter, 1989). A wide range of types of impairment can be subject to anosognosia; we will briefly discuss those involving visual abilities.

Two common consequences of brain injury are paralysis to one side of the body (hemiplegia) and blindness in part of the field of vision (often affecting the entire left visual field or the entire right visual field; termed a hemianopia). Most patients accept the existence of such impairments, but not all (Raney and Nielsen, 1942). Further, lack of awareness of hemiplegia and hemianopia can dissociate. That is, patients may be aware of a hemiplegia but unaware of a hemianopia, or vice versa (Bisiach et al., 1986). Thus, unawareness of impairment does not result from a general change in the patient's state of consciousness, but can be *specific to particular disabilities.*

The classic observations of unawareness of visual impairment date back to Von Monakow (1885) and Anton (1899), who described patients who *denied their own blindness.* One of Von Monakow's (1885) patients had extensive bilateral brain lesions, and did not respond to lights flashed in his eyes or to violent gesticulations made in front of his face. Although he complained about other problems, he never admitted to being blind. The interpretation of the case is complicated, though, by the fact that there was apparently some residual vision; it was noticed that this patient could walk around obstacles put in his way.

Although his name has become associated with denial of blindness, two of the three cases in Anton's (1899) report involved denial of deafness. The second case he described, however, was that of a 56-year-old woman who suffered a progressive visual field defect culminating in apparently complete blindness. She complained bitterly about her other problems, but did not seem to take any notice of her blindness. When questioned about her vision she maintained that it was not as good as when she was younger, but that she could still see. Like Von Monakow's, the case is complicated by the fact that some form of residual vision may well have been present.

There have been numerous subsequent reports of Anton's syndrome, as it has come to be known (see McGlynn and Schacter, 1989). Most emphasize that the patients are unaware of their blindness, behave *as if* they can see, and may even confabulate 'visual' experiences (Raney and Nielsen, 1942; Redlich and Dorsey, 1945). The question of the significance of any residual visual abilities remains unresolved, but it is clear that the patients have little or no insight into their very severe visual problems. There are, though, some cases in which insight is achieved. Raney and Nielsen (1942, p. 151) described a woman who, after a year of apparent lack of insight into her problems, exclaimed 'My God, I am blind! Just to think, I have lost my eyesight!'

Unawareness of visual recognition impairments has also been noted. Bonhoeffer (1903) described a patient unable to identify words after a left hemisphere injury who showed no awareness of his reading problems but was aware of his right hemianopia. Landis et al. (1986) reported six cases of prosopagnosia, four of whom showed unconcern or denial of their face recognition problems. A detailed description of a case, SP, involving unawareness of impaired face recognition is given by Young et al. (1990). In contrast to her lack of insight into her face recognition impairment, SP showed adequate insight into other physical and cognitive impairments produced by her illness, including poor memory, hemiplegia and hemianopia. These findings bear out the point that unawareness of impairment does not result from any overall change in the patient's state of consciousness, but can be specific to particular disabilities.

Lack of insight is also often found in cases of unilateral neglect, and can exasperate relatives who fail to understand why it is so difficult to get the patient to notice the mistakes that she or he is constantly making.

Unawareness of memory impairments is also regularly noted, and its causes have been evaluated by McGlynn and Schacter (1989). The presence or absence of awareness of impaired memory is not solely attributable to the *severity* of the memory impairment. That is, it is not simply the case that people with poor memories forget the occasions when they failed to remember things, and thus feel that their memories are unimpaired (see McGlynn and Schacter, 1989). Instead, unawareness of memory problems seems to form another example of a deficit-specific anosognosia.

Lessons from the Neuropsychology of Visual Awareness

It is clear that visual awareness can break down in a number of different ways after brain injury. Patients may continue to be able to make accurate responses to stimuli they are no longer aware of 'seeing' (blindsight), or they can show responses indicating the continued operation of face or word recognition mechanisms that seem to them to be entirely disrupted. In impairments of visual attention, processing of 'extinguished' or 'neglected' stimuli can continue to relatively high levels, even though they do not enter awareness. Amnesic patients can be shown to retain some type of visual memory capacity on implicit tests.

For each of these types of impairment there does not seem to be any global change of consciousness. Instead, *the loss of awareness is usually highly selective*, and confined to a particular aspect of visual experience (such as awareness of recognizing a familiar face).

Paralleling all of these forms of visual impairment are conditions in which people who have suffered brain injuries seem to be unaware of their own problems (anosognosias), which they ignore or actively deny. Patients with manifestly poor vision may insist that they can still see normally. Patients who can no longer read, or who fail to recognize familiar faces, may deny their visual recognition difficulties. Lack of insight can also characterize patients with problems involving visual attention or memory.

We consider that these deficit-specific anosognosias reflect the existence of the need to monitor our own performance in everyday life (Young et al., 1990). Monitoring is necessary to correct errors we sometimes make, and also because different types of information must sometimes be intentionally combined and evaluated. For instance, if you see what looks to be your father standing outside the Post Office when you thought he was at work, you must weigh up the degree of visual likeness of the seen person to your father against the probability that it could be him given your other knowledge; further examples of this type are given by Young et al. (1985). Similarly, Thomson (1986) mentions a 'field study', in which the daughter of an Australian couple was asked to stand outside a London hotel when her parents thought she was in Australia. They recognized their daughter, but when she (deliberately) did not respond, her father apologised; 'I am terribly sorry, I thought you were someone else.'

Impairment of such monitoring and decision processes is, in our view, what gives rise to anosognosias. As Bisiach et al. (1986) point out, the existence of deficit-specific anosognosias suggests that this monitoring does not involve a common 'central' monitoring mechanism, but is to some degree 'decentralized'.

Although there are a number of conditions which can be considered as much *impairments of visual awareness* as impairments of visual perceptual mechanisms *per se*, it should not be assumed that all visual impairments fall into this category. Coexisting with the types of problem we have concentrated on in this chapter are other conditions in which there does seem to be a genuine breakdown of perceptual mechanisms, and the patients perform poorly both to explicit and to implicit tests of the ability in question (e.g. Newcombe et al., 1989). The use of implicit tests to tease apart different types of impairment, that can otherwise appear rather similar in terms of the patient's problems on explicit tests, forms one of the most interesting developments in contemporary neuropsychology.

As concerns our understanding of awareness, the principal implication of findings from studies of vision after brain injury is that awareness is *not* integral to the operation of many perceptual mechanisms. This conclusion is at variance with what Marcel (1983a, b) calls the 'identity assumption', which postulates that the same processes subserve stimulus analysis and awareness. Instead, awareness seems to depend on different neural mechanisms from those involved in determining the properties of visual stimuli. Although we remain as mystified as everyone else concerning *what awareness is needed for*, it does seem to us that it is difficult to continue to view it as an epiphenomenon if dissociable neural mechanisms are involved. To maintain the epiphenomenalist stance, one would have to argue that awareness is epiphenomenal only to *certain types* of neural activity.

A recurrent feature of the conditions we have described is that the patient's performance takes on a more 'normal' pattern on implicit tests, while being severely impaired to explicit tests. It is thus attractive to view these conditions as forming a group of neurological impairments having a common functional basis, but arising at different loci in the visual system. Schacter et al. (1988) suggest that they can all be characterized as involving *failures of access to consciousness*. Schacter et al. (1988) propose that conscious or explicit experiences of perceiving, recognizing, remembering, and so on, all depend on the functioning of a common mechanism which can normally accept inputs from a variety of processing modules that handle specific types of information. If brain injury disconnects one of the processing modules from the conscious mechanism, the consequence will be an impaired performance of explicit tasks while performance of implicit tasks (which are not considered to require active involvement of the conscious processor) remains relatively intact.

We have considerable sympathy with Schacter et al.'s (1988) position. It certainly seems that the preserved abilities found on implicit tests reflect those aspects of the visual system whose operation is quite automatic in nature, and not subject to conscious control. In addition, we have argued that the pattern of preserved performance is more easily considered as reflecting disconnection from awareness than impairment to perceptual mechanisms *per se*. Our reservation concerning Schacter et al.'s (1988) hypothesis is that we are not yet convinced that it is necessary to think in terms of *one*, centralized conscious mechanism. It seems to us equally likely that there may be multiple systems responsible for different aspects of awareness, which could mean that the complete pattern of possible disconnections might be very complicated. This is, of course, an empirical question, to be settled by further investigations.

Before such issues can be satisfactorily resolved, though, two theoretical developments are needed. First, we need to have a more objective way of making the distinction between implicit and explicit tests. At present, the distinction is convincing in many cases, but there is also a rather worrying 'grey area' in which a test can be allocated to the implicit or explicit category according to the pattern of performance obtained. The use of forced-choice, for instance, characterizes many implicit tests, yet forced-choice determination of familiarity is one of the tasks at which the prosopagnosic patient, PH, is very poor (Young and de Haan, 1988). A lot of the difference may well lie in the *attitude* with which a particular patient approaches a specific task; i.e. whether it is one of 'guessing' (a word which often crops up in descriptions of preserved abilities) or of working hard to try to solve it (which is likely to increase dependence on defective explicit abilities).

The second necessary theoretical development is that we need to have a more sophisticated conception of the way in which input processing modules can access different types of output and response systems. Often it is *verbal* responses that seem to be impaired on explicit tests, and manual responses (such as pointing) that are preserved. Yet we also know that some implicit measures can successfully make use of verbal responses. How? Are they the same implicit abilities which can be accessed by different types of response? If so, why does visual location seem to be more accurate for pointing responses than for eye movements in blindsight patients (Weiskrantz et al., 1974)? And so on.

So there is still much work to do before we can really understand the neuropsychology of awareness. In the meantime, though, the realization that these types of impairment can occur has important implications for how we think about the effects of brain injury, and ultimately awareness itself.

Acknowledgements

Our work on visual impairments has been supported by grants from ESRC (C 0023 2246 to Andy Young and Hadyn Ellis, R 00023 1922 to Andy Young Rick Hanley and Freda Newcombe), MRC (PG 7301443 to Freda Newcombe and John Marshall, G 8519533 to Andy Young, and G 8904698 to Edward de Haan and Andy Young), and the Nuffield Foundation. We are very grateful to many colleagues who have helped us in this work, but especially to Freda Newcombe.

3

The Construction of Subjective Experience: Memory Attributions

COLLEEN M. KELLEY AND LARRY L. JACOBY

A central question now being asked about consciousness was also considered at the turn of the century: is consciousness a passive spectator to behaviour, or is consciousness instrumental in the adaptation of an organism to its environment (e.g. Dewey, 1963)? Along with many others (e.g. Helmholtz, 1968; Marcel, 1983b; Mandler and Nakamura, 1987), we treat conscious experiences as constructions based on inferences (Jacoby et al., 1989a).

By a constructivist view, it is important to specify the cues that serve as the basis for particular classes of subjective experience. In this chapter, we consider the bases for the subjective experience of remembering. Our analysis is similar to Brunswik's (1956) ecological approach to perception. By his model of perception, perceptual experiences such as depth and size constancy derive from inferences based on cues in the environment. In our analysis of memory, the experience of remembering also derives from inferences, but the cues that are the basis for those inferences are aspects of one's own thoughts and behaviour, such as the ease with which ideas come to mind. We will illustrate the importance of inference in the subjective experience of remembering by showing errors of inference. One type of error produces unconscious influences of memory, effects of prior experience that are not accompanied by the subjective experience of remembering. We also show that illusions of memory can be produced, and we discuss the importance of those illusions for uncovering the bases for the subjective experience of remembering.

In a constructivist view, conscious experience follows changes in performance rather than directs performance. In a sense, the constructivist view treats consciousness as a spectator, although not a strictly passive one that 'copies' objective reality. Rather than being identical to earlier unconscious processing, consciousness depends upon an active interpretation of that processing (Marcel, 1983b). Furthermore, in everyday life, people often make conscious awareness a prerequisite for intentional actions. In a second major section of this chapter, we consider intention with reference to both conscious and unconscious influences of the past. We argue that conscious intentions do sometimes direct behaviour and describe an experimental method that we have found useful for separating conscious from unconscious effects.

Unconscious Influences of the Past

People commonly use the term 'memory' to refer to conscious remembering. I remember what I had for breakfast this morning, where I was on 15 January this year, and what the weather was like the day I graduated from college. However, the past can also affect us unconsciously. For example, amnesics often cannot remember events, but nonetheless their behaviour reveals the influence of past experience (Warrington and Weiskrantz, 1974; Cohen and Squire, 1980; see also chapter 2). A classic anecdote illustrates this phenomenon. The French neurologist Claparede (1951) hid a pin in his hand and then shook hands with a woman amnesic patient. The next day, he extended his hand in greeting, but she refused to shake hands with him. When pressed for an explanation, she clearly could not remember having shaken hands with him the day before, although she finally justified her behaviour by saying 'Sometimes pins are hidden in people's hands.' Her behaviour indirectly revealed memory for the prior incident, but in the absence of conscious recollection.

Such a dissociation between conscious remembering and unconscious effects of the past can also occur in people with normally functioning memories. For example, reading a list of words increases the likelihood that people can later read them when those words are flashed very briefly on a computer screen. Interestingly, successful identification of the briefly presented words can be independent of the ability to recognize them as words studied on the list (Jacoby and Dallas, 1981). In this example, the recognition test is a direct test of memory (Johnson and Hasher,1987; Richardson-Klavehn and Bjork, 1988) because the instructions refer to a target event in the personal history of the subject (earlier reading of a list of words). In contrast, the perceptual identification task is an indirect test of memory because the instructions refer only to the task at hand and do not refer the subject back to a particular prior event, even though performance on the task is affected by the prior experience. A variety of tasks indirectly reveal memory by enhanced performance due to past experience: perception of briefly presented words or visually degraded pictures (Jacoby and Dallas, 1981; Jacoby and Brooks, 1984), completion of word fragments (Tulving et al., 1982) or word stems (Graf et al., 1982), solution of problems (Jacoby and Kelley, 1987), and speeded reading of text (Kolers, 1976).

Early studies of direct versus indirect memory tests yielded exciting findings. Organic amnesics are typically more impaired on direct tests of memory than on indirect tests. Indeed, in some cases, amnesics perform as well as normal subjects on indirect memory tests. In people with normally functioning memories, performance on direct tests of memory is often stochastically independent of performance on indirect tests of memory (Jacoby and Witherspoon, 1982; Tulving et al., 1982). For example, the probability of completing a fragment or identifying a briefly presented item is no higher for items that have been recognized than for unrecognized items (Jacoby and Witherspoon, 1982; Tulving et al., 1982). A number of experimental variables differentially affect performance on direct as compared to indirect memory tests. For example, studying items by meaningfully elaborating upon them versus simply reading them substantially improves memory performance as measured by recall or recognition, but seems not to affect performance on indirect tests such as fragment completion or the ability to identify briefly presented words.

Finally, performance on direct tests typically requires that people consciously reinstate a past episode, whereas facilitation on indirect tests of memory is not necessarily accompanied by conscious awareness of the past. This difference in subjective experience may ultimately be the most important. Past research on human memory neglected the subjective experience of remembering in favour of objective performance. Conscious remembering was considered irrelevant phenomenology, an epiphenomenon that accompanied correct recall or recognition. Ironically, it was the *absence* of the subjective experience of remembering on indirect tests that illuminated its importance for memory theories. Without the subjective experience of remembering we would be as amnesics: uncertain about the basis for our actions and unaware of how the past has influenced our current experiences. It is important to understand what gives rise to the subjective experience of remembering.

Most researchers in memory agree that direct versus indirect tests differentially reveal two forms or aspects of memory. These two types of memory have been variously termed memory with awareness versus memory without awareness (Jacoby, 1984), conscious versus unconscious memory (Jacoby and Kelley, 1987; Mandler and Nakamura, 1987; Mandler, 1989), and explicit versus implicit memory (Schacter, 1987). In this chapter, to stress the importance of subjective experience, we will use the terms 'conscious' and 'unconscious'.

What could produce the differences between conscious and unconscious memory? One approach assumes that the differences reflect separate memory systems with separate neuroanatomical substrates (e.g. Cohen and Squire, 1980; Tulving, 1983). One system supports conscious recollection, whereas the other system supports unconscious influences of the past. One system is capable of representing aspects of experience such as contextual and temporal information which later give rise to the experience of remembering, whereas the other is not. By this account, the subjective experience of remembering totally reflects properties of the memory trace, so that having and using a memory trace is necessary and sufficient to produce remembering. An inability to experience remembering would be due to the absence of a corresponding representation. For example, an amnesic incapable of remembering may lack the ability to represent particular aspects of episodes, such as time and place.

However, the mapping between representation and subjective experience is far from perfect. Even when memory functioning is normal, people can use memory representations without experiencing remembering, e.g. performance on indirect tasks reveals unconscious effects of prior events. Furthermore, the memory representations involved in unconscious effects of the past are not abstract and stripped of contextual details, but often contain very specific contextual information, such as visual versus auditory modality of presentation (Kelley et al., 1989). The contrasting case of 'remembering' without using a memory representation also occurs. Following certain neurological disorders and head injuries, patients confabulate fantastic events that never occurred (Baddeley and Wilson, 1886; Stuss and Benson, 1986). Confabulation also occurs in people with normal memory, as we shall discuss later. Although representations obviously play a role in remembering, the presence of a memory representation is neither a necessary nor a sufficient condition for the subjective experience of remembering.

What, then, leads people to experience their thoughts as remembering, rather than imagining, perceiving or thinking? We argue that the feeling of remembering is based on an inference or attribution (see also Johnson, 1988). People interpret particular aspects of their present experience as either reflecting past experience or as due to current conditions. An attribution to the past gives rise to the subjective experience of remembering, which may be correct (veridical remembering) or incorrect (confabulation or memory illusions); conversely, an incorrect attribution of effects of the past to current conditions can alter subjective experience of the present.

Bases for the Subjective Experience of Remembering

We start by noting that past experience influences present performance on a variety of tasks. In learning theory, those influences are termed transfer effects. Many indirect tests of memory (fragment completion, identification of briefly presented items, reading speed and comprehension) can be viewed as cases of positive transfer, in that past experience allows the task to be performed more efficiently or fluently. Differences in performance of the sort produced by transfer could serve as the basis for the subjective experience of remembering. People might learn to interpret variations in their performance on current tasks as a sign that they are using the past, much as they may learn to interpret environmental cues to produce perceptual experiences such as depth perception and size constancy (Brunswik, 1956).

To assess whether such an inferential or attributional basis for remembering is feasible, we need to ask whether effects of the past typically revealed by indirect tests (what we are calling transfer effects) could serve as a sufficiently diagnostic basis for the experience of remembering. Recent work in memory development suggests that early experiences show transfer effects of extreme specificity. Rovee-Collier (1989) tested infants' memory by conditioning them to kick in the presence of a particular crib mobile. She arranged it such that the infants' kicking made the mobile spin, an intriguing event for a 6-month-old. Rovee-Collier and her colleagues assessed the infants' memory for this experience by returning up to two weeks later, attaching the mobile to the crib, and observing the infants' rates of kicking. The infants showed much better memory than anticipated. Most interesting to us is the extraordinary specificity of their memories. Changing even small features of the mobile eliminated transfer of the kicking response to the new mobile. Effectively, the infants behaved as though they recognized the old mobile and could discriminate it from very similar foils. Although no one knows whether the infants experienced this as remembering, the study reveals that effects of the past on behaviour can be extremely diagnostic of a particular past experience. The development of remembering might involve increasing sophistication in interpreting one's own behaviour and qualities of one's thoughts as reflecting past experiences (for a related argument, see Lockhart, 1984).

Following Helmholtz's (1968) analysis of perception, and Baldwin's (1906) analysis of memory development, we expect that a variety of cues engender remembering. One common effect of past experience is more fluent perception and thinking. Words read once are more easily perceived later; an idea formulated once comes to mind more readily later. We take fluent processing to be a primary cue in the construction of remembering, and hypothesize that the feeling of familiarity in recognition is sometimes based on an inference about the ease or relative fluency of perceptual operations. We noted earlier that perceptual identification of briefly presented words is an indirect test of memory. Reading a word allows one to perceive it more readily later. Jacoby and Dallas (1981) proposed that this ease of perceptual processing could be experienced as familiarity. In support of this idea, Johnston et al. (1985) found a correlation between ease of perception (assessed by probability of identifying briefly presented items) and recognition memory judgements for pseudo-words. Items that were readily perceptually identified were more likely to be judged as 'old'.

The feeling of remembering is enhanced when we can follow up one idea with supporting details (cf. Baddeley, 1982). Each detail brought to mind increases our confidence that we are remembering rather than inventing. Nonetheless, even the feeling of 'really remembering' that one has when recalling details of an event involves an inference process, rather than being an intrinsic property of the memory representation. As such, the experience of remembering is open to error, as in the case of confabulation and errors of reconstruction.

As an example, Ross (1989) found that memories can reflect people's theories as much as their past experience. In one experiment, women remembered experiencing pre-menstrual syndrome when those symptoms were assessed retrospectively. However, daily records kept by the same women (who did not know that the study involved menstrual symptoms) revealed no such syndrome. Ross argues that people's autobiographical memory is partially constructed on the basis of their beliefs about the world. Widespread beliefs in PMS lead to widespread 'remembering' of pre-menstrual symptoms. People's theories of what must have happened lead them to think fluently of those outcomes when they attempt recall, and fluently generated thoughts may be misattributed to past experience.

Another quality of thoughts that may serve as a cue that we are using the past is the vividness of an image. Brewer (1988) studied undergraduates' memory for randomly sampled events in their lives. Students wore beepers set to signal them about once every two hours, at which time they were to record what they were doing and thinking. Their memories were tested up to fifty-five days later. The subjects were most confident that they were remembering when they had vivid visual imagery for the event, rated as 'complete re-experiencing of the particular visual experience' (Brewer, 1988, p. 67). People learn to use the presence of vivid imagery in a thought as a cue that they are recalling, rather than imagining. People also use such cues in the reports of others to infer that they are really remembering. Schooler et al. (1986) found that people use the amount of sensory detail in the memory reports of others to distinguish memory for actual events from memory for suggested events. Similarly, Johnson and her colleagues (Johnson and Raye, 1981; Johnson et al., 1989) have found that people use the amount of sensory detail in a memory to infer that they are remembering an event that they actually experienced, rather than one they simply imagined or dreamed about.

In summary, the conscious experience of remembering is not to be found in a memory trace. Rather, remembering is an inference based on internal and situational cues. A fundamental cue for such an inference is what we have termed fluency, the fluent perception of objects, the easy generation of ideas and details. In general, fluency is a reliable cue to the past, because past experience does facilitate present re-experience, and these transfer effects are remarkably specific. An attributional theory of remembering also predicts errors of attribution. We consider such evidence in the next section.

Misattributions and Memory

Much as perceptual psychologists have used perceptual illusions to investigate the information used to construct perceptual experiences, we have used memory illusions to investigate the information used to construct memorial experiences. We also study misattributions that lead to unconscious influences of the past.

Memory Illusions

If ease of perceptual processing is a cue that can serve as the basis for the experience of remembering, then experimental manipulations of perceptual processing should influence the subjective experience of remembering. That is, one should be able to create memory illusions by altering perceptual processing independently of past experience. Jacoby and Whitehouse (1989) manipulated the ease with which words on a recognition memory test were perceived in an attempt to create memory illusions. They briefly presented the same word (match) or a different word (mismatch) immediately prior to the recognition test item. These context words were flashed so briefly that subjects were unaware of their presentation. For both old and new words, a matching context word *increased* the probability of judging an item 'old', whereas a mismatching word *decreased* the probability of judging the item 'old'. The matching word facilitated perceptual processing of items and so increased subjects' feeling of familiarity.

Another condition in the Jacoby and Whitehouse (1989) experiment illustrates the importance of attributions in determining subjective experience. Subjects' interpretation of their fluent perception of recognition test words varied depending on whether or not they were aware of the briefly presented context word. When the context words were presented for a longer duration such that they were clearly seen, the results were opposite to those described above: people were actually *less* likely to call either an old or new recognition test word 'old' when the context word matched the test word than when no context word or a mismatch context word was presented. When they were unaware of the context word, people mistakenly attributed their enhanced processing of the test word to having read it on the study list, and so judged it old. In contrast, when aware of the context word, people attributed their enhanced processing of the test word to having just read it as a matching context word. Subjects in the *aware* condition actually tended to over-correct for the effect of the matching word, and so were less likely to judge the test word old than if no context word had been presented.

Placing the effects of aware versus unaware processing in opposition is a key feature in the experiment described above. Conscious versus unconscious perception of the context word produced different attributions of the subsequent fluent processing of the test word. The opposition technique reveals unconscious perceptual processing that is not simply conscious processing that has gone undetected by the experimenter. We will discuss the importance of placing conscious and unconscious processes in opposition in a later section of the chapter.

The notion that fluent processing is a cue that one is using the past is not restricted to perceptual processing. The familiarity of arguments, ideas and other commonplace activities can also stem from an inference regarding the ease with which we follow the argument or conjure up an image. When people are asked to recall, they tend to accept ideas that come readily to mind as remembered ideas. We predicted that the ease of producing an item during recall attempts would correlate with the likelihood of experiencing that item as remembered. Certainly such a correlation would not compel an attributional analysis of remembering. For example, remembering could be a phenomenological correlate of trace strength: items with strong traces would both be readily available and give rise to a strong feeling of remembering. However, the notion that the ease with which ideas come to mind is the basis for the feeling of remembering implies that we should be able to *manipulate* the ease with which ideas come to mind and so create illusions of remembering.

We had subjects study a long list of five-letter words and then tested their ability to recall the words when given cues (Kelley et al., forthcoming). The cues were fragments of the to-be-recalled words. Some of the fragments were easy to complete (one letters missing, e.g. *b_rch*), and others were relatively difficult to complete (two letters missing, e.g. *b_rc_*). After generating an item, subjects described their subjective experience as 'clear memory', 'feels familiar' or 'no memory'. Unbeknown to subjects, a small proportion of cues on the cued recall test were fragments that could only be completed with new words, that is, words that were not on the study list. Of those new targets, half were cued with easy-to-generate fragments and half were cued with difficult-to-generate fragments. As predicted, the ease with which words came to mind in response to the fragment cues influenced the subjective experience of remembering. There were significantly more reports of 'feels familiar' and 'clear memory' for words produced given the easy cues than for words produced given the difficult cues. What is critically important in this study is that the effect of ease of generation occurred even for new items, those that had never been studied on the list. Thus ease of generating contributed to subjects' experience of remembering and produced illusions of remembering.

Effects of the Past on Subjective Experience of the Present

Others have suggested that the differences between conscious memory and unconscious memory result from separate memory systems. In contrast, we see conscious and unconscious memory as tightly linked. Both reflect changes in processing given past experience; in particular, increases in the fluency of thinking and perception. On a direct memory test, the situation directs subjects to make a particular inference regarding fluent operations – that they are due to past experience. However, the same fluent operations may be misattributed to other factors and so change subjective experience of the present.

To illustrate such misattributions, consider the case of the misattribution of ease of perceptual processing of words or sentences due to past reading. Witherspoon and Allan (1985) had subjects first read a list of words on a computer screen, and later judge the duration of presentation of words presented individually on the screen. Subjects judged the exposure duration as longer for old words (read on the list in the first phase) than new words, although the actual duration was identical. They misattributed their fluent perception of old words to a difference in duration.

Similar effects of the past on perception were found by Jacoby et al. (1988). Subjects listened to old and new sentences against a background of white noise and judged the noise level. They estimated the background noise as less loud when old sentences were presented in the foreground than when new sentences were presented. Subjects apparently misattributed their enhanced perception and comprehension of old sentences to lower levels of background noise.

In the above experiments, subjects were biased towards interpreting changes in ease of processing due to prior experience as changes in physical characteristics of the present. In other experiments, we found that problems were made easier when subjects read the answers in an earlier phase of the experiment (Jacoby and Kelley, 1987). However, the subjects experienced their own facile solution of the problems as due to a characteristic of the problems – that they were easy. The experience of the problems as easy led subjects systematically to underestimate their difficulty for others. The experiment is analogous to a problem inherent in teaching: how do we judge the difficulty of material for our students? When teaching new material, we may successfully use our own subjective experience of difficulty to estimate what the students will find difficult. When teaching material that we have long-since mastered, our subjective experience is a poor basis for predicting students' difficulty: we may experience the material as simple and the students as dull-witted. In so doing, we are guilty of egocentrism of the sort exhibited by children (Piaget and Inhelder, 1956).

Potentially, any effect of past experience on performance could be misattributed to factors other than the past. Thus, the past is a pervasive source of unconscious influence (Jacoby and Kelley, 1987) that can change our interpretations of the perceptual world, our comprehension and evaluation of events, and our prediction of the future. If the current situation directs one towards the past, then it is likely that an idea that comes to mind readily will be attributed to past experience. However, if the situation directs one to another goal, such as solving a problem, then the effects of past experience may be misattributed to other factors such as the relative difficulty of the problem. The seemingly trivial difference between interpreting a change in behaviour as reflecting past experience (and so remembering) or as reflecting current conditions can lead to substantially different experiences and have substantially different implications for later behaviour.

The Role of Intention

We have described the difference between direct and indirect tests as primarily a difference in subjective experience. On direct tests, people attribute changes in their performance to the past and so experience remembering, whereas on indirect tests people attribute those effects of the past to contemporary factors. Although subjective experience is important, it is clearly not the whole story with regard to conscious versus unconscious memory. Amnesics do not simply fail to make particular inferences regarding effects of the past. They lack the ability to form an intention to remember and to engage in special activities that would allow them to carry out that intention (Baddeley, 1982; Warrington and Weiskrantz, 1982).

In this section, we begin by considering the relation between intentional control and memory. First, how does the intention to remember modulate memory performance? Second, how can other behaviours be controlled by memory? One role credited to consciousness in general is that of a higher-order executive function (Shallice, 1972; Johnson-Laird, 1988). We argue that behaviours can also be controlled by unconscious memory for similar episodes. However, one cannot distinguish between the two types of control by simply asking people why they did something, because intention itself is an attribution that can follow behaviour as well as direct it.

Intention as Necessary for an Act

Intentional Control of Memory

People can exert conscious control over their memory performance in several ways. When remembering is unintentional, the retrieval cues are given by the current situation (including one's thoughts and feelings). Those cues lead to a particular idea popping in to mind. People can, however, attempt to elaborate upon an idea in ways that increase the likelihood that particular ideas or images will come to mind. This strategic generation of cues in intentional recall is evident in M. D. Williams' (1976) study of people's attempts to recall the members of their high school class. People consciously attempted to reinstate various contexts, such as imagining a history class or a particular beach frequented by classmates, and then reported the names that came to mind after focusing on those cues.

In intentional remembering, conscious activities generate cues for retrieval. Such intentional control can be mimicked by structuring the retrieval environment for a person. Many neuropsychologists credit the frontal lobes with being the location of executive functions such as planning, restructuring and monitoring (Stuss and Benson, 1986). For some time, the importance of those executive functions was not appreciated because people with frontal lobe damage, including frontal lobotomy patients, could perform normally on memory and intelligence tests. Their loss of executive functioning was masked during those highly structured test situations because the psychological examiner effectively served as the patient's frontal lobes.

During retrieval, the intention to remember structures the retrieval environment and, thereby, guides processing. In indirect tests, the structure of the task guides processing (Jacoby, 1984), and retrieval follows incidentally. Perhaps that is why the performance of many amnesics is so much better on indirect than direct tests (Moscovitch, 1984). There is a similar distinction between incidental and intentional control at encoding, that is, at the time of entering a representation into memory. In intentional encoding, people deliberately memorize by actively engaging in activities that will produce good memory. But encoding can also be an incidental byproduct of a task. In some populations, including children (Flavell and Wellman, 1977) and depressives (Hertel, in press) encoding that is structured by the situation leads to far better memory than does encoding that is structured by the subject. Clearly, the control one has over memory depends upon knowing effective strategies and initiating those strategies, both at encoding and retrieval.

Memory in the Control of Behaviour

From the perspective of the actor, the most salient form of control over one's behaviour appears to be consciously held intentions. However, behaviour can appear organized and goal-directed even when not under conscious control. As suggested by James (1890), habit replaces intention and the conscious control of behaviour. Extended practice results in one responding 'automatically' without conscious intervention. Even amnesics are capable of improving with practice on a task, although they are unable consciously to recollect the particular experiences that gave rise to learning (Warrington and Weiskrantz, 1974).

According to a recent theory of automaticity, automatic responses may actually be unconsciously mediated by memory for specific prior episodes. Logan (1988) presents evidence that automaticity comes about when people change over from computing responses algorithmically to relying on memory for a past response. As in our earlier discussion of indirect memory tests, memory for a prior experience can influence later performance even in the absence of conscious recollection of that earlier experience. The correct response on the current task simply pops to mind. Automaticity thus reflects the use of memory for particular prior experiences rather than the use of an abstract habit that accumulates across many experiences.

A crucial question regarding intentions is the level at which behaviour is controlled. When control is conscious, it is in a sense extrinsic, imposed upon the situation and the responses one would automatically make. When control resides in unconscious memory for prior episodes, it is intrinsic to the situation. Details of the current situation serve as cues for the retrieval of memory for similar experiences, and those experiences then unconsciously guide performance. Behaviour that appears orderly and goal-directed can emerge from unconscious influences of memory for prior episodes.

Intention and the Attribution Process

Intentions are conscious experiences and so are themselves also subject to inference and attribution. An observer often cannot tell whether behaviour is intentionally and consciously controlled or unintentionally guided by unconscious influences of prior experiences. But an actor's report that a particular action was consciously intended is not a reliable guide, because that intention could be an attribution that followed the behaviour rather than caused it. In addition, intentions can enter into the construction of conscious experience by serving as a context for attributions. We will first give an example of intention as a *context* for attributions, and then discuss intention as a *product* of attributions.

Consider the role of the intention to remember in the construction of the conscious experience of remembering. When people are asked to remember, they are biased to interpret evidence such as fluent perception as reflecting the past. If people are asked to estimate duration, they will be biased to interpret fluent perception as reflecting characteristics of the stimulus (Witherspoon and Allan, 1985). Thus, the goal held by subjects influences their interpretation of the same evidence.

In addition to biasing one towards attributing thoughts to the past, the intention to remember may also enter in as a component of the subjective experience of remembering. Talland (1968) interviewed an amnesic man about his family, including details about the forthcoming wedding of the amnesic's younger brother. In response to Talland's detailed questions, the amnesic was able to provide a full report of the wedding plans. Because the man was quite concerned about his memory disorder, Talland complimented him on his performance. The man replied, 'I didn't tell you about the wedding, you told me.' Talland speculated that this misattribution was caused by the highly structured nature of the interview that 'programmed the patient's responses step by step' (1968, p. 154). To experience remembering, ideas that come to mind must be attributed to one's own efforts, rather than to the situation. The intention to remember can be part of the experience of remembering.

Are intentions themselves subject to attribution and inference? We do not always plan and then act. We often act and then concoct an explanation. Munsterberg's motor theory of consciousness held that conscious intentions are actually a *post hoc* interpretation of the behaviours they are assumed to produce. Leahey (1987, p. 269) provides a vivid example:

> Thus, I might announce that I'm going to stand up from my chair, not because I've reached a decision to stand but because the motor processes for standing have just begun and have entered consciousness. I feel my will to be effective because generally the incipient tendencies to act are followed by real action, and the former trigger memories of the latter.

By the motor theory of consciousness, the actual causes of the behaviour are not incorporated into one's conscious construction of the experience.

Similarly, a recent body of research reveals that people are often unable to specify the factors that are important for controlling their behaviour (e.g. Wason and Evans, 1974; Nisbett and Wilson, 1977; Bowers, 1984). When asked to explain their behaviour, people report *a priori* cultural theories or hypotheses that may bear little relation to the variables that psychologists know to be controlling the behaviour (Nisbett and Wilson, 1977). One part of cultural theory for Westerners is that behaviour is ordered by intentions and plans. When people reflect on their behaviour and describe it in terms of their intentions at the time, the intentions may actually exist only retrospectively. That is, an intention may be an attribution about a behaviour, rather than a cause of the behaviour.

We acknowledge that conscious intentions may at times be necessary for action and other times be simply a *post hoc* interpretation of behaviour. The important issue then becomes separating the two. As Nisbett and Wilson (1977) point out, people's *post hoc* theories about the causes of behaviour may be correct, not because they have conscious access to those causes but because the two happen to coincide. When a conscious intention would cause the same behaviour that would be produced unconsciously, it is impossible to know which is controlling behaviour. In the next section we will describe a method that we have found useful for separating conscious and unconscious influences of memory.

The Advantages of Opposition

The indistinguishability of conscious and unconscious processes that are in the same direction has led to a history of research marked by supposed demonstrations of unconscious influences followed by further research to uncover methodological flaws in those supposed demonstrations. Experimental demonstrations of unconscious perception (e.g. Marcel, 1983a) have been criticized on the grounds that the experimenter has mistakenly measured conscious rather than unconscious performance (see chapter 1). Holender (1986) argues that there is so far no convincing evidence for unconscious perception. Similarly, in studies of memory, performance commonly ascribed to unconscious forms of memory may be contaminated by conscious recollection (Richardson-Klavehn and Bjork, 1988). For example, the enhanced completion of word fragments for old words relative to new may be accomplished by intentional conscious retrieval of studied words.

We have avoided relying on differences in threshold or sensitivity of tests as a way of separating conscious from unconscious influences. Instead, we have adopted the strategy of placing conscious and unconscious processing in opposition. In several studies (Jacoby and Whitehouse, 1989; Jacoby et al., 1989b), we arranged it such that subjects made opposite responses depending on whether they were aware or unaware of a prior event. For example, in the Jacoby and Whitehouse (1989) study described earlier, when subjects were unaware of the matching context word that preceded a recognition test item, they were more likely to judge that item 'old', whereas if they were aware of the context word, they were less likely to judge the item 'old'. This rules out the possibility that unconscious effects are simply conscious effects that the experimenter is unable to detect, and allows a clear separation of the two.

The strategy of looking for opposite effects is a variant of the strategy of searching for qualitative differences in performance produced by conscious versus unconscious perception or memory (e.g. Dixon, 1981; Jacoby and Dallas,

1981; Tulving et al., 1982; Marcel 1983a; Cheesman and Merikle, 1986). The opposition strategy is also a variant of methods that pit an unintended process against one's conscious intentions, as in the Stroop test (see chapter 1). Holender (1986) dismissed evidence of qualitative differences as a basis for separating unconscious from conscious perception. Qualitative differences are primarily revealed by an interaction of the conscious versus unconscious measure with some other variable. As Holender (1986) points out, interactions do not necessarily reveal separate processes, but can be interpreted by a variety of single process theories. What Holender neglects to point out is that interactions are important when they derive from a coherent theory.

The opposition of conscious and unconscious influences is more than a methodological tool: an important function of consciousness is to oppose unconscious influences. A commonplace example of such a function is the problem of avoiding repeating oneself. One effect of telling a story is to make that story come more readily to mind later (and, perversely, to do so most often with the same audience). Conscious recollection can be used to oppose this effect of the past. Similarly, conscious awareness can oppose the effects of unconscious perception. The fear of subliminal messages seems to be based on the notion that people cannot resist influences of which they are unaware. A subliminal message to 'Drink Coke' could be mistakenly taken as one's own desire for a drink.

To set conscious and unconscious influences of memory in opposition, we have used a phenomenon that we call the 'false fame' effect. In the first phase of these experiments, people read a list of non-famous names, such as 'Sebastian Weisdorf'. In a second phase, those old names were mixed with new famous and new non-famous names in a test of fame judgements. The fame test served as an indirect memory test: names that were read earlier were more likely to be judged as famous than were new names, even if those names were actually non-famous. We consider this an unconscious influence of prior reading of the names, because the names are often falsely experienced as famous, rather than remembered from the list (Jacoby et al., 1989b).

Subjects could avoid the false fame of recently encountered non-famous names by directing their attention to the past. We correctly informed subjects that all of the names they had read in the first list were non-famous, so if they recognized a name on the fame test as from the first list, they would know it is actually non-famous. In this way, conscious memory for a name from the list would oppose the effect of unconscious memory on fame judgements.

The fact that the fame paradigm separates conscious remembering from unconscious influences of the past allowed us to look for principled differences between the two that followed from our conception of consciousness. Historically, the unconscious and the conscious were considered qualitatively different (e.g. Ellenberger, 1970; Dixon, 1971). Conscious processes were thought to be more active whereas unconscious influences were more likely to emerge when one was relaxed or inattentive. Our distinction between memory-as-tool versus memory-as-object partially captures these distinctions

(Jacoby and Kelley, 1987). Memory can be used unconsciously as a tool to perform a task without any analysis or activity beyond performing the task itself. In contrast, treating memory as an object of conscious reflection generally requires more active processing.

We predicted that conscious remembering of the names from the first phase in the fame paradigm would require a separate, attention-demanding act. Therefore, if subjects are required to divide their attention between the fame judgement test and another task (detecting sequences of digits presented auditorially), they should be less able to use conscious recognition to oppose the false fame than subjects who devote their full attention to fame judgements. That was indeed the case (Jacoby et al., 1989b). Subjects in a divided attention condition were particularly susceptible to the false fame effect – they were *more* likely to call old non-famous names 'famous' than new non-famous names, whereas the opposite was true for subjects in a full attention condition. Making the past an object of conscious reflection requires a different focus of attention than using the past as a tool.

Conclusion

In one sense, recent studies of the unconscious effects of the past add more fuel to Nisbett and Wilson's (1977) arguments that we tell far more than we know about our own behaviour. Past experiences affect the perception and interpretation of later events even when a person does not or cannot consciously recollect the relevant experience. Those unconscious influences of the past undoubtedly exert pervasive influences on our behaviour. However, we think that such a focus on unconscious influences neglects the equally pervasive effects our conscious constructions have on subsequent behaviour.

Memory experiments, our own included, typically investigate the effects of events in a first phase on performance in a second phase. For example, reading a list of non-famous names in phase I leads subjects to judge those names as famous in phase II (Jacoby et al., 1989b). We view this as an unconscious influence of the past because subjects are not comprehending that the increased familiarity of the names is due to their prior reading of them in phase I. If we had asked subjects to explain why they thought a particular name was famous, they might say 'I think she's some sort of athlete' or 'I think he's an actor.' From Nisbett and Wilson's (1977) perspective, it would be another instance of consciousness not reflecting reality. However, in real life, there is a phase III, as well as a phase I and phase II. While conscious awareness in phase II does not always accurately reflect the influences of phase I variables, conscious awareness itself has consequences for later behaviour. The consciously constructed interpretation of one's experience is the basis for later intentional behaviour. If I think a couple on an airplane look familiar because they are famous, I may behave quite differently towards them than if I think they look familiar because I saw them earlier on the airport shuttle bus.

Marcel (1988) makes a similar argument about the causal status of consciousness based on his observations of patients with blindsight. The subjective experience of these patients is that they are blind, yet they can accurately make some visual discriminations when forced to make choices. One might argue that this also is a case in which conscious experience does not accurately reflect the facts of perceptual processing. However, as Marcel points out, blindsight patients are loath to base any intentional behaviour on their visual processing. Marcel argues that there are two reasons for this. First, a conscious intention cannot be formed if a logically necessary part of that intention (e.g. its referent) is not conscious. So, a blindsight patient cannot form an intention to reach out and pick up a glass if they are not consciously aware of the glass. Second, when people are mindful of their behaviour, they do not perform actions without reason. People may or may not be capable of deliberately responding in the absence of conscious referents, but in our culture, they do not. By Marcel's account, consciousness is causal, even if its causal role derives solely from a culturally held belief that consciousness is causal.

Similarly, the conscious experience of remembering is causal even though conscious remembering does not perfectly map onto past experience. People often do not remember past experiences that nonetheless affect them, and they can also 'remember' events that never happened. We give great weight to remembered experiences, even though those memories are often in error. Analogous to Marcel's blindsight patients, we are much more willing to base behaviour on clearly remembered events than on vague feelings of familiarity. In the domain of eyewitness testimony, judges and jurors give memories an evidentiary status that exceeds their reliability (Loftus, 1979). Bruner (1987) makes a similar point that 'in the end we become the autobiographical narratives by which we "tell about" our lives' (p. 15). Bruner is only partially correct; at any point, we are only aware of a part of who we are and what controls our behaviour. However, our conscious construction of ourselves nonetheless influences who we may become.

Acknowledgements

This research was supported by a grant to Larry L. Jacoby from the Canadian National Science and Engineering Research Council. We thank Steve Lindsay for suggestions concerning the manuscript.

4

Freud's Cognitive Psychology of Intention: The Case of Dora

KEITH OATLEY

Cognitive Psychology as Natural Science and Human Science

What makes human action meaningful is that it is intended. This, according to Weber, distinguishes human or social science from natural science. A term used in this context is *Verstehen*, meaning interpretive understanding gained by imaginatively entering into the position of another person to re-live for ourselves some aspect of his or her experience. It is human intention that necessitates *Verstehen*.

To have an intention is to have a conscious goal. Intention is intentional in the philosophical sense of implying a mental state that is about something (the terms are irritatingly the same though their meanings differ). So intentionality implies believing that something, desiring that something, intending that something and so on. I shall argue that Freud's work, though it has met with scepticism, none the less allows us to understand some bases of intention, and hence of an aspect of conscious intentionality.

In this chapter, I present a psychoanalytic case history to show how one of Freud's primary concerns was to understand Dora's action in terms of intention. He tried to understand actions not just as produced by mental mechanisms, correctly functioning or otherwise. Instead, he sought to assess the extent to which there was an element of deliberate intention, and the extent to which mental states were conscious. More radically, of course, if Freud were successful in understanding actions of his patients as being intended, he as an analyst and we as readers could understand our actions as intended too. I shall discuss this question as it bears on the problem of insight.

Putting this in another way, most academic psychology is technical in the sense that its style and content imply being able to understand mental mechanisms and if possible to undertake well-informed manipulations of them. But if we enquire into intentionality, into beliefs, desires and so on, then it is no longer clear that the technical language of psychology is appropriate. What I propose here does not deny the technical, but I point out, as it were, an alternative interpretation of an ambiguous figure. I shall do this by concentrating not on mental mechanisms but on content and meaning, not by describing experiments, but by discussing a narrative. Thereby I hope to indicate the kinds of insight that may allow us to improve our mental models of self. What I hope, then, is by delineating an aspect of our psychological enterprise that is less often recognized in academic circles, to take a small step towards integrating it with the mainstream concerns of cognitive psychology.

I approach these issues by acknowledging that the scepticism of Freud's critics is justified on many grounds – indeed, I shall discuss some of them – but I also argue that important foundations of a psychology of intention were laid by Freud. I propose to treat Freud like most other important figures in the history of ideas. He was not someone who got it all right or all wrong. Instead, I shall argue that he put in place certain ideas and findings that can be usefully built upon.

The direction I shall take is to indicate how Freud's methodological concerns are central to the understanding of narrative as currently investigated in cognitive science. I also claim that the main bases of his work on intention are not subject to the kinds of criticism that have been made validly against many of the tenets of psychoanalysis.

A Psychology of Intention

What might a psychology of intention be about? A full human intention has several elements. It implies a goal or objective, that the goal is conscious, that it has been explicitly adopted by the agent, who believes that he or she can achieve the goal by means of a possible place. The idea of intention poses a problem, however, because although some actions may be fully intended in this sense, others lack some feature of full conscious intention. This lack can make actions puzzling. Often effects are achieved, but it is not clear whether a goal was deliberately adopted, or planned for.

I shall use 'intention' as a bridge between the term 'goal' as used in cognitive science and Freud's term *Wunsch* (wish). We can think of intention, then, in two senses. In a basic sense it is equivalent to 'goal', without commitment to whether it is consciously articulated, or whether it implies any deliberate plan. In the full sense it is conscious, and does imply a deliberate plan. Freud's therapeutic aim, of course, was to enable basic intentions to become full, conscious intentions.

Freud investigated the implications of basic intentions. He began to move away from the idea, prevalent in his time as in ours, that psychology was to be understood purely in terms of neural mechanisms (see also Parisi, 1987). He began to open up a psychology of intention alongside the psychology of mental mechanisms. All his objects of close investigation such as dreams, slips of the tongue, jokes, psychiatric symptoms, free associations, are about ambiguous pieces of behaviour on the border between the intended and the unintended, in which some but not all the attributes of full conscious intention are present.

The procedure that Freud began, and that has not been negated by subsequent criticism, is that of listening to his patients. If we are interested in the mechanisms of mind, then natural scientific methods such as experimentation are appropriate. If we are interested in intention, other methods, including listening, become important. Freud stopped inspecting patients to see what was wrong with them, and began to listen to them with 'evenly suspended attention' (Freud, 1958a, p. 111). It occurred to him that symptoms are not so much seen, but that they speak. To understand them he must learn their language. He asked his patient to tell his or her own story, and to engage with him in dialogues, in which symptoms were part of the language being spoken.

The Case of the Missing Intentions

In this account I shall discuss the case of Dora (Freud, 1953c; except where otherwise indicated, page numbers refer to this publication). In keeping with a psychology intended to be insightful, rather than just technical, I have written in a style that is itself closer to a story than to quantitative arguments – moving away from the almost exclusive (academic) interest in form and process, towards content.

Freud started his account with the problem of gaps in narrative. He says he began by asking the patient 'to give [him] the whole story of [her] life and illness'. He continues: 'As a matter of fact the patients are incapable of giving such reports about themselves . . . their communications run dry, leaving gaps unfilled, and riddles unanswered' (p. 16). These gaps were fundamental for Freud, as they are for cognitive psychology: what is left out are principally the intentions that would make sense of the stories. In Freud's hands the case history became a detective story (cf. Meyer, 1975) in which he set out to solve the puzzles left by the gaps in the patient's narrative. The case history of Dora is the first in this genre that goes beyond short story length.

First, here are its *dramatis personae*.

Dora: The patient, suffering from hysteria. She is aged 18 at the time of the analysis, described at the beginning of the story by Freud as 'in the first bloom of youth, a girl of intelligent and engaging looks' (p. 23).

Freud: The analyst, aged 44, armed with a 'collection of picklocks' (Freud, 1985, p. 427) for penetrating the unconscious, and hoping after several false starts to make a reputation for himself.

Dora's father: A wealthy industrialist living with his wife, son and daughter (Dora herself), but having a love affair with Frau K.

Dora's mother: Treated contemptuously by Dora, by Dora's father and by Freud who dismisses her as an obsessional housewife of no account.

Herr K: Friend of Dora's parents. He connives at Dora's father's affair with his wife, and pays courtly attentions to Dora.

Frau K: Wife of Herr K and lover of Dora's father. She also befriends Dora.

Governesses: In Dora's family and in the K family who become embroiled in family affairs.

The Story of Dora

Dora was referred to Freud by her father. She was distressed and had been at odds with her parents. Her complaints included a periodic loss of voice, a nervous cough, and loss of appetite. She had had what seemed like a fit. Now she was irritable and low in spirits. A suicide note had been found in her writing desk, and this had prompted her father to consult Freud.

Dora's father said that Dora's depression and irritability were linked with an incident two years previously. The family had been staying with the K family, who had a holiday house at the Alpine lakeside resort of L_. Dora had told her mother that Herr K 'had had the audacity to make her a proposal while they were on a walk after a trip upon the lake' (p. 25). She had wanted to leave the Ks' house immediately, with her father. Frau K had told her father that Dora had been reading sexually explicit books. He told Freud that these had over-excited her. Probably she had imagined the proposal. Immediately we find ourselves in ambiguity. Was Dora a woman to whom an abusive suggestion had been made, or a romantic adolescent imagining sexual liaisons with an older man? Neither explanation seems quite adequate. Freud investigates further.

Dora had entreated her father to break with the Ks. He told Freud how unreasonable this was. He said he was bound by ties of honourable friendship to Frau K who had nursed him during an illness some years previously. Freud lets us know that the illness, for which he had previously treated Dora's father, was probably syphilis.

Here then is the setting: a woman aged 18 is depressed and has apparently hysterical ailments. She is passed by her father to Freud. Dora and Freud become caught up in the story as it emerges in their dialogue.

The story begins to reveal certain possibilities about Dora's intentions. These possibilities at first are indirect, arguably because Dora herself was unable to experience them directly. They were, so to speak, unconscious. They had to be spoken at first in evasions and displacements; to put it bluntly, in lies. But the lies were beginnings of truths about Dora's deeper concerns, which, by their discovery, might transform Dora's sense of herself.

An insightful approach is, with Lacan (1982), to read this text as a dialogue, or as Lacan calls it, a dialectical exchange. We can then see how this dialogue form is appropriate to an analysis of intentions.

Approaching a Truth

Lacan describes the story as a series of dialectical reversals, by which a displaced truth is gradually approached. Dora's father's account is followed by what Lacan calls a first development: Dora describes her father's affair.

Freud had said Dora left gaps in her narrative. Now he points out that, in contrast to her vagueness about her own life, Dora's memories of her father's affair with Frau K were very distinct. The affair had become obvious to Dora four years previously, on a holiday taken by the two families in a hotel, which involved changes of rooms by Dora's father and Frau K that would not have been out of place in a theatrical farce.

Dora knew that her father had connived at a relationship between Herr K and herself. It kept Herr K and herself quiet while allowing the affair between her father and Frau K to progress. When Dora was 14, this 'odious exchange', as Lacan (p. 65) calls it, involved Herr K trying to kiss her. She felt disgust, which, Freud surmises, she displaced into symptoms of disinclination for food and ailments of the alimentary canal and respiratory tract. With her disgust displaced, she could continue on warm terms with Herr K. We may wonder whether Dora's father is now handing Dora to Freud, because again she might make difficulties for his affair with Frau K.

Dora's denunciation of her father and his affair are followed by what Lacan calls the first dialectical reversal: Freud, without denying Dora's accusations, asks her whether she might not also be reproaching herself in the same way that she is reproaching her father. Was she not perhaps also engaged in a cover-up? What was her involvement in all this?

This questioning gives way to a second development, in which it emerges that Dora had wanted the attentions of Herr K. He had sent her 'flowers every day for a whole year while he was in the neighbourhood' (p. 35), given her valuable presents, spent all his spare time in her company. Dora was enlivened by their relationship, but somehow, as with the kiss, she displaced its implications.

Not only had Dora known of her father's affair, but by looking after the Ks' children she had enabled Frau K to spend time with her father. Perhaps her youth kept from her the implications of her involvement. But when, at the age of 16, in the scene by the lake, it occurred to her that Herr K was not just making a proposal but also a proposition, she finally was horrified.

Dora angrily assaults Freud with a crescendo of reproaches against her father while using various means, including the argument of her symptoms, to try to get her father to break with the Ks. What enrages Dora more than anything is her father's idea that Herr K's proposal was just her imagination.

Lacan writes that this gives way to a second reversal: Freud observes that this seems like jealousy. Might not such jealousy more appropriately have been expressed by Dora's mother? Dora was behaving as if she were her father's deceived wife. She wanted to be reassured of his love. To do this he must end his affair with Frau K.

The third development begins. There is an indication of Dora's attachment to Frau K. They shared a bedroom on family holidays (Herr K being quartered elsewhere). Frau K had confided in her in terms of closest intimacy. Dora 'used to praise [Frau K's] "adorable white body" in accents more appropriate to a lover than to a defeated rival' (p. 61).

But the question, in Lacan's (1982, p. 67) words, of what 'the real value of the object which Frau K [was] for Dora', is never asked. The analysis is unfinished. Dora left after only three months.

Dora's Intentions

The dialogue returns again and again to Dora's intentions. Freud's interjections, marking what Lacan calls the reversals, are psychoanalytic interpretations. When a gap occurs, the analyst's inference is that something is unconscious, and an interpretation is offered to fill the gap. According to some commentators, interpretations can be anything to fill such gaps. This is misleading. Central to Freud's theories, and to the bridge to cognitive science, is the idea that interpretations are principally about intentions. In psychiatric disorders, actions occur apparently involuntarily. Intentions have gone missing. So Freud says to Dora: 'Is there an intention to reproach yourself as you reproach your father?', and 'Are you not jealous, intending as a wife might, that your father should end his affair?' Among Dora's conflicting goals are: 'I want Herr K's courtship', 'I do not want the implications of male sexuality', 'I want my father to love me best.'

Similar questions are raised by identifications. In an identification an action is copied, but without necessarily having a goal similar to that of the person from whom it was copied. So, for instance, it emerged that Dora had identified with Frau K: she had been almost a mother to Herr K's children with its connotations of being almost Herr K's wife. There were also strong hints that she identified with her father in his affair with Frau K.

Here in identifications is again the pattern of action with some of its effects not consciously intended. Intentions make actions meaningful and rational, and it is the attribution of intentions to actions that allows understanding, *Verstehen*. On the largest scale, it is in terms of intentions that our lives make sense, the 'alternative being 'a tale told by an idiot, full of sound and fury, signifying nothing' (Shakespeare, *Macbeth*, 5, 5).

Multiple Intentions and the Repercussions of Conflict

Part of Freud's hypothesis about intention was that action does not always have a single causal intent. We are creatures of multiple motives, a point reiterated by Neisser (1963), though often neglected in cognitive science.

Perhaps Freud's most basic hypothesis was that conflict of important motives is common and can engender neurosis. To resolve conflicts we may try to make a motive invisible to other people, and thereby lose sight of it ourselves. It becomes, so to speak, unconscious. The very imagery of this idea, of invisibility and of unconsciousness, indicates the difficulty for an empirical science to conceptualize or investigate this problem.

How then, may we understand conflicts of intention? Freud described them as inherent in being human (see e.g. Laplanche and Pontalis, 1980). He thought dreams were fundamental because conflicting intentions become discernible in them. He wanted to expound this idea in the case of neurotic conflict. This was what made Dora's case important to him. The centre of the case history is the analysis of two of her dreams.

In the first, which she had had on several occasions, she dreamed of a house on fire, of her father standing beside her bed and of her mother wanting to save her jewel case. Freud asked Dora to free-associate, to say whatever came to mind when she thought of each image in the dream in turn. He pieced together how it was linked to the scene at L_ by the lake two years earlier, where Herr K had proposed. In giving each association, a new piece of dialogue opened out to confirm that the dream related to the proposal, as Dora described something she had not told Freud before, and that filled a gap in her account. One such was that when she returned after the proposal, she had gone to lie down in her bedroom. She had woken to find Herr K standing beside her. 'Just as you saw your father standing beside your bed in the dream' remarked Freud (p. 66). Dora had been frightened that Herr K might take advantage of her. It became imperative to leave. That night, she said, she had dreamed this dream for the first time.

Six lines of the dream in Freud's text are followed by twenty-nine pages of virtuoso interpretation. He ranges from the theme of the proposal, to childhood enuresis from which her father used to save her by waking her up at night. Then comes the jewel case, representing the female genitalia, and jewels in the shape of drops to represent both drops of semen and vaginal discharges. Dora had said her mother suffered from discharges, and Freud asked whether she did also: she said she did, and Freud writes that he was surprised she knew that her father had a venereal infection – she assumed that somehow he had passed this unclean affliction on to her. Although Freud thought about Dora's sexual exploitation by Herr K, he stopped short in his case history of asking whether she had been sexually abused by her father. Is this, perhaps, another example of what Masson (1984) called an assault on truth?

Freud steers in another direction, not necessarily incompatible with the foregoing. The analysis moves towards Dora's conflicting intentions. In Dora's dream, her father stands beside her bed, as Herr K had in the house at L_. She wants her father to save her from danger though he is also the one to escape from. It is he who has brought the danger in the first place. Freud is most keen to stress that the danger may also be of her own desires.

This is a classical psychoanalytic conflict, but its existence is open to question. We may be intrigued by Freud's suggestions. But in a detective story there needs to be some corroboration of the detective's reconstruction. Here there is none. How is this method sufficient for us to know what the truth might be when the evidence is a story full of gaps, suffused with ambiguities that can seldom be resolved?

I have proposed that Freud founded a psychology of intention, but is it not subject to criticisms that are justly made of Freud's work? Some of his interpretations were corroborated, at least in part, by what Lacan called new developments. But some of the interpretations of Dora's first dream were uncorroborated: Freud describes Dora as rejecting his suggestion that although she feared Herr K and her father she was more afraid of her own desires. We are left thinking that the dream could indicate conflicting desires. It could also indicate Freud's enthusiasm for his own ideas. We should consider the criticisms that have been made of Freud's approach.

Criticisms of Freud

The most thorough of Freud's recent critics has been Grünbaum (1984, 1986), who has argued that Freud's concepts may be contaminated by suggestion, a problem that was raised by Freud himself. Psychoanalysis, Freud said, may be like a relationship of student and teacher, where the compliance of the student can be taken to imply that the teacher is right. In this case it would be no more than another suggestive treatment 'and we should have to attach little weight to all that it tells us about what influences our lives' (Freud, 1963, p. 452).

Freud sought to rebut this by arguing that the veracity of psychoanalytic interpretations is warranted by whether they tally with something real in the patient. We can know whether this has occurred by conflicts being resolved. Grünbaum says this is the most important methodological statement in Freud's work. It provides an objective criterion that does not depend on analysts' accounts. Freud thereby committed his epistemology to evidence that psychoanalysis uniquely relieves disabling conflicts.

It is here that natural scientific criteria are appropriate. We can compare, in experimental designs, outcomes for people having psychoanalytic therapy, with control groups having no therapy or some other therapy. Since Freud's time there have been many such comparisons. They show that psychoanalysis is about as good as methods such as behaviour therapy (see e.g. Smith et al., 1980; Lambert et al., 1986).

Thus far psychoanalysis has therefore not been shown to be unique, but there is a *caveat*. Perhaps we should not expect more than suggestive effects from the short therapies studied experimentally so far. Comparisons of longer therapies, with random assignment to psychoanalysis or comparison groups have not been made. It may be, as many analysts maintain, that it takes years rather than months to resolve transferences.

Cognitive Understanding of Narratives

There is an alternative approach. Our understanding of Freud's case histories can be related to criteria for understanding narrative in general.

When we read narratives we find that they all have gaps. A narrative is like a net, with more gaps than substance. Narrative supplies the barely sufficient clues for a reader or listener to construct a model of the world and the trajectory of characters' actions within it. It is we, the human readers, who supply the world from our knowledge and from our ability to see actions as connected by plans with intentions. Computer programs that could understand narratives would need similarly to supply such a world of understanding. Then, when there are inferences to be made about what might fill gaps in the text, the program could make them from a model of what is being described.

This argument has been put by Wegman (1985) using Schank and Abelson's (1977) work on scripts, which are representations of recurring sequences. He has sketched a computational understanding of a Freudian case history of the British governess Miss Lucy R (Freud and Breuer, 1955). If a narrator mentions something that invokes a script then inferences can be made to fill gaps in the sequence left by things not mentioned. Using this and related ideas, Wegman showed how such inferences could be made in Miss Lucy's case history.

Consider, for example, an incident where Miss Lucy's employer, a wealthy widower, had a visit from a lady. A visit includes arrival, conversation, departure – this sequence is inferred from a visit script, whether or not all its parts are mentioned. At the end of her visit, the lady kissed Miss Lucy's charges. After the lady had gone Miss Lucy's employer flew into a rage, threatening to dismiss her if she ever let anybody kiss the children again.

Issues for psychoanalytic interpretation and for narrative understanding, whether by computer or human, are similar. What do we make of this unscripted, seemingly incomprehensible, event in Miss Lucy's account? Wegman treats it in two stages: first he considers why kissing the children is mentioned. If it is simply a parting ceremony it would be taken care of by the visit script. That the story-teller mentions it at all, indicates it may be significant. A story understanding program would set a flag to indicate that it may be, as Schank and Abelson say, 'weird', and needs to be noticed as such. The program would search its knowledge base for what it knew about kissing. It might find that as well as a greeting or parting, kissing could be a mild health threat, a means of affirming a relationship, a sexual gesture . . . . Next comes Miss Lucy's employer flying into a rage. This too cannot be assimilated to a script. The mention of anger would therefore trigger a search for an intention. One inference is that a goal of the angry person has been frustrated, another is that the person to whom the anger is directed is the cause of this goal frustration. Again, the program has to search for evidence to fill the gaps.

This is similar to Freud's procedures. With Miss Lucy, Freud inferred from her depressed state, from incongruities in her story, and her associations to certain events, that she had fallen in love with her employer – her distress at his anger was due to her wish for more tender exchanges, though she had tried to put any such idea out of mind. We can ask: is this the sort of thing that might happen to a young governess working for a widower? Might such a wish, in conflict with an opposite intention to keep out of mind that it has been crushed by a violent outburst, explain Miss Lucy's depression? If so we can consider the 'weird' event of her employer flying into a rage. We can ask whether the idea that Miss Lucy's wealthy employer had become sensitive to possible designs of his lady visitor, and perhaps of Miss Lucy herself, gaining a foothold in his affections via his children, would explain his outburst.

For any understanding whatsoever of such a story the issue is to fill the gaps. Just as at the centre of a detective story is the issue of motive, so at the centre of such a gap-filling process, is the same question: what intentions, or conflicts of intentions, would make sense of this action? This question brings together issues that have seemed far apart: mechanism (as in computers) and meanings of human actions; the structure of discourse and the content of stories; natural science and human science.

Confusion between Natural Science and Human Science

Now comes a possible confusion between natural and human science. If, in the natural scientific sense, we ask whether Dora had really been jealous, or whether her vaginal discharges had been caused by sexual penetration, we do not know. We cannot exclude alternative hypotheses. We cannot tell generally from individual case histories whether conflict causes symptoms, whether sexual abuse in childhood makes adult anxiety states more likely, or whether psychoanalysis resolves conflicts. The story form does not validly permit such inferences. Such questions need empirical enquiries with appropriate controls or comparisons. But within the terms of human science, an interpretation can be acceptable and important in two ways.

First, for us readers, it provides an explanation that we might not have thought of, that allows us to understand the story, to make sense of the language of Dora's complaints. The question of intention is not just ambiguous in the sense of whether an action had an intention but also in the sense of which of many intentions could possibly fit a particular action. Since this is not always obvious, we may need suggestions. As Wilensky (1978) says, in understanding a story, it is not that we are trying to predict what will happen, but we try to summon a range of explanations to make sense of what does happen. Such explanations typically concern intentions.

Second, there is the effect of an interpretation on the patient. If an interpretation is accepted, it helps the patient build a model of his or her interacting goals, a model of self to which there is conscious access.

In neither case is there a guarantee against suggestive contamination. A reader, by imaginatively entering into the life of the patient, might have felt moved, and might have realized something about people in general, and him or herself in particular. A patient might have had an insight about his or her own intentions. But such insights will be relative to that person only. They will be more ambiguous, objectively, than a technical result. The criteria for judging their truth admit ambiguity. This is acceptable since the inference or interpretation is just one part. The other part is whether this inference allows an increase in personal understanding, an insight that resolves an inner inconsistency, fills an inner gap.

By contrast, the results of natural science are exportable from situations in which they are demonstrated. Technical effects must be reproducible independently of persons. So technical writing must exclude ambiguities.

Personal insight, derived from human science, is thus complementary to technical truth. This is not to say that the methods of human science are for ever separated from the quantitative, the formal and the empirical. On the contrary, we must construct links, because as psychologists we are interested both in insight and technical truths.

Whose Intentions?

Dora left analysis after three months, perhaps, as Freud suspected later, because he had by 'premature communication of a solution brought the treatment to an untimely end' (1958b, p. 140). Many people leave consideration of psychoanalysis for a similar reason: Freud's fondness for believing himself to be right without presenting convincing evidence.

If what is recounted in a case history is implausible, the step of applying it to an understanding of self is not made. We sense instead that there is something wrong with the story or its teller. Freud says Dora did not accept his interpretation of her first dream as a conflict of fear and her own sexual desire. A structure in which interpretation is followed by corroboration later in the dialogue has been proposed as an objective basis for recognizing the validity of certain kinds of interpretation in transcripts of psychoanalytic sessions (Luborsky et al., 1986). But here no new piece of dialogue opens up, nor does anything else in the case history corroborate this interpretation. Readers may therefore be reluctant to accept it as insightful.

And yet for Freud to leave behind such writings as Dora's case is to provide evidence for others to analyse his own text using methods that he himself pioneered. It is because we are prompted by him to seek intentions in actions, that we ask: 'What was Freud's involvement in all this?'

Freud called his text a fragment pointing out, rather baldly one might think, that it had gaps. He too tells a story. We, his readers, discover not just minor gaps, but rather large ones. Might they occur for the same reasons that he supposed hysterics left gaps, because of conflicts? The unreliability of Freud's narrative affronts us as natural scientists, but it can prompt us as human scientists to apply interpretive methods to it.

One of the gaps is that, although Freud was at first attracted to this young woman 'of intelligent and engaging looks' (p. 23), the text indicates that he came to like her less (Marcus, 1974), but he did not say why. Perhaps he preferred women to be more pliant. In the end he, too, let her down. He had an ulterior motive, the prospect of becoming famous. Not far beneath the surface of this text, we see indications that his goal was to convince himself, then force his ideas upon Dora, then tell us readers of his theories.

Can we make sense of the gap between Freud's hope of establishing his work as natural science and his disregard of the criteria of science, by enquiring into his intentions? Freud was, in his own words, a man with a 'thirst for grandeur' (Freud, 1953a, p. 192), a 'conquistador' (Sulloway, 1979, p. 216). Kardiner remembers him saying, twenty years later, more modestly: 'I have several handicaps that disqualify me as a great analyst . . . I am much too much occupied with theoretical problems . . . rather than paying attention to the therapeutic problems' (Kardiner, 1977, pp. 68–9).

Dora's Second Dream

Freud's involvement is clearest in his account of Dora's second dream: she was walking in a strange town, and came to a place where she lived to find a letter from her mother saying her father was dead and that she could come if she liked. She visited a station, entered a wood, met a man who said 'Two and a half hours more' (p. 94), and offered to accompany her. Then she reached home to find that her mother had left for the cemetery. Freud did not finish interpreting this dream because Dora left after only two further sessions. He inferred that it included a theme of revenge: she wished her father dead.

In her associations Dora recognized the phrase 'if you like' (p. 98) as coming from the letter from Frau K that had contained the invitation to L—. So this dream too led back to the scene on the lake. Again, a new memory opened up: Dora remembered that, in that scene, Herr K had said 'I get nothing out of my wife' (p. 98) and that she had slapped his face. She had walked away and intended to walk alone back around the lake to the Ks' house. She had asked a man how long this would take: 'Two and a half hours' (p. 99) was the reply so she decided to go back on the boat, meeting Herr K again there, where he had apologized to her.

On the third day after this dream, Dora began 'with these words: "Do you know that I am here for the last time today?" – "How can I know, as you have said nothing to me about it?" – "Yes, I made up my mind to put up with it till the new year. But I will wait no longer than that to be cured"' (p. 105). Freud asked how long ago she had decided. She said two weeks.

Freud, in a barely credible intuitive leap, remarked that this sounded like the length of notice given to a maidservant or governess, and asked whether anything came to mind about a governess. The great detective had hit upon the right question. Its answer cleared up some of the mystery of Dora's case. She said there had been a governess of the Ks who gave two weeks notice when they were at L—. She had confided in Dora, a day or two before the scene at the lake, that Herr K had made advances and had sexual intercourse with her. He had said to her that he got nothing out of his wife.

Said Freud: 'These are the very words he used afterwards when he made his proposal to you and you gave him the slap in his face' (p. 106). He inferred that among the causes of Dora's outrage at Herr K was that she was being treated like a governess, a servant. Accompanying this is a footnote to the effect that Dora's father had also said he got nothing from his wife.

Freud explained to Dora that before this she had thought that Herr K would divorce and marry her. Her father could then marry Frau K. Her disappointment was more serious than had appeared. No wonder she had been enraged that her father had discounted the idea of Herr K's proposal. Now the reason why she wanted her father to end his affair with Frau K was also clearer. She felt envious of her father and Frau K continuing their affair now that she was excluded from the arrangement she had imagined. Dora had taken the possibility of a proposal from Herr K seriously for a long time. When it came it was horribly transformed by the governess's confidences.

Freud added that Dora 'had listened to [him] without any of her usual contradictions. She seemed to be moved' (pp. 108–9).

Freud Dismissed

Gallup (1982) describes how, despite Freud's immediate grasp of the significance of two weeks as the period of notice given to a governess, he did not grasp its implications for him. Freud was paid for his services, just as governesses are paid. It was Freud who had been given two weeks notice. It was he who was being thrown out. Clement and Cixous (cited by Gallup, 1982) use, for this throwing out, the vulgar idiomatic French expression 'foutu à la porte' (chucked out at the door). ' "Foutre" which no longer has a literal sense used to [be a term for sexual intercourse]'. What Freud could not tolerate was to have been 'foutu à la porte' (Gallup, 1982, p. 147).

The governess is a figure who appears often in Freud's works, insecure in her employment like Miss Lucy, liable to being foutu, as was the Ks' governess, and seen as getting up to things. But it is not governesses only who are foutu à la porte. It is women in general. In Dora's case there is a series of instances in which women are declared nothing. Dora's father and Herr K declare that their wives give them nothing, perhaps are nothing. Might Dora have realized that it was only a matter of time before this fate would befall her too? Was the label 'hysteria' a further attempt to nullify her refusal of the consequences of the kind of male sexuality that turns a woman from a thing into a nothing? Freud did not want to realize himself in the role of a governess, meaning a nothing. He avoided recognizing that Dora was saying that she intended that it was he who was to be foutu à la porte.

The End of Dora

The end of the story for Dora and Freud is that neither of them was cured by their dialogue. Freud recounted how Dora returned fifteen months later. Her visit was prompted by her seeing his name in the newspaper – no doubt the news of his professorship (footnote to p. 122). Dora's symptoms had improved. An opportunity had arisen to visit the Ks, following the death of one of their children. She told Frau K that she knew of the affair with her father. She got Herr K to admit that the scene by the lake was not her imagination. This she told her father. Subsequently she did not resume relations with the K family.

Dora was recognized twenty years later by Deutsch (1957) from the story of her early life given by a woman who consulted him. She was pleased to be recognized as the famous Dora, but she was still beset with serious psychosomatic symptoms. Not long after her last visit to Freud she had married. To Deutsch she denounced her husband as 'selfish, demanding and ungiving' (1957, p. 161). She was fond of her brother, by that time a prominent politician. He, though saying that she was a difficult woman 'who distrusted people and tried to turn them against each other' (Deutsch, 1957, p. 162), saw her frequently and was kind to her. Some 30 years later still, Dora died of a bowel cancer, having emigrated to New York. It shocks us to read, in an echo of what has gone before, that Deutsch's informant of her death utters a contemptuous phrase, denouncing her as of no account.

Freud went on from Dora's case with his system largely in place. It was allowed to change later so long as he made the changes. But from then on, he seems to have been unchanged. Among the characteristics that persisted, as Forrester (1984) and others have pointed out, was Freud's unwillingness to see himself as feminine in any way. In our society, for those with a certain kind of ambition, to be feminine is not such a good role. It can mean being passed over, being given a couple of weeks' notice.

Freud's ideas about this culminated in his lecture on 'Femininity'. Although, he says, the hysteric's ideas of male seduction turned out to be largely fantasy, the real cause of all the trouble is the seductive action of the mother. This is grounded in reality. She had caressed the child and then in various ways been disappointing. He says: 'Women have made few contributions to the discoveries and inventions in the history of civilization' (Freud, 1964, p. 132), but they may have invented weaving – a kind of cultural equivalent of pubic hair to cover up the shame of having no penis. Freud was not on any account going to be like that. He was going to make sure that he was cock of the roost, and to be quite shameless about it. He continued to be domineering when his schemes were at stake. Later, when any substantial disagreement with his views occurred, he was the one to give the dissident notice to quit (see for instance, Gay, 1988).

Marcus (1974) points out that Freud's story ceases to be about Dora. It is about himself and his ideas. Dora leaves without being able to fill her gaps or tell her story. By contrast, Freud filled the gaps left by his hitherto unfulfilled desire for recognition, and told his story many times.

Insight and Models of the Self

Where does this leave us? We could do any of the usual things such as idealize Freud or dismiss him. But if, instead, we involve ourselves not so much as observers in a commanding position with respect to the observed, or as natural scientists asking whether in psychopathology some mechanism is at fault, if we take the intentional stance seriously, if we listen to this story, and take part ourselves in it, then a remarkable thing may happen. From the dialogue of an outraged woman and an ambitious man in 1900, there may come alive a world in which we are all still involved, of multiple conflicting intentions for which there is no necessary resolution. We want to be loved and respected, but we fear to be made a convenience of. We fear to be *foutu à la porte*. Such conflictual intentions make the story recognizably human, and their recognition in ourselves may provoke insights.

Freud's striking proposal is that in a dialogue, that can be retold in story form, about abuses of power, about imperfections and evasions, we can take a few steps towards truths that may be transformative. It was this idea that Freud glimpsed; even if not quite clearly enough to transform himself.

Cognitive psychology is not just a basis for cleverer and more complex technical innovations. Many, perhaps most, of its practitioners expect it also to help us understand ourselves better – to afford us insights. Yet cognitive psychology is almost exclusively technical: its literature helps us do repeatable things to the outer world. It does not often encourage insights that enable us to change things in our inner world.

I have proposed (Oatley, 1987) that psychology is unique among academic disciplines in that it provides a natural scientific basis for useful technological development, while at the same time, within terms of human and social sciences, it aims to be insightful about ourselves. Human science, as an interpretive discipline is not so much under-represented, as unintegrated with modern psychology's main edifice based on natural science. But to achieve the integration means that we should concern ourselves with meaning as well as with mechanism.

Mechanisms of mind no doubt contribute to the phenomena of intentionality, and of course mental mechanisms are interesting to psychologists. But what I have proposed here is that they are not our exclusive interest. If we admit intentionality we admit meaning, and if we admit meaning then we are also concerned with insight.

We are not in a position to stand outside all this and say: 'Well, Freud was such and such, and Dora was so and so, but I, on the other hand . . .'. Freud, Dora and we are all involved. The possibility, indicated in this fragment of a story, is that even if truth may not set us entirely free, there may be a possibility of reappropriating missing intentions that we are tempted to project and displace, that tend to be chucked out of the door. By this means we may have some partial success in coming to know consciously our own intentions, and integrating them into models of self.

Acknowledgement

A version of this chapter was given at the British Psychological Society Annual Conference, 31 March to 3 April 1989, at St Andrew's University.

5
The Intentionality of Animal Action

CECILIA HEYES AND ANTHONY DICKINSON

In the preface to his *Psychosemantics*, Fodor (1987) tells us that he has a strikingly intelligent cat that goes by the name of Graycat. By 'intelligent' what Fodor means is that Graycat has a mental life built on the rational interactions of intentional states, such as beliefs and desires, and which, Fodor believes, is manifest in Graycat's behaviour. He tells us that 'In the morning, at his usual feeding time, Graycat prowls the area of the kitchen near his feeding bowl. When breakfast appears, he positions himself near his food bowl in a manner that facilitates ingestion' (p. ix). From this and other similar observations, Fodor concludes that 'The reason, for example, that Graycat patrols his food bowl in the morning is that he wants food and believes – has come to believe on the basis of earlier feedings, that his food bowl is the place to find it' (p. x).

Although we suspect that Fodor himself would not claim that simple observations, such as that of Graycat's feeding activities, are sufficient to establish the cognitive status of an action, contemporary 'cognitive' ethologists have attributed intentional states to animals on the basis of passive observation of their behaviour under free-living conditions (e.g. Griffin, 1984; Whiten and Byrne, 1987). We shall argue in this chapter that such observation, however careful, can be misleading; that intentionality is not directly 'manifest' in behaviour and that the attribution of intentionality to animals should be based upon specific behavioural criteria that cannot be applied through passive behavioural observation in an uncontrolled environment.

Thus, our purpose in this chapter is to specify the behavioural criteria that have to be met if an action is to warrant an intentional account. To do so, we must first provide an analysis of what is involved in claiming that an action is intentional. We have not tried to justify this analysis, to make it comprehensive or even innovative. Instead, we have simply developed the account to the point where it provides an adequate introduction to the second section of the chapter in which we discuss the application of the criteria. Finally, we will consider several potential objections to our approach to the study of intentionality in animal action, focusing on the extent to which it is consistent with our understanding of both human intentionality and evolution.

The Intentional Account of Action

In developing this account we have adopted a blatantly 'realist', rather than 'instrumentalist' view of intentionality (Bechtel, 1985). For the present purposes, this means that we regard an intentional account of action as a variety of causal explanation, and in order to test most causal explanations, including intentional ones, it is necessary to translate them, implicitly or explicitly into counterfactual claims. Thus, in the case of an animal action, an intentional account must be translated into claims about what the animal would have done if its circumstances had been different in certain, specifiable respects from those in which the action actually occurred (e.g. Millikan, 1984; Lockery, 1989). The central problem with attributing intentionality on the basis of naturalistic observation alone is that such observation seldom provides the opportunity to evaluate these claims. This is a direct and inevitable consequence of the fact that in the field, rather than laboratory, it is rarely possible to observe an action under more than one set of circumstances, let alone under circumstances that are known to vary in a systematic way.

In order to specify the nature of the counterfactual claims that we take to be involved in an intentional explanation of animal action, we must first outline the general character of an intentional theory of action. Consider, once again, hungry Graycat's approach to his food bowl. An intentional account of Graycat's act has three main components:

1 *Instrumental beliefs.* Graycal must believe that approaching the bowl causes access to food. For expository purposes we shall represent the content of mental states in terms of PROLOG, a programming language designed, at least in part, to simulate cognitive processes. The assumption then is that Graycat has a belief with the content *cause (approach,access(food))*. .

2 *Desires.* Graycat must have a desire, and since he is hungry we can assume that he wants access to food, a desire the content of which can be represented as *access(food)*. .

3 *Practical inference process.* Finally, an intentional account has to specify how the instrumental belief and the desire interact to produce the action. We shall assume that the presence of a mental state, an intention to perform an action A, is sufficient in the present context for the execution of the action. We shall represent the content of this intention in PROLOG in the form of the command, *perform(A)*. . Thus, two mental states, a belief and a desire, are assumed to interact by a process that conforms to a rule of practical inference to produce a third mental state, an intention. The rule

describing the practical inference process can be represented in PROLOG by

perform(A):-cause(A,access(O)),access(O). .

By this process of practical inference, an animal that had the belief *cause (approach,access(food)).* and the desire *access(food).* would also have the intention *perform(approach). .*

There are two features of this explanation that are noteworthy. The first is that it is causal in the sense that it is the interaction of the belief and desire in the practical inference process that determines the content of the intention. Without the appropriate belief and desire, the animal would not have the relevant intention. Second, the explanation portrays the action as rational. Thus, the practical inference rule is such that if the belief *cause (A,access(O)).* is true, and the intention *perform(A).* is executed (i.e action A is performed), then, other things being equal, the desire *access(O).* must be fulfilled. Of course, there is nothing about PROLOG that would prevent us from specifying a rule of the form

perform(R):-cause(A,access(O)),access(O).

where R is an action unrelated to A and without consequences with respect to O. Such a rule could not, however, be part of intentional account of action because the performance of R would be in no sense rational with respect to the belief and desire that caused its execution. It is this 'rationality assumption' (Dennett, 1987, p. 185) that gives intentional accounts of animal behaviour explanatory power by making them subject to empirical evaluation. If it were assumed that intentional states participate in non-rational interactions, it would be impossible to predict the outcomes of their interactions and therefore impossible to test those predictions through observation.

Of course, this intentional account is rudimentary in the extreme and represents little more than a starting point for a proper cognitive theory of action. For instance, it takes no account of the quantification of beliefs and desires, nor does it specify how competing intentions are resolved in action. Even so, this primitive theory is sufficient for the present purpose, namely that of specifying behavioural criteria for the attribution of intentionality.

Behavioural Criteria

There are two counterfactual claims supported by this intentional account, namely that the target action would not have occurred in the absence of (a) the appropriate belief and (b) the appropriate desire. These claims imply that two corresponding behavioural criteria, the belief and desire criteria, have to be met in order to justify an intentional attribution.

The Belief Criterion

According to the intentional account, Graycat's approach to his food bowl is caused by a belief *cause(approach,access(food))*. . If this is so, the action should not persist in a world where approach no longer gives access to the food bowl. Suppose we placed Graycat in the world faced by Alice when she went through the looking glass; a world in which goals recede when you walk towards them, but draw nigh when you attempt to retreat from them. The contingencies of such a world would not support a belief that would make the approach of a hungry animal to its food bowl rational. Consequently, if Graycat's action is intentional he should, like Alice, adapt to this environment by, at least, removing *cause(approach,access(food))*. from his corpus of beliefs. Thus, we would have grounds for asserting that Graycat's approach behaviour in the normal environment is mediated by an appropriate causal belief if he adapts to the looking glass world by no longer attempting to walk towards his food bowl. This would show that a necessary condition for approach is that the environment provide contingencies that would support the belief required by an intentional account.

Of course, we cannot know what Graycat would do in a looking glass world, but there is evidence to suggest that he might persist in attempting to walk towards his bowl. Hershberger (1986) arranged a looking glass environment for some chicks: their food bowl receded from them at twice the rate they walked towards it, and approached them at twice the rate they retreated from it. In spite of the fact that they could easily have gained access to food by walking away from the bowl, the chicks persisted in chasing the bowl away. After 100 trials the chicks succeeded in gaining access to the food bowl only 30 per cent of the time. Thus, an action, which appears to be intentional on the basis of passive observation, loses this property when there is a simple reversal of the environmental contingencies.

It could be argued that Hershberger's study indicates, not that the chicks lacked a belief about the relationship between approach and access to food, but that this belief was highly resistant to change. There is some force to this argument because outside Hershberger's apparatus the chicks will have continually contacted contingencies supporting conventional beliefs about the consequences of walking towards objects. This argument, however, could not account for maladaptive approach when the behaviour was originally acquired within the experimental situation itself. It is a common procedure in the animal psychologist's laboratory to study signal learning by measuring approach during a signal for food. In this procedure hungry rats are presented with some food pellets every few minutes, and each presentation is announced by a signal, say a tone, that comes on a few seconds before the food is delivered into a bowl. Across successive pairings of the signal and food presentations, the rats learn to approach the bowl during the signal so that they are adjacent to it at the time of presentation. An intentional account would argue that the development of this behaviour reflects the acquisition of a belief *cause(approach-tone, access(food))*., namely the belief supported by the tone-food contingency to the effect that approaching the bowl during the tone causes access to food. However, it is easy to show by an implementation of the looking glass world that this account cannot be sustained. If we simply arrange that from the outset of training the presentation of the food is omitted whenever the rats approach the bowl during the tone, the animals can never experience a contingency that would support the appropriate causal belief for approach during the tone. Despite the lack of this experience, the animals do acquire approach under this 'omission schedule'. Holland (1979) found that rats lose a significant proportion of the rewards available to them by acquiring and persisting in approach during the tone, a behavioural pattern completely at variance with the rationality posited by an intentional explanation of approach behaviour.

We know of no evidence indicating how Graycat and his feline fellows would cope with an omission contingency but, if they are anything like rats and chicks, it is unlikely that their approach behaviour would support the intentional explanation that Fodor, and many other cat lovers, would like to give it. However, just because things look bleak for an intentional account of Graycat's approach behaviour, it does not mean that *none* of his actions are intentional. While the rat's approach responses appear to be relatively insensitive to their causal consequences (and therefore appear to be non-intentional), there is no doubt that rats are capable of at least one action that *is* sensitive to its consequences and therefore meets the belief criterion. If rats are simply trained to press a lever for food, they will refrain from pressing when the schedule is subsequently changed so that the food is delivered independently of whether or not they press (e.g. Rescorla and Skucy, 1969).

This contrast, between approach and lever-pressing behaviour, underlines the fact that intentionality is primarily a property of an agent with respect to a particular action rather than of the agent *per se*. Of course, there may be species of animal that are incapable of any intentional actions, but it is equally clear that the capacity for one kind of intentional action does not guarantee that all, or indeed any, of the animals' other actions are intentional. This is apparent when one considers the human case. Few people doubt that humans are capable of intentional action, but even we have difficulty in adapting to certain omission schedules. This is a claim, however, that we can only substantiate by anecdote. Consider the case of a friend of ours, Tony, who became amorously involved with a young lady who was particularly susceptible to 'macho' displays. Unfortunately, Tony's disposition was to display affection and courtesy when in love. His girlfriend rapidly became bored by this lack of the machismo spirit and rejected his subsequent advances, a rejection that so hurt and angered Tony that the next time they met by chance he was cool and offhand. This display was, of course, irresistible to the lady in question, who instantly revived the relationship, and thereby initiated the whole cycle over again. Tony went through a number of such cycles with her before he realized that his affection was in fact under an omission contingency; the display of affection caused the loss of the desired goal. However, this realization did not help Tony to cope with the schedule because his affectionate behaviour was not under rational, intentional control. The only solution was to break out of the schedule altogether, thereby ensuring that he was never again exposed to this powerfully attractive stimulus.

In summary, the first criterion that must be met if an action is to warrant an intentional account is a belief criterion. The behaviour must be sensitive to whether or not the environmental contingencies will support a belief with the appropriate causal content. Other things being equal, if an action is acquired under contingencies that would support a contradictory belief, this action does not warrant intentional characterization.

The Desire Criterion

Although our discussion of the belief criterion has left us with doubts about the intentionality of Graycat's approach behaviour, we have at least one animal action that has been shown to be sensitive to the relevant instrumental contingencies, namely lever pressing for food by hungry rats. However, even this action has a further test to pass before we can conclude that it is intentional. The intentional account assumes that an action is mediated not only by an instrumental belief but also by a desire; in this case, a desire with the content *access(food)*. . Consequently, if the desire is eliminated or, at least, diminished, then the performance of the action should, other things being equal, decline.

At first sight, it appears to be easy to devise a behavioural criterion corresponding to this counterfactual. Surely all we have to do is to reduce the desire for food by simply ensuring that our rat is well fed before we test him? Under these circumstances no one would be surprised to find that the animal has little inclination to press the lever, but a moment's reflection shows that the desire criterion cannot be met so easily. The problem with this test is that it does not ensure that 'other things are equal'. A hungry rat is likely to differ from a satiated rat in a number of respects other than in his desire for food. For example, a satiated rat may be more inclined to sleep, and its slumbers, rather than its weaker desire for food, may result in relatively little lever pressing.

Animal psychologists have thought long and hard about how to demonstrate that a change in the desirability of a goal or an incentive can affect instrumental action, although they have seldom expressed the problem in these terms. One of the procedures they have come up with goes by the cumbersome name of the 'irrelevant incentive test'. First, consider two groups of hungry rats all of which are trained to press a lever and pull a chain concurrently for two food rewards, dry food pellets and sugar solution. The only difference between the two groups is that lever pressing is rewarded with the pellets in one group but with the sucrose solution in the other. In both groups chain pulling is trained with the other incentive. All the animals are then sated for food and their propensity to press the lever is assessed when they are thirsty, and in the absence of any rewards. According to an intentional account of this action, the group trained with the sugar solution for lever pressing should press more than the one trained with the food pellets. The shift from hunger to thirst should reduce the desirability of the dry food pellets, while maintaining that of the sugar solution, an incentive for which rats will work when thirsty. This is precisely the outcome observed under certain circumstances (see below) by Dickinson and Dawson (1988, 1989).

The significant feature of this irrelevant incentive effect is that it demonstrates an apparent effect of changing the desirability of a goal under conditions in which other, non-intentional factors appear to be equated. Both groups are in the same motivational state at the time of test, and both received comparable training under hunger. The latter is demonstrated by the fact that if the animals are tested in the absence of any rewards while hungry, rather than thirsty, they press at similar rates (Dickinson and Dawson, 1987a). Thus, the difference observed during the test under thirst must be due to the animals being in that motivational state.

This irrelevant incentive design also ensures that the effect of the motivational manipulation intended to change the relative strengths of the desires for the two incentives is mediated by the instrumental contingency between lever pressing and the incentives. This requirement is implicit in the claim that an intention to act is the product of the interaction of a desire and a belief about this contingency in the practical inference process. Two features of the design meet this requirement. If we had presented the sugar solution and the dry food pellets on test, when the animals were thirsty, any variations in performance could be explained by differences in the immediate impact of the two incentives. By testing in the absence of any rewards, we ensured that any difference in the performance of the two groups was due to the 'information' acquired during training, namely the instrumental belief about the consequences of lever pressing. Second, the concurrent training procedure in which both groups received the same exposure to the two incentives, but contingent upon different actions, ensured that the only difference between them was the content of the instrumental beliefs supporting their training schedules.

In conclusion, the rat's lever-pressing behaviour can fulfil the desire criterion; the animal's actions adjust appropriately to manipulations that should change its desires in a way that depends upon the training schedule supporting the appropriate instrumental beliefs. We have discussed the application of the belief and desire criteria in some detail because we feel that it is important to appreciate that an animal action warrants an intentional explanation only if it fulfils certain quite specific requirements. It is somewhat ironic that the only example of an animal action that has, as far as we know, met both criteria is the behaviourist's prototypical example of a non-intentional, stimulus-response habit – rats' lever pressing in a Skinner box.

Potential Objections

Our analysis suggests that in order to find out whether any given example of animal action is intentional it is essential to measure the effects on that action of changes in the animal's environment which could be expected to alter the content of the animal's mental states. Many behaviours, that appear to be intentional on the basis of simple observation, fail to change in appropriate ways under the influence of new environmental contingencies, and therefore, if our analysis is correct, naturalistic observations of behaviour provide no reliable information about the intentionality of animal action. But is our analysis correct? We will now consider briefly several potential objections to our approach, each of which alleges either that we have not taken sufficient account of what is known about human intentionality, or that we have disregarded the facts of evolutionary biology. Thus, we will attempt to defend ourselves against allegations of both 'species-ism' and anthropomorphism.

Manipulating Mental States

First, it could be argued that inherent in our analysis is an anthropomorphic bias against recognition of intentionality in animals; that it will tend to yield 'false negative' conclusions because it presupposes that, if an animal has any beliefs and desires, then a scientist can reliably identify environmental contingencies and manipulate motivational states that will affect their content. Our short response to this allegation must be 'Guilty, m'lud'. Our approach does require the identification of conditions that will alter the content of mental states, and we recognize that there are major obstacles to such identification. We shall argue, however, that the difficulties associated with the manipulation of desires are greater than those encountered when trying to implement the belief criterion.

In the case of beliefs, the contentious issue is conceptual rather than empirical. In withholding an attribution of intentionality unless an animal adapts to a reversal of the instrumental contingency, we are demanding evidence not just that the animal has beliefs, but that it has veridical or true beliefs. It could be argued that the very fact that the rat approaches the food bowl during the tone is the strongest evidence we could have for a belief *cause(approach-tone,access(food))*. . According to this view, acquisition of this behaviour under an omission schedule merely shows that the content of the animal's belief does not veridically represent the contingencies in the world. For us, however, this argument undercuts the whole concept of representation. Unless a system appears to be capable of detecting the extent to which the contents of its mental states actually match or represent states of affairs in the world, and of adjusting the content to bring about a degree of correspondence, we should certainly be cautious about according the determinants of its behaviour representational, let alone intentional, status.

The requirement that a system should meet the belief criterion in order to qualify for intentional status is also consistent with the consensus view of certain test cases. For example, in effect it is the application of the belief criterion that leads most people to deny that simple homeostatic mechanisms, such as thermostats, are intentional systems. In the case of a thermostat we could measure performance against the belief criterion by rewiring its connections to the boiler so that the output that previously switched the boiler on, now switches it off. This rewiring would reverse the instrumental contingencies operating on a thermostat, just as an omission schedule reverses the instrumental contingencies operating on the rat's approach response. The fact that a simple thermostat would never adapt to such a reversal is consistent with the widespread intuition that a thermostat does not have a representation of the instrumental contingency between its output and the temperature of its environment.

It should be made clear that we are arguing that it is necessary in *practice*, as part of an empirical programme designed to assess the intentionality of animal action, to treat all beliefs as veridical. Of course, this is not entirely satisfactory because *two* inseparable possibilities are implicit in the concept of representation: that representations can be true and that they can be false. There is no doubt that both animal and human beliefs about even simple instrumental contingencies are not always veridical. For instance, if we simply introduce a short delay between the performance of an action and its outcome, both animals, in terms of their performance (e.g. B. A. Williams, 1976), and humans, in terms of their causal judgements (Shanks et al., 1989), fail to distinguish this relationship from a truly non-contingent schedule. However, the implications of these contingency judgement studies are rather different from those, described above, showing that animals can acquire a maladaptive behaviour on an omission schedule. In both cases the subjects could be said to have acted on the basis of a false belief, but the origins of the false belief are mysterious only in the case of the omission schedule. When, as in the contingency judgement studies, the presence of a contingency has no effect on behaviour, it suggests that the subject has failed to form certain true beliefs that its environment would, in fact, support. On the other hand, when the contingency *does* affect behaviour, but the behaviour is maladaptive, as in the omission schedule experiments, it suggests that the subject has formed a belief that is inconsistent with any true belief that the environment would support. How could such a false belief come about? The onus is surely on those who would like to explain such maladaptive behaviour in intentional terms to provide a principled answer to this question.

The interpretation of failures to meet the desire criterion is far more problematic. What are we to make of an action if its performance does not adjust appropriately to a manipulation designed to change the mediating desire? Does this mean that the action is non-intentional, or that the manipulation has failed to change the animals' desires as anticipated? There seems to be no principled way of deciding this issue. Of course, one chooses one's manipulations in the light of what is known about the animal's physiology, ecology and behaviour, but that this is not necessarily a reliable guide can be illustrated by reconsidering the irrelevant incentive effect. It seems reasonable to suppose that shifting an animal's motivational state from hunger to thirst will lead to a greater desire for sugar solution, a hydrating fluid, than for dry food pellets. However, if that is all one does, then an irrelevant incentive effect will not be observed; the rats trained to lever press for the food pellets on the concurrent schedule will respond just as much under thirst as those rewarded with the sugar solution for lever pressing during training (Dickinson and Dawson, 1987a). In order to observe an irrelevant incentive effect, Dickinson and Dawson (1988, 1989) found that the rats had to be given the opportunity to consume the sugar solution and food pellets under thirst at some point prior to the instrumental test. Rats appear to have to learn about the relative desirability of the two incentives under the motivational state of thirst. Only after this incentive learning will a shift in motivational state bring about an appropriate change in behaviour.

Although in retrospect it seems that we should have realized that incentive learning might play a role in controlling desires, there was no *a priori* basis for certainty. Rats could have been, and other species might be, 'prewired' to desire certain fluids when thirsty. The dependence of the irrelevant incentive effect upon incentive learning is simply an empirical discovery. The implication of this example is that we must remain agnostic about the intentional status of actions that meet the belief criterion but not the desire criterion because in such cases we may simply have failed to manipulate desires appropriately.

Direct Perception of Intentionality

In the foregoing section we have tried to indicate why we think that the belief and desire criteria are necessary, and how they should be used to avoid false-negative bias. Now we turn our attention to a more specific, empirically based, potential objection to our approach. It could be argued that, regardless of the details of our analysis, it must be wrong because it yields a conclusion that can be at odds with the results of recent experiments on human perception. Many of the experiments in question use Johansson's (1973) 'patch-light' technique. Subjects are exposed to the trajectories of lights attached to the joints of an actor, and on the basis of this information alone they can report accurately the content of certain of the actor's mental states. For example, Runeson and Frykholm (1983) have shown that when the actor is observed preparing to lift a box, the observer can detect what the actor expects the box to weigh, what the box actually weighs, and what the actor intends the observer to believe about the weight of the box. Our analysis suggests that intentionality is not necessarily manifest in behaviour, while experiments like these apparently indicate that intentionality can be 'directly perceived' even under impoverished stimulus conditions.

If intentionality is defined with reference to rational interactions among mental states, covert states with representational content, and if what is meant by 'direct perception' is that the observer cannot be misled, then experiments of this kind certainly do not show that intentionality can be directly perceived. The potential for illusory attributions of intentionality is apparent when one considers the experimental technique itself. While Johansson and his followers happen to have generated their patch-light displays through the performance of intentional actions, there is no reason why the same displays could not be generated artificially without destroying the phenomenological percept. Under these circumstances, the observed movements would be perceived to be intentional although they would have, at best, 'derived' intentionality; i.e. they would be the products of intentional action on the part of, for example, the person who programmed the visual display.

It could be argued that the perception of intention in an artificially generated display is not illusory, that derived intentionality is intentionality-in-good-standing, or that, while it *is* illusory, such non-veridical attributions do not present any challenge to the claim that intentionality is manifest in natural behaviour under normal viewing conditions. Implicit in the latter argument is an appeal to evolutionary considerations to support the idea that intentionality can be directly perceived. While we agree that it can be helpful to think about the detection of intentionality in evolutionary terms, we suspect that, if anything, an evolutionary perspective casts doubt on the view that *human* observers can directly perceive intentionality in *animal* behaviour. Adopting such a perspective, Runeson and Frykholm (1983) suggest that direct perception of intention is unlikely to be possible when (a) it would not bestow any fitness advantage on the perceiver, because the perceptual apparatus necessary to exploit the information in the stimulus array will not have evolved, and (b) there is a reliable cost to the actor of having his intention directly perceived. In the latter case, mechanisms camouflaging the intention are likely to have evolved. Now, with respect to how many animal actions is it likely to be the case that direct perception of their intentionality (a) *would* bestow adaptive advantage on a human observer, and (b) would *not* have any cost to the animal observed? Our guess would be that the answer to this question is 'precious few'. Consider, for example, species that are preyed upon by humans. Selection pressure might well favour perceptual mechanisms that would allow people to perceive their intentions, but this, in turn, would favour the evolution of camouflage processes on the part of the prey.

Of course, by responding in this way we may have mistaken the implications of the direct perception research altogether. The claim inherent there may be, not that certain mental states are manifest in behaviour, but that what were once thought to be mental states are in fact properties of behaviour. Thus, the Gibsonians might well be in the process of redefining intentionality in such a way that it is *necessarily* observable. Tolman, the prophet of cognition in animal behaviour throughout the dark-ages of behaviourism, often seemed to be attempting the same kind of redefinition:

We, the observers, watch the behavior of the rat, the cat, or the man, and note its character as getting to such and such by means of such and such a selected pattern of commerces-with. It is we, the independent neutral observers, who note these perfectly objective characters as imminent in the behavior and have happened to choose the terms *purpose* and *cognition* as generic terms for such characters. (Tolman, 1932, p. 13)

Any attempt to 'reduce' intentional states to behaviour is likely to meet strong opposition on many grounds (e.g. Montefiore, 1989), and indeed there is good evidence that Tolman himself was not committed to a behaviourist interpretation (see Amundson, 1986). For the present purposes, however, we need only note that a claim for the priority of manifest intentionality based upon a behaviourist interpretation of cognition simply misses the point of the present argument, an argument predicated upon a 'realist' view of mental states and their causal properties.

Intentionality in the Lab and in the Field

We have used an evolutionary argument in an attempt to show that our approach to the investigation of animal intentionality is not inconsistent with data on human perception. A cognitive ethologist might be surprised, if not indignant, to find us using an evolutionary argument because, he or she might claim, the fundamental weakness of our approach lies in its failure to consider the possibility that animals are less likely to provide evidence of intentionality in the laboratory than in the field, i.e. when they are under free-living conditions. Dennett (1983) makes this claim explicitly, and his view has been echoed by Whiten and Byrne (1987). Dennett believes that behaviour, like lever pressing, which is the product of hundreds of training trials, is very unlikely to warrant intentional characterization because it will probably be explicable in terms of 'rival, conditioning hypotheses' (Dennett, 1983, p. 348). It is not clear to us why Dennett, and others, hold this view; why they think that the existence of a 'prolonged training history' is inconsistent with the attribution of intentionality. One possibility is that they assume that unlike, for example, stimulus–response habits, beliefs are formed quickly, on the basis of minimal experience.

There may well be some truth in this assumption in certain specific cases. Adams (1982) investigated the effect of changing rats' desire for sucrose after training them to lever press for it. Instead of changing the desire by shifting motivational state, he established an aversion to the sucrose by associating its consumption with the induction of gastric illness. When their propensity to press the lever in the absence of any incentives was subsequently assessed, those that had received only 100 rewards pressed less than a control group who had not been averted to the sucrose, a finding that fulfils the desire criterion. By contrast, after 500 training rewards, lever pressing was unaffected by decreasing the desirability of the sucrose. Adams's (1982) finding should not lead us to assume, however, that overtraining automatically robs an action of its intentional status. In an experiment similar to that of Adams, Colwill and Rescorla (1985) found that overtrained lever pressing fulfils the desire criterion if trained on a concurrent schedule with chain pulling. What it is about the training schedule that determines the intentionality of an instrumental action remains unclear (but see Dickinson, 1989).

Even if it is true that the intentional status of an action is determined by its training history, it is not clear why this would make the field a better place to look for animal intentionality than the lab. Free-living animals may not have been trained by human hand, but their behaviour surely has a 'history'; quite possibly a long one. We can think of only one line of reasoning that would lead one to expect to find more evidence of animal intentionality in the field than in the lab: if intentionality is an attribute that has evolved, then it may only be present in animal species that have experienced certain selection pressures, and only then when the animals are under conditions resembling those that constituted the selection pressure. If this reasoning is correct, it could have turned out to be impossible to study intentionality in the lab, i.e. it may have been impossible to find a laboratory trained animal action that fulfilled stringent criteria for intentionality. The fact is, however, that at least one such action *has* been found.

Causal Judgement and Intentional Action

Finally, our analysis may be faulted on the grounds that it says nothing about the conscious experience of animals. There is no doubt that one reason for endorsing the 'realist' view of the intentional causation of action is that, at least sometimes, we are aware of the instrumental beliefs and desires implicated in this account. This immediately raises the question of whether animals can be similarly aware of their intentional states.

Basically, we think that this is an irresolvable issue; the best that can be done is to bring tangential evidence to bear. One such line of evidence comes from the fact that variations in the major parameters of an act–outcome relationship affect in a similar manner both rat's lever pressing behaviour and human judgements about the causal effectiveness of an action (Dickinson and Shanks, 1985). We have already noted that animal performance and human judgements about the causal effectiveness of an action demonstrate a comparable sensitivity to the delay between action and outcome. Even more striking is the parallel observed in the face of variations in the so-called act–outcome contingency. If the probability of an outcome that is temporally contiguous with the action [$P(O/A)$] is kept constant, then the causal effectiveness of the action can be systematically degraded by increasing the probability of an outcome in the absence of an action [$P(O/-A)$] until, when $P(O/A)$ equals $P(O/-A)$, performing the action has no effect on the likelihood of an outcome. Both rats' lever pressing (Hammond, 1980) and human judgements about the causal effectiveness of pressing a key on a computer console (e.g. Shanks, 1987) show a similar decline when the act–outcome contingency is degraded by increasing P(O/-A).

It is, however, the non-contingent schedules, in which P(O/A) equals P(O/-A) and the action is without any causal consequence, that provide the most compelling evidence for a commonality. When exposed to a non-contingent schedule, humans judge that they have more control over the high rather than low-frequency outcomes (Shanks, 1987) just as rats press more on a non-contingent schedule with high outcome probabilities (Hammond, 1980). Moreover, an illusion of control can be induced in both cases by the same operation. If outcomes that occur in the absence of an immediately preceding action are signalled by a brief stimulus, such as a light or tone, the degradation of performance produced by a non-contingent schedule is ameliorated (Dickinson and Charnock, 1985). Correspondingly, signalling non-contiguous outcomes induces the illusion of control in humans (Shanks, 1989).

At the very least, these parallels suggest that common processes underlie human judgement and rat performance in certain situations. The implication is that rats detect the causal relationship between their actions and associated outcomes by psychological processes analogous to those mediating the acquisition of simple instrumental beliefs in humans, the content of which can be reported in the form of a judgement. To the extent that this is so, rats at least have some of the necessary processes for causal judgement. Beyond this we cannot go.

Concluding Comments

We have argued that an intentional account of an animal action is only warranted if it can be shown that the action meets two behavioural criteria. Assessing the belief criterion requires that performance of the action is investigated in an environment that differs from the target context only in the content of the instrumental belief that it will support. If action is acquired in a context that will not support the appropriate belief, an intentional account is unwarranted. Second, it must be demonstrated that the performance of the action adjusts appropriately to manipulations designed to alter the desire for the outcome. Furthermore, the desire criterion requires that the adjustment is demonstrated to depend upon training contingencies that support the appropriate instrumental belief. Applying these two criteria has revealed that the simple instrumental act of lever pressing performed by rats in the laboratory can support an intentional account.

Moreover, experimental analysis suggests that a strict application of these criteria is necessary because animals are endowed with non-intentional processes that under simple observation, and even cursory analysis, appear to generate intentional action. We have already noted the operation of such a process in the case of goal approach. It is important to appreciate, however, the subtlety of such non-intentional processes, a point that can be illustrated by reconsidering the application of the desire criterion through the irrelevant incentive effect. To recap, Dickinson and Dawson (1988, 1989) were able to demonstrate that the rat's lever press meets this criterion once they discovered that changing the relative desirability of sucrose solution and food pellets under thirst depends upon giving animals prior experience with these incentives in this motivational state or, in other words, upon the opportunity for incentive learning. The importance of incentive learning was not immediately appreciated, however, because apparent intentional control was exhibited with a simpler training procedure. If one group of hungry rats is simply trained to lever press for the sucrose solution and another for the food pellets, the sucrose-trained animals will press more when tested thirsty (Dickinson and Dawson, 1987a), even though they have had no prior opportunity for incentive learning.

At first sight this simple procedure looks like a perfectly good implementation of the desire criterion. This is not so, however; with the simple training procedure, the two groups differ not only in the instrumental belief supported by the schedule, namely that lever pressing causes the delivery of sucrose solution in one case and food pellets in the other, but also in their exposure to the two incentives during training. The groups are exposed selectively to either the sucrose solution or the food pellets. As we have already noted, when the exposure is equated by using a concurrent training procedure in which all animals received both incentives but contingent upon different actions, the irrelevant incentive effect disappears in the absence of the opportunity for incentive learning. It turns out that on further behavioural analysis the effect observed with simple training, although apparently rational and goal-directed, is in fact mediated by a non-intentional process operating through the association of the contextual stimuli and the incentives (Dickinson and Dawson, 1987b).

These examples clearly demonstrate that there is often a conflict between the intentionality manifest in behaviour and the outcome of a strict application of our criteria. Given this conflict, we argue for the precedence of the criteria because the argument linking these criteria to intentional states and processes has a stronger rationale than the claim that cognition should be manifest in behaviour. Indeed, once we accept that there are complex and subtle non-intentional processes, such as those mediating basic goal-approach and the adjustment to changes in motivational state, that can mimic true intentional control in many situations, we can understand why the propensity to perceive actions as intentional may have developed. Given that either there is nothing in the stimulus input *per se* to distinguish intentional from non-intentional behaviour or that such a discrimination yields little of consequence in most situations, it may well pay the perceiver to treat both classes of behaviour as intentional in predicting the subsequent course of events. Indeed, as Dennett (1987) has argued, the intentional 'stance' can be the best standpoint from which to predict the behaviour of complex, non-intentional systems.

Having waded through our arguments for these conclusions, the reader may well be left wondering why we have concentrated exclusively on simple instrumental acts at the expense of careful, controlled demonstrations of more impressive cognitive feats, such as the ability of Gillan et al.'s (1981) chimpanzee, Sarah, to solve analogical reasoning problems or Pepperberg's (1987) parrot, Alex, to match by attribute. We have no quarrel with a cognitive account of performance in these and other tasks for in each particular instance there are no obvious psychological explanations which do not appeal to intentional or representational states. But any intentional account of these higher 'cognitive' processes must in the end assume that they are expressed in behaviour through an instrumental act; such acts must be the final common pathway in any intentional account of behaviour. Thus, until we are convinced that animals are capable of simple, intentional acts and understand how intentional states and processes can control such actions, any cognitive account of higher functions will remain divorced from the behaviour that is their only form of expression in animals. It is this fact that gives the simple instrumental action, however prosaic it might seem, priority. We suspect that many ethologists and comparative psychologists of a cognitive persuasion believe that the intentional status of such actions is not in dispute. Our analysis demonstrates, however, that it is indeed an issue.

Finally, many readers may be puzzled about why we should be concerned about the intentional status of simple instrumental actions when it is to be supposed that there are many non-intentional explanations of how an animal's behaviour could fulfil the belief and desire criteria. But, as far as we know, there are no such adequate accounts (see Sutton and Barto, 1981, for the best attempt). Whether or not it is possible to explain the intentionality of instrumental action in terms of a psychological *mechanism* must at present remain an open question.

6
On Leaving Out What It's Like

JOSEPH LEVINE

Among the reasons for doubting the adequacy of physicalist theories of the mind is the charge that such theories must 'leave out' the qualitative, conscious side of mental life. One problem with evaluating this objection to physicalism is that it is not clear just what physicalist theories are being charged with. What is it for a theory to 'leave out' a phenomenon? My project in this chapter is threefold: First, I want to clarify the anti-physicalist charge of 'leaving out' qualia, distinguishing between a metaphysical and an epistemological reading of the objection. Second, I will argue that standard anti-physicalist conceivability arguments fail to show that physicalist theories 'leave out' qualia in the metaphysical sense. But, third, I will also argue that these conceivability arguments do serve to establish that physicalist theories 'leave out' qualia in the epistemological sense, because they reveal our inability to explain qualitative character in terms of the physical properties of sensory states. The existence of this 'explanatory gap' constitutes a deep inadequacy in physicalist theories of the mind.[1]

The Metaphysical Reading

To begin, let us focus on the metaphysical reading of the phrase 'leave out'. In this sense, to say that a theory leaves out a certain phenomenon is to say that there are objects, events or properties to which the descriptive apparatus of the theory cannot refer. For instance, on Descartes's view, since the mind is composed of a non-physical, unextended substance, there is no way to use the predicates that apply to extended objects to refer to the mind. Property dualist views are similar in this respect. For a property dualist, there is no way of constructing descriptions using physical predicates[2] that apply to mental properties.

At least since Descartes, anti-physicalist arguments have taken roughly the following form. It is alleged that certain situations are imaginable, conceivable etc., and then a metaphysical conclusion is drawn. So, Descartes claims that from the fact that he can coherently conceive of the situation in which his body does not exist – for example, he may be deceived by an evil demon – and from the fact that he cannot conceive of the situation in which his mind does not exist (i.e. consistent with his having his current experiences), it follows that his body and his mind are not identical.

A look at the current state of the debate shows that anti-physicalist arguments have not advanced significantly beyond Descartes's. In particular, I want to focus on the two most prominent contemporary anti-physicalist arguments, those of Saul Kripke (1980) and Frank Jackson (1982).

Kripke's Argument

Kripke argues that there is an important asymmetry between purported mental–physical identity statements and those that derive from other scientific reductions. In both cases, if the identity statements are true, they are necessarily true. Also, in both cases, the identity statements involved appear contingent.[3] The asymmetry arises when we attempt to explain away their apparent contingency. Whereas the apparent contingency of other scientific identity statements can be explained away adequately, this cannot be done for mental–physical identity statements.

Suppose we compare a standard scientific identity statement like (1) below to a mental–physical identity statement like (2) below:

1   Water = H_2O
2   Pain = the firing of C-fibres

Since neither statement is known *a priori*, they are both imaginably false. Yet, if they are true, they are necessarily true – they are not even possibly false. How do we reconcile the apparent contingency with the actual necessity? According to Kripke, this is easy to do in the case of (1). When we think we are imagining a situation in which water is not H_2O, in fact we are imagining a situation in which some substance which behaves superficially like water – but is not *water* – is not H_2O. On the other hand, a similar account will not work to explain the apparent contingency of (2), for to imagine a situation in which one is experiencing a state superficially like pain *just is* to imagine a situation in which one is experiencing pain. Conscious mental states are unlike external objects in that the standard distinction between how they appear and how they really are does not apply.

Many responses to Kripke's argument have appeared over the years. Early on it was pointed out that materialism does not entail the sort of type–type reductionism of the mental to the physical that is manifested in statements like (2). Rather, mental states are higher-order functional states, which can be realized, at least in principle, in a wide variety of physical systems. Hence, it is quite consistent with materialism that it is possible for one to experience pain and yet have no C-fibres whatever to fire.

However, functionalism itself has come under attack from Cartesian-style objections, particularly the inverted and absent qualia hypotheses.[4] The essence of these objections is that it seems perfectly imaginable that there could be creatures functionally alike who nevertheless differed in the qualitative character of their experiences; or, even worse, that there could be a creature functionally like ourselves who had no qualitative experiences at all. One line of response to either or both of these objections is to retreat to a physiological reductionist view with respect to qualia. That is, instead of identifying qualia with functional states, we identify them with the neurophysiological states that play the relevant functional roles in human beings, which would explain the possibility of both inverted and absent qualia.[5] Of course, this just brings us back to where we started.

I favour another strategy in response to Kripke's argument. Suppose he's right that we can coherently imagine feeling pain without having C-fibres firing. What's more, suppose he's right that this coherently imagined scenario cannot be explained away in the manner in which we explain away imagining that water is not H_2O. Still, what is imaginable is an *epistemological* matter, and therefore what imagining pain without C-fibres does is establish the *epistemological* possibility that pain is not identical with the firing of C-fibres. It takes another argument to get from the *epistemological* possibility that pain is not the firing of C-fibres to the metaphysical possibility, which is what you need to show that pain isn't *in fact* identical to the firing of C-fibres.[6]

Kripke, following Descartes, seems to rely on the idea that when you have a really 'clear and distinct' idea you have access to how things are, metaphysically speaking. If one believes in this sort of access to metaphysical facts, it then makes sense to use the Kripke test, by which I mean the test that determines whether the imagined scenario can be explained away appropriately, to determine whether one has hold of a genuine metaphysical possibility or not. So, in the water/H_2O case, Kripke shows that, as it were, when your idea is made properly clear and distinct, you see that what you are really entertaining is the thought that something that behaves like water is not H_2O. Notice that the situation satisfying this description is indeed metaphysically possible. Since the same move doesn't work for the pain/C-fibres case, we conclude that there is a metaphysically possible world in which pain isn't the firing of C-fibres.

But suppose we reject the Cartesian model of epistemic access to metaphysical reality altogether. One's ideas can be as clear and distinct as you like, and nevertheless not correspond to what is in fact possible. The world is structured in a certain way, and there is no guarantee that our ideas will correspond appropriately. If one follows this line of thought, then the distinction Kripke points out between the pain/C-fibres case and the water/H_2O case turns out to be irrelevant to the question of what is or is not metaphysically possible. Thus, for all we know, pain *just is* the firing of

C-fibres or, if functionalism is right, the realization of a certain functional state.

Early identity theorists, in their response to Cartesian conceivability arguments, protested that they only intended their theory to be empirical, and therefore it was not subject to objections from what was conceivable or not.[7] Kripke correctly pointed out the error of that sort of response. Empirical or not, if they were making identity claims, then a consequence of their theory is that it is not possible for some mental state not to be identical to its physical or functional correlate. But the basis of Kripke's objection lies in a strict distinction between metaphysical and epistemological possibility. Once we appreciate that distinction, the physicalist can return to her original ploy, i.e. to say that metaphysical consequences cannot be drawn from considerations of what is merely conceivable. Thus, without an argument to the effect that what is metaphysically possible is epistemologically accessible, the Cartesian argument fails.

Jackson's Argument

A similar problem – that is, a reliance on the Cartesian model of epistemic access to metaphysical reality or, in other words, using epistemological premises to support a metaphysical conclusion – seems to infect Frank Jackson's well-known 'knowledge argument' against materialism. Jackson takes the thesis of physicalism to be the claim that 'all (correct) information is physical information' (Jackson, 1982, p. 127). Of course, his use of the notion of information here is already fraught with ambiguity as between matters epistemological and metaphysical, a point to which I will return shortly. His argument against physicalism revolves around examples like the following:

> Mary is a brilliant scientist who is . . . forced to investigate the world from a black and white room *via* a black and white television monitor. She specializes in the neurophysiology of vision and acquires . . . all the physical information there is to obtain about what goes on when we see ripe tomatoes, or the sky, and use terms like 'red', 'blue', and so on
> . . . .
> What will happen when Mary is released from her black and white room or is given a color television monitor? Will she *learn* anything or not? It seems just obvious that she will learn something about the world and our visual experience of it. But then it is inescapable that her previous knowledge was incomplete. But she had *all* the physical information. *Ergo* there is more to have than that, and Physicalism is false. (Jackson, 1982, p. 130)

There have been a number of replies to Jackson in the literature, and the sort of reply I am most interested in is exemplified by Horgan (1984a). Horgan argues that Jackson is equivocating on the notion of 'physical information'. In one sense this might mean information expressed in terms used in the physical sciences. In another sense it might mean information about physical facts, processes etc. It is only in the second sense that any reasonable physicalist is committed to the claim that all information is physical information. Of course, in this sense, the thesis could be better put by just saying that all token events and processes are physical events and processes – by which one means something like, they have a true description in the terms of the physical sciences. (Actually, I think any interesting doctrine of physicalism is committed to more than this, though it's difficult to pin down exactly how much more. At any rate, it doesn't affect the present point.) But no plausible version of physicalism is committed to the claim that all information is physical information in the first sense: in the sense that it is expressed in (or translatable into) the terms of the physical sciences.

What Mary's case shows, argues Horgan, is that there is information Mary acquires after leaving the room that isn't physical information in the first sense, but not that it isn't physical information in the second sense. Certainly, she may think something like, 'Oh, so *this* is what red looks like.' Her experience of *learning* something new shows that she now knows something she didn't know before. She now knows what it's like to see red, which she didn't know before. But it doesn't follow that her new information isn't physical information in the second sense: that is, that it isn't information about a physical event or process. On the contrary, the case of Mary typifies the phenomenon of there being several distinguishable ways to gain epistemic access to the same fact. One cannot infer from a variety of modes of access to a variety of facts being accessed.

A similar emphasis on the distinction between the epistemology and the metaphysics of the matter underlies the following sort of reply to Jackson. What the case of Mary shows is that one can know which physical (or functional) description a mental state satisfies without knowing what it's like to occupy that state. But of course! After all, in order to know what it's like to occupy a state one has actually to occupy it! All Mary's newly acquired knowledge amounts to is her new experience, which is indeed new, since she didn't have those experiences until leaving the room. So it remains perfectly possible that what she learns is what it's like to occupy a certain physico-functional state. There is no threat to physicalism here.

Two Metaphysical Anti-Physicalist Replies

The common thread in the responses to both Kripke and Jackson is that their thought experiments demonstrate only an epistemological divide between different modes of access to what may, for all we know, be the very same phenomenon. On the one hand, we have certain physico-functional descriptions of certain states occupied by psychological subjects. On the other hand, we have whatever descriptions are derived from one's first-hand experience of these states. If these thought experiments show that physicalism leaves something out, it can't be in the sense that there are facts that physicalistic descriptions fail to pick out, since we have no argument to show that the two sorts of descriptions just cited do not refer to the same facts.

I will briefly consider two replies on behalf of the metaphysical anti-physicalist. First, perhaps Cartesian conceivability arguments can't demonstrate that qualia aren't physical states or processes, but they at least throw the burden of argument back onto the physicalist to show why we should think they are physical states or processes. The physicalist strategy presented above only opens a space for the physicalist hypothesis, but it doesn't give us any reason to believe it.

Fair enough. That's all it was intended to accomplish. The main burden of the physicalist argument is borne by considerations of causal interaction. If qualia aren't physical processes (or realized in physical processes), then it becomes very difficult to understand how they can play a causal role in both the production of behaviour and the fixation of perceptual belief. Jackson himself admits the cogency of this argument, and therefore bites the bullet by endorsing epiphenomenalism. Those who don't find that bullet particularly appetizing, must either show how the requisite mental–physical causal relations are possible on a dualist account or endorse physicalism.

The second reply on behalf of the metaphysical anti-physicalist goes like this.[8] Take some identity statement that is not epistemologically necessary, like (3) below:

3   The Morning Star = the Evening Star.

Though one might accept Kripke's claim that (3) is necessarily true if true at all, still one has to explain its apparent contingency. The way we do this is to say that what is contingent is that the very same heavenly body should appear where Venus does in the morning and also where it does in the evening. Notice that our explanation of the apparent contingency of (3) adverted to a real distinction between two of Venus's properties: namely, appearing at a certain heavenly location in the morning and appearing at a certain heavenly location in the evening. That is, we can explain the epistemological state of conceiving of the Morning Star and the Evening Star as two distinct objects, despite their identity, by reference to two distinct properties through which we have epistemic access to the one object.

Suppose one grants that the absent qualia argument does indeed establish at least the epistemological possibility that a qualitative state and a functional state are distinct, even though they are in fact identical. In order to explain how it is possible to conceive of this one state as two distinct states, we must assume that there are (at least) two 'modes of presentation' under which we apprehend this one state. Let us call them the 'first-person mode of presentation' and the 'third-person mode of presentation'. But now we seem committed to the claim that there are at least two distinct properties of the state corresponding to the two modes of access, akin to the two spatiotemporal properties of Venus by which we gain epistemic access to it in the morning and in the evening. If so, this shows that qualitative character, the property by which we identify a conscious state in the first-person mode of access, is distinct from the property of playing a certain functional role, the property by which we identify that conscious state in the third-person mode of access. So, we seem to be back to deriving a metaphysical conclusion from an epistemological premise, namely, that the property of having a certain qualitative character is distinct from the property of playing a certain functional role (or being in a certain neurophysiological state).[9]

The physicalist, however, can reply as follows. Certainly whenever we conceive of a single object in two distinct ways – sufficiently distinct ways, in fact, that we believe we are conceiving of two distinct objects – the object in question must possess (at least) two distinct properties that correspond to these different modes of presentation. But whether or not we now have a problem for physicalism depends on which two distinct properties we find ourselves committed to. This requires some elaboration.

What the physicalist needs to maintain is that having a certain qualitative character is a physical or functional property. This reduction of qualitative character is necessary in order to account for the causal role that qualia play in the fixation of perceptual belief and the production of behaviour. So, if the argument above could establish that having a certain qualitative character is a property distinct from a mental state's physical and functional properties, that would be the sort of metaphysical conclusion the anti-physicalist is after.

However, the argument above does not in fact establish the non-identity of having a certain qualitative character and any of a state's physical or functional properties. The argument begins with the premise that there must be two properties of the one state, providing two epistemic paths by which the subject conceives of that state, in order to account for the fact that it is epistemologically possible for someone to experience qualitative character without occupying the relevant physico-functional state. We can accept this premise and yet refuse to grant the conclusion – that having a certain qualitative character is irreducible to a state's physico-functional properties – by finding two other properties to provide the requisite epistemic paths. For instance, we can account for the conceivability of experiencing a certain quale without occupying the relevant physico-functional state by noting that the two relational properties, being thought of under the description 'what I am now consciously experiencing' and being thought of under the description 'the state that normally causes [such-and-such behavioural effects]', are not identical. However, there is no reason for the physicalist to claim that *these* two properties are identical, and therefore the argument above fails to mount a challenge to physicalism.

The Epistemological Reading

I have argued that on a metaphysical reading of 'leave something out', Cartesian conceivability arguments cannot establish that physicalist theories of mind leave something out. However, there is also an epistemological sense of 'leave something out', and it is in this sense that conceivability arguments, being epistemological in nature, can reveal a deep inadequacy in physicalist theories of mind.

For a physicalist theory to be successful, it is not only necessary that it provide a physical description for mental states and properties, but also that it provide an *explanation* of these states and properties. In particular, we want an explanation of why when we occupy certain physico-functional states we experience qualitative character of the sort we do. It's not enough for these purposes to explain the contribution of qualitative states to the production of behaviour, or the fixation of perceptual belief; this is a job that a physicalist theory can presumably accomplish. (At least there is no reason stemming from conceivability arguments to suppose that it cannot.) Rather, what is at issue is the ability to explain qualitative character itself; why it is like what it is like to see red or feel pain.

Conceivability arguments serve to demonstrate the inability of physicalist theories to provide just this sort of explanation of qualitative character. To see this, consider again the disanalogy Kripke draws between statements (1) and (2) above. Kripke bases his argument on the fact that both statements appear contingent, and then distinguishes between them by pointing out that the apparent contingency of (1), but not of (2), can be explained away. My strategy is quite different. I see the disanalogy between the water/H_2O case and the pain/C-fibres case in the fact that there is an apparent *necessity* that flows from the reduction of water to H_2O, a kind of necessity that is missing from the reduction of pain to the firing of C-fibres.

The necessity I have in mind is best exemplified by considering statement (1'):

1'   The substance that manifests [such-and-such macro properties of water] is H_2O.

On Kripke's view, (1') is in fact contingent, and it is the contingency of (1') that explains the apparent contingency of (1). So, on his view, (1') and (2) are on a par. Yet, it seems to me that there is an important difference between them. If we consider the apparent contingency that attaches to (2), we notice that it works in both directions: it is equally conceivable that there should exist a pain without the firing of C-fibres, and the firing of C-fibres without pain. However, the apparent contingency of (1') only works in one direction. While it is conceivable that something other than H_2O should manifest the superficial macro properties of water, as Kripke suggests, it is not conceivable, I contend, that H_2O should fail to manifest these properties (assuming, of course, that we keep the rest of chemistry constant).

This difference between the two cases reflects an important epistemological difference between the purported reductions of water to H_2O and pain to the firing of C-fibres: namely, that the chemical theory of water explains what needs to be explained, whereas a physicalist theory of qualia still 'leaves something out'. It is because the qualitative character itself is left *unexplained* by the physicalist or functionalist theory that it remains conceivable that a creature should occupy the relevant physical or functional state and yet not experience qualitative character.

The basic idea is that a reduction should explain what is reduced, and the way we tell whether this has been accomplished is to see whether the phenomenon to be reduced is epistemologically necessitated by the reducing phenomenon, i.e. whether we can see why, given the facts cited in the reduction, things must be the way they seem on the surface. I claim that we have this with the chemical theory of water but not with a physical or functional theory of qualia. The robustness of the absent and inverted qualia intuitions is testimony to this lack of explanatory import.

Let me make the contrast between the reduction of water to H_2O and a physico-functional reduction of qualia more vivid. What is explained by the theory that water is H_2O? Well, as an instance of something that's explained by the reduction of water to H_2O, let's take its boiling point at sea level. The story goes something like this. Molecules of H_2O move about at various speeds. Some fast-moving molecules that happen to be near the surface of the liquid have sufficient kinetic energy to escape the intermolecular attractive forces that keep the liquid intact. These molecules enter the atmosphere. That's evaporation. The precise value of the intermolecular attractive forces of H_2O molecules determines the vapour pressure of liquid masses of H_2O, the pressure exerted by molecules attempting to escape into saturated air. As the average kinetic energy of the molecules increases, so does the vapour pressure. When the vapour pressure reaches the point where it is equal to atmospheric pressure, large bubbles form within the liquid and burst forth at the liquid's surface. The water boils.

I claim that given a sufficiently rich elaboration of the story above, it is inconceivable that H_2O should not boil at 212°F at sea level (assuming, again, that we keep the rest of the chemical world constant). But now contrast this situation with a physical or functional reduction of some conscious sensory state. No matter how rich the information processing or the neurophysiological story gets, it still seems quite coherent to imagine that all that should be going on without there being anything it's like to undergo the states in question. Yet, if the physical or functional story really explained the qualitative character, it would not be so clearly imaginable that the qualia should be missing. For, we would say to ourselves something like the following:

> Suppose creature X satisfies functional (or physical) description F. I understand – from my functional (or physical) theory of consciousness – what it is about instantiating F that is responsible for its being a conscious experience. So how could X occupy a state with those very features and yet *not* be having a conscious experience?

One might object at this point that my position presumes something like the deductive-nomological account of explanation, an account that is certainly controversial.[10] In fact, I quite openly endorse the view that explanations involve showing how the explanandum follows from the explanans. I believe that the deductive-nomological model, in analysing explanation in terms of exhibiting a necessary connection between explanans and explanandum, is certainly on the right track.

I am not committed, however, to the view that all explanations take the form of the 'covering law' model described by Hempel (1965) in his classic account of explanation. For instance, Robert Cummins (1983) has argued that some explanations take the form of 'property theories', in which the instantiation of one sort of property is explained by reference to the instantiation of some other properties. So we might, for example, explain a certain psychological capacity by reference to the physico-functional mechanisms that underlie it. In such cases we are not explaining one event by citing initial conditions and subsuming it under a law, so it does not quite fit the traditional deductive-nomological model.

I have no problem with Cummins's objection to the covering law model. Yet even in his example – explaining how a psychological capacity is instantiated by reference to the underlying mechanisms – the element of necessity is there, even if there is no subsumption under laws. For it is clear that if citing the relevant underlying mechanisms really does explain how the psychological capacity in question is instantiated, then it would be inconceivable that some creature should possess these mechanisms and yet lack the capacity. If not, if we could conceive of a situation in which a creature possessed the relevant underlying mechanisms and yet didn't possess the capacity in question, then I would claim that we haven't adequately explained the presence of the capacity by reference to those mechanisms. For we are still left wondering what distinguishes the actual situation, in which the creature possesses the capacity, from those conceivable situations in which it (he/she) does not.

The Conceptual Basis of the Explanatory Gap

I have argued that there is an important difference between the identification of water with H_2O, on the one hand, and the identification of qualitative character with a physico-functional property on the other. In the former case the identification affords a deeper understanding of what water is by explaining its behaviour. Whereas, in the case of qualia, the subjective character of qualitative experience is left unexplained, and therefore we are left with an incomplete understanding of that experience. The basis of my argument for the existence of this explanatory gap was the conceivability of a creature's instantiating the physico-functional property in question while not undergoing an experience with the qualitative character in question, or any qualitative character at all.

In order fully to appreciate the nature and scope of the problem, however, it is necessary to explore in more detail the basis of the explanatory adequacy of theoretical reductions such as that of water to H_2O, as well as the difference between these cases and the case of qualitative character. I can only begin that project here, with the following admittedly sketchy account. We will see that an adequate account must confront deep problems in the theory of conceptual content, thus drawing a connection between the issue of intentionality and the issue of consciousness.

Explanation and Reduction

To begin with, it seems clear that theoretical reduction is justified principally on the basis of its explanatory power. For instance, what justifies the claim that water is H_2O anyway? Well, we might say that we find a preponderance of H_2O molecules in our lakes and oceans, but of course that can't be the whole story. First of all, given all the impurities in most samples of water, this may not be true. Second, if we found that everything in the world had a lot of H_2O in it – suppose H_2O were as ubiquitous as protons – we wouldn't identify *water* with H_2O. Rather, we justify the claim that water is H_2O by tracing the causal responsibility for, and the explicability of, the various superficial properties by which we identify water – its liquidity at room temperature, its freezing and boiling points etc. – to H_2O.

But suppose someone pressed further, asking why being causally responsible for this particular syndrome of superficial properties should be so crucial.[11] Well, we would say, *what else* could it take to count as water? But the source of this 'what else' is obscure. In fact, I think we have to recognize an *a priori* element in our justification. That is, what justifies us in basing the identification of water with H_2O on the causal responsibility of H_2O for the typical behaviour of water is the fact that our very concept of water is of a substance that plays such-and-such a causal role. To adopt Kripke's terminology, we might say that our pretheoretic concept of water is characterizable in terms of a 'reference-fixing' description that roughly carves out a causal role. When we find the structure that in this world occupies that role, then we have the referent of our concept.

But now how is it that we get an explanation of these superficial properties from the chemical theory? Remember, explanation is supposed to involve a deductive relation between explanans and explanandum. The problem is that chemical theory and folk theory don't have an identical vocabulary, so somewhere one is going to have to introduce bridge principles. For instance, suppose I want to explain why water boils, or freezes, at the temperatures it does. In order to get an explanation of these facts, we need a definition of 'boiling' and 'freezing' that brings these terms into the proprietary vocabularies of the theories appealed to in the explanation.

Well, the obvious way to obtain the requisite bridge principles is to provide theoretical reductions of these properties as well.[12] To take another example, we say that one of water's superficial properties is that it is colourless. But being colourless is not a chemical property, so before we can explain why water is colourless in terms of the molecular structure of water and the way that such structures interact with light waves, we need to reduce colourlessness to a property like having a particular spectral reflectance function. Of course, the justification for this reduction will, like the reduction of water to H_2O, have to be justified on grounds of explanatory enrichment as well. That is, there are certain central phenomena we associate with colour, by means of which we pick it out, such that explaining those phenomena is a principal criterion for our acceptance of a theoretical reduction of colour.

The picture of theoretical reduction and explanation that emerges is of roughly the following form. Our concepts of substances and properties like water and liquidity can be thought of as representations of nodes in a network of causal relations, each node itself capable of further reduction to yet another network, until we get down to the fundamental causal determinants of nature. We get bottom-up necessity, and thereby explanatory force, from the identification of the macroproperties with the microproperties because the network of causal relations constitutive of the micro level realizes the network of causal relations constitutive of the macro level. Any concept that can be analysed in this way will yield to explanatory reduction.

Notice that on this view explanatory reduction is, in a way, a two-stage process. Stage 1 involves the (relatively? quasi?) *a priori* process of working the concept of the property to be reduced 'into shape' for reduction by identifying the causal role for which we are seeking the underlying mechanisms. Stage 2 involves the empirical work of discovering just what those underlying mechanisms are.[13]

A Digression about Concepts

In order to clarify the sense in which it is inconceivable that something should be H_2O and not be water, I have had to slip into talking about concepts; even worse, talking about analysing the contents of concepts. This is unfortunate for my position, since the whole topic of concepts is filled with controversy, and I do not yet see how to construct a theory of conceptual content that will do the work, briefly outlined above, that needs to be done. Let me briefly indicate where the problems lie.

In the literature on concepts and contents, various distinctions have emerged which are useful to our concerns here. First of all, we can distinguish between a concept's[14] 'narrow content' and its 'broad content'.[15] A concept's broad content is its satisfaction conditions. This is the referential component of its content. The notion of narrow content is meant to capture that aspect of its content that is psychologically significant and independent of facts external to the subject. With regard to the famous Twin Earth example, narrow content is what my concept of water and my twin's concept of water have in common.

It is, of course, controversial whether or not it is narrow content that is relevant to the individuation of psychological states, or even whether there is such a thing as narrow content. However, I believe there is something psychologically significant that I and my twin have in common when we entertain the concept of water and, moreover, it is this aspect of our concept that seems relevant to the question of explanatory reduction. I will not defend this claim here, I will just presume it.

So, how do we characterize the narrow content of our concept of water? On one view, the 'functional role' view,[16] narrow content is determined by the cluster of beliefs involving the concept of water that determine the inferential relations among them. On this view, to analyse the concept of water is just to present those central beliefs. Our concept of water is the concept of a substance that . . . , where statements about the typical behaviour of water fill in the blank. On a functional role view, then, to say that our concept of water can be analysed as the concept of a causal niche is just to say that the beliefs which go into the blank all involve the causal role of water.

Thus a functional role view of narrow content seems quite amenable to my needs. However, there are real problems with this view. In particular, there is the problem of holism. That is, if you change any element of the description of causal relations definitive of the concept, you change the concept. Now, in the course of scientific investigation, we can expect to revise our beliefs about these causal connections as we learn more about the phenomenon under investigation. If such changes counted as changing the concept, then it wouldn't be *water* we were learning about when we discovered that water was H_2O. This would seem to be an intolerable consequence.

There are three ways one might deal with this problem. First, just bite the bullet and admit that our concepts are hopelessly holistic. Second, attempt to distinguish those elements of the functional role that are essential to the concept from those that are accidental, so that only changes in the essential elements constitute changes in concept. Third, find a different theory of narrow content.

One might argue that biting the bullet is not as bad as it seems on the grounds that we are only talking about *narrow* content. So long as we are atomistic about reference, we can still make sense of the claim that two theories contain conflicting claims *about water*, since they are talking *about* the very same thing. However, what we are looking for here is a notion of conceptual content suitable for grounding the explanatory relation, and this is clearly a matter of narrow content. Unless we can build stability into the notion, it is unclear how to make sense of the idea that the chemical theory of water explains why water behaves the way it does.

The second sort of strategy has a sad history, and I do not see how to make it work. For any element of the functional role you pick as essential, there always seems to be a story you can tell in which that element is missing and yet it seems intuitively right to claim that the subject still has the concept in question. As for a different theory of narrow content, the only one I know, that departs radically from the functional role theory, is Fodor's (1987) theory of narrow content as a function from contexts to broad contents. It is not at all clear to me how the notion of a conceptual content as the specification of a causal niche could be made to work on this view.

To sum up, there seems to be a need for a theory of conceptual content that both grounds explanatory reductions on the basis of some sort of functional/causal analysis of the requisite concepts, and yet does not entail holism. I do not have such a theory, and so must content myself with merely characterizing this desideratum on a theory yet to be developed.

Qualia Again

If we apply the same model of explanatory value to the theoretical reduction of qualia as we used for the reduction of water, then we need to look for a property that is being reduced and then a property, or set of properties, by which the to-be-reduced property is normally picked out. Of course, this raises a problem. When it comes to something like the qualitative character of a sensation of red, what other property could we point to to play the role of the reference-fixer? We seem to pick out this property by itself. The distinction between the property to be reduced and the properties by which we normally pick it out, or its superficial manifestation, seems to collapse. (Obviously this is connected to Kripke's point about the appearance/reality distinction not getting a hold in this case.)

There are, of course, other properties of qualia that we can expect a theoretical reduction to explain; namely, those properties associated with their causal role in mediating environmental stimuli and behaviour. It is precisely on the grounds that a particular physico-functional property can explain the 'behaviour' of qualitative states that we would endorse an identification between a particular quale and that property. Furthermore, if that were all there were to our concept of qualitative character – as the analytical functionalist maintains – then there would be no difference between the theoretical reduction of water and of qualia with respect to explanatory success. But the very fact that one can conceive of a state playing that role and yet not constituting a qualitative experience shows, or at least so I have argued, that causal role is not all there is to our concept of qualitative character.

What seems to be responsible for the explanatory gap, then, is the fact that our concepts of qualitative character do not represent, at least in terms of their psychological contents, causal roles. Reduction is explanatory when by reducing an object or property we reveal the mechanisms by which the causal role constitutive of that object or property is realized. Moreover, this seems to be the only way that a reduction could be explanatory. Thus, to the extent that there is an element in our concept of qualitative character that is not captured by features of its causal role, to that extent it will escape the explanatory net of a physicalistic reduction.

Conclusion

I will conclude by drawing out another consequence of this discussion of the explanatory gap. It is customary to attack the mind–body problem by a divide-and-conquer strategy. On the one hand, there is the problem of intentionality. How can mere matter support meaning; how can a bit of matter be *about* something? On the other hand, there is the problem of consciousness; or, to be more specific, the problem of qualitative character. How can there be something it is like to be a mere physical system? By separating the two questions, it is hoped that significant progress can be made on both.

Certainly in recent years we have come to have a deeper understanding of the issues surrounding the question of intentionality, and this progress has been largely the result of divorcing the question of intentionality from the question of consciousness.[17] However, if I am right, there may be more of a connection between the problem of qualitative character and the problem of intentionality than it is fashionable now to suppose. It is not that one needs to be capable of experiencing qualia in order to bear intentional states, as Searle would have it. Rather, since the problem of qualitative character turns out to be primarily epistemological, the source of which is to be found in the peculiar nature of our cognitive representations of qualitative character, a theory of intentional content ought to explain what makes these representations so uniquely resistant to incorporation into the explanatory net of physical science.[18] Thus the problem of qualia threatens to enlarge into the problem of the mind generally.

Acknowledgements

An earlier version of this chapter was delivered at the conference on Mind, Meaning, and Nature, at Wesleyan University, 31 March 1989. The Chapter was completed while I was holding a fellowship from the National Endowment for the Humanities. I would also like to thank Louise Antony, David Auerbach, Martin Davies, and Georges Rey for helpful discussions and critical comments on earlier drafts.

Notes

1 See Levine (1983) where I first argued for the existence of an explanatory gap.

2 Of course, it is a non-trivial question to decide which predicates count as 'physical' predicates, but for present purposes we need not attempt a precise explication of the notion.

3 As Kripke (1980, p. 154) puts it, there is a 'certain obvious element of contingency' about such theoretical identity statements.

4 For extensive discussion of the absent and inverted gualia hypotheses, see Block and Fodor (1972); Block (1978, 1980b); Horgan (1984b); Shoemaker (1984, chs 9, 14, and 15); Conee (1985); Levine (1989).

5 For various versions of this position, see Block (1978, 1980b), Horgan (1984b) and Shoemaker (1984).

6 Given that Kripke is largely responsible for drawing the philosophical world's attention to the distinction between epistemological possibility

and metaphysical possibility, it might seem odd to accuse him of confusing the two in this case. I diagnose his mistake as follows. Since he believes that any state which appears painful is thereby a pain, he infers that there is no appearance/reality distinction with respect to pain, and therefore epistemological and metaphysical possibility collapse in this case. But even if he's right that any state that appears to be a pain is a pain, he still has to justify the premise that it's possible for one to suffer even apparent pain without having one's C-fibres firing, and he can't do that, I contend, merely by noting that it *seems* possible.

7   See, for instance, Smart's (1959) reply to his 'Objection 2'.

8   This objection was suggested to me by a discussion in White (1986). The analogy to the Morning Star-Evening Star case is his.

9   As White explicitly acknowledges, a precursor of this objection can be found in Smart's (1959) famous 'Objection 3'.

10 For the classic presentation of the deductive-nomological model of explanation, see Hempel (1965, ch. 12).

11 Of course, it's possible to imagine situations in which we would accept a theory of water that nevertheless left many of its superficial properties unexplained. However, unless the theory explained at least some of these properties, it would be hard to say why we consider this a theory of *water*.

12 In some cases, for instance with properties such as liquidity and mass, it might be better to think of their theoretical articulations in physical and chemical theory more as a matter of incorporating and refining folk theoretic concepts than as a matter of reducing them. But this is not an idea I can pursue here.

13 To a certain extent my argument here is similar to Alan Sidelle's (1989) defence of conventionalism, though I don't believe our positions coincide completely.

14 Some readers might find my speaking of a *concept's* content, as opposed to a *term's* content confusing. I am interested in the nature of our thoughts, not with their expression in natural language. For present purposes, we can think of a concept as a term in whatever internal, mental language is employed in our cognitive processing.

15 For the source of this distinction, see Putnam (1975b). For further discussion of its significance for psychology, see Fodor (1987, ch. 3) and Burge (1986).

16 See Block (1986) for a defence of the functional role view.

17 For a dissenting opinion on the question of divorcing intentionality from consciousness, see Searle (1989).

18 See Rey (chapter 12) and Van Gulick (chapter 7) for suggestive approaches to just this problem.

7
Understanding the Phenomenal Mind: Are We All just Armadillos?

ROBERT VAN GULICK

Do phenomenal mental states pose a special obstacle to materialism or functionalism? Three main families of arguments in the recent philosophical literature may seem to show that they do: the 'knowledge argument', the 'explanatory gap argument' and the various versions of the 'inverted and absent qualia argument'. However, as I shall show, none of the three in fact presents an insurmountable barrier to materialistic functionalism.

Before turning to the arguments, let me issue one caveat about the use of the word 'phenomenal'. In much of the recent philosophical literature it has been used to refer exclusively to sensory qualia or so-called raw feels, such as the redness of which one is immediately aware when viewing a ripe tomato, or the taste of a fresh mango. Although I will myself spend some time discussing just such sensory qualia, I nonetheless believe it is a serious mistake to equate the phenomenal aspect of mind solely with such properties. We should not forget that the idea of the phenomenal structure of experience entered philosophical thought through Kant, who introduced it in the context of rejecting the sensational theory of experience associated with traditional empiricism. Phenomenal experience is not merely a succession of qualitatively distinguished sensory ideas, but rather the organized cognitive experience of a world of objects and of ourselves as subjects within that world.

Any adequate theory of the phenomenal aspect of mentality should take this richer Kantian concept into account. To focus exclusively on raw feels would be a mistake in at least two respects. First, it would provide too narrow a definition of what needs to be explained; and, second, I doubt that qualia and raw feels can themselves be understood in isolation from the roles they play within the richer Kantian structure of phenomenal experience.

The Knowledge Argument

Let us turn then to the 'knowledge argument'. Its basic underlying assumption is that there is some knowledge about experience that can be acquired *only* by undergoing the relevant experience oneself. In the paradigm case, one can come to know what the character of phenomenal red is only by having a red experience. No *physical* knowledge of what goes on in the brain when one has a red experience will suffice. It is for this reason that Thomas Nagel (1974) believes that no human can ever know what it is like to be a bat. Given our human inability to undergo experiences of the sort the bat has when sensing its surroundings by echo location, the relevant knowledge about bat-type experience is forever beyond us. The relevant facts about what it is like to be a bat are cognitively inaccessible to us in the sense that we are incapable of even understanding them.

To see how this is supposed to lead to an anti-materialist conclusion, let us consider the knowledge argument as presented by Frank Jackson (1982, 1986), certainly the most widely discussed anti-physicalist argument in the American philosophical world during the 1980s. Jackson offers the hypothetical case of Mary the super colour scientist who has spent her entire life within a strictly black and white (and grey) environment. Mary nonetheless (via television) has become the world's greatest expert on colour perception and *ex hypothesi* she is said to know *everything physical* there is to know about what goes on in a normal perceiver when he perceives something red. Yet, Jackson argues, Mary does not know *everything* there is to know about having a red experience, a fact that he believes is obvious if we consider what would happen if Mary were released from her achromatic isolation and shown a ripe tomato for the first time. Jackson's claim is that Mary would come to know something that she didn't know before. But since *ex hypothesi* she already knew *everything physical* there was to know about seeing red, the knowledge or information she gains must be non-physical phenomenal information.

A1   *The knowledge argument*

P1   Mary (before her release) knows *everything physical* there is to know about seeing red.

P2   Mary (before her release) does not know *everything* there is to know about seeing red because she learns something about it on her release.

Therefore:

C3   There are some truths about seeing red that escape the physicalist story.

C4   Physicalism is false and phenomenal properties cannot be explained as (or identified with) physical properties.

This argument has been regarded as a serious threat to physicalism. Indeed, so ardent a physicalist and formidable a philosopher as David

Lewis (1988) has held that if we admit that Mary really gains information when she first experiences red, then physicalism must be false. However, being regarded as a serious threat is not the same as being regarded as a sound argument, and a wide variety of critical objections have been raised against the knowledge argument. We can classify them into groups by use of a few diagnostic questions about Mary (figure 2). They are all variants of the question that riveted the Watergate investigations of Richard Nixon: *what* did she know and *when* did she know it?

> *Question 1*:   Does Mary in fact learn anything or gain any knowledge when she first experiences red?

Most philosophers have been willing to concede that Mary does learn something, but Paul Churchland (1985) has argued that the claim is open to reasonable doubt. Remember that *ex hypothesi* Mary knows *everything physical* there is to know about what goes on in peoples' brains when they experience red. Since our present knowledge of the brain is so far short of what Mary would know, it is difficult to say what she would or would not be able to understand or anticipate. It seems at least possible that when Mary sees her first tomato (rather than expressing surprise) she might remark, 'Ah yes, it is just as I expected it would be.' Thus there is the possibility of undercutting the argument right at the start by simply rejecting its second premise.

But let us follow most philosophers in conceding that Mary gains at least some knowledge and push on to question 2.

> *Question 2*:   What sort of knowledge does Mary gain? Is it strictly *know-how* or does it include new *knowledge* of *facts, propositions* or *information*?

One reply to the knowledge argument, originally proposed by Lawrence Nemirow (1980, 1990) and championed by David Lewis (1983, 1988), is to hold that the only knowledge Mary gains is *know-how*; she gains no new knowledge of facts or propositions. According to this so-called '*ability reply*', she gains only new practical abilities to recognize and imagine the relevant phenomenal properties. If the argument's second premise P2 is thus read as saying only that Mary gains new abilities (new know-how) then its conclusion C3 no longer follows. There need be no truths or information left out of the physicalist story nor out of Mary's prior knowledge. The ability reply thus promises a quick and clean solution to the knowledge argument. But its viability depends on the plausibility of the claim that Mary gains no new knowledge of facts or propositions and, like many other philosophers, I find that claim not very plausible. Part of what Mary gains is know-how, but that does not seem to be all she gains. There seems to be a fact about how phenomenal red appears that she apprehends only after her release. Let us

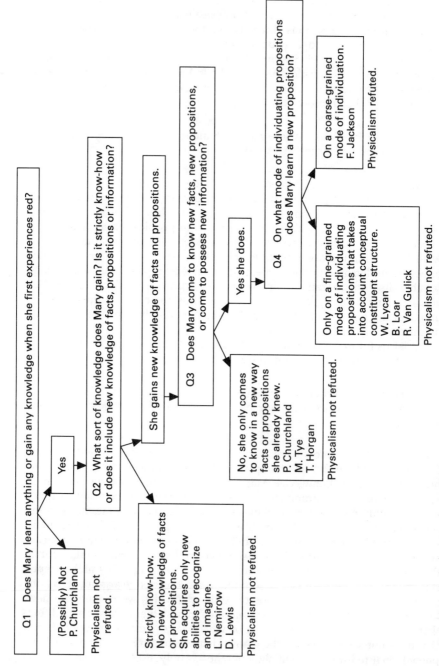

Q1 Does Mary learn anything or gain any knowledge when she first experiences red?

Yes

(Possibly) Not
P. Churchland

Physicalism not refuted.

Q2 What sort of knowledge does Mary gain? Is it strictly know-how or does it include new knowledge of facts, propositions or information?

She gains new knowledge of facts and propositions.

Strictly know-how.
No new knowledge of facts or propositions.
She acquires only new abilities to recognize and imagine.
L. Nemirow
D. Lewis

Physicalism not refuted.

Q3 Does Mary come to know new facts, new propositions, or come to possess new information?

Yes she does.

No, she only comes to know in a new way facts or propositions she already knew.
P. Churchland
M. Tye
T. Horgan

Physicalism not refuted.

Q4 On what mode of individuating propositions does Mary learn a new proposition?

Only on a fine-grained mode of individuating propositions that takes into account conceptual constituent structure.
W. Lycan
B. Loar
R. Van Gulick

Physicalism not refuted.

On a coarse-grained mode of individuation.
F. Jackson

Physicalism refuted.

thus turn to a *similar* sounding but *importantly different* question

> *Question 3*:   Does Mary come to know *new facts, new propositions* or come to possess *new information*?

The difference between questions 2 and 3 is a change in the scope of the word 'new'. In question 2 it qualifies knowledge (new *knowledge*), but in question 3 it qualifies the *object of knowledge* (knowledge of new propositions or new facts). The difference can be significant since there are philosophers who hold that Mary gains new knowledge only in the sense that she comes to know *in a new way* facts and propositions that she already knew. (Churchland, 1985; Tye, 1986) There are various options for unpacking the notion of knowing an old fact in a new way. Mary now knows directly by introspection what she knew before only indirectly by inference. Mary is now able to represent such facts to herself using a basic biological and probably pre-linguistic system of representation quite distinct from the linguistic representations she had to use to represent such facts in the past. Such differences in *mode of access* or *system of representation* might justify us in saying that Mary was now in a new epistemic state and might suffice to explain our inclination to accept the claim that Mary gains new knowledge. Read in this way, P2 again fails to support the argument's conclusion; there need be no facts or propositions that Mary failed to know before her release and thus none that was left out by the physicalist story.

David Lewis (1988) has recently criticized such approaches as inadequate to account for the intuitive appeal of the knowledge argument. He argues that they make the sense in which Mary gains new knowledge from experiencing red no different from that in which she gains new knowledge about her brain when she learns Russian or Urdu and thus acquires a new system of representation. He finds it uncharitable to suppose that the proponents of the knowledge argument have confused so innocuous a sense of 'new knowledge' with any that would support their conclusion. Lewis's criticism strikes me as a bit unfair in so far as the differences between Mary's linguistic and biological non-linguistic systems for representing experiential states seem far greater than those between English and Russian and thus better able to account for our sense that Mary has gained new knowledge, *even if* she has not come to know a new proposition.

There is, however, one last question we need to ask, one which can allow us to concede even the strong claim that Mary learns a new proposition without being forced to an anti-physicalist conclusion.

> *Question 4*:   On what mode of individuating propositions does Mary learn a new proposition? (That is, what counts here as a new proposition?)

Propositions, like beliefs, can be individuated in a variety of fine or coarse-grained ways. Coarse-grained propositions might be taken as functions from possible worlds to truth values. On such a mode of individuation, the proposition that $5 + 7 = 12$ is the same proposition as the proposition that 38 is the square root of 1,444, they are both true in every possible world. And the proposition that water freezes at 32°F is the same proposition as the proposition that H_2O freezes at 32°F. However, one can use a more fine-grained scheme of individuation which treats propositions as having *constituent structure* composed of such things as *concepts* that must also match up if two propositions are to be identified.

Thus, *even if* Mary has come to know a new proposition, that in itself need not undercut materialism *as long as* propositions are being individuated in a sufficiently fine-grained way (Loar, 1990; Lycan, 1990b). I find this reply to the knowledge argument quite attractive, especially as developed in a recent paper by Brian Loar (1990). Indeed, I have made a similar argument in the past in a reply to Thomas Nagel's argument regarding the individuation of facts (Van Gulick, 1985). Loar argues that Mary acquires a new concept, a concept that enters her cognitive repertoire in part on the basis of her newly acquired discriminative abilities. Thus, using this new concept, she is able to apprehend the truth of new propositions. Yet the addition of such a new proposition to her store of knowledge need not cause any concern to the physicalist in so far as the *property* to which her new concept refers can be just some property she referred to in the past by use of a *purely physical concept*, i.e. a concept constructed within the resources of the physical sciences.

What then is the bottom line on the knowledge argument? Despite its widespread intuitive appeal and the air of mystification it produces about the explanatory elusiveness of phenomenal qualities, I think it's pretty clearly a loser as an argument against the possibility of giving a materialist explanation of phenomenal mentality. There are any number of points at which one can cut off the argument. Though I favour a Loar-type solution, I think each of the other replies provides a plausible place at which to draw the line against the anti-materialist attack. Please choose your favourite.

The Explanatory Gap Argument

Let us turn then to our second argument, the 'explanatory gap argument'. It aims at a more modest, though still substantive, result. It does not try to show that materialism is false, but only that with respect to the phenomenal aspect of mind, materialism is in an important sense unintelligible or incapable of being adequately comprehended, at least by us humans. Thus Thomas Nagel writes, 'We have at present no conception of how a single event or thing could have both physical and phenomenological aspects or how if it did they might be related' (1986, p. 47). Joseph Levine puts the point like this:

> there is more to our concept of pain than its causal role, there is how it feels; and what is left unexplained by the discovery of C-fiber firing

(the standard philosophical candidate for the neural basis of pain, despite its total empirical implausibility) is why pain should feel the way it does! For there seems to be nothing about C-fiber firing that makes it naturally 'fit' the phenomenal properties of pain, any more than it would fit some other set of phenomenal properties. Unlike its functional role, the identification of the qualitative side of pain with C-fiber firing (or some property of C-fiber firing) leaves the connection between it and what we identify it with completely mysterious. One might say it makes the way pain feels into merely a brute fact. (Levine, 1983, p. 358)

Levine maintains that psychophysical statements asserting such brute fact identities are unintelligible, they leave an explanatory gap that we have no idea how to fill.

Colin McGinn (1989) has argued that making the psychophysical link intelligible may be beyond our conceptual capacities. We humans should not with hubris assume that every fact about the natural world is within our cognitive capacity to comprehend. Just as monkeys are unable to comprehend the concept of an electron, and armadillos (those ugly armoured ant-eating survivors of an earlier biological era that still inhabit Texas and points south) are not even up to the task of doing elementary arithmetic. So, too, we may all be armadillos when it comes to understanding the link between brain and phenomenal mentality. Or so McGinn suggests.

The explanatory gap argument is not an argument in the sense that the knowledge argument is. Its strength derives not from any path of deductive reasoning but rather from the intuitive appeal of its conclusion, which speaks to our bewilderment about how any physical story about the brain could ever explain phenomenal consciousness. Recall Wittgenstein holding his head in the *Philosophical Investigations* and saying, 'THIS is supposed to be produced by a process in the brain!' (1953, p. 412). None the less, I want to consider one deductive reconstruction of the argument because I think it will help us see what needs to be done to defuse the intuitive appeal of the position. At one point, Joe Levine makes an approving reference to John Locke's seventeenth-century claim that sensory qualia are *arbitrary*:

The point I am trying to make was captured by Locke in his discussion of the relation between primary and secondary qualities. He states that the simple ideas which we experience in response to impingements from the external world bear no intelligible relation to the corpuscular processes underlying impingement and response. Rather the two sets of phenomena are stuck together in an arbitrary manner. (Levine, 1983, p. 359)

Immediately following this passage Levine attempts to support his point by appeal to a standard philosophical case of hypothetical spectrum inversion with red and green qualia switching causal roles in an otherwise normal subject. What is important here is the suggestion that basic ideas, such as colour qualia, are *simples*. They have *no structure*, and since each one is what it is *sui generis*, it is hard to see how their connection to anything could be anything but arbitrary. We might reconstruct the explanatory gap argument as A2:

A2   *The explanatory gap argument*

P1   Qualia such as phenomenal hues are basic simples; they have no structure.

Thus:

C2   Any links between such qualia and the organizational structure of their neural substrates must be arbitrary.

Thus:

C3   The links between qualia and their neural bases are unintelligible and present us with an unfillable explanatory gap.

Formulating the argument in this way suggests a possible line of reply, one that has been made by Larry Hardin (1988). It is the first premise of A2 that we must reject. Hardin argues that the phenomenal hues that philosophers such as Locke and Levine regard as *sui generis simples* are not in fact such, but rather elements within a highly organized and structured colour space. Any attempt to invert them or interchange them *in undetectable ways* would have to preserve that structural organization. More importantly, the articulation of an organized structure among colour qualia provides the basis for establishing *explanatory connections* between them and their neural substrates. The method is the familiar one of explaining higher-order organization in terms of underlying structure. Consider a few brief examples.

1   Some colour qualia are phenomenally experienced as binary (e.g. orange and purple) and others as unary (e.g. red and blue) while other combinations are phenomenally impossible (e.g. a colour that is both red and green in the way purple is both red and blue). This phenomenal organization is explained by appeal to the existence of two underlying opponent colour channels, one subserving red/green discrimination and the other yellow/blue. Since red and green are mutually exclusive extreme outputs of the red/green channel, they cannot be combined; binaries are always combinations of the outputs of the two distinct channels.

2   Some hues are experienced as warm, positive and advancing (red and yellow) and others as cool, negative and receding (green and blue). They have an affective dimension. The warm hues are those that result from increased stimulation in their respective channel, while the cool hues result from decreased stimulation.

3   Phenomenal yellow tends to be 'captured' by phenomenal green in the sense that hues intermediate between yellow and green tend to be perceived as shades of green (rather than of yellow) far more quickly as one moves away from unary yellow than when one moves away from any

other unary hue. This phenomenon has as yet no neural explanation. (All examples are from Hardin, 1988, pp. 134–42)

The three examples allow us to make our two points. First, most (perhaps even all) of the hypothetical spectrum inversions considered by philosophers would disrupt the organization of the phenomenal colour space in detectable ways. One cannot preserve structure while interchanging red with orange or with any other binary hue, nor by interchanging red with the cool hues of green or blue, nor red with yellow given the phenomenon of capture. Second, and of more immediate relevance to the explanatory gap argument, the phenomenal colour space is revealed to have a *complex organizational structure* that allows us to establish *explanatory* rather than simply brute fact connections between it and underlying neural processes.

Our critic may still reply that any explanations we produce will still leave something essentially qualitative unexplained. No matter how much structural organization we can find in the phenomenal realm and explain neurophysiologically, she will insist that the distinct redness of phenomenal red will not have been captured or explained by our theory. For though it may be impossible to map the hues of *our* colour space in a way that rearranges them, while making the change behaviourally undetectable by preserving all their organizational relations, it seems there could be other non-human creatures who had *alien qualia* quite unlike our own, but whose interrelations exactly mirrored those among our phenomenal hues (Shoemaker, 1981a). Red*, their correlate of red, would bear to green* and orange* the same relations that red bears to our phenomenal greens and oranges; yet red* would not be the same as red. If so, then something essentially qualitative would seem to have escaped our explanation (Shoemaker, 1975, 1981b). We might have explained why a given brain process is identical with experiencing red rather than with experiencing orange but not why it is a case of experiencing red rather than red*.

This countercharge needs to be taken seriously, but I think we have altered the nature of the debate. The more one can articulate structure within the phenomenal realm, the greater the chances for physical explanation; without structure we have no place to attach our explanatory 'hooks'. There is indeed a residue that continues to escape explanation, but the more we can explain relationally about the phenomenal realm, the more the leftover residue shrinks towards zero. Though I admit that we are as yet a long way from that.

The Absent Qualia Argument

These considerations bring us to our third family of arguments, those that appeal to the alleged possibility of absent qualia. Such arguments are typically directed against the functionalist thesis that mental states can be type-individuated on the basis of the causal functional relations they bear to each other and to the inputs and outputs of the relevant system. The standard and by now all too familiar absent qualia claim is that given *any* functionally specified organizational structure, it is always possible (at least in principle) to construct realizations of that structure which we have every reason to believe possess *no qualia*: realizations such as Ned Block's nation of China example in which the functional role of each state is filled by a distinct member of the population of China (Block, 1978). It is claimed that the bizarre construction would realize the relevant functional organization, though it is absurd to believe that the overall construction, as opposed to its individual personal parts, actually has any qualia or phenomenal properties.

This line of argument has been much discussed and criticized, at times in subtle and successful ways (e.g. by Sidney Shoemaker 1975, 1981a). But I wish to offer a not very subtle criticism: the argument is *question begging*. Consider how it might look on reconstruction.

A3   *The absent qualia argument*

P1   Any functional model of mental organization will be capable of being realized by systems lacking qualia (or phenomenal properties): the absent qualia claim.

P2   A model M of some feature of the world F explains F (or what F is) only if nothing could be a realization of M without being F.
Therefore:
C3   Functionalism cannot explain (what) phenomenal mentality (is).

The reasoning is valid, but its premises are problematic. One might object to the claim of its second premise that nothing short of a logically or metaphysically sufficient condition counts as an adequate explanation. But the real problem is premise 1. How can the anti-functionalist know *a priori* that *any future* functionalist theory will allow for absent qualia realization? The absent qualia claim is made plausible only by construing functionalism as restricted to a highly abstract sort of *computationalism*, which requires of its realizations only that they mirror in the temporal or causal order of their states the sequence relations specified in the functional model. There is a widespread but mistaken belief that in constructing his model the functionalist cannot appeal to any relations among states other than that of *simple causation* (by which I mean causing, inhibiting or contributing to the joint causation of). So construed, it would seem that a realization by the population of China would always be possible, all we need to do is make sure that each person goes 'on' and 'off' in a way that mirrors the sequence of states in the model. But the functionalist need not and should not accept any such restriction on his theorizing; his job is to characterize the relations that hold among mental states, processes and properties without regard for the austere constraints of purely computational relations or relations of simple causation.

Once such constraints are rejected, the absent qualia claim no longer seems obvious. What we need to determine is whether there are functional relations into which phenomenal states can enter but non-phenomenal states cannot. The burden of proof may lie with the functionalist to show that there are such relations by coming forward with a specific theory about the roles played by phenomenal states, but his attempts cannot be rendered dead before arrival by *a priori* appeals to inevitable absent qualia realizations.

The Functional Role of Phenomenal States: A First Attempt

One way to investigate this question is to consider the psychological roles played by phenomenal states in humans (Van Gulick, 1989). Which of our human psychological abilities, if any, are dependent on our having conscious phenomenal experience? This way of asking the question has its limits. Even if it should be that certain psychological processes cannot operate *in humans* in the absence of experience, it would not follow that phenomenal experience is a necessary condition *in general* for those psychological processes or abilities. The 'necessity' may be only a contingent fact about how those processes are realized in us and nothing more.

That said, let us consider a few abilities that seem *de facto* to require conscious phenomenal experience in humans. Tony Marcel (1988) mentions at least four such abilities. Two concern respects in which human subjects suffer a total (or nearly total) loss of function as the result of losing some aspect of their capacity for phenomenal experience:

1 Loss of the ability to initiate actions with respect to parts of the world lost from conscious experience though still in some sense perceived (as in cases of blindsight with respect to objects located within the blind field of a hemianopic patient).
2 Loss of the ability to form an integrated self-concept in amnesic patients as the result of losing the capacity for episodic memory (i.e. memory of past conscious experiences as such).

Two others concern less pathological limitations:

3 The inability to learn new non-habitual tasks without conscious awareness of task instructions.
4 The inability to form plans of action without conscious thought.

One might ask, 'What, if anything, do these various cases of dependency on phenomenal experience have in common?' A sceptical or deflationary answer would be that they share nothing in common, or nothing more than the brute fact that the particular human representation systems that underlie or subserve those abilities just happen *accidentally* to involve representations with phenomenal content. I think we should resist such a deflationary strategy; at least we should not embrace it until we have made a thorough effort to find some psychologically interesting explanation of *why* the relevant abilities seem to require conscious phenomenal experience in humans.

In his discussion, Marcel at least implicitly suggests that all four abilities require not merely consciousness but some form of *self-consciousness* since the mental states that figure in the relevant psychological processes are all *reflexive* and *meta-cognitive in content*. That is, all the relevant processes require awareness or knowledge about some aspect of one's own mental or psychological organization or activity.

> *Ability 4:*   Both planning and control of plan execution require knowledge of one's goals and their relative priority, as well as knowledge of one's mental capacities and resources and the ability to monitor the ongoing operation of those resources in the course of execution. All of which, as Philip Johnson-Laird (1983, 1988) has argued, involves having a model of oneself.
>
> *Ability 2:*   The lack of personal integration noted in amnesic patients could well result from the inability to construct and update such a self-model.
>
> *Ability 3:*   The inability to acquire new non-habitual task behaviors might be a result of the failure of the same systems involved in action planning.
>
> *Ability 1:*   And even the fact that hemianopic patients do not initiate voluntary actions towards objects in the blind field might be explained on this basis as a deficit in the representation of the *world-in-relation-to-self* that is employed by the action planning system.

While I think that there may be something interestingly right about this suggestion, I find it less than satisfying as an answer to the question of *why* the relevant abilities in humans all seem to require conscious phenomenal experience. The proposed explanation is that they all involve reflexive meta-cognition (or meta-psychological knowledge.) But left unanswered is the question of why such meta-cognition should require phenomenal awareness. Meta-cognitive awareness is a straightforwardly functional process, and one should be able to build such self-directed control and its associated iterative mental states into an organized system without having to give it anything like phenomenal awareness.

One could fall back on a *unitary version* of the *brute fact explanation* by arguing that all the relevant abilities involve higher order meta-cognition and its associated model of the self, and then claiming that it is *just a brute fact* that the self-model in humans involves phenomenal awareness. The final explanation would still terminate in a brute fact, but it would replace four independent brute fact terminations with one making it less *ad hoc*.

I am still inclined to hope for more. The account in terms of functionally defined self-monitoring and self-control offers both too little and too much to explain the role of phenomenal consciousness. Too little because it seems one could get the higher-order cognition without phenomenal experience; too much because it is doubtful that such sophisticated meta-cognitive processes are present in all the non-human animals which we believe to have some form of phenomenal consciousness (see Nelkin, chapter 11).

The Functional Role of Phenomenal States: A Second and More Speculative Attempt

We may gain some insight if we take a somewhat different perspective on the proposal to analyse self-consciousness in terms of reflexive meta-cognition. Most accounts of meta-cognition postulate a set of explicit higher-order processes that are distinct from the lower-level cognitive processes they monitor and control. However, as I have argued elsewhere (Van Gulick, 1988a, b), meta-cognitive understanding can also be implicitly embodied in the very processes that operate on lower-level representations. In particular, a system can be said to possess information about (or understand) the intentional content of its own internal representations, in so far as its internal operations with respect to those representations are specifically adapted to their content.

In brief, this involves two steps. First, one gives a basically functionalist account of what it is to possess information (or understand) some fact in terms of having a capacity specifically to modify one's behaviour in a way which adapts it to that fact, and then one applies that general account of understanding to the special case of understanding facts about the intentional content of one's own internal system of representation (Van Gulick, 1988a, b).

If we expand our account of meta-cognition to cover such cases, we can introduce a notion which may help explain what is special about phenomenal representations. The notion is that of *semantic transparency* and concerns the extent to which a system can be said to understand the content of the internal symbols or representations on which it operates. The basic idea is that the greater the extent to which the system's use of a representation reflects an understanding of its content, the more the representation can be said to be semantically transparent to the system. The relevant behaviour by the system will consist in part of behaviours connecting the symbols with the outside world through input and output relations, but will also include behaviours relating symbols to each other in ways sensitive to their content. The important point is that the understanding is embedded in the organization of the system, that is, in how it is organized to relate symbols to its input, output and each other.

Phenomenal representations, of the sort associated with normal conscious experience, involve a very high degree of semantic transparency. Indeed, they are so transparent that we typically 'look' right through them. Our experience is the experience of a world of familiar objects – of desks, chairs, coffee cups and beech trees. Moreover, this transparency is to some extent an *immediately experienced feature of our conscious life*. On the whole, when we have a conscious experience, we know what we are conscious of (though there are exceptions such as infants, persons newly sighted after a lifetime of congenital blindness or patients suffering from visual agnosia). The phenomenal representations that are constructed or activated in conscious experience are normally transparent to us. We know what they represent in virtue of our capacity instantaneously and effortlessly to connect those representations with other semantically related representations.

My understanding that part of my visual field represents the presence of a telephone is in part a matter of my ability rapidly to connect that representation with a host of others concerning the structure, function and use of a telephone. It is the awareness of these transitions among representations in the seemingly continuous flow of experience that provides the phenomenal or subjective experience of understanding, our conscious feeling that we know what we are thinking about.

A bit of care is needed here. I am not claiming that a system's being able to make such automatic and rapid transitions is in itself sufficient to guarantee that it has a subjective phenomenal life and that there is *something that it is like to be* that system. I am *assuming* that human beings have a subjective life and making the more modest claim that our *subjective experience of understanding* is to be accounted for in terms of the connections and transitions that our underlying organization allows us to make within our experience.

We are now in a position to pose two last *why* questions, which are perhaps the most interesting and the most difficult, though I can at present supply only some sketchy and speculative suggestions in answer. The questions are these:

1   Why do phenomenal representations (normally) involve a high degree of semantic transparency?
2   Why do we humans use representations with phenomenal properties to construct our self-model?

I suggest we take quite seriously the Kantian notion that our conscious phenomenal experience is the experience of a world – a world of objects. Conscious experience involves more than just being in states that represent or refer to objects and their properties. In some sense, which is hard to articulate, it involves there *being* a world of objects *inherent* in the representation. Or perhaps one should say it inherently involves an interdependent structure of conscious subject and world of objects set over against one another since, as Kant taught us, the notions of subject and object are interdependent correlatives within the structure of experience. One might say that conscious phenomenal experience involves the construction of a model of the world that in some sense itself *is a world*, but is so only from the subjective perspective of the self, which in turn exists only as a feature of the organization of experience. The problem is to give some account of the objectivity and concreteness of phenomenal objects, i.e. to give some account of the fact that we *experience* them as concrete, independent and objective. How might trying to solve this problem help with our two questions?

With respect to our first question, the semantic transparency of phenomenal representation might be explained as a consequence of the fact that such representations are *of a world* in the strong sense we have been considering. Part of what makes a world a world in that sense is the density of relations and connections among the objects which are simultaneously the *constituents* of which that world is composed and also *constituted as* the objects that they are by their relations within that world. Put another way, the (experienced) objectivity of phenomenal objects consists in part of the enormous diversity of the perspectives from which they are accessible from within the representation. Any phenomenal object is delimited and defined within the representation in large part through the relations that it bears to other objects, which are in turn defined in part by the relations that they bear to it. It is in part the density of these interdefining relations that gives phenomenal objects their 'thickness', their objectivity. The fact that the phenomenal representation of objects involves such dense and interdependent relations might help to account for its high degree of semantic transparency; any phenomenal representation of an object would of necessity also be a representation of its myriad relations within its world.

Solving our problem and explaining the sense in which conscious phenomenal representations are objective and *of a world* may also help to explain the importance and role of qualia such as colours. As we learned long ago from *The Critique of Pure Reason* (1781), conscious experience requires the presence of an *intuition* in the Kantian sense of the term, that is, a *continuous sensuous manifold*, whether it be the spatial manifold of perception or the merely temporal manifold of inner sense. Without such a particular manifold there is no way in which objects can be present as particular things. Thus the 'thing-liness' of phenomenal experience, the sense in which objects are present to us in experience as real and concrete, requires that there be such an intuition or sensuous manifold within the structure of experience. Indeed, in clinical cases in which there is a loss of part of the sensuous manifold, reports of patients indicate (directly, or indirectly by omission) that it is subjectively as if a portion of *the world itself* has been lost. Consider this autobiographical comment by Oliver Sacks:

> I didn't care to tell Nurse Sulu that she was bisected and half of her was missing. And then suddenly with a most enormous and wonderful relief, I realized I was having one of my migraines. I had completely lost my visual field to the left, and with this as would sometimes happen, the sense that there was (or ever had been, or could be) any world on the left. (Sacks, 1984, p. 97)

Qualia might then be understood as properties by which regions of such manifolds are differentiated and by which objects as particulars are delimited and located within them.

We can thus begin to see a route by which qualia might be connected with semantic transparency via the fact that phenomenal representations are *of a world* in the strong sense we have been discussing. As we noted just above, part of what makes a representation *of a world* in the relevant sense is the density of relations among objects that it specifies. In particular, such a representation should specify in very great detail the spatiotemporal relations holding among arbitrary pairs of objects within the represented world, i.e. it should carry a rich and easily accessed store of information about how any represented object is spatiotemporally related to other objects in the represented world, with perhaps some falling off of detail or precision as we move from an object's immediate neighbours to objects at a greater distance.

Sensuous manifolds provide a medium well suited for the representation of such rich and easily accessed spatiotemporal information. They have a continuous structure isomorphic to the spatiotemporal domains they are used to represent. Thus, by using qualia to delimit regions of such manifolds as representing objects, it is possible to implicitly represent a large stock of information about the relative spatiotemporal relations of those objects.

Indeed, following a suggestion by the ethologist Konrad Lorenz (1973), it is plausible to suppose that the phenomenal representation of space appeared evolutionarily with the transition from organisms whose system of spatial representation was linked to the guidance of specific behaviour patterns (such as taxes) to those with a general representation of space capable of being used to guide a wide range of behaviours in flexible and open-ended ways. Both ants and birds acquire and make use of spatial information. In so far as the ability of ants to acquire and make use of spatial information is restricted to a fairly narrow range of stimulus/response mechanisms, there is little reason to think that they have a general and central representation of space; in contrast, it is hard to imagine how birds could do without one.

What, then, have we shown with respect to our first question? I hope to have shown that in so far as the phenomenal mode of representation is *of a world* in the strong sense and involves a sensuous manifold of representation, it is particularly well suited for the construction of representations with a high degree of semantic transparency. I have not argued that phenomenal representation is either necessary or sufficient for a high degree of semantic transparency. It may be possible for active representational systems to achieve a high degree of semantic transparency using non-phenomenal representations; though phenomenal representations provide *one* design solution to the problem of achieving high semantic transparency, they need not be the *only* solution. And, conversely, it seems possible for phenomenal representations to lack a high degree of semantic transparency as seems to be the case with the visual experiences of those with visual agnosia. Such agnosia appears to result from damage to the association cortex which prevents the establishment of a normal rich network of connections to representations in other modalities; the fact that the agnosic cannot connect the representations in his visual system with those in other systems leaves him in a state of not understanding his visual experiences. For him they become semantically opaque.

Consider in this regard the hypothesis offered by Baars (1988) that one of the functions of consciousness is to 'broadcast' information throughout the nervous system and make that information widely available. Here again there are possibilities for explaining in a more than brute fact way *why* phenomenal representations play the functional roles they do. As we noted above, part of the objectivity of phenomenal representation consists in the density and diversity of ways in which objects are represented. Objects within the phenomenal model are represented from many perspectives and in many different modalities which none the less harmonize and 'agree'. Conscious phenomenal awareness thus likely involves large-scale higher-order patterns of brain activity spanning many different sensory and representational modalities providing a very rich set of active associative links. Thus it becomes quite reasonable to think of conscious awareness as identical with (or at least part of) the process by which information is broadcast. Because of their highly integrated and multimodal content, conscious phenomenal representations require rich associative networks of activation as their basis. Thus, any type of brain activity able to serve as the neural substrate for phenomenal representations would seem of necessity also able to fulfil the function of 'broadcasting information'. Some recent hypotheses about the neurological substrate of consciousness (Flohr, 1991) seem to support just such a link.

With respect to our second question let me make three very brief suggestions.

1 Phenomenal representation probably predates the advent of meta-cognitive self-models in evolutionary development. Since it has the high degree of semantic transparency that is desirable in constructing a self-model, it may have been 'recruited' for that application.
2 We should not forget the Kantian point that the conscious self is implicitly represented in the structure of conscious experience. Thus constructing a model of the self of the sort used in meta-cognitive process is in part a matter of making *explicit* what is at least partly *implicit* in the phenomenal mode of representation.
3 Third is the fact that having a model of the self of the sort that is lost in amnesics seems to require the presence of an intuition in the Kantian sense, that is a sensuous manifold, within which the self can be constructed or located as a self. It need not be a spatial intuition; for Kant it was merely temporal. But it seems that some sort of intuition is required, some structure with particularity, within which the isolated units of experience can be unified into the experiences of a single self. Again, the phenomenal mode of representation satisfies the design requirement for the self-model. The intuition of continuous time associated with phenomenal experience provides the required intuition within which to carry out the construction of a unified self. For amnesics it is not merely the self that is truncated and compressed into the present moment; it is time itself that shrinks.

Conclusion

None of the three families of arguments we have considered succeeds in giving a sound *a priori* reason for concluding that the phenomenal aspect of mind cannot be adequately explained in physical or functional terms. First, the *knowledge argument* turns out to be vulnerable in a wide variety of ways. Second, as long as phenomenal properties are not thought of as basic simples, filling the *explanatory gap* between the phenomenal and the physical (or functional) remains an option by continuing the step-by-step process of articulating structure within the phenomenal realm and mapping it onto the structure of underlying non-phenomenal processes. And, third, only when we have such theories will we be in a position to say without begging the question whether or not non-phenomenal representations (*absent qualia*) can play the same functional roles as phenomenal representations. The ultimate outcome of such theorizing remains an empirical question not open to *a priori* answer. As we saw above, there are reasonable prospects for articulating the structure of the phenomenal colour space, for linking semantic transparency with phenomenal objectivity and for showing why phenomenal representations serve an information-broadcasting role within the nervous system. Thus, there is at least some reason to think that future theorizing will fill the gaps and banish absent qualia.

Acknowledgements

An earlier version of this chapter was presented at the conference on The Phenomenal Mind: How is it Possible? Why is it Necessary? held at the Center for Interdisciplinary Studies (ZiF), Bielefeld University, Bielefeld, Germany, May 1990. The final two sections of the chapter are revised versions of material originally published in Van Gulick (1989); I am grateful to Martin Davies who encouraged me to include them and offered many acute criticisms from which I have benefited in making the revisions.

8
Consciousness and Cosmology: Hyperdualism Ventilated

COLIN MCGINN

Prologue

Something interesting happened to me recently (usually, not much does). Would you like to hear about it? I was dozing in my bed, feverish with 'flu, my mind dwelling obsessively on the topic of consciousness and the brain – how the former springs from the latter and allied conundrums – when I sensed an alien presence in the room, as if a bat had flown in through the window. My consciousness was like something confronted by a consciousness like something other than it.[1] Opening my eyes, I beheld, not a bat, but a numinous volume of light, immaterial-seeming, about the size of a small man. It floated over to me, hovered for a moment, then enveloped me completely. Being the nervous type, I got a little worried at this point: but nothing untoward happened to me – indeed, it felt as if I had been mentally augmented in some way. I was then levitated from my bed, carried out of the window, and whisked (or was it beamed?) to a tremendously remote galaxy in an obscure corner of the cosmos. Yes, really.

It was a matter of seconds before I was face to face with my kidnappers, who looked almost exactly like ordinary human beings, except for a greater serenity about the countenance – and a larger forehead, of course. One of them, evidently in a position of authority, explained to me why I had been brought there: it was in order to talk philosophy for a while. (Why me?, I wondered.) More specifically, he wanted me to explain, and if possible justify, the worldview accepted by us late twentieth-century earthlings; and he desired to put to me the merits of the worldview routinely believed in his sector of the universe. He knew a little about our cosmological theories, he said, but his intelligence reports had made our views sound so incredible that he wished to verify whether we were really serious in holding them and if necessary to enlighten us as to the correct cosmological position. Would I oblige him by entering into a full and frank dialogue, after which I would be safely returned to earth? He understood that I was fairly representative of the standard earthly position.[2] I replied that I would be glad to dispute with him (my 'flu seemed to have flown), confident that *he* would emerge the enlightened one. What follows is a record of our conversation, still fresh in my mind, so that you, loyal fellow human, can judge for yourself which of us was philosophically worsted. Remember, it's your cosmology that's on the line, too. I am CM, my alien interrogator is MC (to be read as 'My Captor').[3]

Cosmology

MC: Let's begin with a brief exposition of your theory as to the nature and origins of the universe, specifically as it relates to the existence of consciousness – about the reality of which I gather there is no disagreement between us.

CM: Certainly not: I take consciousness to be as incontrovertibly real as anything else in the universe – I am no eliminativist. So I'm glad we concur on one thing. I'd have been disappointed if you simply sidestepped the mind–body problem by denying the existence of what creates it.

MC: I can assure you now that you will not be disappointed on *that* score. Quite the contrary, I suspect. We are not shy when it comes to matters of ontology.

CM: Well, our story goes roughly as follows. Long ago an event known as the Big Bang brought the material universe into existence – particles, gravity, electrical energy, space maybe. Large lumps of matter quickly formed and began moving around each other, obedient to the laws of physics. There was, of course, no sentience in the world at this early time: nothing was aware of anything else, nothing mental glimmered. After a while, in certain privileged pockets of the material world, the evolution of life began: matter started to replicate itself, sometimes changing a bit in the replication process, some chunks of it better at reproducing themselves than others, with competition for the materials needed for replication, until some quite fancy lumps of matter were dotted around the place. Still nothing of a mental nature, though. After another lapse of time, a few of the fancier lumps started to acquire mental states, primitive at first but soon pretty impressive because this made the lumps more adept at producing viable copies of themselves. Thus, just as life emerged from matter by natural selection – some say by way of crystals[4] – so consciousness duly emerged from life; and therefore, by the transitivity of the emergence relation, we have it that consciousness emerged from matter. Matter became organized in certain ways, you see, under the impact of natural selection, and as a result consciousness, well, came out of it – if you see what I mean. Matter generated consciousness, brought it into being. This part of the story, I freely admit, is still something of a mystery to us: we call it the mind–body problem – *how* matter found the resources to produce states of consciousness. We don't really yet understand, scientifically or philosophically, by what means or mechanism bunches of particles contrived to generate something so apparently different from themselves: but we don't seriously doubt that they did – and the optimists among us expect that one day we shall understand what the process consists in.[5] Ontologically, then, consciousness is a derived or secondary existent, arriving quite late in cosmic history. Clear?

MC: Your theory is indeed much as it was reported to me. Remarkable! You are certainly audacious thinkers, I'll grant you that: paradox inhibits you not a bit. I hope you will excuse my chuckle when you got to that brilliant part about consciousness being conjured from collections of particles. I had to laugh. Let me now offer you a summary of the way we see things here, so that we can then make a fair comparison. Please try to keep an open mind, because there is a radical divergence in our basic cosmologies, and I know that people are very wedded to their cosmologies – it's almost a religion with some folks! To aid your comprehension, I shall, in deference to certain natural frailties, first describe our system in its theistic version; then we can drop God from the picture to derive the hygenic scientific version. Ready?

In the beginning, God couldn't make up his mind which kind of universe he wanted to create – a material universe or a spiritual one. He was undecided, that is, between creating an insentient world of moving matter in space, on the one hand, and an immaterial world of pure consciousness, on the other. Each seemed to have its attractions. Since he didn't really have to decide, being omnipotent, he opted to create both, so that he could enjoy surveying his heterogeneous handiwork on alternating days, down through all eternity. He put this plan into effect, keeping his two universes entirely separate and insulated from each other; they were set up as closed systems – no causal commerce between them. In the material universe, U1, matter went its mindless way, while in the immaterial universe, U2, conscious events and processes displayed their characteristic subjectivity and intentionality.[6]

After a few billion years of this segregated parallelism, God became a little bored with his pair of artefacts and hungered for cosmic novelty. Should he, he wondered, scrap the two independent worlds he had created and generate a completely new order, or should he tinker with what he already had and transform it into something fresh and interesting? Reluctant to admit that his original works could cease to inspire interest – for he was a proud God – he hit upon a bold plan, with which he was much pleased. He would think of a way to connect U1 and U2! It sounded impossible, he knew, what with U1 and U2 being so different from each other in the kinds of item they contained and in the laws and principles that obtained in them; but he was God, after all, and the impossible had never deterred him in the past (well, there was that unfortunate business with the round squares . . .). He would take it as a challenge to his creative ingenuity. Anyway, he could always resort to his old standby if the project proved too tricky – divine fiat. But it would be aesthetically preferable to forge the link by coaxing his existing creations into making the connection themselves, so that no far-reaching nomological revisions would be required. This was going to need careful thought, so he went back to his original cosmic blueprints and tried to see whether the solution to the 'connection problem' somehow lay hidden in his initial conceptions. *Only connect*, he exhorted himself.

Imagine his delight (and self-congratulation) when he discovered that by jiggling around with his now-dusty designs for U1 and U2 he could forge a causal link between them. He must have known all along, omniscience being what it is, that he would some day want to marry his separate spheres of reality. What he had to do was form a few pounds of ordinary matter into a particular configuration, admittedly not easily predicted from the manner of matter's original spontaneous clumping, and the result would act like a kind of inter-universe radio receiver tuned in to the conscious events and processes already occupying U2. The required configuration would be pretty fiddly to put together and needed a dozen or so strokes of pure genius to get right, but God was confident that the engineering work could be brought off; unless he was very much mistaken – which he seldom, if ever, was. He couldn't wait to see his new device in operation.

So the next day he woke up good and early, honed his divine cuticle, and by lunchtime he had created – a *brain*. It didn't look like much, but he knew that its advent heralded a new phase in cosmic history. He sheathed this piece of apparatus in a body (it looked unsightly in its naked form), flipped a switch, and waited for his two universes to start flowing into each other for the first time since . . . well, time. And sure enough, it worked! The brain, located there in U1, began picking up signals from the conscious events occurring in U2, causing the attached body to twitch in various interesting ways. Moreover – and this also was part of God's clever plan – the form he had given to this brain, which structured matter in a specific and subtle way, a way in which it had not hitherto been structured, *also* worked to give new form to the conscious processes in U2, conferring upon them a complexity and structure they had not possessed up to this time. The brain thus functioned as both a receiving and a combining device with respect to the contents of U2. The form of the brain operated dually to give new shape to both sorts of being – matter and consciousness – so producing an unprecedented hybrid entity: a conscious organism, a psychophysical unit. All the other forms in God's two universes were limited to structuring one or the other kind of 'stuff', but the form of the brain was unique in that it could structure *both* realms simultaneously. Brilliant! Thanks to this universe-straddling form, there was now two-way causal interaction between U1 and U2, made possible by the porthole punched through by the brain. (Even entropy looked momentarily to have met its match, though this appearance dissolved when you looked more closely.) God was thrilled with what he had achieved. And how was he to know what these conscious organisms would get up to as history began to unfold? He really should have been more careful with the free-will part of the design.

CM: That's a very amusing fairy tale, but before I point out some of the obvious plot weaknesses I'd like to be regaled with that sober scientific version you promised – the one that doesn't bring in God's mysterious powers at all the creaky points. You did tell me that your creation story is supposed to be literally true.

MC: I was just coming to that. All you need to do, actually, is imagine essentially the same story without the idea of divine design behind it. Thus, there were originally two universes, causally isolated one from the other, either brought into being by some initiating event like the Big Bang or existing from eternity in a Steady State. This state of independence ended only when brains came into existence as a result of natural selection. There was a genetic mutation one day and by luck, if you can call it that, a physical object came to exist that was capable, as no physical object before had been, of tapping into the other universe. It was like a radio receiver evolving naturally on some planet and picking up frequencies that had always pervaded the atmosphere but had never before been detected; where these frequencies carried biologically useful information, say weather forecasts emanating from earth, so that having one of these receivers about your person enhanced your reproductive capacity. Brains happen to have the unique capacity to act as an interface or conduit between the two universes, structuring and moulding what lies on either side of the dividing line; and this capacity enabled organisms to exploit the resources of mental causation. If you like, the genes began to take advantage of the contents of U2 as well as U1, using brains as their way in: genes for universe-hopping turned out to have survival value, as genes for continent-hopping in birds do.[7]

CM: But how did the universe of consciousness come to exist in the first place? You have given me no account of that.

MC: We have no real idea, but then neither do we – or you – know how the material universe came to exist: not when you get right down to it. We know there was a Big Bang, true, and we know a good deal about its nature, but what produced that initial explosion of being – what preceded it? *Why* did it happen? No one can say. Something has to be taken as given, after all; explanations of origins must come to an end. But we know the material universe came into existence somehow, because here it is; and, similarly, consciousness came into existence somehow, because here *it* is. What we don't know is how or why the conscious universe came to be: what caused it, what its point may be, whether it might one day cease to exist.[8] But, as I say, this is the kind of mystery we have to live with for the material universe too.

CM: But this is just where your story is inferior to ours – not to mention its intrinsic nuttiness, of course. We *can* say where consciousness came from: it emerged from matter, just as living organisms did. *We* don't have to throw up our hands and wallow in mystery.

Emergence

MC: Now here we have the crux of the disagreement, if I'm not mistaken. Earlier you confessed, with commendable humility, that you earthlings have no understanding of *how* consciousness emerged from matter, though you tell me you are confident that it did.[9] So, if we are counting mysteries, that's one mystery each so far, and mine is a mystery of the same kind that we have to live with in respect of matter anyway. But, on closer inspection, your position is really very much worse than ours *because you insist on the reality of something that we know is impossible.* That is, we see no reason to believe that the primitive and underived existence of conscious processes is impossible, but we see every reason to think that extracting consciousness from matter is a real impossibility. You speak, forgive me, somewhat glibly of this 'emergence' of consciousness from matter – sensations from brain cells, thoughts from chemical neurotransmitters – but surely such a feat is quite inconceivable. It reminds me of the old myth of spontaneous generation, though in that case at least we are dealing with two kinds of physical thing. You might as well assert, without further explanation, that space emerges from time, or numbers from biscuits, or ethics from rhubarb . . . or matter from consciousness. Isn't it perfectly evident to you, as it is to us, that consciousness simply *could* not be produced by mere combinations of particles, no matter how subtle the combination? Matter is just the wrong *kind* of thing to give birth to consciousness. How can physical properties of the brain generate phenomenal features? From what magical crevice in the cortex derives the peculiar subjective homogeneity of an impression of red? How can the enormous variety of sensations be produced by the dull uniformities of neural structure? Where in consciousness do we find the spatial character of the brain's structures, and why isn't this spatiality preserved in the process of emergence? Isn't it as plain as the smell in the nose on your face that we are speaking here of two radically distinct kinds of being? The physical brain just doesn't have the resources to do the kind of generative work you are asking of it: it's not a miracle-box, you know. The great merit of our cosmology, as against yours, is that we are not compelled to make a leap of faith into a palpable absurdity. We grant consciousness the kind of ontological autonomy it so clearly demands.

CM: Hang on a minute: admittedly, we don't know how the emergence is brought about, but neither do you have any account that I have heard of how this 'brain receiver' works – of how the inter-universe link is mediated. Isn't there going to be a mystery about the psychophysical nexus whatever your underlying cosmology? It shouldn't be taken as an excuse to multiply universes.

MC: That is a fair point, but I don't think you have yet grasped quite how fundamentally we disagree with your understanding of the mind–brain relation. It isn't that we think the emergence of consciousness from matter is a numbingly difficult problem, nor even that it is insoluble by thinkers with our, or your, kind of conceptual/cognitive architecture, as we think the problem of interaction may well be. No, what we hold – and are amazed that you cannot see – is that it is clearly and incontrovertibly the case that consciousness *could* not owe its *existence* to the properties of matter. It could not be some kind of byproduct of matter, owing its very nature and being to the operations of the physical world. Our cosmology is expressly designed to avoid commitment to such an impossibility. Why cling stubbornly to the dogma that there is only one universe, the material one, when this means crediting it with magical powers? Why not drop the voodoo science and go with the double universe hypothesis? To us, your emergence thesis seems as crazy as insisting that there is only the conscious universe and somehow it magically gave rise to the material one – as if matter could emerge from consciousness.[10] Both views are mistaken for the same dualistic reason.

Dualism

CM: Your incredulity has a familiar, if antiquated, ring. As you may know, some earthly philosophers, mainly in days gone by, have shared your misgivings over the idea of emergence, not seeing how things with such apparently different natures or essences could ever stand in a relation as intimate as that – emergence being so close to reduction: dualists, they are called. Not many people hold this kind of view any more, at least within the academy, but even those who do would recoil from the extremes to which you have taken the idea.[11] Their soul-stuff is taken to reside right here in this universe; they don't concoct another universe entirely in which to house it. If you feel the need to be a dualist, why not pare your dualism down a bit – Occam's razor and all that? Even Descartes would have blanched at a whole independent world of consciousness, joined to the material world only after a long stretch of splendid isolation. Why not stick to one individual mental substance for each person, and have these substances come into existence at the same time as the person's brain does – or thereabouts?

MC: I'm not so sure your earthly dualists are as sober (by your standards) as you – or even they – think they are, especially when one examines their view more closely. But yes, I am aware of this tradition among your more rigorous and realistic thinkers, and I wonder why it is so derided nowadays. My own opinion, though I am hardly an expert in the history of human dualistic thought, is that your dualists lacked the courage of their convictions, so they undermined their position precisely by understating it: they hadn't the nerve to go one step further into full cosmological dualism. And, of course, they tended to advance their dualism against a theistic background, which hardly recommends it to a secular age. Without an underlying naturalistic cosmology on which to base their account of the mind–body relation, they left themselves open to objections they could have countered had they gone the whole way with their instincts.

Surely the most troubling aspect of traditional earthly dualism, at least if you're open-minded about it to begin with, is its inability to answer the question of origins. Where do all the individual minds come from? If cerebral matter does not create them, then what does? They can't just miraculously pop into existence at the precise moment a suitable body looms into view, coincidentally developing as the organism does. It therefore seems, on the standard dualist conception, very hard to avoid postulating God as an *essential* cog in your cosmology: *he* is the one who must do the creating of each individual mind, as well as ensuring the ongoing coupling of mind and body. Ordinary biological reproduction generates your body, but it is given to God alone to be the author of your soul.

You might, of course, try saying that individual minds have always existed and only get coupled to bodies late in their careers; they are uncreated substances. But first, this brings the theory close to our form of cosmological dualism, the sempiternality of consciousness being the cornerstone of our position. And, second, it is surely overdoing a good thing to hold that my mind, in all its specificity, has existed for ever, poised to become linked to my body – which itself might never have existed. Why have I no memories of this previous discarnate existence? Why do I begin life with a baby's mind? Isn't it preferable to assume, as we do, that the brain plays an essential role in moulding the individual minds that are associated with specific organisms? What pre-exists my body is not my mind in full bloom, as it were, but rather the primitive materials my brain forms into my mind. The brain, remember, can work as a combinatorial device without being called upon to act as a generative one. It's rather like a living organism and the physical materials its biological form shapes into that organism. What pre-exists me as a psychophysical unit are, in addition to my physical materials, my mental materials, as yet unformed into the individual mind I shall possess – not me as I shall eventually become. Your dualists simply needed to make the same kinds of cosmological assumptions about their mental realm that they were historically poised to make about the material world. They were benighted creationists about both the biological and the mental realms; a better form of dualism needs to extend to the latter realm the kind of evolutionary naturalism we now take for granted for the former realm.

And, finally, dualists should refrain from trying to slot consciousness – bodily, as it were – into the world of tables and chairs. There is no room (or too much room!) for immaterial substances in physical space; it is hardly plausible to think of my mind as a kind of dimensionless point hovering somewhere in the vicinity of my body. Matter belongs in space, but the immaterial has no place there. Certainly, it should not be conceived as a kind of vaporous presence, putting up no resistance to other potential occupants of space. It needs its own dimension. In effect, the logic of dualism leads one irresistably to hyperdualism, but your dualists couldn't quite rid themselves of the prejudice that matter in space is somehow cosmologically basic.

CM: But *isn't* it thus basic? I mean, what about questions of individuation with respect to the denizens of U2?[12] Let me put a dilemma to you about the contents of that other alleged place. Either it contains only mental universals (or types) or it contains both mental universals and mental particulars (or tokens). If the former, then hyperdualism is equivalent to mere property-dualism, given realism about mental properties and an irreducibility thesis. But this is relatively trivial ontologically and hardly warrants the inflated terms in which you are apt to characterize U2. On the other hand, if you wish to allow for a type-token distinction for items in U2, so that there can be many mental tokens of the same type, then you owe me an account of what this might consist in: what *makes* one mental token differ from another of the same type if it is not something about their spatial location or material incarnation? How, in short, do you get mental particularization in a world without matter and space?

MC: First, let me be clear that we do intend to populate U2 with tokens as well as types; so our view is not just a notational variant of a platonic conception of (irreducible) mental universals or properties. Accordingly, we accept that there is a question to be raised about the individuation of mental tokens. And the more analytically inclined among our philosophers have provided an answer to this question. In the first place, U2 has a temporal dimension, so that the same type can be instantiated at distinct times; and there may also be some analogue of the notion of self in U2, so that tokens could be distinguished by occurring in distinct selves (or proto-selves).[13] But, in the second place, and more important, the question you raise presupposes the very prejudice I mentioned, as I hope the following line of questioning will reveal to you.

How do *you* distinguish physical tokens of the same type – let's say particular events or processes? You may say in terms of their causes and effects; but we can say that of mental events too: and in both cases the individuative circle is extremely tight.[14] To avoid the circle, you might say the events occur in distinct continuant substances. But we can now ask what makes material substances distinct. You might say that they are made of different material constituents, which just raises the question what differentiates these constituents. A natural reply then is that they are at different locations, so that spatial distinctness lies at the bottom of material distinctness. This must already seem suspect, since it isn't that material things *are* regions of space. But now we cannot avoid this final question: what distinguishes one region of space from another? Either we have to circle back to material objects or we have to take spatial individuation as primitive. This is how it goes, right?

The point of rehearsing this familiar story is just to show that in the end you either accept the circularity or take something as individuatively basic, space usually. But if that is so, then what is to stop us from taking the distinctness of mental particulars as basic? Only, it seems, the prejudice that spatial individuation is somehow privileged – that it is self-explanatory, and hence a satisfactory individuative terminus. But *we* fail to see why space should be unique in this respect: we don't see why the distinctness of one mental token from another of the same type shouldn't be taken as primitive, as not admitting of any reduction to some *other* kind of item. So we see no big problem about insisting on a robust type-token distinction for U2, even before the hook-up to the spatial world occurs.

CM: Okay, I can see you have a line to push on the individuation issue. Let me try a blunter kind of objection, though I think I can anticipate your reply from what you've already said. This is just that it's hard to make *sense* of the idea of immaterial things: one can form no clear conception of what is meant, except as the negation of the idea of a material thing. Isn't U2 ontologically weird?[15]

MC: I was wondering when you would get around to rolling out that old chestnut. I am afraid we don't take such worries terribly seriously here, as indeed many of your own pre-modern thinkers did not. We think you are in the grip of an ontological prejudice produced by excessive attention to the deliverances of sense (as well as being smitten by physics idolatory, it goes without saying). You think that if you can't perceive it that's in itself a reason to say it isn't there, even that it's not coherent. The senses do indeed detect (directly or indirectly) many of the properties of matter, but there is much else in reality that they are silent about. In particular – and this is a subject we shall need to return to – you also have a similar bias against the abstract world. Indeed, the ontological revulsion you just voiced concerning the contents of U2 can be reproduced in respect of numbers and the like, since they too have non-spatial immaterial existence. Numbers don't emerge from matter either, *pace* some nominalists, though they are as real as material things: here too we hold that ontological duality is unavoidable. So we simply don't share your neurosis about abstract entities, any more than we do your anxieties concerning discarnate consciousness. Just as we are dauntless dualists, so we are proud platonists. And we resist your ontological cavils against hyperdualism in the same kind of way we resist nominalism. We point out the descriptive and explanatory benefits of a broader ontology than the merely material; we invite you to provide us with an untendentious argument against this broader ontology; and we stress its rootedness in common sense, in contrast to the contortions of an overambitious materialism.[16] We have a saying here: never reject a useful entity just because it doesn't mimic the entities you're already comfortable with.

CM: I grant you the issues of dualism and platonism are rather similar, and I suppose there is always refuge in numbers. I don't really feel up to getting into the platonism issue now, but your raising it does prompt the following question: where do numbers and other abstracta belong in your big scheme?

Abstract Emergentism

MC: I'm glad you asked me that, because there is a further component to our position – or at least that of some of our more adventurous thinkers – which brings numbers and other abstract entities into the very centre of the picture. But before going into that, let me first offer a simple answer to your question: the abstracta exist in U2, or in its general vicinity, along with episodes of consciousness. God couldn't very well install them in U1 next to matter, on account of their non-spatial immateriality, so he deposited them in the world already devised for states of consciousness. Numbers lack the mutability of consciousness, of course, but the two are alike in not requiring a spatial receptacle. So we prefer not to add a third universe to the two we have already. Two seems enough, does it not?

Let me note, parenthetically, that once U1 and U2 come to be causally connected by virtue of brain activity, it becomes strained to speak of there any longer being *two* universes, since the criterion of identity for universes plausibly consists in considerations of causal relatedness. This causal leakage from one to the other creates a single inclusive closed system out of two hitherto separate closed systems. But let's not embroil ourselves in pedantic questions about how many universes there strictly are on the hyperdualist view: the theory can be allowed to speak for itself. The important point is that numbers and states of consciousness are alike in their immateriality – and this despite their standing in various interesting kinds of relation to concentrations of matter in space.

CM: By all means let's avoid those questions, of which the well-trained analytical philosopher is so fond. What peaks my interest is how you conceive the relation between the abstract and the conscious in U2. Do they just sit beside each other there, minding their own business? Or is there some more intimate relation between them? How intertwined are the essences of the abstract and the mental, on your view?[17]

MC: I see that you are beginning to develop a feel for the cosmological picture I am urging on you: that is just the kind of question you should be asking. The short answer is that these essences are far more closely related than are the essences of matter and consciousness. There is ontic harmony here, if not ontic penetration. Our thinkers actually divide into two distinct schools on this question. The conservative school, known as the primitivists, holds that the abstract and the conscious merely exist alongside each other, leading quite separate and extrinsic careers – aside, that is, from the odd spot of abstract intentionality. The primitivists thus maintain that consciousness is an underived existent, having no essential nature other than that peculiar to it – as ontologically basic as matter or number. By contrast, the progressive school, known as the abstract emergentists, holds that there is a relation of ontological dependence between the mental and the abstract: the nature of the one involves that of the other. So –

CM: Then you aren't really platonists at all! You are conceptualists or intuitionists or something of the sort, since you think numbers and so on are mental products. In effect, you hold that the abstract emerges from the mental, and so you situate both in the same strip of reality.

MC: You have got hold of the wrong end of the stick. The ontological dependence doesn't run that way; it goes the other way around. It is the mental that depends upon the abstract, while the abstract depends upon nothing but itself. Consciousness, contend some, is an emergent characteristic of abstract entities and their properties and relations; so the abstract lies at the heart of the mental. As you believe that mind emerges from matter, and so has a physical essence, so some of us think that it emerges from the abstract realm, deriving its essence therefrom. So we are platonists in the full sense. If I were to state this abstract emergentism in Plato's idiom, I should say that it is the thesis that consciousness is a byproduct of the World of Forms. The slogan is: consciousness is the abstract in process.

CM: I thought your hyperdualist cosmology far-out enough, but this abstract emergentism business sounds like the kind of thing people used to think up under LSD. Let me get this clear, because I must have misunderstood you. You go along with Plato and Frege and others in thinking that the abstract is not a creature of the mind, holding instead that the mind is a creature of the abstract. Numbers sort of get together in platonic heaven and somehow emit states of consciousness. You multiply 13 by 27, say, and get pain. Is that it?

MC: Crudely put, that is indeed the theory the progressives think has the most chance of being true – explains the most and has the greatest internal coherence. The only major adjustment I would make to your satiric formulation is that the abstract entities are held to be *dispositionally* the basis of mind – the mental is *latent* in the abstract. There has to be some outside trigger, or occasion, for this disposition or potential to become manifest: something has to engage the abstract entities in a temporal and causal process of the right sort. There has to be, as we say, a 'realization' of the abstract reality before you have mentation. The abstract world supplies, as it were, the original materials from which minds are constructed. God recycled his prior abstract creations as the building blocks of mind, involving them thus in a temporal process. A mental event is basically the temporal tokening of an abstract fact.

CM: You make it sound like some kind of bizarre Pythagoreanism of the mind – as if thoughts and sensations were literally composed out of abstract entities. Pain isn't neural excitation, it's arithmetical multiplication!

MC: I'm surprised you're having so much trouble coming to grips with abstract emergentism. Isn't essentially the same idea familiar on earth under the title 'the computational theory of mind', at least when properly conceived?[18] Don't some of you hold that it is necessary and sufficient for something to have mental processes that it realize a computer program – that mental types are programme types, and that mental tokens are these types incarnated? And what is such a program if it isn't just an algorithm defined over abstract objects – numbers, functions, propositions and so on? A computation, literally, is a kind of calculation, and a calculation is precisely an operation whose objects (directly or indirectly)[19] are abstract entities. A computer program typically consists in a sequence of instructions to perform certain abstract operations, like addition, on certain abstract entities, like numbers. Or again, the rules (NB) are defined over a domain of propositional entities, and the program specifies (say) the numerical probability of one proposition being represented given that certain others are. A platonist will accordingly conceive of realizing a program as a matter of standing in a set of relations to the denizens of the abstract world; and if mentation is computation, then mentality itself consists in standing in just such relations. Of course, the abstract system has to be implemented in some concrete way in order to get an actual computation going, this being a type of action or event rather than a purely mathematical fact; but still, according to computationalism, the essence of the mental process consists (at least partly) in abstract facts. The implementation may be of a physical nature but, as some of the more clear-sighted computationalists have pointed out, this is strictly incidental to the central thesis: *any* implementing process, even an ectoplasmic or divine one, could serve to bring the abstract facts to mental life.[20] The type of hardware (or ectoware) is contingent to the mental state; it is the abstract software that is of the essence. What is this but abstract emergentism?

Note here that what cannot be allowed is that the abstract facts should themselves be construed as products of mind, on pain of circularity in the explanation of the mental in terms of the abstract: you can't be, say, an intuitionist about the abstract and a computationalist about the mental. Note too that it is necessary to distinguish between an object's performing a computation and its having a computation performed on it, on penalty of finding mentality wherever mathematics is applied to objects, as in ordinary physical measurement: here the object doesn't perform the numerical operation – we do.

So, you see, your computationalism is a special case of the kind of view our progressives espouse: the mental is latent in the abstract and needs only an implementing process to become temporally tokened. In U2 there exist such processes, though they are not, of course, of a physical nature: these processes are the trigger that elicits mental events from their dispositional basis in abstract entities, and gives to these events their causal potential.

Some of our theoreticians maintain, additionally, that what mediates between U1 and U2 is precisely the circumstance that the brain performs mathematical operations: its physical processes thus map onto the abstract world and hence (indirectly) bring mental states into alignment with the brain, these states being originally emergent upon the abstract realm, which has already turned mental in virtue of the eliciting processes in U2. The brain, as it were, makes a detour through the abstract, reaching consciousness through its basis in that domain. Psychophysical correlations are thus abstractly mediated. However, this is all pretty speculative stuff and isn't part of our orthodox sober hyperdualism.

CM: I suppose I do now see an affinity between your abstract emergentism and our computationalism, though I doubt that our theorists would care to reveal the metaphysical picture implicit in their supposedly hard-headed approach so explicitly.

MC: People do tend to keep their metaphysical assumptions quiet, don't they?

CM: Like guilty secrets, yes. The main problem I see with abstract emergentism, ours or yours, is explaining clearly just *how* it is that the abstract could be sufficient, in conjunction with a suitable realizing process, to produce states of consciousness. Isn't there a rebarbative bruteness to the postulated dependence, redolent of the kind of magic you excoriate in our idea of material emergence?

MC: I grant you that. But my polemical aim was to get you to compare the two theories of emergence, so as encourage a more impartial view of the options. And you have to admit that the mental and the abstract are closer ontological neighbours than the mental and the material; there is thus less of a gap to be crossed by the emergence relation in the former case. I ask you at least to try to give the view a fair hearing: philosophical progress can sometimes come from the least likely directions.

CM: I promise I'll try. I can see you've got quite a system going here, each part cohering with the rest. I suppose it would be *nice* if it were true. But aren't there just too many unanswered questions?

Methodological Queries

MC: You have to expect unanswered questions in these areas. Wouldn't it be strange if all the ultimate cosmological questions could be answered by tiny bounded mortals like us? Here, any knowledge at all is to be marvelled at. Ignorance comes with the cosmic territory. Quantum theory, for example, would never have gained general acceptance if unanswered questions were sufficient to undermine a theory. You should ask yourself what overall picture of the universe provides the best general account of the phenomena to which we have access, limited as these phenomena are. What makes for the most coherent *fit* between the basic categories of reality? Which theory ascribes the most intelligible pattern to the universe as a whole? As far as I can see, our hyperdualist cosmology – with or without abstract emergentism – is superior on these counts to your matter-obsessed monistic mystery story. Come on, isn't it only ontic prejudice and the dead weight of (recent) tradition that makes you prefer your theory to ours? Show me one non-question-begging respect in which your view has the theoretical advantage over ours. And don't just say ours is bizarre!

CM: Let me think – what *are* the problems with your theory? Well, to begin with, isn't it very uneconomical? I mean, two universes instead of one – it's not terribly parsimonious, is it? Our theory is ontologically simpler than yours.

MC: True enough, if the sheer number of basic categories is your measure of theoretical simplicity. But at what cost do you restrict the number of universes to one? Simplicity of this kind is no virtue if the simpler theory fails to explain what the more complex theory does, and *a fortiori* if the simpler theory contains a screaming absurdity – like the idea of material emergence. Besides, there are members of your intellectual community, quite respectable ones too, who advocate world multiplication, prompted by considerations of explanatory power and theoretical adequacy. There are the possible worlds theorists, who embrace an infinity of existent (though non-actual) worlds in addition to the one we witness with our senses.[21] And there are even some physicists, the thinkers you earthlings seem to revere most in the current epoch, who propose a theory known the 'many-worlds hypothesis', where these worlds are taken as not only existent but actual.[22] World plurality is practically *de rigueur* in some earthly circles. And ontological economy easily slides into sheer mean-mindedness – it's not as if the worlds are being rationed! Besides, as I remarked earlier, once the brain has punched its way through from U1 to U2, we may as well say that we have only the one universe on our hands, causal closure being the operative criterion of identity here.

CM: All right, but hyperdualism is also highly unempirical: no one has ever had, nor could have, any experience of U2 except as it bears upon his or her own consciousness and that of other conscious organisms situated here in U1. According to the theory, as I understand it, we are all little pockets or packets of consciousness selected from a much more extensive conscious reality, but we have no access to that larger reality. Except for the little specks of consciousness that find their way into us, as it were, the contents of U2 are completely unverifiable.

MC: I'm surprised to find you still so much in the sway of the empiricist outlook. Think of your own theories for a moment: the world-multiplying ones I just mentioned, as well as quantum theory, relativity theory, string theory, evolutionary theory, and so forth. You can't always get direct empirical access to realities that are needed to make the best sense of the world as you find it. Explanatory power is the thing, not sensory convenience. Antirealism and idealism are especially out of place in cosmological discussions. And, as I have already argued, the individual pockets on their own raise the origin problem in an insoluble form. Good theory construction, here as elsewhere, calls for the postulation of unobservables.

I suspect you are being misled by a feature of your predicament as a sentient organism that you are failing to interpret correctly. Since you are partly a physical entity, existing in U1, your access to what transpires in U2 is restricted to what your brain – a selective receiving instrument – can resonate to: the rest of U2 lies outside its powers of transduction. Your brain cannot tune in to the same constituents of U2 as, say, a bat's brain can – not to mention the constituents of U2 that no extant brain can tune in to. And this makes you conclude, erroneously, that there is nothing more to consciousness. But that is to inflate a merely epistemological point into a metaphysical or cosmological one. It is like thinking the electromagnetic spectrum is no broader than the band of light visible to terrestrial eyes, yours or those of other species. In fact, theory requires that we recognize that brains dipped into consciousness late in the history of things and quite fortuitously, so that there is bound to be much of it that is not connected to any physical organism. Indeed, what is really remarkable, to a larger view, is that *any* of it should be so connected, given the correct cosmological conception. Our brains are, as it were, windows onto the contents of U2, but they are windows that offer only a partial vista of the full terrain. There is thus an illusion of dependence on the material world, prompted by this very partialness, which is perhaps (partly) why you people are prepared to live with the paradox of material emergence. If you could survey U2 from a perspective outside of your own brain and that of other brains, then you would have no tendency to subscribe to the myth of material emergence. You would *see* that brains are just local sumps into which the vast ocean of consciousness only partially drains.

Panpsychism

CM: You're beginning to sound mystical in your desire to shun the magical. Your theory reminds me of a theory some of our more extravagant and mystically inclined thinkers have purported to believe: namely, panpsychism.[23] Panpsychism also takes consciousness to extend very much further than we usually suppose, regarding the psychic raw materials from which individual conscious minds are built as pre-existing those minds. Primitive mentality is thus held to pervade the physical universe: rocks instantiate mental properties. But at least this view, unlike yours, confines the proto-conscious basis to this universe, tying conscious states down to ordinary lumps of matter. Why not take a leaf out of the panpsychists' book and insert your wider conscious reality snugly into the material world? Why have your irreducible conscious properties instantiated by immaterial particulars in U2 instead of material ones in U1?

MC: Now you are asking a perfectly reasonable question, one that proceeds from the right first principles. The panpsychists are, of course, absolutely right to despair of the material emergence idea, which is why they take consciousness to have its basis in something of the appropriate kind to produce it, viz. itself. And viewing the structure of the brain as essentially combinatorial with respect to primitive conscious ingredients, instead of as magically productive of consciousness, accords closely with our own conception: no conscious output without conscious input (setting side abstract emergentism for the moment). They are also large-visioned enough to grasp that this requires a novel conception of reality as a whole, not merely of that small part of it wherein brains reside, in which consciousness is not really the late and parasitic arrival it has seemed to some to be. Consciousness must indeed be seen as a more basic or primordial feature of the universe than your modern materialistic thinkers have hypothesized. (These latter thinkers, by the way, are the true mystics: they remind me of nothing so much as fakirs claiming to make carpets levitate by blowing into flutes – where the flute tunes are neural volleys and the floating carpets are the conscious states that correlate with them.)

The panpsychists go wrong principally because they lack the imagination, or the nerve, to locate their conscious materials outside the spatial world of coagulated particles, to be connected up with that world only subsequently. They seem to assume that conscious properties could not be instantiated save by extended physical things; when the truth is that, strictly speaking, physical things never *instantiate* conscious properties – they merely correlate with items that do. Because of this basic mistake, panpsychism runs into problems that cannot be surmounted under its assumed cosmology. In particular, it cannot explain why it is that these alleged properties of non-cerebral matter make no difference to the way this matter behaves – why particle physics, say, can do without attributing psychic properties to atoms in addition to their physical properties. There is simply no description of the behaviour of a hydrogen atom under which its trajectory needs to be explained by the postulation of intrinsic conscious states – in contrast to the movements of cerebrally guided systems such as ourselves. The panpsychist's alleged proto-conscious states of atoms, tables and black holes have no causal powers in respect of those physical objects that are held to instantiate them. And this is why there is no *evidence* that such objects possess states of consciousness – they behave precisely as if they do *not* possess such states. In addition, of course, this impotency ill suits these properties to yield mental states as we know them, since these states do have causal powers. The problem here stems, clearly, from the panpsychist's insistence on situating his wider conscious reality within the physical universe: the problems go away when you give consciousness its own universe in which to be independently instantiated. So you don't have to spread conscious properties all across a physical world in which they palpably play no role; you can spread them instead across their own universe, making causal connections only where they are there to be seen. If only the panpsychists, with their wider conscious reality and combinatorial picture of the brain, had put their heads together with the Cartesian dualists, with their appreciation of the need for non-physical instantiation, and then had given a little thought to cosmology, *then* they might well have arrived at the correct hyperdualist theory. Hyperdualism, after all, is really just regular earthly dualism combined with panpsychist elements and then taken cosmic – if that makes it seem any more palatable to you. The truth was thus within earthly reach, if only you humans had the courage to *think big*. When it comes to the problem of consciousness, pusillanimity is the chief foe of progress.

Brain Power

CM: You are certainly not afraid to boldly go wherever the problem may lead you: whatever I pose as a difficulty you embrace as a virtue! Let me try to bring a final objection that is far more concessive to your basic cosmological outlook but which it seems to me you haven't yet properly addressed. This is simply that hyperdualism runs the risk of leaving the essential problem where it was to start with, by allowing that the brain plays a major sustaining role in shaping or organizing the conscious stuff onto which it hooks in U2. Isn't this action of constituting conscious stuff into specific minds, either of individuals or species, just the same old problematic emergence you are so anxious to reject? The brain, a material thing, is still doing essential constructive work in bringing consciousness into the form in which we experience it; it isn't, on your view, a mere passive receiver. Now, isn't this generativity uncomfortably similar to the kind of material generation we favour?

MC: Again, you are now asking the right questions: that is, indeed, an issue over which we have lost sleep. You are, of course, correct in saying that, on our view, the structure of the brain is capable of producing conscious novelty

– in somewhat the way natural selection can produce physical novelty. That is, its combinatorial powers can yield new forms of consciousness. However, the generativity envisaged here is of a different order altogether from that imagined by your kind of material emergence. You think the brain's physical form can act as a kind of (computable?) function from the instantiation of physical properties to the instantiation of conscious properties – that it can span this vast ontological divide. But we maintain only that it can act as a function from one kind of conscious property to another; as I keep saying, its role is purely combinatorial, not foundational or ultimately creative. It is, indeed, a big scientific question how in detail the combinatorial conversion is effected, but this is a question that begins from sound cosmological assumptions: it makes the brain very clever without requiring that it perform magic tricks. The brain receives and organizes prior conscious components, but that is by no means the same as somehow extracting these components from within itself, as if conscious states could be mined from its neural substrata like precious stones from rock. The brain performs a kind of mental chemistry, yes, selecting its raw materials from U2; but it contains no al-chemical capacity – no power to get something from nothing.

The question that most exercises our mental scientists nowadays is whether conscious processes as we encounter them can be somehow analytically broken down into simpler components in the way that we know matter can. What is the deep nature of our states of consciousness? Is there perhaps a table of elements for consciousness as there is for chemicals? Are the conscious states we experience ultimately made up of complexes of these fundamental elements? Are there natural laws prevailing in U2 that govern the way conscious primitives can combine and associate with each other to produce the flora and fauna of consciousness that our brains present to us? What, in short, does the natural science of U2 look like? Does it have the kind of depth and difficulty that the natural sciences of U1 display? Is there, say, a mental analogue of the quark? Might there be fundamental indeterminacies in U2? These are the kinds of question we would like to answer.

The trouble we have in answering these questions, of course, is that our concepts of consciousness are geared directly to the way consciousness strikes us introspectively and through its behavioural expression, which might be but the final result of a complex process of natural construction. These concepts don't, as it were, go straight to the cosmic source, bypassing the brain's complex contribution; it is almost as if the brain disguises from us what the contents of U2 are like in their elementary form. Our concepts seem to represent many conscious states – pain, for example – as if they were unanalysable simples, one-dimensional, as it were – but these concepts may not do justice to the underlying natural structure of the phenomena. Our concepts of consciousness might be deeply superficial, if you follow me, limited by the manner in which our brains serve conscious states up to us. On general theoretical grounds, it seems attractive to think of U2 as having the kind of natural nomological depth exhibited by the denizens of U1, but it is surpassingly difficult to develop concepts of consciousness able to depict such depth.

Ironically enough, then, our brains may be preventing us from achieving a scientifically powerful theory of the deep workings of U2, and indeed of the manner of its connection with U1. The messages they send to us from U2 are in all likelihood elaborately coded, are perhaps not even decipherable from our restricted standpoint. We can't infer the ground from the upshot.

This is frustrating, though we are not such idealists as to infer from this lack of accessibility that U2 *could* not have the kind of natural depth I have just been speculating about. It might indeed have a rich and surprising nature that is quite far removed from the ways in which we habitually conceptualize our own little strips of consciousness. And this nature, real though it is, might be quite unknowable to the kinds of being who benefit (if that is the word) from its manifestations.[24] Who knows what possibilities might be realized out there in the objective world? I mean, the world doesn't care whether we can figure it out or not, does it?

CM: I see that you are not only unapologetic dualists and unblushing platonists but also unabashed realists. In fact, now that I think of it, your entire position depends upon a firm adherence to realist principles, does it not? You put the metaphysics first and let the epistemology take care of itself – if it can.

MC: Absolutely right; and perhaps it is the inveterate tendency of human beings to fight shy of realism that leads to their persistent cosmological blunders – if I may speak candidly. Your species seems determined to believe that objective reality is somehow limited to that small portion of it on which it can train its meagre epistemic faculties. This is not only metaphysically preposterous; it also reveals a degree of egocentricity that comports all too easily with the dearth of virtue so conspicuous on planet earth. Have some humility! Try not to see everything from your own limited viewpoint! Respect the non-human world!

CM: You won't find me dissenting from those worthy precepts, nor from the realism you prize so highly. I've always tried to consider the bat's point of view, in more ways than one. But I can't assent to your cosmology simply because it has the *ethical* advantage over ours. Isn't it also a form of idealism to suppose that the natural is shaped by the moral? Still, you have my promise that I'll think carefully about it. Anything that cuts human beings down to size has got to be worth serious consideration. You have certainly given me much food for thought, so much so that I can feel an attack of intellectual dyspepsia coming on. Hyperdualism is going to take some digesting. Can I go home now?

MC: By all means: we have no wish to hold you against your will. We merely thought that a candid exchange of philosophical opinion might prove beneficial to all concerned. I have to say, though, in that spirit of honesty, that you have said nothing to change my original impression that human thinking on these matters is woefully misguided. I had half-supposed that you might be able to say something to remove the appearance of paradox that so glaringly afflicts earthly orthodoxy, and to put up some kind of cogent case against our hyperdualism. But – no such thing.

CM: You have, I must confess, made me ask myself what *does* justify my firm commitment to the monistic cosmology I have hitherto taken for granted, in the light of the alternative you have pressed upon me. I shall have to decide whether, after mature reflection, there really is any rational foundation for my long-held conviction. Who knows, maybe in twenty years I might be able to see my way clear to joining you in hyperdualist heaven! (Somehow I doubt it, though.)

MC: Then we have achieved our purpose in bringing you here. It has been trying for us to observe a race of otherwise relatively intelligent creatures persisting in such perverse error. I hope that you will endeavour, upon your return to earth, to bring the hyperdualist creed to the attention of your fellows, so that they may assess it for themselves. They may, indeed, find it more eupeptic than you . . . . You may now board the neutron transporter and return to earth. Bon voyage!

Aftermath

And so I was returned safely to my home planet, physically all in one piece, though mentally shaken up (= order in U1, chaos in U2). I still suffer from insomnia worrying about the mind–body problem, but now at least I have another position to occupy my thoughts. It feels strange, though, to lie there in the dark, focusing hard on my consciousness, and to think of it as a kind of fortuitous infusion from another dimension, sucked through by my overactive brain: I am a hybrid being whose nature is to bestride two universes that were never intended to cross paths. While all around me the other material objects are confined to just the one universe. Where exactly am *I*? It gives new meaning to the phrase 'to have your head in the clouds'. My brain is a key for opening the combination lock to a different world. Am I glad that nature invented this key? What if it hadn't? And, what happens to me when I die? But at least I'm not the only one to exist in this divided condition: if hyperdualism is true, then you are all in the same boat as me – we all live on the border of two worlds. Our nature as conscious organisms is to bring two autonomous spheres into unlikely propinquity. That would explain a lot, philosophically and otherwise.

Notes

1 These higher-order subjective states have received little attention, in contrast to the first-order subjective states discussed (say) in Thomas Nagel's 'What Is It like to be a Bat?' (1974). Are there specific qualia whose intentional objects are other qualia? How does externalism about content bear upon that question? Is there really a distinctive subjective state corresponding to the apprehension of subjective states that one cannot grasp: the 'alien subjectivity quale'? And so on. These questions belong to what might be called the phenomenology of other minds.

2 Readers can gauge how representative by consulting my *The Problem of Consciousness* (1991). In that book the assumption of material emergence is central to the argument; in the present chapter this assumption will be brought into question (though not by me). I am (currently) inclined to think that the view offered by my eccentric host is the strongest alternative to the position I defend in the aforementioned book. It should be clear that I don't *want* this alternative to be viable. But the opposition must be given its day.

3 The most proximate cause of this chapter was a remark Peter Unger made to me (quoting Michael Lockwood, I gather): he said that the trouble with the usual theories of the mind–body relation is that they aren't crazy enough. Being sympathetic to this remark, I set myself the task of devising a theory in which craziness was at a premium: a no-holds-barred theory. Intrinsic plausibility (by earthly standards) was to be ruthlessly sacrificed to weird internal coherence. Call this craziness requirement 'Convention C': a materially adequate and formally correct theory of consciousness must be as wild as possible while still observing minimal standards of explanatory power. As will become apparent, My Captor's theory certainly conforms to Convention C. For comments on an earlier draft I thank my Rutgers colleagues Jerry Fodor, Barry Loewer, Brian McLaughlin and Tim Maudlin, as well as Peter Unger, Consuelo Preti and Galen Strawson.

4 See Richard Dawkins's discussion of Graham Cairn-Smith's crystal theory of pre-DNA replicators, in *The Blind Watchmaker* (1986), ch. 6. First mud; then crystals; eventually us. (Then probably back to mud again.)

5 I am not myself one of these cheerful utopians, convinced *a priori* that human science will inevitably lead to total knowledge of everything. Cognitive pessimism is the prevailing mood of *The Problem of Consciousness* (McGinn, 1991).

6 Cf. Nagel's 'all-pervading world soul, the mental equivalent of space-time, activated by certain kinds of physical activity' (1986, p. 30).

7 Obviously, this analogy should not be taken literally: birds really do migrate from one place to another, but brains don't actually travel from U1 to U2, they exploit the contents of U2 while staying put in U1. Still, both sorts of relation to a distant zone (careful!) have proved biologically useful.

8 So consciousness does not exist for the same kind of reason that hearts and brains do, i.e. on account of biological utility. Consciousness is not inherently biological, according to hyperdualism: the genes exploited its prior existence, as they do many other kinds of intrinsically unbiological material. In this respect, consciousness is more like water than blood; less like an organ and more like what composes an organ.

9 This is my position in *The Problem of Consciousness* (McGinn, 1991): certainty about the fact of emergence coupled with admitted nescience about the mechanism.

10 This is not the same as Berkeley's (far more defensible) thesis that what we *call* 'material objects' are really ideas in our minds or in the mind of God. Rather, it is the thesis that matter *in the sense Berkeley repudiated* is an upshot of mind, i.e. that alleged substance whose nature differs radically from the nature of mind. What MC can't understand is how you can combine irreducibility (a kind of dualism) with emergence – *either* way round. Once reduction has been roundly rejected, he thinks you have to go the full dualist route and not mystify yourself with talk of emergence. In other words, straightforward materialists and idealists are entitled to the notion of emergence, but no one else is.

11 Academic dualists include Karl Popper and John Eccles: see *The Self and its Brain* (Popper and Eccles, 1977).

12 Fodor urged me to consider this kind of objection, which I am glad to do. Such concerns are familiar from Peter Strawson's *Individuals* (1959), in which the primacy of space in individuation is pressed.

13 This, in effect, is how Berkeley distinguishes tokens of the same mental type: they occur in distinct selves. Of course, you get a circle if you go on to individuate selves in terms of mental events. Whether this is bad depends upon your individuative ambitions.

14 Donald Davidson proposes a causal criterion of event identity in 'The Individuation of Events' (1980). The circle here arises through the obvious fact that the causes and effects of token events are also token events.

15 Orthodox opposition, along these lines, to dualistic immaterialism can be found, for example, in my *The Character of Mind* (1982), ch. 2.

16 I don't know if MC has had access to Hartry Field's *Science Without Numbers* (1980), in which the virtues of nominalism are hymned: but if he has, he clearly wasn't persuaded (different form of life, I suppose).

17 I was prompted to consider this question by a lecture given by Roger Penrose at Rutgers in 1990. Penrose asked how we might integrate matter, mathematics and mind into a single coherent worldview.

18 That is, functionalism of the computer-model variety: see Hilary Putnam (1975a) and the mighty throng of his followers.

19 I mean: even if a computation is conceived as an empirical operation on numerals, construed as particular inscriptions, it is still the case that computation is indirectly number-involving, since numerals denote numbers. In fact, of course, it is far more natural to conceive addition, say, as an operation performed on numbers themselves (no doubt mediated by non-abstract entities like marks on paper).

20 Thus Putnam: 'the functional-state hypothesis is *not* incompatible with dualism!' (1975a, p. 436).

21 See, for example, Lewis (1986).

22 Otherwise known as the Everett–Wheeler–Graham interpretation of quantum mechanics. For a popular account see *The Dancing Wu Li Masters: an Overview of the New Physics* by Gary Zukav (1979).

23 See Nagel (1979a).

24 The idea that consciousness might have an unknowable hidden nature is defended in my 'The Hidden Structure of Consciousness', in McGinn (1991). This conception of consciousness is not, then, the exclusive property of material emergentists: dualists can be noumenalists too. Indeed, they might need to be in order to deal with the problem of interaction, which MC concedes to be daunting.

9
Consciousness and Objectivity

JOHN I. BIRO

The Neglect of Consciousness in Recent Philosophy of Mind

'Consciousness is what makes the mind–body problem really intractable.' Thus Thomas Nagel begins his well-known paper, 'What is it like to be a bat?' and goes on to claim that current discussions of the mental, when not altogether ignoring or side-stepping consciousness, 'get it obviously wrong'.[1] Nagel is far from alone in voicing this sort of complaint, and it is one that appears to strike a chord in many philosophers who share his feeling that an account of consciousness must be central to any adequate theory of the mind. Yet it turns out to be surprisingly difficult to discover exactly what this complaint amounts to, and even more difficult to decide whether it is well founded. In fact, as we will see, a number of different intuitions are at work in giving rise to the sort of misgiving expressed by Nagel, and more than one argument has been based on one or the other of these, without enough care being taken to distinguish either intuitions or arguments. I believe that doing so is essential before we decide whether to accept or reject the sweeping metaphysical conclusions many, including Nagel, are prepared to draw from the alleged intractability of the problem of consciousness: that the inability to fit consciousness into a scientific account of reality reveals that our very conception of reality has been fundamentally flawed.

Impressive, though still controversial, as they have been, recent advances in theorizing about the mind have come largely by focusing on aspects of mentality other than consciousness, leaving that allegedly central, but baffling, phenomenon largely untouched. There are, of course, many difficulties still to be resolved before arriving at a satisfactory theoretical understanding even of these other aspects of the mind. A host of questions about intentionality and its role in the explanation of behaviour, about the difference between mere behaviour and action, about the nature of mental operations and processes, and about many other equally puzzling matters are far from settled.

Yet there is a widespread conviction that some progress has been made, and some optimism that we know how to maintain it. By contrast, there is a queasy feeling that with consciousness we do not even know where and how to begin. This leads sometimes to an ostrich-like attitude of simply avoiding the subject, sometimes to an airy, hand-waving sort of faith in some as yet un-glimpsed future approach and – most relevant to our purposes – sometimes to an all-too-ready concession of both the intuitions and the conclusions mentioned above. These conclusions are at odds with the ideal of a science of the mind to which much of science and philosophy has always been committed. While the realization of such an ideal is easily conceded to be far off, accepting that it is in principle unrealizable is quite another matter. Yet it is often maintained that giving consciousness its due would show just that: that there is no hope of a theory or science of the mind which can account for it. This means, of course, that there is no hope for a science of the mind at all. Even if there were in fact a true naturalistic theory of consciousness, it may be that *we*, as conscious beings, are not in a position to develop, or even understand, one. The fact that there are truths about consciousness of the form an objective theory would state is no guarantee that beings who instantiate it are in a position to discover or even comprehend such truths. And if they are not, as some people suspect, they will not be in a position to develop a science of the mind nor, *a fortiori*, a complete theory of the world.

In this chapter, I would like to make a start on sorting out and evaluating some of the arguments that have been offered on behalf of this pessimistic conclusion. These arguments all have as their basis the kind of vague and general unease about theorizing about consciousness to which writers such as Nagel appeal. They exploit that unease to persuade us of the *sui generis*, essentially theory-resistant, character of the phenomenon, in the face of the perennial philosophical and scientific drive for a unified account of all of reality. Since Nagel's original formulations of these arguments have been so influential, I shall focus mostly on these, though I hope that the results will be generalizable to a whole family of arguments reflecting the same outlook.

Points of View and Subjectivity

If most discussions of consciousness get it wrong, the way at least to begin to get it right, according to Nagel, is to recognize its essential *subjectivity*, a characteristic that makes it impossible to place it in any *objective* framework. There are obviously two questions to ask in beginning to explicate and evaluate such a claim: what are we to understand by 'subjectivity' and what should the contrasting term 'objectivity' be taken to mean?

'Subjectivity', it turns out, covers more than one idea; correspondingly, we have to distinguish a number of different senses of 'objectivity'. The clues Nagel offers are all metaphorical and need considerable unpacking. They include his provocative 'What is it like to be . . .?' test and the introduction of the related notion of a *point of view*, something all and only conscious beings have. A point of view, it is claimed, gives its owner access to a special kind of fact that is different from, and irreducible to, any other fact or set of facts equally available to others. It is only from a point of view that such facts are accessible; but it is these facts that are the essence of consciousness. Similarly, it is only from a creature's own point of view that the 'What is it like to be ...?' question *for that creature* can be answered, and that answer, disclosing 'the subjective character of the creature's experience', is what expresses that essence.

Let me illustrate these claims with a couple of brief quotations, since they are central to Nagel's formulation of the anti-objectivist argument:

> The fact that an organism has conscious experience *at all* means, basically, that there is something it is like to *be* that organism.
> ... fundamentally an organism has conscious mental states if and only if there is something that it is like to *be* that organism – something it is like *for* the organism. (Nagel, 1974, p. 436)

Leaving aside the 'basically' and the 'fundamentally' – one is not sure whether these are here for emphasis or as qualifications – the thing to note here is that the 'means' in the first quotation suggests that the 'if and only if' in the second should be taken in the strongest possible sense, as expressing an analytical thesis. This makes sense of treating the something that it is like to be – the so-called subjective character of experience – as the essence of consciousness. Now, to quote Nagel again:

> ... every subjective phenomenon is *essentially* connected with a single point of view, and it seems *inevitable* that an objective, physical theory will abandon that point of view. (Nagel, 1974, p. 437; emphasis added)

This unpacking of 'subjectivity' in terms of points of view leaves open the question, which we will soon see to be centrally important, of whether we are supposed to be thinking about a *kind* of point of view, one that more than one individual could, at least in principle, occupy or about a single, unique one that by definition only one being has or even could have. But before turning to that question, let us note that, as the last of the above quotations from Nagel makes clear, we are not dealing with an accidental failing of the actual theories of consciousness that philosophers and scientists happen to have been drawn to, remediable by constructing different and better, more sophisticated ones. Theories by their very nature *aim* at leaving particular points of view behind (Nagel, 1974, p. 444). Thus, in so far as it is such special, point-of-view-dependent facts that constitute the essence of consciousness, objective theories are in effect *designed* to miss the mark, being unable to recognize, let alone to explain, them. ('Fact' here must be taken in the ontological sense, as an existing state of affairs with certain properties. The mere – and banal – fact that all facts are *epistemically* perspectival would not, in and of itself, present a barrier to a theoretical treatment of the actual facts in this context any more than in any other.) The only reason that currently fashionable reductionistic theories have any plausibility is that they overlook or deny the reality of these facts and thus *mis*-analyse what they then set out to reduce. But reduction of the mental *sans* consciousness, even if successful, is not interesting and does not bear on the mind–body problem to which the reductionist theory purports to be a solution. In effect, such theories change the subject. What *would* be interesting would be a reduction of the mental *including* consciousness. But once we recognize the essential subjectivity of consciousness, we will see that that kind of reduction is a will-o'-the-wisp.

Just what kind of thing is this essentially subjective experience, on whose reality Nagel insists, and which constitutes the essence of consciousness? One thing we should not confuse it with is the *intentionality* of much of what we count as mental. Nagel quite cheerfully concedes – though possibly only for the sake of the argument – that the intentionality of such things as beliefs and desires may be accounted for in an objective theory (Nagel, 1974, p. 436).[2] Beliefs, desires and the like are, on any going account, mental states. But they need not be conscious and need not involve any episodes of *experiencing* with any qualitative character, episodes on which their subject might report. Hence the modifier 'conscious' in the first two quotations above: it is only a certain kind of mental state that has the peculiar characteristic Nagel is interested in, and it is only that kind of state that is claimed to be essentially theory-resistant. Paradigms of this kind of state are sensations of various sorts, such as sense perceptions and pains and itches, as well as what one might call images of these (Hume's *simple* ideas), as in memory and, perhaps, in anticipation. What these states are like, only the creature who has them (or, perhaps, creatures sufficiently like it) can *know* – and, most importantly, no objective theory can *say*.[3]

Point-of-view Types and Tokens

I shall shortly return to the question I posed above, of whether we should take the notion of a point of view, and thus that of subjectivity to which it is the key, in a type or in a token sense. But first, let me note that merely to emphasize the subjectivity of some facts is not, *eo ipso*, to commit oneself to any particularly daring metaphysical thesis. One might see what Nagel is doing as merely drawing attention to, and emphasizing, the importance of empathy and imaginative projection in all one's attempts to understand others, whether they are like one or different. (Something much easier, of course, in the former than in the latter case.) So construed, Nagel is invoking the remote and unimaginable inner life of bats merely as a heuristic aid in reminding us that even with a fellow human being what matters is his perspective and that understanding him requires assuming a perspective as similar to his as possible.[4] Of course, our ability to do this, even with members of our own species, let alone with those of another, varies greatly, according to our own individual imaginative capacities (partly given, partly learned) and the degree of similarity between us and our subject in terms of physical constitution, conceptual resources, cultural background and personal history. But no abandonment of an objective metaphysics (however that is to be understood) seems forced on us simply by an appreciation of the importance of empathy.

A much more radical project confronts us if we take seriously some of the broader claims Nagel makes about the connections between the essential subjectivity of conscious experience, on the one hand, and the nature of enquiry, knowledge and reality, on the other. Here is what, according to Nagel, would follow if we did 'get consciousness right': We would realize, first, that not all knowledge is objective knowledge (and would consequently reassess the status of science, whose domain is limited to such objective knowledge); second, that there is in fact an inescapable, but ultimately healthy and potentially fruitful, tension between the scientific and whatever non-scientific modes of knowledge and pictures of the world there may be; third, that there is no single *account* possible of the way things are; and, finally, that there is in fact no single way things *are*. It is the case neither that reality is essentially the way it appears in experience and conception nor that it is essentially as it is in itself no matter how it appears.[5]

At different places in Nagel's work, one or other of these two, very different, strands comes to the fore.[6] The first, more modest, one goes more naturally with construing points of view as types, as perspectives characterized in terms of the typical experience of a kind of being – or even if in terms of the experience of a particular individual, that experience thought of as repeatable in another of the same species. Taken either way, nothing essentially non-reproducible is involved – hence even the possibility of cross-species reproduction through imaginative effort is left open. No matter how difficult such reproduction may be, it is not clear that any (type of) fact available from one type of point of view is inherently shut off from creatures whose natural (type of) point of view is different. And this means that something like the transcendence of one's limited point of view, required by the ideal of an objective science aiming at an account of reality independent of particular points of view, is, at least in principle, possible. The other, more radical, strand, by contrast, suggested by Nagel's occasional use of expressions like 'a single point of view', makes what a point of view yields *essentially* unshareable, even with members of one's own species, even with the utmost effort at empathy. This construal would yield a notion of radical subjectivity that could indeed support Nagel's more extreme epistemological and metaphysical claims. Here would indeed be a limitation that none of us could transcend; spectacles, as it were, that none of us could remove. And along with a recognition of such a limitation would have to go the admission that if there are indeed facts that can be seen only through such spectacles – whose very nature, indeed, consists in being so seen – they will forever elude the grasp not only of science, but of all attempts at communicating them to others.

Much of what Nagel says about the irreducibility of consciousness to physical properties is consistent with attributing to him only the weaker of the two lines of thought just distinguished. To say that 'realism about the subjective domain . . . implies a belief in the existence of facts beyond the reach of human concepts' (Nagel, 1974, p. 441) and that facts about the subjective domain 'are facts that do not consist in the truth of propositions expressible in *human* language' (1974, p. 441; emphasis added) suggests that the subjectivity captured by a point of view is species-relative, rather than individual-relative. Furthermore, since it leaves it unclear whether Nagel thinks that the linguistic and conceptual limitations are contingent and possibly temporary, or necessary and inescapable, it does not, as such, rule out the logical possibility even of intra-species objectivity. It also allows us to make some sense of Nagel's own suggestion that we may be able to develop 'an objective phenomenology not dependent on empathy or the imagination . . . whose goal would be to describe, at least in part, the subjective character of experiences in a form comprehensible to beings incapable of having those experiences' (Nagel, 1974, p. 449). This would amount to finding 'new theoretical forms' that would enable us to describe *in our language* similarities between our experience and those of a different species, even to the extent of, in so doing, capturing the latter's subjective character. The details of this new method are left, to say the least, sketchy; it is said that it might involve objective descriptions of 'structural features of perception', common to its various modes (Nagel, 1974, p. 441).

Whatever one thinks of such speculations, they seem incompatible with the other, stronger, line that surfaces from time to time, one on which the very idea of describing experience (or those features of it that only a *single* point of view can disclose) in *any* language or concepts seems excluded. Indeed, there is perhaps nothing objective to describe: 'experience does not have, in addition to its subjective character, an objective nature' (Nagel, 1974, p. 443).

This line issues naturally from thinking of points of view as tokens. We have seen Nagel insist that 'every subjective phenomenon is essentially connected with a *single* point of view' (Nagel, 1974, p. 437; emphasis added), and the intuition-pump question, 'What is it like to be . . .?' is typically completed by '*that* organism' (e.g. Nagel, 1974, p. 436; emphasis added again), rather than by 'that *kind of* organism'. He also emphasizes that 'the problem is not confined to exotic cases . . . for it exists between one person and another' (if their respective perceptual apparatūs differ; Nagel, 1974, p. 440).

Still, Nagel is often explicit that he wants to base his argument for the inaccessibility to objective theorizing of experience on considerations of point-of-view type (Nagel, 1974, pp. 438, 441), rather than point-of-view token. So, in this chapter, I shall not consider the merits of the individualistic alternative, even though I suspect that a conflation of the two is partly responsible for the intuitive appeal of anti-objectivist claims.[7]

Senses of 'Objectivity'

I have talked, as does Nagel, about science embodying an ideal of objectivity, without thus far attempting to take a closer look at *that* notion to see whether it can be made precise enough to bear the burden of some of the claims made concerning its inapplicability to consciousness. It is time to do so, before we can decide what to make of the argument that the subjectivity of points of view, understood as tied to types or species of cognizer, presents a problem for objective theorizing about the mental in general, and for reductionistic programmes in particular. In this section, I want to distinguish between a number of different ideas that may be involved in the, sometimes somewhat loose, talk of objective facts and theories.[8]

What makes a fact, a description of a fact, or an account of a phenomenon, objective? We may distinguish three different conceptions of what makes a fact an objective fact according to what it is thought to take for the language in which it can be stated to be objective. (We have, I think, no conception of a fact that is not statable in *some* language.) These three conceptions differ in what accessibility relations they require between experience types and languages. The first is that a fact is objective only if it is statable in a language accessible from any experience type. For a language to be accessible from an experience type, in turn, the terms of the language must express concepts that are correlated with the qualitative properties that define the experience type. (I am using 'experience type' here as a label for a set of different particular kinds of experiences, e.g. of a blue flash or a shrill noise, each of which must be considered as itself a type). Just what 'correlated' means here is difficult to spell out in any detail, but the intuitive idea is that for some concept C, that concept is correleated with some quality Q if and only if the semantic content of C is derived from the experience of Q.[9] If there is a language accessible only from a single experience type, in the sense that at least some of the concepts its terms express (that is, the qualitative ones) are derived from only one experience type, then it will follow that no language correlated with some other experience type will be able to state some facts about that experience type. It is this that Nagel's bat example seems intended to illustrate: our lacking a sensory modality possessed by bats presumably deprives us of the concepts necessary for us to state, indeed, to imagine or conceive of, some of the facts that typify the bat's experience. It further follows that for any language thus correlated with an experience type, there may be unstatable, even unthinkable, facts correlated with any other distinct experience type.[10]

A second proposal for spelling out the sense of objectivity involved in these arguments might be the following. For a fact to be objective, it must be statable in a language that is formed by conjoining all the languages accessible from all different experience types. This as it stands cannot, of course, be what Nagel has in mind, since it would make every fact an objective fact. It would mean that any creature capable of having any of the experience types with which one of the conjoined languages is correlated would be capable of understanding and describing any fact about any of those experience types. So, there must be some limitation placed on the languages to be conjoined. What might this be? Presumably something to do with a creature's being stuck in a given location in experiential space, as it were, a location from which such a conjunction of languages could not be understood. We must envisage some incompatibility between experience types, such that a creature who happens to possess one is incapable, even in principle, of possessing (some of) the others and is thus incapable of understanding at least some of the things sayable in a language objective in this sense.

This last line of thought suggests a third possible conception of objectivity: a fact is objective if and only if it is accessible from the maximal set of mutually accessible experience types. This additional restriction would still allow any fact expressible in a language based on concepts derived from any of these mutually accessible experience types to be an objective fact, even if it is a fact about just one of these experience types. Of course, every speaker of such a language would have to meet some general cognitive conditions and would have to share the non-qualitative concepts required for the language to be adequate for an objective, scientific account of anything. But that is only to say that only intelligent beings can theorize. It is not likely that bats can do so about facts concerning our experience; on this account, however, that is not because they cannot *have* our experience but, rather, because they suffer from cognitive shortcomings of a more general kind.

On the other hand, we *can* theorize about their experience, in spite of our not having (one just like) it. Only if we *could not* have it, would we be prevented from doing so. But, as I shall now argue, Nagel could claim that *that* is the case only at the cost of endorsing a physicalistic reduction, the very thing whose possibility he wishes to question.

The central example on which Nagel's argument rests exploits the natural idea that what sensory apparatus a kind of creature has puts strong constraints on what concepts it is capable of having. But it should be clear that this idea is not one of which an anti-reductionist can avail himself. For doing so threatens to commit him to just the kind of nomological physicalistic reduction against which his entire argument is directed. If we can individuate experience types *only* in terms of physiological differences, we have already embraced a kind of physicalism, indeed, one might think, something perilously close to a reduction. To suppose, as Nagel does, that it is obvious that because bats have a different physiology from ours, the same physical input must yield different qualitative states in them, is to suppose that the relevant differences at the experiential level are lawfully correlated with differences at the physiological level. It is not that this is an unreasonable thing to believe; only it is incompatible with a simultaneous deployment of an anti-reductionist argument, an argument insisting on the *absence* of psychophysical laws. If qualia really were nomological danglers, one would not expect a creature's physiology to imply *anything* about its experiences. So, the fact that bats are physiologically different from us cannot be used by the anti-reductionist to establish that their experiences are different. For all *he* knows, bat experience may be just like ours, in spite of the physical differences!

None of this is to claim that it is impossible that there might be creatures with experiences quite unlike ours. Indeed, it is not only possible but highly likely that there are such. But the anti-reductionisit needs to show that the differences are of a sort that make each experience type conceptually inaccessible from the other. For this task, appeals to differences in physiological type are not enough. Further, the anti-reductionist needs to individuate experience types in a way that does not depend on considerations of physiology. It is not at all clear to me that this is possible. Attempts to do so from the inside, as it were, in terms of features identified purely qualitatively, run the risk of begging the question against the objectivist, as well as sliding into the construal of points of view as tokens in the absence of any general characterization of the putative types of experience.[11] And while he may be able to describe one experience type (his own) in this way, what – except by some *via negativa* – can he say about any other? Finally, even if he could describe different experience types, he would still need a way of specifying which are accessible from which. Debarred from an appeal to physiology, what resources would he have left?

Objectivity, Accessibility and Possibility

The next question we need to consider is what kind of modality is involved in the accessibility relation we have considered as a possible key to objectivity. For all three options we have discussed, we can ask whether we are supposed to consider only actual experience types, or also all nomologically possible, or all logically possible, experience types. We then need to ask (a) in which, if any, of the senses of 'objective' spelled out in these different ways are scientific theories supposed to be objective; and (b) in which, if any, of these senses are there facts that are not objective. My suspicion is that Nagel thinks that a scientific theory must aim for objectivity in the sense of describing the world in a language accessible from all possible experience types and that the bat example shows that this aim cannot be fulfilled. The trouble with this (leaving aside the worries noted in the last section) is that, first, it is not clear that science does aim for objectivity in *this* sense and, second, it *is* clear that the most the bat example shows is that there may be facts inaccessible from a language correlated with an actual experience type (ours). On the first score, it is plausible to think that the most objectivity science ever lays claim to is captured by the last proposal understood as limited to using a language accessible from the maximal set of all nomologically mutually accessible experience types. On the second score, it is not obvious that the experience types of bats and humans, respectively, *are* nomologically incompatible. Indeed, if we remember that we are not supposed to appeal to physiological differences in individuating experience types, it is not clear that there is any content left to the notion of nomological incompatibility, leaving only logical incompatibility as a possible barrier to members of different species being speakers of a language objective in the second sense specified above. What grounds, however, might be offered for a claim that two different experience types are logically incompatible so that a creature who happens to possess one *could* not (come to) possess (the concepts correlated with) the other? I cannot imagine.

A straightforward conception of the kind of objectivity involved in science is that scientific theories must be expressed in a language that any *intelligent* being could understand. Such a language would be accessible to any creature with the requisite *conceptual* equipment, whatever its point of view, including its position in sensory space, as it were. Accidental limitations resulting from one's position in sensory space are to be transcended in the same way as accidental limitations in terms of one's position in physical space: by moving. (If you cannot see around the corner, *go* around it, and you will.)

Is it, though, possible that there are positions in sensory space that not every intelligent being could occupy? If so, there *will* be facts of which objective scientific knowledge is not possible. I have not offered any arguments to establish that this is not *in fact* the case, let alone that it *could* not be. But Nagel and his supporters seem to think that they have offered evidence that it *is* the case – and I have been arguing that they have not really done so just by appealing to the intuitions that are, admittedly, readily prompted by examples such as that of the bats. The claim they are making is much stronger than can be sustained on such evidence alone. It requires that we believe that some locations in *sensory* space make it impossible, logically or nomologically, for an individual who occupies them to move to another location, this in turn making it impossible for that individual to occupy certain locations in *conceptual* space. But we have not been given any grounds for thinking that this is so, at least not any that do not suggest the very reductions proponents of these arguments are so concerned to disown.

Imaginability, Analogy and Indirect Description

As noted before, at least part of Nagel's purpose seems to be to remind us of the effort of imagination needed to understand another person, to stress the importance of assuming the other's perspective. Yet he also insists that because of the differences in perceptual apparatus we cannot *imagine* what the experience of bats is like. What kind of, and how serious, a handicap is that in trying to *understand* a creature? Throughout his discussion, Nagel uses the terms 'imagine' and 'conceive' interchangeably (e.g. Nagel, 1974, pp. 439, 442, n. 8). It is because of our limited powers of imagination that we cannot now or ever 'conceive', 'comprehend', 'represent' or 'express' the facts whose knowledge would constitute an understanding of a different species. But this identification of conceiving with imagining seems as unwarranted here as in general. Notoriously, imaginability is a poor criterion of conceivability. Nor can it be predicted how our powers of imagination may change, as they clearly do for many reasons, not least as a *consequence* of additions to our knowledge and understanding. We have already noted that for Nagel the inter-species and the intra-species problems are supposed to differ only in degree (Nagel, 1974, p. 440). But what one finds imaginable with respect to others at least of one's own species is quite variable and malleable (and it is clearly physiologically based only in those special cases where radical sensory deprivation is involved, as with the congenitally blind and the like).

Perhaps there are more severe limitations on our imagination with non-human creatures. Still, even in those cases where imagination really fails, what that may mean is only that we cannot somehow vicariously undergo or duplicate the experiences of the other creature. It need not mean that we cannot arrive at a conception of them and express that conception in a language accessible to creatures who do not have the experiences in question. And the more we learn about the perceptual apparatus and, equally important, the form of life, of the other creature, the more informative such descriptions can be. They can then appeal to whatever analogies there may be between those experiences we have which seem to be correlated with similarities in these respects between ourselves and the other species. If there are none – very unlikely, in fact – our indirect description will, it is true, be a mere schema.[12] But in so far as there is still a *de re* component of our description – the experience described is taken to be experience of the same thing we experience – and in so far as the other species is part of a continuous biological world, it cannot be that the schema will be completely empty. Things may be a bit different with putative aliens of a radically different sort, though even here chemical and at least physical continuities are likely to remain. But, of course, the wilder the science fiction, the less room for analogical content; so with a 'creature' that shares not even basic physical properties with us, the method of indirect description will break down. So what? As we noted in the last section, it is implausible to think that scientific objectivity requires the ability to give a theory of all *logically* possible experience types. Anyhow, it is not at all clear that there is any content to the notion of such a radically different creature, and thus of such a radically different experience, in the first place.

But bats, different as they are, are physically, chemically, biologically and even physiologically continuous with us, so there is something for analogy to get started on. (As noted previously, understanding Nagel's own proposals for an 'objective phenomenology' requires taking such continuities seriously.) Much more, of course, can analogy yield content in the intra-species situation. Here, the perceptual apparatus and form of life of the describer and the described are sufficiently alike in the relevant respects that an indirect description can be highly informative (even if fallible).

So the inability to imagine an experience different from one's own need not stand in the way of describing it, in one intelligible sense of 'describe'. But then we can also construct theories of it. It is not reasonable to demand of a theory that it should do more than *say* what something is. That is what theories are for. They are not for recreating the things they are theories of, or for manufacturing *ersatz* versions of them.

Qualia and the Knowledge Argument

What gives Nagel's thought experiment with bats much of its plausibility is that we are asked to imagine that the *qualities* the bats find in their experience are very different from those in ours (even though it is just as important that we cannot really imagine *what* those qualities are!). It is not clear, as noted before, whether such differences, if they exist, are best thought of in terms of some notion of subjectivity (Biro, 1991a). Be that as it may, there is a temptation to draw anti-objectivist and anti-scientific conclusions simply on the basis of the seeming intractability of the qualitative aspects of experience. These aspects – *qualia*, as they are sometimes called – are supposed to be theory-resistant since, as is often claimed, there are no psychophysical laws to connect them with our fundamental theories. We cannot deduce the qualitative states (if any) of an organism from the facts we may have about its physical states. Also, the familiar arguments from the alleged possibility of absent or inverted qualia are taken to show that no matter how much we might know about the innards of a creature, as long as that knowledge is in terms of physical concepts (and what else could it be in terms of?), it will not yield knowledge of what, if any, qualia the creature has.[13]

I shall discuss one argument along such lines, the so-called 'knowledge argument' – shortly, to see if it can be used to buttress the anti-reductionist's position. But first let me note some other problematic features of these arguments, features they share with the line of thought we have found in Nagel. First, in so far as they are used to support the claim that qualia are not in some metaphysical sense real or objective (recall the metaphysical consequences I reported Nagel as drawing from his argument), they embody the assumption that being so requires law-likeness, indeed, law-likeness of a particular sort (i.e. deducibility from physical laws). This is an assumption we may not feel compelled to make. Second, *token* physicalism asserts only that every mental state (including every qualitative experience), whatever (if anything) it is like to be in it, is identical with some physical state. This can be true even if we cannot get *any* principled way of getting psychophysical pairings, let alone if the problem is only not being able to get them deductively. All that is required is that there be no *more* mental states than there are physical states. For this reason, imagined cases of absent or inverted qualia are not to the present point: the only relevant kind of case would be one where a quale was *present* and yet no candidate physical state existed with which to identify it.[14] But it is very much less clear that such cases are possible than that cases of absent or inverted qualia are. Short of showing – without begging the question – that they are, we cannot rely on the more familiar thought experiments to rule out the possibility that at least token-physicalism is true.

Third, one may see no reason not to be satisfied with what we *can* get, namely, inductive correlations between physical states and mental states. Consider (a) our expectations based on experience that certain physical effects in us will be accompanied by certain sensations and (b) our willingness to extend these to others believed to be similar to us. (Notoriously there is no agreement on how far these extensions should reach – witness the disagreement on the treatment of slaves, once, and animals, now.) One need not see the fact that this is the way in which we come to know what qualia are correlated with what physical states as having any implication for the ontological status of the former. It does not follow that the nature of qualitative states cannot be physical, *even if* the physical states that are thought to be their nature can exist without their existing. For it is no part of the token physicalist's claim that the essence of these physical states themselves is to be, or to be correlated with, mental states.

Friends of qualia will nonetheless argue that when we give a physical description of a person, however exhaustive that description might be, something is left out, something that *should* not be left out. Theories are supposed to give us knowledge of the thing they are theories of, and a complete theory of a person should give us complete knowledge of every fact about him. Since a physical theory that fails to 'capture' qualia does not do that, it cannot be a complete theory of a subject with conscious experience.

An argument of this sort has been put forward by Frank Jackson (1982). He calls it 'the knowledge argument', and its gist is that since it is possible to imagine a person making sensory discriminations where we can make none, such a person must be thought of as *knowing* something we do not, namely, the more finely discriminated qualities his experience offers him. For example, Fred might see two distinct colours where we see only one, so that some tomatoes will look red$_1$ to him, others red$_2$ – and for each such discrimination he makes, he knows what the difference is, while we do not. So, no matter how much we know about such a person's body, behaviour, dispositions and so on (and let us imagine that we know all there is to know), there are things about him and his experience that we do not and cannot know. This means that even an ideally complete physical-cum-behavioural theory of such a person will be necessarily incomplete as a theory of his experience: it will inevitably leave something out.

But this cannot be all there is to Jackson's argument, for this is merely to insist on the familiar point that no psychological propositions follow from purely physical ones: if the vocabulary of our physical theory does not include phenomenal predicates, it follows straightaway that it will not entail any description that does. (On this point, compare Levine in chapter 6.) If there is a point to be made by an appeal to Fred's discriminatory abilities outstripping ours deeper than just this one about disjoint vocabularies preventing cross-theoretic inferences, it is difficult to see how it can be different from that made by Nagel in the arguments already discussed. The point must be that the kind of fact about Fred that is involved in his having certain qualia cannot be accommodated in a scientific account of the world. And that is because a scientific language must be objective in the sense of not including terms that express concepts not accessible from any experience type. But this is no different from the sort of point made by Nagel that we have already discussed.

Jackson, however, is concerned to distinguish his knowledge argument from the 'What is it like to be . . .?' argument. He says, after discussing what we might learn from a physical theory of his imagined superior experiencer, Fred: 'I was not complaining that we weren't finding out what it is like to *be* Fred. I was complaining that there is something *about* his experience, a property of it, of which we were left ignorant' (Jackson, 1982, p. 132).

It is far from clear that this way of separating Jackson's argument from Nagel's can succeed. Grant, for the sake of argument, that there is something we do not know in Fred's case. The question is, what is the best description of our ignorance? First, note that there is a sense in which we know exactly what it is Fred knows that we do not: namely, the difference in colour between two tomatoes we see as uniformly red. What we cannot find out from a physical description of Fred (or of anyone else) is what it is like to *have* such experiences, what it is like to *see* such different colours. But from this it does not follow that we do not know *what* the person who knows what that is like knows. I know what it is that a person who knows Sanskrit knows, though I do not know what it is like to know Sanskrit. And so for all sorts of skills, activities and experiences.

Not knowing what it is like to *have* a certain kind or piece of knowledge or a certain kind of experience is, I suggest, more like not knowing what it is like to be someone who has it than it is like not knowing what it is that someone has. So, contrary to Jackson's claim, what we do not get from a physical description of Fred *is*, after all, more like what it is like to *be* Fred, than anything else. Jackson is right in insisting that there is more to our ignorance than just the inability to have Fred's experience 'from the inside', as it were. That nobody but Fred has *that* ability is true, but uninteresting. It is not Fred's ownership of his experience that is supposed to matter here, but, as Jackson puts it, its 'special quality' (Jackson, 1982, p. 132). But 'knowing' what that special quality is can still come to two very different things. It can mean being able to *say* (or think, in concepts that are in principle shareable) what it is, or it can mean being able to *have* an experience with that same quality.[15]

Still, one could question the legitimacy of separating the ability to describe experience (even in this indirect way, let alone in some more full-blooded sense) and the ability to actually undergo it. Is it not the case that any *description* of experience, no matter how thin, must make use of some concepts derived from that experience, on pain of missing its target altogether? And if experience-based concepts *are* needed, will someone who does not have the experience in question not lack them and fail to have the resources for describing it?

This insistence on the importance of experience-based concepts serves only to bring out again that at bottom Jackson's argument is no different from Nagel's. There it was because we lacked the bat's experience that we were supposed to lack the concepts needed to describe it. It is really no different with Fred: lacking his experience, we are thought to lack concepts adequate for describing it. (One difference is that, in being of the same species, Fred is less plausibly different from us experientially than were Nagel's bats. While it is obviously possible for a person to make finer sensory discriminations in one sensory modality or another than the rest of us – think of painters, musicians, wine-tasters – it is unlikely that these heightened abilities, even when natural, rather than learned, *could* not be had by any of us. Only a typing of experiences so fine-grained that no two individuals could share the same experience type could ensure *that*, but this would take us, again, towards the token interpretation of points of view set aside earlier as unproductive.)

So, whether we take the knowledge argument as involving the ability to describe an experience, or the ability to have it, we do not seem to get anything that helps the anti-physicalist. Understood in the first way, it cannot show that we know less than Fred does about what he is experiencing. As Jackson tells us, Fred is experiencing two different colours, the ones *he* sees when he looks at the tomatoes *we* see as uniformly coloured. A physicalist theory has no difficulty in stating this and in explaining it in terms of Fred's physiology. In fact, it is hard to see what more any theory could be expected to say about any case of perception. No story different in kind can be given concerning *our* seeing of the red we see when we look at the tomatoes Fred sees as having two different colours. The defender of qualia will say here, triumphantly, 'You see! That's just my point: such theories always leave something out.' But that begs the question: conceding that there are qualia in both cases (and that they are different) need not lead us to concede that we do not know (and that our theories cannot say) *what* these are.

Understood as involving the possibility not of describing but of having another's experience, on the other hand, the argument misses its target. True, Fred *has* the quale in question, whereas we do not. He has experiences with certain properties the like of which we do not and, perhaps, given enough physiological differences, could not have. In one sense, we indeed do not know what it is like to have those experiences. We do not know what it is like to *be* Fred because we *are not* Fred, and we do not know what it is like to *have* experiences like Fred's because we are not *like* Fred. I have argued that from this it does not follow that we cannot know what those experiences are, even what they are *like*, as long as this is not taken to be equivalent to knowing what it is like to *have* them. My present point is that while Jackson can distinguish the knowledge argument from one relying on the first of these indisputable facts (the token-subjectivity discussed above), he cannot distinguish it from one trading on the second. And an argument of *that* sort is still essentially a 'What is it like to be . . .?' argument, one vulnerable to the same objection as any other version. That objection, put in summary form is this: if I know *what* X perceives and I know all there is to know about X's perceptual apparatus, I know all there is to know about X's experience, whether X is a member of my species or not.[16] I do not, thereby, *have* that experience, nor do I have one just *like* it. Why should having a theory be expected to enable me to do *that*? Why should it be thought that a theory or a description need or could yield knowledge by acquaintance?

Defenders of the knowledge argument find a certain, intuitively plausible, rhetorical question compelling: if when all the physical facts about a person are known – as their description of cases like Fred's postulates – something still remains unknown, how can that something be a physical fact? My response has been that there is no reason to think that if all the physical facts *were* known, anything *would* remain unknown. To assume that something would begs the question against physicalism.

Theories and Understanding

Lastly, a brief word about the weakest interpretation of Nagel's argument I mentioned at the beginning. We may call this the *Verstehen* version; what is going on according to this interpretation is a kind of education of sensibilities, by way of graphic illustrations, which make us realize that all understanding must be in some sense from the inside, through empathy and imaginative projection. Nagel's real concern is then seen to be not physicalistic reduction and not sense-perception particularly. It is, rather, the need for identification (in some sense) in our attempts to understand the point of view – now in the *broad* sense I distinguished earlier, only to set it aside – of other people and groups socially and culturally different from us. So it is not the metaphysical conclusions Nagel draws that are important but the epistemological ones, and these have to be understood in a rather special way. It is not so much that I cannot know – in a perfectly objective way – what someone else's beliefs, opinions, preferences, even feelings are. In a sense I often *do* know, though it is true that it requires an effort of imagination to '*really* know' what it is like to have these. And perhaps that does mean in some sense replicating the same (*type* of) experience, requiring what looks like, but is not really, knowledge by acquaintance.

I actually think that there is much in this, though one has to be careful about just how one spells it out. But I think Nagel sets us off on the wrong scent in making it look as if the difficulties involved in the *Verstehen* enterprise were rooted in differences in physical and perceptual facts and were identical with the difficulties encountered in seeking a scientific understanding of the latter. The two issues are, as far as I can see, completely independent of each other, and treating them as one does not advance our understanding of either.

Acknowledgement

I have been fortunate to be the recipient of helpful responses to forerunners of this chapter by a number of audiences and colleagues. I am particularly grateful to Ariel Campiran and Raymundo Morado, my commentators at the SOFIA conference on consciousness in 1989, to Richard Hare, Chris Swoyer and, most especially, to Kirk Ludwig.

Notes

1 Nagel (1974). See also Nagel (1979b). Others voicing similar complaints include Jackson (1982), McGinn (1983) and Searle (1990b, 1992). Among those untroubled, sometimes for reasons similar to those to be offered here, are Russow (1982), Maloney (1985), Van Gulick (1985) and Foss (1989).

2 It is interesting to compare Nagel's position with that taken on the question of intentional content in some recent papers of Brian Loar's. For Loar, a recognition of the importance of individual perspective should lead to a view of even the contents of the attitudes as essentially subjective and thus not capturable, as is commonly assumed, in the ordinary idiom of that-clauses; see, for example, Loar (1989). Other champions of intentional explanation, such as Jerry Fodor, also see intentional content (of the genuinely explanatory kind) as inexpressible in ordinary descriptions. See, among other places, Fodor (1987). For criticisms of such a line, see Biro (1991b, 1992). Others argue that the separation of intentionality from consciousness is a mistake, involving as it does the failure to recognize a deep connection between the two kinds of phenomena. For vigorous arguments to this effect, see Searle (1990b). On this issue, see also chapters 6 and 11 in this volume.

3 I shall discuss Jackson's so-called 'knowledge argument' below in the section 'Qualia and the Knowledge Argument'.

4 An interesting discussion of how far this is possible can be found in Vendler (1988). See also Vendler (1984) and Hare's response to the former paper (Hare, 1988). I address the question, with respect to intentional states, more fully in Biro (1991a). As far as Nagel's views are concerned, the passages most suggestive of this weak interpretation occur in Nagel (1974, pp. 441–2). It is easy to slide from such an emphasis on the importance of individual perspective into a radical individualism on which such a perspective is forever inaccessible to others. I explain why this is a mistake with respect to intentional explanation in Biro (1991b, 1992). On the innocuousness of the emphasis on the importance of respecting perspective in interpretation, as long as such a slide is avoided, see also my final section below, 'Theories and Understanding'.

5 For more on these general claims, see Nagel (1979b, 1986).

6 The former, innocuous, line surfaces more in Nagel (1974) the latter, more dramatic, one in (1979b, 1986). Even in the first of these, however, there is vacillation between the two, as we will see in this section.

7 I do discuss it in Biro (1991a). A particularly explicit version of the

individualistic conception of subjectivity can be found in Searle (1992, ch. 4).

8 My discussion here owes a great deal to exchanges with Kirk Ludwig.

9 It is important to note that this conditions may be satisfied without every element of the content of *C* being related to (an element of) *Q* by qualitative resemblance. (For a fuller discussion of this issue, in a somewhat different context, see Biro, 1985, pp. 263–8.) Stipulating that this could not be the case would be both unmotivated and question-begging.

10 Note that the argument requires that a creature lack some substantive experience-based concepts another creature has. Only then will it even be plausible that the former's other concepts, ones that it shares with the latter, might not suffice to capture everything that is *non-trivially* different about the latter's experience. The mere fact that one set of experiences is one creature's and the other the other's is trivial. Mere ownership does not suffice to yield any *content* to the notion of subjectivity, of the sort required for the argument that there is something qualitative in subjective experience that cannot, but should, be captured by objective description. For arguments in support of this claim, see Biro (1991a).

11 For more on this point, see Biro (1991a).

12 Nagel concedes that we can 'form a schematic conception' of the bat's experience. His speculations, noted earlier, about the possibility of devising 'a new theoretical form' to capture these (Nagel, 1974, p. 445) and about 'an objective phenomenology' (p. 449) suggest at least a partial concession to the kind of objectivist account being sketched here.

13 Analogous arguments have, of course, been mounted against functionalist accounts of both qualitative and intentional states. For examples, see Shoemaker (1975), Block (1978) and Searle (1980); for resistance, see Dennett (1988).

14 One can read Descartes' *Meditations* as leaving him unable to escape a generalized version of this possibility.

15 It is instructive to compare Hume's discussion of what it takes to have an idea of a certain property. (For references and discussion, see Biro, 1985). Hume distinguishes between just having an idea, which one can do without a personal encounter with the property, from having a 'just' idea, which, perhaps, one cannot. But he insists that the former is sufficient for communication, just as I am urging that it is sufficient for *description* (and he does so for very similar reasons). Compare also Austin's remarks on the difference between the relative and the interrogative construals of expressions containing 'knowing what' (see Austin, 1946). He reminds us that 'I know what (it is that) he is feeling' formulates a different claim from that formulated by 'I know (= feel) what (= that which) he is feeling.' The former, says Austin, is equivalent to 'I know the answer to the question "What is he feeling?"', and for this I do not have to (be able to) feel what he is feeling. The key to avoiding confusion

here is to resist being trapped by the direct-object parsing into thinking that the sense of knowledge involved here is necessarily that of acquaintance (see also Foss, 1989).

16 I have gone along with putting the argument in terms of knowledge, though I think it would be more helpful to speak of justified belief. Knowledge-talk in this context can easily encourage thoughts of privileged access and incorrigible first-person authority, ideas that can prejudice the issue in favour of the anti-objectivist.

10
Thinking that One Thinks

DAVID M. ROSENTHAL

There are two distinct kinds of thing we describe as being conscious or not conscious, and when we describe the two kinds of thing as being conscious we attribute two distinct properties. The term 'conscious' thus conceals a certain ambiguity.

In one use, we speak of mental states as being conscious or not conscious. Mental states, such as thoughts, desires, emotions, and sensations, are con-, scious if we are aware of them in some intuitively immediate way. But we also apply the term 'conscious' to the creatures that are in those mental states. A creature's being conscious consists, roughly, of its being awake and being mentally responsive. Plainly, this property of being conscious is distinct from the property a mental state may have.

It is the notion of a mental state's being conscious that occasions such difficulty in understanding what consciousness amounts to. It is the consciousness of mental states, as Thomas Nagel (1974) points out, that makes understanding the nature of those states seem difficult, or even impossible. If we bracket or ignore the consciousness of mental states, the problem of how to explain their nature will no longer seem intractable. Our explanation will then proceed simply in terms of the intentional or sensory content mental states have, without reference to their being conscious. Because the notion of consciousness that applies to mental states is the more difficult to explain, it is that notion which I shall be concerned with in what follows.

By contrast, no special problems impede our understanding what it is for a creature to be a conscious creature. A creature's being conscious means that it is awake and mentally responsive. Being awake is presumably an unproblematic biological notion. And being mentally responsive amounts simply to being in some mental states or other. That will occasion no special difficulty unless those states are themselves conscious states, and if they are we can trace the difficulty to the notion of a mental state's being conscious, rather than a creature's being conscious.

It is possible, however, to dispel our sense that special difficulties face any explanation of what it is for mental states to be conscious. The sense that such consciousness is somehow intractable derives at bottom from the tacit, and unnecessary, assumption that all mental states are conscious states. If being a conscious state did coincide with being a mental state, we would then be unable to rely on any prior account of mentality in trying to explain what it is for mental states to be conscious. For if the concept of mind we started from had consciousness already built in, the resulting explanation would be circular, and if it did not, our explanation would rest upon a conception of mentality that, by hypothesis, is defective. There is no third way; we plainly can explain consciousness only in terms of what is mental. So if mental states are all conscious, no informative, non-trivial explanation of such consciousness is possible.

This result perfectly suits Cartesian theorists. If we can give no informative explanation of consciousness, the gulf that intuitively separates mind and consciousness from the rest of reality will seem impossible to bridge. Our explanations will thus be limited to tracing the conceptual connections holding among such terms as 'mind', 'consciousness', 'subjectivity' and 'self'. Cartesians such as Nagel (1974) and Colin McGinn (1991) encourage us to embrace this limitation by evoking that sense we have of ourselves on which consciousness is the most central feature of our existence. If consciousness were the most basic aspect of our nature, why should we expect to be able to explain it in terms of anything more basic?

The sense that consciousness is thus basic is closely tied to the idea that mental states are all conscious states. And if mental states are not all conscious, the foregoing difficulty dissolves. We can then seek first to explain the nature of those mental states which are not conscious, and build on that understanding of non-conscious mental states to arrive at an informative account of what it is for a mental state to be conscious. In particular, if consciousness is not essential to a state's being a mental state, we can reasonably identify a state's being mental with its having either intentional or sensory character. And this account does not presuppose that such states are conscious. A mental state's being conscious, moreover, is our being aware of that state in a suitably immediate way. So we can then go on to argue that a mental state's being conscious is its being accompanied by a roughly simultaneous higher-order thought about that very mental state. On this account, not all mental states are conscious, and we can explain how the conscious ones differ from those which are not. It is this hypothesis which I shall defend here.

On this account, we explain the property of a mental state's being conscious in terms of our being conscious of that state. In general, being conscious of something means having a thought about it or a sensation of it. One may be conscious of a chair, for example, by thinking something about the chair or by having some sensation of it. Sensations will not help with the present concern. Although discussions of consciousness often make metaphorical appeal to so-called inner sense, no such sense actually exists. We may conclude that mental states are conscious by virtue of our having suitable thoughts about them.

It might be supposed that higher-order thoughts can help explain introspective or reflective consciousness, but not the so-called simple consciousness our mental states have in virtually every moment of our waking lives. Indeed, the connection between higher-order thoughts and introspection has sometimes been drawn. Writers such as D. M. Armstrong (1968, pp. 94–107, 323–38; 1980, esp. pp. 59–63), Daniel C. Dennett (1978b, esp. pp. 216–22), David Lewis (1966, p. 21; 1972, p. 258) and Wilfrid Sellars (1963, pp. 188–9, 194–5) have urged that being introspectively aware of a mental state means having a roughly simultaneous thought about that state. And Dennett (1976, esp. pp. 281–6), in a probing discussion of higher-order thoughts, uses that notion to explicate the concept of a person.[1]

If higher-order thoughts could explain only introspective consciousness, that would not do much to dispel the apparent difficulties in the notion of what it is for a mental state to be conscious. Introspective consciousness occurs when we pay deliberate, reflective attention to some mental state. That is relatively rare, and is a lot more elaborate than the non-reflective, phenomenologically immediate awareness we have of mental states in everyday life.

I have argued elsewhere (1986, 1990a), however, that we can in fact explain the ordinary, non-introspective consciousness of mental states in terms of higher-order thoughts.[2] On my account, a mental state is conscious – non-introspectively conscious – just in case one has a roughly contemporaneous thought to the effect that one is in that very mental state. Since not all mental states are conscious, it is open for not all of those higher-order thoughts to be conscious thoughts, though having such a thought will always mean that the lower-order thought it is about is conscious.

An account of introspective consciousness follows naturally. Introspection is the attentive, deliberately focused consciousness of one's mental states. So introspecting a mental state is not just being aware of it, but being actually conscious that one is thus aware. Since a state's being conscious is its being accompanied by a suitable higher-order thought, introspective consciousness occurs when a mental state is accompanied both by such a second-order thought, and also by a yet higher-order thought that one has that second-order thought. A mental state is conscious, but not introspectively conscious, when the higher-order thought it is accompanied by is itself not conscious. Introspective consciousness is the special case in which that second-order thought is also conscious. It is only if we assume that higher-order thoughts themselves must all be conscious that higher-order thoughts will seem useful in explaining introspective consciousness, but not ordinary non-introspective consciousness.

In previous work (1986, 1990a) I have mainly argued that an account of consciousness in terms of higher-order thoughts can save the phenomenological appearances and explain the data of introspection even more successfully than the traditional Cartesian view. Here I develop a wholly different kind of argument – one that more directly and decisively supports an account in terms of higher-order thoughts. The next section sets out the background and premises of this argument, and the section after that puts forth the actual argument. The last three sections, then, defend the argument against various objections.

ARG   for   HI - ORDER   w/C

Expressing and Reporting   Background + premise of arg

Saying something and thinking it are intimately connected (see Sellars, 1964; Vendler, 1972, chs 1–3; Searle, 1983, ch. 1; Rosenthal, 1985). If one says something meaningfully and sincerely, one thereby expresses some thought that one has, and the thought and speech act will have the same propositional content. The speech act and thought will also in cases of sincere speech have the same force; both, that is, will be a matter of affirming, suspecting, wondering, denying, doubting, and the like. We usually speak of people expressing their thoughts; by an innocent metonymy, it is natural to talk also of a person's speech act as itself expressing, or giving expression to, the person's thought.[3]

But it is also possible to communicate what we think in another way, by saying something that does not literally express the thought we have. Instead of expressing our thoughts, we can describe them. If I think that the door is open, for example, I can convey this thought to you simply by saying 'The door is open'; that speech act will express my thought. But I could equally well convey the very same thought by saying, instead, 'I think the door is open'. Similarly, I can communicate my suspicion that the door is open either by expressing my suspicion or by explicitly telling you about it. I express the suspicion simply by saying, for example, that the door may well be open, whereas I would be explicitly telling you that I have that suspicion if I said that I suspect that it is open.

In every case, the speech act that expresses my thought has the same force and the same propositional content as the thought itself. But, if I say that I think the door is open, the propositional content of my speech act is not that the door is open; it is that I think it is open. And if I say I suspect the door is open, my speech act tells of a suspicion. But my speech act then has the force, not of a suspicion, but of an assertion. In saying I suspect something, I report, rather than express, my suspicion.

In general terms, then, I can convey my thought that *p* either just by saying that *p*, or by saying that I think that *p*.[4] These two distinct ways of conveying our thoughts to others are plainly distinct; still, it is easy to conflate them. This is because the conditions in which I could assert that *p* are the same as the conditions in which I could tell you that I think that *p*. Any conditions that warranted my saying that *p* would equally warrant my saying that I think that *p*, and conversely. Things are the same for other speech acts, and the mental states they express, even when their force is not that of asserting something. The conditions for appropriately expressing doubt, suspicion or wonder are the same as those for explicitly reporting that one is in those mental states, at least when such social considerations as tact and discretion are not at issue.[5]

But the truth conditions for saying that p and saying that one thinks that p are, of course, dramatically different. That these truth conditions differ, even though the corresponding performance conditions are the same, is vividly captured by G. E. Moore's observation that the sentence ⌜p, but I don't think that p⌝, though not literally a contradiction, is still plainly absurd.[6] Such a sentence cannot have coherent conditions of assertibility, since the thought I seem to express by saying that p is precisely the thought I deny I have by going on to say that I don't think that p. Parallel remarks hold for speech acts other than assertions; I cannot, for example, coherently say 'Thank you, but I am not grateful.'[7] And, though I can perhaps actually have both thoughts simultaneously, I could not coherently convey both at once. Nor could I think them in, so to speak, the same mental breath. If the truth conditions for reporting thoughts and expressing them were not distinct, Moore's example would be not merely absurd, but an actual contradiction. We can infer to the distinction between expressing and reporting propositional states as the best explanation of why Moore's paradox is not an actual contradiction.[8]

Moore's paradox also helps with an earlier point, that all sincere speech acts express mental states with the same force and propositional content. If reporting and expressing were the same, Moore's paradox would be contradictory. If, on the other hand, I could say that p without thereby expressing the thought I have that p, Moore's paradox would not even be problematic, in whatever way. There would be no difficulty about saying that p and going on to deny that I have any such thought. We can thus infer to the claim that sincere speech acts express corresponding thoughts as the best explanation of Moore's-paradox sentences' being in some way absurd.

In ordinary conversation, however, we typically focus more on conditions of assertibility and other conditions for correct performance than on truth conditions. And as just noted, this may lead us to elide the difference between expressing our mental states and reporting them. This point will be crucial to dealing with certain objections in the last three sections. For now, an example will do. People untrained in logic generally regard literal contradictions as meaningless. It is wrong, however, to suppose, as many do, that this betrays some confusion of meaning with truth. It is simply that, until we are taught otherwise, we tend to rely on conditions of assertibility, rather than conditions of truth. Since a contradictory sentence lacks coherent conditions of assertibility, we can perform no meaningful speech act with it. The sentence itself is false, and so must have semantic meaning. But nobody could mean anything by asserting it.

The distinction between expressing and reporting is pivotal to the argument I want to advance for the theory that a mental state's being conscious consists in its being accompanied by a suitable higher-order thought. So it is important to see whether that distinction applies not only to our thoughts, doubts, suspicions and the like, but to all our conscious mental states.

It turns out that it does. One way to convey one's desires and emotions is to express them (see, for example, Hampshire, 1971). One does this both by the things one says and by one's facial expressions, gestures, choice of words and tones of voice. But one can also communicate these states by explicitly reporting that one is in the state in question. In the case of one's thoughts, the thought and its expression are about the same things, and the two have the same propositional content and the same truth conditions – they are true under the same circumstances. This holds also for emotions and desires; to the extent to which one's desire for food or fear of a tiger are about the food and the tiger, one's expressions of these states will be as well.[9] The same goes for whatever propositional content these states may have. But one's report of being in such a mental state is never about the very thing that the mental state itself is about. Rather, any such report must be about the mental state, and its propositional content is that one is now, oneself, in that very mental state.[10]

Sensations are a special case. Sensations have no propositional content, and are not therefore about things. Still, there is one kind of sensation that we plainly express non-verbally, namely, our bodily sensations such as pain. And these sensations may even be expressible in speech. We use various interjections, for example, to express pains, and perhaps this counts as speech. If so, such an expression of a bodily sensation would not diverge from the sensation expressed in respect of propositional content, since neither the sensation nor its expression has any propositional content. And reports of bodily sensations, such as 'It hurts', are about those sensations, and have propositional content in a way exactly parallel to reports of other mental states. So it is not surprising that the sentence 'Ouch, but nothing hurts' is like a standard Moore's-paradox sentence in being absurd, but not contradictory.[11]

Whereas bodily sensations are plainly expressible non-verbally and possibly verbally as well, neither sort of expressing is possible in the case of perceptual sensations. No speech act or other form of behaviour can express, for example, a sense impression of red. At best, a sense impression may occasion the comment that some observable object is red or, more rarely, that one has a red after-image or hallucination. But such remarks at best report red objects or red sense impressions; they will not express any sensation at all, but rather a thought about a red object or red sense impression. Perhaps it seems that one expresses a perceptual sensation when a startled cry is provoked by one's sensing a sharp or rapidly moving object. But this is hardly a clear case of one's expressing a perceptual sensation, as opposed to expressing, for example, one's feeling of fear. Or it may seem that saying 'Ah' as one savours a wine or settles into one's bath should count as a verbal expression of the relevant perceptual sensations.[12] But it is perhaps more reasonable to regard such borderline cases as expressing a bodily sensation of pleasure that accompanies the perceptual sensations in question.

The problem is that perceptual sensations seldom have any effect on our behaviour except when they are part of our perceiving something. But when one perceives something, one's behaviour, both verbal and non-verbal, expresses the propositional content of the perception, and not its sensory quality. One can always isolate the sensory content for special attention. But even then, what one says and does will express one's thought about the sensory quality, and not the quality itself.

Sense impressions enter our mental lives, therefore, in a kind of truncated way, compared with other sorts of mental states. We express every other kind of mental state in fairly standard ways, sometimes even when we are not conscious of that state. Perhaps it is this odd feature of perceptual sensations that has made some follow Descartes in doubting whether sensations are mental states at all.

But our concern is with the distinction between reporting and expressing. In particular, we want to know whether expressions of mental states invariably have the same content as the states themselves, whereas reports of mental states always diverge in content from the states they are about. And the foregoing considerations show that sense impressions are not counterexamples to this generalization. Even though we speak of perceptual sensations as being 'of' various sorts of perceptible objects (see Sellars, 1963, pp. 154–5), such sensations are not actually about anything. And reports of sense impressions are, again, about those impressions, and their propositional content conforms to the pattern described earlier.

There is a view often associated with Wittgenstein that might be thought to cast doubt on the distinction between expressing and reporting one's mental states. In *Philosophical Investigations* Wittgenstein (1953) seems to have held, roughly, that although one can report that some other person is, for example, in pain, in one's own case one can only express the pain, and not report it as well.[13] If so, sentences like 'I am in pain', which ostensibly report bodily sensations, actually just express them.

But however suggestive this idea may be, it is plainly possible to report explicitly that we are in such states. And it is indisputable that others sometimes assert of us that we are, or are not, in particular mental states, and we sometimes explicitly contradict what they say. It is not just that we undermine what they say, as I might by saying 'ouch' when you say I am not in pain. Rather, we literally deny what others say about us. If we were unable to report on our own states of mind, but could only express them, this direct denial of the ascriptions others make about us would be impossible. If you deny that I am in pain and I simply say 'ouch', we have not thus far contradicted each other.[14]

We may thus conclude that, for creatures with the requisite linguistic capability, reporting mental states is possible, and that such a report differs in content from a verbal expression of that state. Not all types of mental state can be verbally expressed; perceptual sensations, for example, cannot be, and it is not clear what to say about bodily sensations. But creatures with the requisite linguistic ability can verbally express all other types of mental state, and in every case the verbal expression has the same propositional content as the state being expressed, and an illocutionary force corresponding to the state's mental attitude.

The Argument

Distinguishing clearly between expressing one's mental states and reporting them has important consequences for consciousness. Whenever one says something meaningfully and sincerely, one's speech act expresses some thought that one has. Speech acts that do not express one's thoughts either are parrotingly produced, as in something recited by rote, or else are cases of intent to deceive or dissimulate. So, whenever one meaningfully and sincerely reports being in some mental state, one's very report invariably expresses some thought that one has.

Moreover, speech acts that are meaningful and sincere express thoughts that have the same propositional content as the speech acts. So whenever one meaningfully and sincerely reports being in some particular mental state, one thereby expresses one's thought that one is, oneself, in that mental state. Unless one's words expressed that higher-order thought, the ostensible report would fail to be an actual speech act, rather than a piece of parroting behaviour. The ability to report being in particular mental states requires the ability to express higher-order thoughts that one is in those states. Clarity about the distinction between expressing and reporting points towards those very higher-order thoughts needed for the theory of consciousness I am defending.

There is an even more intimate tie, however, between the question of what it is for a mental state to be conscious and the distinction between expressing and reporting mental states. The ability to report being in a mental state of course presupposes moderately sophisticated capacities to communicate. But, given that a creature has suitable communicative ability, it will be able to report being in a particular mental state just in case that state is, intuitively, a conscious mental state. If the state is not a conscious state, it will be unavailable to one as the topic of a sincere report about the current contents of one's mind. And if the mental state is conscious, one will be aware of it and hence able to report that one is in it. The ability to report being in a particular mental state therefore corresponds to what we intuitively think of as that state's being in our stream of consciousness.[15]

But the ability to report being in a particular mental state is the same as the ability to express one's thought that one is in that mental state. So a mental state's being conscious will be the same as one's having the ability to express one's higher-order thought that one is in that mental state. It is unclear how one could have the ability to express some particular thought without actually having that thought. The best explanation of our ability to express the higher-order thought in question is plainly that one actually has that thought.

The converse holds as well. When a mental state is not conscious, we cannot report on it, and thus we cannot express higher-order thoughts about it. The best explanation of our inability to express higher-order thoughts about non-conscious mental states is that when the states are not conscious no such higher-order thought exists. And, if conscious mental states are invariably accompanied by suitable higher-order thoughts, but non-conscious mental states never are, we have every reason to conclude that a mental state's being conscious consists simply in its being accompanied by such a higher-order thought.[16]

If a mental state is conscious, one can both express that state and report that one is in it. But when a mental state is not in one's stream of consciousness, even though one cannot then report being in that state, one can often still express it, at least non-verbally. One's non-verbal behaviour often betrays non-conscious scious mental states, by giving unwitting expression to them. A person may sometimes even explicitly deny being in a particular mental state whose presence is made overwhelmingly obvious by some non-verbal expression of it; we have all had occasion to remark, with the Queen in *Hamlet*, that somebody 'doth protest too much' (III, ii, 240).[17] This kind of occurrence shows that the abilities to express and report one's mental states need not coincide, any more than the mere ability to express a mental state non-verbally implies that that state is conscious.

The kind of consciousness we are focusing on is that special awareness we all have of our own mental states which is intuitively immediate, and seems to require no particular act of attention. Common sense puts few constraints on what positive account we should give of this intuitive immediacy. But part of our sense of immediacy plainly results from the awareness's being independent of both inference and observation, at least as these are ordinarily conceived.[18] And we must exclude both proprioceptive and visceral observation, as well as observation by way of the five exteroceptive senses.

Because our behaviour can express mental states we are unaware of being in, others can learn about such states by observation and inference. So occasionally others can point out to us that we are in some mental state we had not previously noticed – say, that we are irritated or pleased. But the feeling of pleasure or irritation is not a conscious mental state if one's awareness of it relies solely on ordinary observation and inference, as the other person's knowledge does. The feeling would become conscious only if we also came to know, non-observationally and non-inferentially, that the other person's comment is correct. For my mental state to be conscious, my higher-order thought about it must not be based on inference, at least not on any inference of which I am aware.[19]

Typically one's higher-order thoughts are not themselves conscious thoughts. Indeed, our feeling that the consciousness of mental states is somehow immediate is most vivid in just those cases in which the higher-order thought is not conscious. This is because conscious higher-order thoughts normally distract us from the mental states they are about,[20] so that those states no longer occupy centre stage in our stream of consciousness. But when we are unaware of having any higher-order thought, we lack any sense of how we came to know about the conscious mental state. It is this very feeling of mystery about how we come to be aware of conscious mental states which encourages us to regard such consciousness as phenomeno-logically immediate.[21]

Is it necessary for a creature to have something as elaborate as human linguistic ability to be able to report its mental states? It is sometimes urged that we would not regard a creature's signals as making assertions unless those signals were embedded in something like human language. If so, non-human terrestrial animals would be unable to report their mental states.

But the ability to make assertions may well not require such elaborate resources. In particular, the syntactic complexity and semantic composi-tionality that permit the prodigious expressive powers characteristic of human language may not be necessary to performing simpler speech acts. It is far from obvious that a creature must be able to express the seemingly unlimited range of things that humans can to be capable of performing any speech acts at all. One factor that is more important is whether the creature can differentially express distinct mental attitudes. This ability seems more important to the core idea of what is involved in performing a speech act than the range and complexity of thoughts a creature can express. Another factor is whether there is some measure of conventionality about what various signals convey and a suitable degree of deliberate, voluntary choice about when the signal is used.[22]

It will take more, however, to report one's mental states than to be able to perform other sorts of speech acts. Unless a creature's signals exhibited a fairly sophisticated compositional structure, perhaps nothing would justify us in concluding that it was reporting its mental states, rather than just expressing them. Norman Malcolm's well-known distinction between thinking and having thoughts (1977, §II) seems to capture the distinction. Malcolm contends that non-linguistic animals can think, but cannot have thoughts. As he describes the difference, thinking seems to correspond to intentional states one can express but not report, whereas having thoughts corresponds to those one can report as well.[23] So what Malcolm calls thinking will be non-conscious thinking, and the having of thoughts will be conscious thinking.[24]

In any case, even if reporting one's mental states did require a commun-icative system with the full resources of human language, that would not show that creatures that cannot report their mental states have no conscious mental states. Being able to report a mental state means being able to express a higher-order thought about that state. Most creatures presumably have far more thoughts than they can express; the inability to express a thought hardly means that no such thought occurs. So if a creature were unable to express any of its higher-order thoughts, that would not imply that it had none.

The ability to report mental states is important here only because we understand what it is for a mental state to be conscious by appeal to crea-tures who can say what mental states they are in. We fix the extensions of terms for the various types of mental state by way of the conscious cases. We understand what it is for a mental state to be of this type or that by reference to conscious examples of that type of mental state, both our own and those of others. But we often fix the extensions of terms by way of a range of phenomena narrower than those to which the terms apply. So using the conscious cases to fix the extensions of our terms for mental states does not show that all such states are conscious.

Similarly, we fix the reference of the term 'conscious' itself, as it applies to mental states, by the special case of creatures like ourselves that can report being in such states. But this does not show that creatures that cannot make such reports cannot be in conscious mental states. The connection between a state's being conscious and our being able to report that state reflects the fact that conscious states are accompanied by thoughts about those states and we can express those thoughts. In the human case, we may describe the ability to have higher-order thoughts in terms of the language system having access to certain mental states (see, for example, Dennett, 1978b, §§3–4). But what matters to a state's being conscious is the higher-order thought, not the resulting ability to report.[25]

A Dispositional Alternative

On the foregoing argument, conscious mental states are those mental states we are able to report, and any such report must express a higher-order thought about the conscious state in question. It may seem, however, that these considerations do not support the conclusion that higher-order thoughts actually accompany all conscious states. Rather, they may support only the weaker conclusion that a higher-order thought must be able to accompany every conscious state. If so, the foregoing argument would show, instead, that a mental state's being conscious consists only in a disposition to have such a higher-order thought, and not in its actual occurrence.

This conclusion seems to receive support from an independent line of argument. Conscious mental states are mental states we can readily introspect, pretty much at will. So it is reasonable to think of a mental state's being conscious as a matter of our being able to become introspectively aware of it; conscious states are normally[26] introspectible states. Moreover, it is natural to think of being introspectible as a dispositional property. So it may seem but a short step to the conclusion that a mental state's being conscious is, itself, a dispositional property: a disposition to have higher-order thoughts about one's mental states. Similarly, conscious states are those we can report, and it is natural also to think of being reportable as a dispositional property.[27]

These considerations recall Kant's (1781, B131–8; cf. B157–9, A122–3, B406) well-known claim that the representation 'I think' must be able to accompany all other representations. Kant insists that the representation 'I think' be a non-empirical (B132) or transcendental representation (B401, A343); the possibility of its accompanying all other representations is a condition for those representations all being mine, united in one centre of consciousness (B132–5, esp. B134; on mental states' belonging to a subject, see note 21). But this qualification is irrelevant for present purposes, since the reflexive representation Kant has in mind is presumably like other, more mundane thoughts in that a sincere, meaningful speech act could express it.

Kant does not say in so many words that a representation's being conscious is due to its being able to be accompanied by the representation 'I think'. But there is reason to think he holds this. The representation 'I think' must accompany all other representations because we could not otherwise explain what it is for my representations to be mine. And he seems to hold that a mental state's being mine coincides with its being conscious.[28]

Kant's dictum therefore suggests an account of a mental state's being conscious in terms of higher-order thoughts. But Kant does not say that the representation 'I think' actually accompanies all other representations, but only that it must be able to do so. His view is therefore a version of the dispositional account just sketched: A mental state's being conscious is not its being actually accompanied by a suitable higher-order thought, but its being able to be thus accompanied.

This dispositional view, however, does not readily square with our intuitive idea of what it is for a mental state to be conscious. A mental state's being conscious is our being conscious of being in that state in a suitably immediate way. And being conscious of things generally is occurrent, not dispositional. On the present theory, we are conscious of being in mental states when they are conscious states because we have higher-order thoughts about those states. Merely being disposed to have such thoughts would not make us conscious of the states in question; we must have actual, occurrent higher-order thoughts. Having a disposition to have a thought about a chair could not make one conscious of the chair; how could having a disposition to have a higher-order thought about a mental state make one conscious of that state? This conclusion accords well with our common-sense intuitions, on which, whatever being conscious may amount to, it seems to be a clear case of a non-dispositional, occurrent property of mental states.

Moreover, the fact that conscious states are all introspectible and reportable does not show that a state's being conscious is solely a dispositional matter. Being conscious can perfectly well be a non-dispositional, occurrent property of mental states and yet involve dispositions. One and the same property can often be described in both dispositional and occurrent terms. Something's being red plainly involves various dispositions, such as causing bulls to charge. And perhaps something's being flammable or soluble consists in something's having a certain physical make-up, though we pick out those properties by way of a disposition to burn or dissolve. Similarly, a mental state's being conscious is an occurrent property, even though it involves such dispositions as being introspectible and reportable.[29]

Positing occurrent higher-order thoughts as accompanying all conscious states also readily explains why those states are introspectible and reportable. It is my ability to express my thoughts verbally that enables me to report on the mental states my higher-order thoughts are about. And it is because my higher-order thoughts can become conscious that I can come to introspect the mental states those thoughts are about. This second point will figure below toward the end of this section.

On the present theory, a mental state's being conscious is a relational property – the property of being accompanied by a higher-order thought. This accords poorly with common sense, which seems to represent being conscious as non-relational. Why should it matter, then, that common sense represents a mental state's being conscious as occurrent, and not dispositional?

Common-sense considerations are hardly decisive, and may well be overruled by theory. But we should try to do some sort of justice to those intuitions. There are different ways to do this. The present theory preserves the intuition that consciousness is occurrent. And, though it does not preserve the idea that consciousness is non-relational, the theory does explain why that idea is so appealing. Consciousness seems to be non-relational because we are generally unaware of the higher-order thought that makes a mental state conscious, and thus unaware of the relation by virtue of which that consciousness is conferred.

An apparent advantage of the dispositional view stems from the difficulty in accepting the existence of so many higher-order thoughts. At most waking moments we are in a multitude of conscious states; it seems extravagant to posit a distinct higher-order thought for each of those conscious states. When a mental state is conscious, we plainly have the ability to think about it, but it seems equally plain that we do not actually think about all our conscious states. A dispositional account circumvents this difficulty by requiring only that we be disposed to have a higher-order thought about each conscious state, and not that we actually have all those thoughts.

But this line of reasoning rests on a mistake. Thinking about something is not just having a train of thoughts about it, but having a conscious train of thoughts about it. We seldom think, in that way, about any of our conscious states. But the higher-order thoughts the theory posits are typically not conscious thoughts. The intuitive difficulty about how many higher-order thoughts we could have arises only on the assumption that those thoughts must be conscious; higher-order thoughts of which we are unaware will pose no problem. The worry about positing too many higher-order thoughts comes from thinking that these thoughts would fill up our conscious capacity, and then some; we would have no room in consciousness for anything else. But this is a real worry only on the assumption that all thoughts are automatically conscious thoughts.[30]

A mental state's being conscious consists in one's being conscious of being in that state. Being conscious of being in a mental-state type will not do; I must be conscious of being in the relevant token of that type. A dispositional account faces a difficulty here, since it is far from clear how a disposition to have a higher-order thought can refer to one mental-state token rather than another. Perhaps a dispositional account will require not that the disposition refers to a mental-state token, but that it is a disposition to have a higher-order thought that refers to it.[31] Still, if such a disposition is responsible for a mental state's being conscious, the disposition must somehow connect with the right mental state, and it is unclear how that can take place.

This problem becomes especially intractable in the case of sensations. No higher-order thoughts could capture all the subtle variations of sensory quality we consciously experience. So higher-order thoughts must refer to sensory states demonstratively, perhaps as occupying this or that position in the relevant sensory field. It is especially unclear how mere dispositions to have higher-order thoughts could accomplish this.

A headache or other bodily sensation may last an entire day, even though one is only intermittently conscious of it. The point is not merely that one introspects or pays attention to headaches only intermittently; a day-long headache is unlikely to be constantly in one's stream of consciousness in any way at all. And, in general, sensory states need not be conscious states. The distinctive sensory qualities of such states are simply those properties in virtue of which we distinguish among sensations as having distinct sensory content. There is no reason to hold that these differences can obtain only when the sensation is conscious. The distinctive sensory properties of non-conscious sensations resemble and differ in just the ways that those of conscious sensations resemble and differ, differing only in that the one group is conscious, whereas the other is not.[32]

Explaining the intermittent consciousness of such a headache is easy if we appeal to occurrent higher-order thoughts; occurrent thoughts come and go. So one and the same mental state, such as a headache, could persist, sometimes accompanied by a higher-order thought, sometimes not. Mental states would accordingly enter and leave our stream of consciousness. Dispositions seem less well-suited to this task. Because they are more long lasting, dispositions seem intuitively less likely to come and go with the desired frequency, as occurrent higher-order thoughts might.

The argument of the previous section also tells against a dispositional account. A mental state's being conscious is manifested by reports that one is in that state, and to be meaningful these reports must express corresponding thoughts about those mental states. And speech acts plainly do not express mere dispositions to have thoughts.[33]

Conscious states can normally be introspected. And one might argue that even though this does not imply a dispositional account, a dispositional account is necessary to explain why it is so. But that is a mistake. A state is introspectible if it can become an object of introspection. And introspecting a state consists in being aware of that state, and also being conscious that one is thus aware. So introspecting is having a conscious thought about a mental state. On the present theory, a state's being conscious is its being accompanied by a suitable higher-order thought. Those higher-order thoughts are typically not conscious; but once one has such a higher-order thought, it can itself become conscious. And its being conscious results in the mental state it is about being introspectively conscious. Conscious states are introspectible because higher-order thoughts can themselves become conscious thoughts.

If all mental states were conscious states, however, this explanation would be unavailable. There would then be no difference between having a conscious thought about one's mental state and having a thought about it, *tout court*. So one could not explain why a state's being conscious coincides with its being introspectible by saying that the accompanying higher-order thought is not conscious but can become so. Moreover, introspecting would simply be having such a thought, and a mental state would be introspectible just in case one were disposed to have such a thought about it. A state's being non-introspectively conscious could not then consist in having a higher-order thought, on pain of collapsing the distinction between being introspectively and non-introspectively conscious. We would thus have to say that a state's being non-introspectively conscious consists in one's being disposed to have such a thought.

The idea that a state's being a conscious state consists in a disposition to have a suitable higher-order thought does not explicitly presuppose that mental states are always conscious. But the foregoing considerations suggest that this Cartesian picture may underlie much of the appeal a dispositional theory has. Only if we tacitly assume all mental states are conscious will the dispositional account be needed to explain why conscious states are introspectible. But the assumption that all mental states are conscious is plainly question-begging in the context of evaluating the present theory.[34]

Are Higher-order Thoughts Possible?

The objection just considered sought to show that conscious mental states need not be accompanied by occurrent higher-order thoughts. But there are other considerations that seem actually to cast doubt on whether such higher-order thoughts are possible at all. When a conscious mental state is a thought, the mental analogue of performance conditions will be the same for that thought as for the higher-order thought about it. No circumstances exist in which I can appropriately think that *p*, but not appropriately think that I think that *p*. Perhaps, moreover, the right way to individuate mental states is by reference to these mental analogues of performance conditions. If so, the ostensibly higher-order thought would be indistinguishable from the thought it purports to be about; the conditions for having a thought about a thought would be the same as those for just having that thought. The very idea of distinct higher-order thoughts about other thoughts would accordingly be incoherent.

Brentano (1973, p. 127) actually advances just such an argument, applying it even to the case of perceiving.[35] Thus he maintains that my hearing a sound and my thought that I hear it are one and the same mental act. And he goes on to insist that the very content of that perception must be contained in the content of any higher-order thought about it, thus reasoning from performance conditions to mental content. Accordingly, he concludes, every mental state is, in part, about itself; in his words, all mental acts 'apprehend [themselves], albeit indirectly' (1973, p. 128). Every mental state, in addition to having its standard nature, will also function as a higher-order thought about itself.

This idea is not uncommon. Locke seems to express it when he writes that 'thinking consists in being conscious that one thinks' (1700, II, i, 19; cf. Locke, 1700, I, ii, 5; II, i, 10–12; II, x, 2; and IV, vii, 4; on Locke's reflexive model of consciousness see also: 1700, II, xx, 1 and II, xxvii, 9). Some such idea seems also to underlie Descartes' and Hobbes's insistence that it is absurd to suppose that one thought could ever be about another.[36] If higher-order thoughts must be a part or aspect of the mental states they are about, an account of consciousness in terms of distinct higher-order thoughts will be unintelligible.[37]

It is useful to see Brentano's argument as the mental analogue of Wittgenstein's (1953) idea that meaning is use.[38] Understanding how sentences are correctly used is knowing their performance conditions. So focusing on use will suggest typing speech acts by reference to performance conditions, rather than by such semantic features as truth conditions or propositional content. This fits well with Wittgenstein's suggestion, noted at the end of the earlier section entitled 'Expressing and Reporting', that one cannot report, but can only express, one's own pains and other bodily sensations. 'I am in pain' is indistinguishable from 'ouch' in respect of performance conditions; so if one focuses solely on performance conditions, it is natural to type the two together.

This has consequences for how we think about consciousness. 'It hurts' and 'I am in pain' plainly have propositional content; they are about one's pain, and thus express one's thought that one is in pain; that is, they express one's awareness of being in pain. And saying 'ouch' plainly expresses one's pain. So if 'I am in pain' were on a par with 'ouch', it too would express one's pain, as well as expressing one's awareness of being in pain. Accordingly, sentences such as 'I am in pain' and 'It hurts' intuitively seem to yoke together the pain and one's awareness of it, suggesting that the two actually cannot occur separately.[39]

But there is more to a mental state than the mental analogue of its performance conditions. When we individuate mental states, we must also take into account their truth conditions, if any, and their propositional content. Two states are the same only if their semantic properties and performance conditions are the same. Brentano's argument hinges on the idea that it is sufficient for two states to be the same that they have the same mental analogue of performance conditions. That argument cannot therefore be sustained, and there is thus no incoherence in the idea of higher-order thoughts distinct from the thoughts they are about. Indeed, mental attitude is by itself sufficient to undermine Brentano's argument. Suppose the higher-order thought is about a suspicion or doubt; that state will perforce have a mental attitude distinct from any higher-order thought, since higher-order thoughts will invariably have the mental attitude corresponding to an assertion.

There is in any case a somewhat idle air to Brentano's claim that higher-order thoughts are part of the mental states they refer to. How could we ever show, in a non-question-begging way, that a higher-order thought is part of the mental state it is about, rather than that the two are just distinct, concurrent states? It would be more tempting to hold this if all mental states were conscious. If we trace a state's being conscious to the presence of a higher-order thought and every mental state is conscious, there will be a higher-order thought for every mental state. Since no mental state would then occur without its higher-order thought, it might seem inviting to hold that higher-order thought to be part of the state itself. But, if higher-order thoughts are distinct mental states, we can explain why we are generally unaware of them only by saying that such thoughts are usually not conscious thoughts. And this explanation would be unavailable if all mental states were conscious. It begs the question against the present theory to suppose all mental states are conscious, and in any case we have excellent reason to hold that mental states exist that are not conscious states.

There is an even more dramatic way to see how the view suggested by Brentano and Locke goes wrong. If every mental state is conscious and every conscious mental state is, in part, about itself, every mental state without exception will, in part, be about itself. Those who endorse this reflexive model of consciousness presumably find this consequence acceptable. But there is a further implication that has generally not been noted. To say anything meaningfully and sincerely, one's speech act must express some thought that has the same force and the same propositional content. So, if every mental state is, in part, about itself, it will be impossible to say anything at all that is not, in part, literally about one's own mental states.

Locke actually seems to endorse something like this when he claims that the primary use of words is to refer to the ideas in one's mind.[40] Indeed, in advancing this view, Locke seems deliberately to assimilate expressing one's ideas to reporting them. As he puts it, 'the *Words* [a person] speak[s] (with any meaning) . . . *stand for the* Ideas *he has*, and which he would express by them' (1700, III, ii, 3).[41] Words, on this account, are about the very ideas they express.

This assimilation of reporting and expressing recalls Locke's reflexive model of consciousness, though his doctrine about words and ideas derives not from that model but from his views about meaning. Locke's semantic theory thus fits well with his views about consciousness. Because words apply primarily to the speaker's ideas, all speech acts will be about the speaker's mental states. It is interesting to note in this connection that J. R. Ross (1970) has argued, on grammatical grounds, that the deep structure of every declarative sentence is dominated by the pronoun 'I' plus some verb of linguistic performance, as though every such sentence implicitly reported its own illocutionary force and meaning.

But just because particular grammatical or semantic theories fit neatly with the reflexive model of consciousness does not mean that those theories provide any support for that model. The conclusion that the reflexive picture of consciousness forces on us is truly extravagant: Every speech act, to be meaningful and sincere, must literally refer to one of the speaker's own mental states. It is hard to see how any grammatical or semantic theory could render this claim acceptable.

Is Reporting Distinct from Expressing?

Stressing performance conditions over propositional content raises doubts about whether a higher-order thought can really be distinct from the thought it is about. But there is another source for such doubts. We sometimes use verbs of mental attitude in ways that may appear to undercut the sharp distinction between expressing and reporting, on which the argument three sections back (in the section entitled 'The Argument') relied. And if reporting and expressing a mental state are the same, a speech act such as saying 'I think it's raining', will indifferently express both the ostensible higher-order thought that I think it's raining and the thought that it's raining. Those thoughts will then arguably be the same, since an unambiguous speech act presumably expresses a single thought.

The problem is this. I can express my doubt about something by saying, for example, that it may not be so. But, even when I say 'I doubt it' or, more explicitly, ⌜I doubt that p⌝, it seems natural to take me to be expressing my doubt, and not just reporting what mental state I am in. Similarly, if I say that I suppose or choose something, or sympathize with somebody, it is natural again to see this as actually expressing my supposition, choice or sympathy, and not just telling you about the contents of my mind (cf., for example, Alston, 1965, esp. p. 16). A parody will illustrate the point especially vividly. If you ask me whether it is raining and I say 'I think so', it would be bizarre to take me to be talking about my mental state, rather than the weather (see note 13).

This challenge is important. Higher-order thoughts entered our account of consciousness because conscious mental states are those we can report non-inferentially. And those putative reports will not be actual speech acts unless they express thoughts about the conscious mental states in question. But if such ostensibly higher-order remarks are not really second-order reports about our mental states at all, but only express those states, those remarks will not express any higher-order thoughts.

This conclusion would thus vindicate the Cartesian claim that consciousness is intrinsic to mental states. The second-order character of such remarks would be a surface illusion, and would not imply the existence of any distinct second-order thoughts. More important, these ostensibly second-order remarks would presumably also report the very mental states they express. The speech act 'I doubt it' would both express and report one's doubt, so that the doubt itself would have both the content of the doubt and the content that one had that doubt. Every conscious mental state would be, in part, about itself; consciousness would be a reflexive feature of mental states, in Ryle's apt words, a matter of their being 'self-intimating' or 'self-luminous' (1949, p. 159). We would then have no choice but to swallow the strikingly unintuitive consequence noted earlier about sincere speech acts' invariably referring to the speaker's own mental states.

It is worth noting that not all ostensible reports follow the pattern illustrated above. If I say that I gather, deduce, covet or recognize something, it is not all that tempting to hold that I thereby express, rather than report, my mental state. And if I say that I expect, want, understand or suspect something, it is plain that I am then explicitly talking about my mental states, and not merely, as we say, 'speaking my mind' – not just expressing those states.

But even in cases such as saying that I think, doubt, suppose or choose something, the tendency to take my remarks to express, rather than report, my mental states misleads. As already noted, that temptation stems from focusing on the performance conditions of such sentences at the expense of their distinctively semantic characteristics – their truth conditions and propositional content. The sentences 'I doubt it' and 'I think so' may superficially seem to express one's doubts and thoughts, and to be about whatever those doubts and thoughts are about. But this is because the circumstances in which one can appropriately say that something may not be so are the same as those for saying that one doubts it; similarly for saying that something is so and saying that one thinks it is.[42]

Once again, meanings and truths conditions tell a different story. If I am asked whether it is raining and I say I think so, my remark is not semantically equivalent to saying 'Yes, it's raining'.[43] The sentence 'It's raining but I don't think so' is absurd, but not contradictory; the sentence 'I think it's raining but I don't think so', by contrast, is an actual contradiction.[44] Moreover, if you say that I believe, doubt, suppose or choose something, I can deny what you say, and in so doing I would contradict what I would have said if instead I agreed with you. And agreeing with you would naturally take the form of saying that I believe, doubt, suppose or choose that thing.

The distinction between reporting and verbally expressing one's mental states is crucial to the argument of this chapter. Given the failure of the most plausible attempts to undermine that distinction, we may conclude that the argument successfully supports a theory of consciousness in terms of higher-order thoughts.

Acknowledgements

Much of the work on this chapter, resulting in the penultimate draft, was done while I was a fellow at the Center for Interdisciplinary Research (ZiF), University of Bielefeld, Germany, in 1989–90. I am indebted to the Center for generous support and exceptionally congenial and stimulating surroundings. Previous drafts were read at Tufts, Columbia, The University of Wisconsin at Milwaukee, and the August 1989 Joint Conference of the Sociedad Filosófica Ibero-Americana and the Sociedad Argentina de Análisis Filosófico, in Buenos Aires. I am grateful to friends and colleagues in those audiences for helpful reactions, and to Martin Davies for useful comments on the penultimate draft. Special thanks to Daniel Dennett.

Notes

1 D. H. Mellor appeals to higher-order believing to explain not merely our introspective consciousness of beliefs, but the ordinary, non-introspective consciousnes beliefs often have (Mellor, 1977–8, 1980). But he holds that this view, for which he argues forcefully, applies only to the case of conscious believing, and not to other mental states as well.

2 Dennett (1978b) develops a related strategy for avoiding the difficulty about consciousness being an intrinsic feature of mental representations.

3 There are differences. If the expressing is deliberate, it may be more natural to say that the person expresses the mental state; otherwise one may say instead that the person's behaviour expresses that state. On these two ways of speaking, see Alston (1965, esp. pp. 17–8, 23–6). (I use 'thought' throughout as a generic term covering all types of propositional mental states, and 'say' as a generic verb to cover all kinds of speech act, whatever the illocutionary force.)

4 Cf. Dennett's related distinction between reporting and expressing in (1969, esp. §13), though Dennett's concern there is with introspective, rather than simple, consciousness.

5 Strictly speaking, it may be that the performance conditions for saying that one thinks that p are not identical with, but rather include, the performance conditions for saying that p. This refinement is irrelevant in what follows.

6 Moore (1942, p. 543; 1944, p. 204). Moore uses believing, rather than thinking, as his example, but the point is the same. On Moore's paradox (so called by Wittgenstein, 1953, II, x), see Black (1954), Burnyeat (1967–8), and Wittgenstein (1953, II, x).

7 *Pace* Mellor, who claims that Moore's paradox 'has no analogue for the other attitudes' (1984, p. 38). Mellor also restricts his account of consciousness to the case of believing (see note 1 above). As will emerge in the next section, the generalization of Moore's paradox shows that this restriction is unwarranted.

8 It may seem possible to explain this absurdity without appeal to any such distinction. On a Gricean view, my sincerely saying something involves my intending that my hearer believe that I believe what I say. Such a view thus implies that I cannot at once sincerely say that p and say that I do not believe it (see Mellor, 1977–8, pp. 96–7; cf. 1980, p. 148). But Moore's paradox strikes us as absurd independent of any context of communication; it is absurd because it lacks coherent conditions of assertibility. Insincere speech on the Gricean picture involves my intending you to believe that I believe something that in fact I do not (see Mellor, 1980, p. 148). But it is more reasonable to regard insincere speech

acts as in fact a degenerate kind of speech, similar to reciting lines in a play. Like play acting, insincere speech is a kind of pretence; in both cases, one in effect pretends to perform normal speech acts. Thus Austin (1946, pp. 69–71 in 1961 reprinting, pp. 101–3 in 1970 edition) describes a sense of 'promise' and related words in which if I speak insincerely I do not promise. Compare Austin (1962, pp. 48–50, 135–6; pp. 48–50, 136–7 in 1975 edition) in which he urges that an insincere speech act, though it succeeds, is defective (1962, pp. 15–6 and Lecture IV, esp. pp. 39–45 in 1975 edition). Also see Rosenthal (1985), esp. §§2, 3 and 5, and the 1989 postscript. There is also nothing automatically problematic about one's speaking insincerely in ways that betray that insincerity. So one cannot express the absurdity, as Moore once proposed (1942, pp. 542–3), as due to one's betraying one's insincerity if one says something with the form of Moore's paradox.

9   This is plainly true of verbal expressions, and it is plausible for non-verbal expressions as well.

10 It is not sufficient that the report be about somebody who happens to be oneself. Rather, the report must be about oneself, as such; that is, it must be a report that the being that is in the mental state is oneself. See Castaneda (1968), Anscombe (1975), Lewis (1979), Perry (1979), Boër and Lycan (1980) and Chisholm (1981) for discussions of the special sort of reference involved.

11 Care is necessary here. Sentences such as 'It hurts' may at first glance seem to express pains, rather than report them. But since 'Ouch' if anything expresses one's pain rather than reporting it, it is reasonable to explain why 'Ouch, but nothing hurts' is not contradictory by taking 'It hurts' as reporting one's pain, and not expressing it.

12 This was suggested by Daniel Dennett.

13 Wittgenstein (1953, I, §§244, 256, 310, 377); cf. Malcolm (1963a, pp. 138–40; 1963b, pp. 105–17). In an illuminating discussion, Rosenberg (1977) argues that it is characteristic of speech acts such as 'I am in pain' that we have no criteria for their being true independent of our criteria for their being performed truthfully, i.e. sincerely. He concludes that such avowals are 'report[s] judged as ... expression[s]' (1977, p. 159). This suggestion goes far in capturing Wittgenstein's idea, while still recognizing the reporting status of the relevant speech acts. Intuitively, it seems out of place to evaluate expressions of feelings with respect to their cognitive credentials and success, as one might evaluate reports. Accordingly, Wittgenstein's view seems to capture whatever sense we have that speech acts such as 'I am in pain' have some special epistemic privilege. Wittgenstein actually seems to extend the expressive theory beyond the case of sensations. See Wittgenstein (1953, II, §x, p. 190): 'the statement "I believe it's going to rain" has a meaning like, that is to say a use like, "It's going to rain".' Sentences that ostensibly report one's own beliefs, like those which ostensibly report one's own sensations, would then really just express those beliefs and sensations.

14   Parallel remarks hold for Wittgenstein's claim about 'I believe it's going to rain'. See also the final section of the present chapter. It may seem that the expressive theory works better with 'I am in pain' and its kindred than with 'I am not in pain'. Perhaps one can contradict such negative remarks, but not the affirmative counterparts. Moreover, 'I am not in pain' must express my thought that I am not in pain, since if I am not in pain, there is nothing else for it to express. But in both cases, whatever inappropriateness exists in my contesting your word about your own mental states disappears if we imagine that I speak first. There is nothing intuitively amiss if I say you are not in pain and you insist you are, or I say you are and you deny that. Moreover, you would then be contradicting what you would say if, instead, you agreed with me that you are not in pain. Even if the expressive theory applies only to affirmative sentences, it cannot accommodate these facts. Although 'I am in pain' and $\ulcorner$I think that $p\urcorner$ express thoughts about my pain and my thought that p, they may still have the same force as 'ouch' and 'p', respectively. My saying that I am in pain or that I think that p will then be appropriate when, and only when, I am in pain or think that p. These considerations would explain our sense that these speech acts are somehow privileged, and even capture the kernel of truth in Wittgenstein's stronger claim that we never report, but only express, our bodily sensations.

15   Cf. Dennett (1969, ch. 6; 1978b, esp. §§3–4). Robert Van Gulick has urged that we detach self-consciousness from the ability to report (1988a, p. 160). But Van Gulick identifies self-consciousness in terms of the subpersonal possession of 'reflexive meta-psychological information' (1988a, p. 160ff.); self-consciousness occurs whenever a mental state has informational content that involves some other mental state. This notion covers far more than the intuitive notion of a conscious mental state, which is under present consideration. So even if Van Gulick's defined notion is independent of any abilities to report, nothing follows about our intuitive notion of a conscious state.

16   In an earlier publication (1986, p. 339) I assumed that a mental state's being conscious required not only that it be accompanied by such a higher-order thought, but also that it cause that higher-order thought. This causal requirement may seem natural enough; after all, what else would cause that higher-order thought? But the requirement is unmotivated. Being a conscious state requires only that one be conscious of being in that state; the causal antecedents of being thus conscious do not matter to whether the state one is conscious of being in is, intuitively, a conscious state. The causal requirement may seem tempting as a simulation of the essential connection Cartesians see between mental states and their being conscious. But this weaker connection is still problematic. If mental states cause accompanying higher-order thoughts, why do many mental states occur without them? We might posit causal factors that block the causal connection, but that wrongly

makes being conscious the normal condition for mental states. It is more natural to suppose that higher-order thoughts are caused by a coincidence of mental factors, many of which are causally independent of the state in question.

17 Sometimes even one's speech acts will give unwitting expression to mental states one is not conscious of; Freudian slips are the obvious example. But here things are more complicated. When a speech act unwittingly expresses a non-conscious mental state, one is aware of the content of one's speech act. So the content of the speech act is distinct from the content of the non-conscious state it betrays. Indeed, it is probable that, with systematic exceptions, whenever one expresses a thought verbally, that thought will be conscious. (On the explanation of this generalization, and on why it does not threaten the argument of this section, see Rosenthal, 1990b, 1991b.) It is therefore natural to understand these cases on the model of non-verbal expressing. One's speech act reveals one's non-conscious state not by functioning linguistically, but by being a piece of non-verbal behaviour that gives non-verbal expression to that state.

18 Perhaps, as Gilbert Harman (1973) convincingly urges, much of our knowledge derives from non-conscious inference. If so, such non-conscious inference may well underlie the presence of the higher-order thoughts that make mental states conscious. Such non-conscious inferences are not precluded here, since they would not interfere with the intuitive immediacy of such consciousness.

19 Dennett has remarked (personal communication) that there will be penumbral cases in which one simply cannot tell whether or not one's higher-order thought is based on inference, so understood. This is no problem; in such cases one will plausibly also be unsure whether or not to count one's mental state as a conscious state.

20 As Ryle (1949, p. 165; cf. p. 197) in effect observed, though he talks simply of higher-order mental activities, and omits the qualification that they be conscious. It is important for a theory of consciousness in terms of higher-order thoughts that non-conscious higher-order thoughts do not distract one from the mental states they are about.

21 There is another way in which the consciousness of conscious mental states seems intuitively immediate. In the case of non-conscious mental states, it is arguable that their belonging to a particular subject is no more problematic than the bond between physical objects and their properties. But when a mental state is conscious, it is tempting to insist that there is more to say about how it belongs to a particular subject. The present theory explains what is phenomenologically special about the way in which conscious mental states belong to their subjects. Propositional states, both conscious and non-conscious, intuitively seem bound to their subjects by their mental attitudes; the attitude is a kind of relation joining a thinking subject to its thoughts. And sensory mental states, whether conscious or not, seem similarly tied to their subjects by occurring within a field of experience, which connects these mental states

to others of the same and different sensory modalities. But conscious states seem tied to their subjects in some way above and beyond the bond they have in common with non-conscious states. We can explain this additional tie that such consciousness seems to add as due to the content of the accompanying higher-order thought. That higher-order thought is a thought to the effect that one is, oneself, in the mental state in question. Because such higher-order thoughts are both about oneself and the mental state one is in, they carry with them the sense that the tie between one's mental state and oneself is stronger when the state is conscious than when it is not.

22   When the means of expressing thoughts is not all that systematic, as with all the non-human terrestrial animals we know about, we will want to see more conventionality and deliberateness to be convinced that speech acts are occurring.

23   Malcolm would not put it this way, since his (1977) inclination towards an expressive theory of first-person ascriptions of mental states leads him, in effect, to assimilate reporting and expressing. And this, together with a view of expressive ability modelled on human language, lead him in turn to a rather restrictive view of the mentality of non-human animals (1977, §iii).

24   As noted above (note 17), verbally expressed thoughts are typically conscious. But when a creature lacks the ability to report its mental states, verbally expressing them may well imply nothing about whether the state expressed is conscious. This point is exploited in Rosenthal (1990c).

25   Indeed, Dennett in (1978b, e.g. p. 217) also puts his point in terms of the having of thoughts – what he calls 'thinkings'. These considerations show that, *pace* Van Gulick (1988a, p. 162), the fact that many mental states of non-linguistic creatures are conscious provides no reason to deny the connection between a state's being conscious and the ability for creatures with suitable linguistic endowment to report on that state.

26   I.e. normally for creatures like us that have the capacity for being introspectively conscious of their mental states.

27   I am especially indebted to Daniel Dennett for pressing on me the virtues of some form of a dispositional view, and also for many other helpful reactions to drafts of this paper.

28   Kant explicitly allows that I need not be conscious of my representations as being mine (B132). So, if its being mine is its being non-introspectively conscious, my being aware of it as mine would be my introspecting it.

29   There are additional sources of confusion. Something can plausibly be dispositional from the point of view of common sense and occurrent from the point of view of a scientific treatment, or conversely. Similarly, something can count as an occurrent property from the vantage point of science and common sense but figure dispositionally within a functional or computational description, or again conversely. Moreover, it is sometimes difficult to draw any useful distinction between short-term dispositions and occurrent properties. In claiming that a mental state's

being conscious is its being actually accompanied by a suitable higher-order thought, the present theory is operating with our ordinary folk-psychological categories and concepts. Still, such higher-order thoughts might correspond to something dispositional when we move to scientific theory.

30 One might hold that the distinction between occurrent thoughts and dispositions to have them coincides with the distinction between conscious and non-conscious thoughts. If so, occurrent thoughts could never be non-conscious. The only way, then, to put the present theory would be in terms of dispositions to have higher-order thoughts, since these thoughts are typically non-conscious. (I am grateful to Ernest Sosa for pressing this point.) But it is not easy to see how one might independently substantiate this Cartesian denial of non-conscious occurrent mental states.

31 I am grateful to Martin Davies for this point.

32 For more on sensory quality see Rosenthal (1986, §iii; 1990a, §ii; and 1990b). Norton Nelkin, if I understand him, holds that sensory states, though they can occur non-consciously, always have what he calls phenomenologicality, and thus are invariably felt (Nelkin, 1989b, p. 139). It is unclear in what sense non-conscious states might be felt. Apart from these issues, Nelkin presents a view very similar to that defended here, though he advances different arguments for it.

33 The argument that speech acts express corresponding thoughts relied on Moore's paradox; 'It's raining but I don't think so' lacks coherent performance conditions because one cannot meaningfully say it's raining and not think it is. So one could argue that meaningful speech acts must express dispositions to have the relevant thought, since 'It's raining but I'm not disposed to think so' also lacks coherent performance conditions. But this shows at best that meaningful speech acts express both corresponding thoughts and dispositions to have such thoughts, since whenever the dispositional version of Moore's paradox works, the non-dispositional version will as well. Indeed, the dispositional version works presumably only because the corresponding non-dispositional version does. Since 'I'm not disposed to think so' is stronger than 'I don't think so', if 'It's raining but I don't think so' is problematic 'It's raining but I'm not disposed to think so' must be as well. So the reason meaningful speech acts are accompanied by dispositions to have higher-order thoughts is that they are accompanied by the actual thoughts themselves.

34 Introspecting a mental state means having a conscious higher-order thought, and non-conscious mental states are presumably unaccompanied by higher-order thoughts, whether conscious or not. Moreover, a state's being non-introspectively conscious involves less than its being introspectively conscious, but more than its not being conscious at all. So it may seem that only a disposition to have a higher-order thought could fit in between a conscious higher-order thought and its absence. But the Cartesian assumption that all mental states are conscious again figures

in this reasoning. Such a disposition is the natural intermediate between a conscious higher-order thought and none at all only if we tacitly rule out the possibility of a higher-order thought that is not conscious.

35   As Brentano puts it, we must choose whether to individuate propositional mental states (presentations) in terms of their (propositional) object or the mental act of the presentation. Brentano credits Aristotle with the idea. Aristotle's actual argument (1907, III 2, 425b13–4), which Brentano adapts, is that if the sense by which we see that we see is not sight, then the sense of sight and the other sense would both have colour as their proper object, and distinct senses cannot share the same proper object.

36   For both, see *Third Replies*, Descartes (1964–76, vol. VII, p. 175; 1984–91, vol. II, p. 124); though see also *Seventh Replies* (1964–76, vol. VII, p. 559; 1984–91, vol. II, p. 382).

37   This conclusion echoes a certain interpretation of the thesis that knowing implies knowing one knows. On that interpretation, there is nothing to such second-order knowing above and beyond first-order knowing itself. Here, too, stressing performance conditions over propositional content seems to be at issue: the force of saying or thinking that I know is equivalent to that of saying or thinking that I know that I know, even if their propositional contents differ. Historically, however, this view has generally encouraged claims about the transparency of mind to itself, rather than vice versa. And if knowing can be tacit, the idea that knowing implies knowing one knows is independent of such claims of transparency.

38   Applied, however, to sentence-sized, rather than word-sized, mental units: 'The meaning of a word is its use in the language' (1953, I, §43). See also note 13. Wittgenstein's denial that there is anything to meaning above and beyond use amounts, in effect, to denying that anything other than performance conditions figures in these issues. In that respect, Brentano's argument is less clean, since he allows an independent role for propositional content. Just as Moore's paradox helps show that reporting and expressing are distinct (see p. 201), so it helps show that content is distinct from force, or performance conditions. It seems impossible to explain the difference between 'It's raining but I don't believe it' and 'It's raining and it's not raining' without invoking some distinction between force and content. Rosenberg's idea that our criteria for the truth of avowals are the same as our criteria for the truthfulness of their performance (note 13) also involves a move from semantics to performance conditions.

39   Another consequence of the Wittgensteinian focus on performance conditions, and the consequent idea that ostensible reports actually express one's sensations has to do with J. J. C. Smart's well-known topic-neutral translations of sentences that refer to sensations. According to Smart, the statement 'I have a yellowish-orange afterimage' is roughly equivalent to 'Something is going on in me like what goes on in me when I am visually stimulated by an orange' (Smart, 1959, p. 167). Smart's critics

have rightly stressed that these sentences differ in truth conditions, but perhaps they are, after all, equivalent in respect of performance conditions. Smart sometimes describes the relevant sentences as reports (1959, p. 168; cf. pp. 170–1), but he also concedes finding congenial the ' "expressive" account of sensation statements' often attributed to Wittgenstein (1959, p. 162; see the next paragraph in the text). Seeing these statements as expressions rather than reports of perceptual sensations may explain Smart's persistence in casting his topic-neutral accounts in the first-person singular, a feature of Smart's treatment that other advocates of the topic-neutral approach have not followed, and that critics have not noted. Still, since statements such as 'I have a yellowish-orange afterimage' report, rather than express our sensations, this reconstruction cannot justify Smart's topic-neutral programme.

40 I owe this observation to Margaret Atherton. See Locke (1700, III, ii, 2–3); words all 'apply to' (III, ii, 2), 'are signs of', 'signify', only one's own ideas. Note, however, that Locke's claim is that terms refer to the ideas they express, and is not directly about complete sentences.

41 'Nor can any one apply them . . . immediately to any thing else, but the *Ideas*, that he himself hath' (Locke, 1700, III, ii, 2).

42 Cf. Vendler's argument: 'the utterance *I say that I order you to go home* (if it is acceptable at all) amounts to the same speech-act as the utterance *I order you to go home*. Similarly, to think that *p* and to think that one thinks that *p* (if we can speak of such a thing) are the same thought' (1972, pp. 193–4; see also pp. 50–1). Vendler is plainly relying here on performance conditions and their mental analogues. The same holds for a related matter. If one held that $\ulcorner$I think that $p\urcorner$ expresses, rather than reports my thought that *p*, one might urge that $\ulcorner$I don't think that $p\urcorner$ expresses my thought that it's not the case that *p*. Perhaps this would explain why we use 'I don't think . . .' and its kindred not to deny we think that *p*, but to say we think *p* isn't so. But again, performance conditions explain this more successfully: It is normally appropriate to deny we think that *p* only when we think it isn't so.

43 As Austin points out, 'I think he did it' can be a statement about myself, in contrast to 'I state he did it', which cannot (1962, p. 134; p. 135 in 1975 edition).

44 Similarly, as noted above (p. 202), 'Ouch, but I'm not in pain', unlike 'I'm in pain, but I'm not in pain', is like a standard Moore's-paradox sentence: absurd but not contradictory. See also note 11 and pp. 203, 212.

11

The Connection between Intentionality and Consciousness

NORTON NELKIN

The following claim contains a serious mistake:

> 'Life' is a functional concept, in part because there need be nothing it is like to be alive. There is nothing it is like to be a living tulip or potato. 'Intentionality' (that our thoughts and perceptions are *about* something or other), on the other hand, is not functional exactly because *there is* something it is like to be in an intentional state. An intentional state is essentially a conscious state, and there could be no good functional account of consciousness.

This claim is at least implicit in Searle (1980, 1982, 1983, 1988, 1989, 1990b), in Nagel (1974, 1979a, 1986), and in McGinn (1988, 1989), among others.[1] The comparison between 'life' and 'intentionality' goes back at least to Leibniz (1714), who held that neither concept is functional. One way of attacking this claim is to agree with Leibniz that there is an analogy between life and intentionality and to argue that since, *pace* Leibniz, it turns out that 'life' is functional, we should expect 'intentionality' to be functional as well. However, the focus of this chapter will not be on the issue of whether there is a functionalist account of intentionality or of consciousness, but on the claim that there is an essential link between intentionality and consciousness. I will argue, mostly by presenting actual cases, that there is *no* such essential link.

One view that defenders of the consciousness–intentionality link (I will call the position that defends this link 'C–I') share in common is that consciousness is a unitary, indivisible state. Searle (1990b, p. 635), for instance, says, only somewhat metaphorically, that being conscious or unconscious is a matter of a switch's being on or off. I have argued previously (1987b, 1989a, b) that this view of a unitary, indivisible consciousness is mistaken, that when we talk about 'consciousness' there are really three different sorts of states to which we might be referring: (a) phenomenal states (or phenomenological states),[2] (b) intentional states, and (c) introspective states. We distinguish ourselves from things like rocks or roses in all three ways; and, perhaps because they each play this similar role, we call each of them 'states of consciousness'.

Before accounting for how conflating these states gives rise to C–I, let me say a little more about what I mean by these terms. By a *phenomenal* state, I mean the 'feel' of an experience: feeling hot water just feels different from feeling cool water; experiencing a red after-image just is different from experiencing a green one. Phenomenal states best exemplify Nagel's (1974) slogan about consciousness: to be conscious is for there to be something it is like to be in that state.

By calling a state *intentional*, I mean to capture the notion that many of our mental states are 'about' something or other, i.e. they have content. For instance, if I think that the book is on the table, my thought is *about* a book and a table. There are obviously other uses of the English word 'intentional' for describing mental states, as in having in mind to do a certain action (intending to go to the store), or as in the notion of an action's being purposive ('she snubbed him intentionally'). I am talking about these latter uses only in so far as they are instances of the broader use of 'intentional'.

When I talk about an *introspective* state, I mean only that state by which we are non-inferentially aware that we are in one of the first two sorts of states. For instance, when we are seeing a book, or thinking about one, we are often aware, not only of the book, but also of the fact that we are seeing it, or thinking about it – as opposed to touching it, say. Again, it is important to stress what I do *not* mean by 'introspection'. First, I do not mean to imply that introspection is like a perceptual state. Since there is no 'organ' of introspection, I doubt if introspection works at all like perception. Second, one can be introspectively aware, in the sense I mean, without attending to that of which one is introspectively aware: for instance, in looking at a book, one is aware of seeing it, rather than feeling it, even if one's attention is focused on the book.[3]

This discussion of being aware of *seeing* the book, even when one's attention is focused elsewhere, provides a useful introduction to certain claims that lie behind C–I and that I take to be true. First, that ordinary perceptual experience we are most familiar with involves all three types of consciousness. In an ordinary perceptual state, such as seeing the clock on Big Ben, (a) we experience certain phenomenal states (experiencing Big Ben's clock is just a different sort of experience from visually experiencing our watch – the two experiences just 'look' different); (b) our perceptual state is *about* a clock on a tower; (c) we introspect our *seeing* the clock as opposed, say, to hearing it.

Second, intentional states involve more than low-level representation.[4] Among other things, for a representation to constitute an intentional state, the representation has to be a representation *for* the organism, which is, then, the 'representer'. How this notion of *'for* the organism' is to be parsed is beyond the scope of this chapter. While I would agree with this claim of C–I, I would not agree with the further claim that attempts to account for this 'more than covariance' by adding on to a covariance account, or by giving a functionalist story in addition to the covariance one, will not provide a plausible account of intentionality. Such attempts *may* be mistaken; but, if so, it is not for the reasons given by C–I.[5] I would agree with C–I this far: no very good account of intentionality has thus far been given.

Third, we discover our intentional states by being conscious of them. We might have to infer that others have intentional states, but we do not have to infer that we do. Consciousness just reveals intentional states to us. Without being able to take this first-person stance (Searle, 1988, p. 528), we would have nothing to discuss.

I will not defend these claims in this chapter. The thesis of the chapter is that even if we accept all three points, there is still good reason to think C–I mistaken.

The Diagnosis

As I have said, C–I takes consciousness to be a unitary, indivisible state. My claim is that there are, instead, three different states called 'conscious', and that C–I results from conflating these three states. Searle (1990b, p. 635) says being conscious is like having a switch turned on. Of course, he never very carefully describes what turning on the switch results in, except for claiming it is essential to there being intentional states. But it is difficult to see what turning on a switch would have to do with a state's being a representation, even a representation for the organism. The 'switch' metaphor, I suggest, comes from thinking of phenomenal states as the paradigms of conscious states. But our conviction that we have intentional states, a conviction which is non-inferential, arises, instead, from taking introspection as the paradigm conscious state.[6]

Since I do divide 'consciousness' into three sorts of states, and one of these sorts consists of intentional states, then, of course, in one sense, I agree that all intentional states are conscious states. But it is obviously more than this sense of 'consciousness' that C–I means. C–I wants to tie intentionality essentially to phenomenality (or to phenomenologicality) and to introspection. The clinical cases and thought experiments I present will point to dissociations between intentionality and introspection, and between intentionality and phenomenality. These dissociations will support the view that we mean three different states by the term 'conscious(ness)', that there is no unitary, indivisible, turn-the-switch-on state of the kind dreamed of in the philosophy of C–I, and that intentionality, whatever the correct understanding of it, is not essentially tied to either introspection or phenomenality.

Since Searle's arguments are, perhaps, the best known, I will focus on them, though I will have something to say about one of McGinn's claims below. There are four claims that Searle puts forward which play a significant role in the discussion to follow. First, Searle claims that a feature that essentially characterizes intentionality is possessing an aspectual character (similar to what others have labelled 'referential opacity': all intentional states are from a point of view; 1980, 1983, 1989, 1990b). Second, he takes ordinary, familiar perceptual staes to be intentional states (1983). Third, he claims that intentionality is *essentially* connected to consciousness (1989, 1990b). And, fourth, Searle claims that unconscious states are intentional only because, and in so far as, they could become conscious (1989, 1990b). I will argue that there are empirical reasons to deny that the last two claims are true, especially if we accept the first two. In the next section, the connection between intentionality and introspective consciousness will be considered. Following this, the connection between intentionality and phenomenality will be considered.

Intentionality and Introspection

Introspection alone reveals genuine intentionality. That fact about conscious states underlies Searle's insistence that a first-person stance is required for psychology. In situations where a third-person stance is appropriate, 'mere' neural accounts are adequate to account for subsequent behaviour (1990b, p. 588). By a 'mere' neural account, Searle seems to mean something similar to what I am calling a low-level representation account, one in which, if there are representations involved at all, they are not representations for the representer – at least not in a relevant sense.[7] For instance, according to Searle (1989, 1990b), mere neural states are adequate for accounting for any 'representation' state that is unconscious in principle (i.e. could not, in principle, become conscious), because only third-person stances are possible toward unconscious states (at least, occurrent ones). For instance, Searle believes that blindsight, if it is, in principle, unconscious, must be accounted for as a mere neural state. We could not then posit intentionality as a property of blindsight. Ordinary perceptual behaviour, on the contrary, is fully understandable only when perceivers are understood as taking their 'representations' *as* representations. Searle is not claiming that there are no unconscious intentional states (1990b, p. 632). He claims that there are such states and that they retain their aspectual nature, even when unconscious (1990b, p. 632). What allows for them to be intentional is that they can, in principle, become conscious. They can, in principle, cause the switch to be turned on. If Searle is right, then there would be no compelling reasons to posit intentionality at the in-principle unconscious level. Intentionality and consciousness would go hand-in-hand.

Before we turn to cases, several general remarks need to be made. First, Searle confuses our means of discovering intentionality – introspection – with intentionality itself. That we have to take a first-person stance (introspection) to discover intentionality does not mean that intentionality itself is not understandable in third-person scientific terms.[8] Second, if the aspectual nature of states that are not conscious is retained even when they are not conscious, especially if they can occur without ever having been conscious, then it is difficult to comprehend what the intentionality of such states has to do with whether the switch is on or not, or even with whether intentional states can be causes of turning on such a switch. If Searle believes their aspectual nature is acquired or retained *out of* consciousness, why is that not an *admission* of the independence of intentionality from consciousness (from *both* phenomenality and introspection)? Third, it is not insignificant that when Searle gives examples of unconscious intentional states, he almost always cites *dispositional* states, such as beliefs, and not *occurrent* states, such as blindsight experience. The claim that occurrent unconscious intentional states are potentially conscious is, in many cases, much more tendentious than the claim that dispositional states are. There are reasons to think that Searle's claim that all occurrent, in-principle unconscious states must be mere neural states is empirically false. At least, it is plausible to read intentionality into the relevant cases.

First, in blindsight cases, when a patient denies seeing anything but 'guesses' that there is an X in his or her 'blind' field of view, the patient is not conscious in the sense that the patient can introspect his or her seeing. Yet the patient's correct 'guess' makes good sense if there is intentionality operating at the level of the unintrospected occurrence, with the patient's unintrospected representational state *meaning* an X to the patient, i.e. being taken by the patient, at some level of mental awareness, though not at an introspectible level, *as* a representation. One might claim that there is no aspectual nature involved here; but since the patient 'guesses' the *letter* 'X' (as opposed to the *letter* 'O'), why is there not exactly whatever aspectual nature there is when a normal-sighted person *sees* an 'X'? Since Searle (1983) claims that cases of normal perception are paradigms of intentional states, it is difficult to find a principled difference between these two cases. Most importantly, if this blindsight perception *is* an intentional state, then it is doubtful that there is any interesting sense of 'potential' in which this unconscious state is potentially conscious (i.e. introspectible). There is no evidence that it is the kind of state anyone has ever introspected or, given our neural system, could introspect. There is even reason to believe that blindsight does not involve the cortical pathways of normal vision (Weiskrantz, 1977, 1986). If different pathways really are used, the representational system employed may be of a kind that can never become conscious. If Searle means by 'could' merely that it is logically possible, his claim would be completely uninteresting. He must mean 'could' in some stronger sense. But, in fact, it looks as if it may be *humanly* impossible for blindsight representations to become conscious to human beings. It may be true that someone could have an experience with the same content ('There's an "X" in front of me') in ordinary visual experience. In that sense, the blindsight representation could be conscious. But the blindsight *representation* of that content *cannot* become conscious. Surely, the fact that we can represent the same content in some other way (in ordinary perception or in speech) is no guide as to whether the blindsight representation is or is not itself an intentional state.

Other blindsight responses still more clearly involve intentionality, as they more clearly involve semantic processing, which exemplifies that aspectual nature which Searle (1983) takes to be essential for intentionality. When blindsight patients are shown a semi-circle in their preserved field of view (the one they acknowledge), they say they see a semi-circle. If shown a semi-circle in their blind fields, they say they see nothing. Yet, if shown a circle, half in the preserved field and half in the 'blind' field, they say they see a circle, even though what is presented to each field is the same semi-circle as in the previous case (Weiskrantz, 1986, pp. 133–5). It seems reasonable to believe that seeing a circle in the last case depends, in part, on 'seeing' a semi-circle in the blind field. This conclusion is surely no less reasonable than concluding that seeing the circle depends, in part, on seeing a semi-circle in the 'sighted' field. At least, there seems no difference other than the patient's being introspectively aware of one representation but not of the other.

Yet a further relevant blindsight case has been presented by Anthony Marcel. He and his co-workers claim to have found semantic priming caused by 'blindsight' vision. If shown in the blind field the word 'river', when asked to associate the word 'bank', the subject was much more likely to respond to the association task with a word having to do with water than with a word having to do with money (Weiskrantz, 1986, pp. 139, 149). One would think such semantic priming would be impossible unless some semantic, i.e. intentional, processing occurred in the 'blind' field, beyond the reach of introspective consciousness. Such processing need not be even in principle introspectible.

One could argue that such priming is not really semantic. While based on semantic features, the processing is merely a kind of lexical, associative, merely 'mechanical' process, not characterizable by intentionality. That is, what takes place in semantic priming cases may be no more *semantic* than is the 'spell-check' feature of my word-processing program.[9] However, even if the association is purely lexical, one might argue that the fact that the printed marks are taken as *words* at all already displays that aspectual nature that Searle takes to be defining of intentionality. Further, it is reasonable to think that, given priming in their introspectible visual field, the subjects' subsequent behaviours would be similar. But if introspectible perception is fully intentional – as it is on Searle's account – then, given that there seem no other differences in the two situations, other than the lack of introspectibility in the blindsight case, there seems no good reason to think that blindsight is not characterized by intentionality if ordinary, introspectible perception is. Granted that the response in the semantic priming cases is 'automatic', even associative, that fact is not incompatible with its *also* being an intentional state, and not merely 'mechanical'.

Of course, these are not decisive reasons for understanding the semantic priming cases as instances of in-principle unconscious intentional states. But

– and this is the critical point – the issue of whether these are such instances seems to be wholly a matter of empirical investigation and theory. These cases make clear that there are no *a priori* reasons to think that the connection between intentionality and introspective consciousness is an *essential* one.

It is my view that Searle thinks the connection to be essential because of his belief that what we refer to by the word 'consciousness' is a unitary state that is intentional, introspective, and – most importantly to the essentiality issue – phenomenal. I will examine this belief more closely in the next section. In the meantime, consider some further cases that make doubtful any essential connection between intentionality and introspection.

Consider a case, not of blindsight, but of prosopagnosia. Prosopagnosics, if asked (even in a forced-choice situation), fail to identify familiar or famous faces. Yet some prosopagnosics show other signs of recognition, such as galvanic skin response or other physiological reactions. One interesting way in which they show recognition is by having their responses on certain kinds of tests facilitated or delayed when shown a picture of a face. For instance, if shown names and asked to categorize the people named (as 'writer', 'politician' and so on), prosopagnosics have no trouble. But if, immediately prior to being shown the name, they are shown faces, the results are interesting. If the face shown does not match that of the category for the name, the response to categorizing the name is delayed, even though the patients deny having recognized the face. Their denial seems sincere since if only the faces are presented for categorization, the subjects' responses are at the chance level. Some prosopagnosics fail these indirect tests as well as the forced-choice, direct tests. Young and de Haan (chapter 2) conclude about these cases – quite correctly, based on the evidence – that those prosopagnosics who pass the indirect tests do not suffer from a lack of face recognition, but from a *lack of awareness* of their recognition, i.e. they are not conscious of their own first-order intentional states. As Young and de Haan point out, categorizing as to occupation requires semantic processing, and Searle himself (1980, 1983) makes semantic processing sufficient for intentionality.

Some cases of hemi-neglect are also best interpreted as instances of intentionality without consciousness. Hemi-neglect patients seem not to recognize the left sides of their own bodies. They will only dress themselves on the right side, they run into things on their left side, and so forth. Some of the hemi-neglect patients also have a left-sided hemianopia. That is, by standard tests, like blindsight patients, these hemi-neglect patients are blind in their left field of view. Marshall and Halligan (1988) showed some hemi-neglect–hemianopic patients pictures with line drawings of houses. The drawings were exactly alike except that the left side of one of the houses was drawn as if on fire. When shown the drawings separately, one side of each picture on each side of the midline of their visual field, and asked to say whether the drawings were alike or different, such patients invariably answered that the drawings were alike. Yet, when asked which house they would rather live in, one of the patients almost always pointed to the one that was not *on fire*, though whenever asked to choose, she said the question was silly since the pictures were exactly alike. Surely, to see the house as *on fire* requires that aspectual nature of a state that Searle requires for intentionality.

Cases of hemi-neglect raise their own issues, for it is not absolutely certain whether these patients are not introspectively conscious of their left sides or are introspectively conscious of them but deny them. Since these patients either have or once had left-sided paralysis, one can understand why they might deny the left sides of their bodies. But it is less psychologically plausible to think that they would deny everything to the left side, including everything in their left field of view. It is possible, of course, that that is what they are doing (they *hate* the left side), but such an explanation surely requires more substantiation before we need accept it. Furthermore, the fact that neglect comes about from damage to a fairly circumscribed area of the brain makes the 'denial' explanation less likely: it would be surprising if that area which accounted for the paralysis also 'controlled' their 'hate' of their left side. Finally, in order to undermine Searle's argument, all I need is that my reading of these cases is an epistemologically possible one (based on the empirical evidence we have now). And it is.

Searle might claim that if it were not for the brain damage, the intentional states of the prosopagnosics and of the hemi-neglect patients *could* become conscious, and so, for him also, these states are genuinely intentional, although unconscious. But it remains an *empirical* question whether the representations employed are even of a kind that ever enters introspective awareness. It is more plausible in these cases, than in blindsight (where the optic cortex has been destroyed), to think that these representations *are* similar and could otherwise possibly become conscious. But so what? These are such clear cases of intentional states that exist outside introspective awareness that their very existence emphasizes the *independence* of intentionality and consciousness. That these states might, without brain damage, become conscious seems a wholly extraneous and minor (though interesting) fact about them.

Further evidence of the separation of intentionality and consciousness comes from visual extinction cases (Volpe et al., 1979). Visual extinction patients, unlike the previous patients, are not hemianopic. Extinction patients can recognize and describe any single object shown anywhere in their visual field. But if shown *two* objects, one in each half of the visual field, these patients claim to see only the object in their right field of view. Yet, in forced-choice tests, the patients are nearly perfect in saying whether the pictures are the same or different. Several of the patients again express their opinion that the tests are silly since nothing was shown to their left field of view. It is hard to know why such unconscious seeing is not characterized by intentionality if, as Searle thinks, conscious seeing is.

Let us now consider a case that does not involve brain damage, although it does involve degraded presentation. Marcel (1980) showed normal subjects strings of letters in a series of three. In each case the subjects were asked to say whether the third string was a word or non-word. In the cases where the third string was a word, there were two sorts of strings, congruent and incongruent ones. In each of these types of cases, the middle string was a polysemous word. In the congruent cases, the first and third words were related to the same meaning of the polysemous word (e.g. hand, palm, wrist). In the incongruent cases, the first and third words were each related to the different meanings of the polysemous word (e.g. tree, palm, wrist). When the polysemous word was shown normally, identification of the third string as a word was facilitated in the congruent cases only. But when the polysemous word was shown in a visually degraded (subliminal) manner, identification of the third string as a word was facilitated in both sorts of cases.

This example of the polysemous words supports our belief in unconscious intentionality-characterized processing, since the processing is semantic. As to there being genuinely semantic, and not merely lexical, processing involved, this case seems even stronger than the previous semantic priming case; for it is somewhat difficult to believe that there could be a very strong *automatic* correlation between 'palm' and 'wrist'. If asked to free-associate the word 'palm', even in the context of a body, my intuition is that few, if any, people would come out with the word 'wrist'.

Consider another case from the subliminal perception literature. Dixon (1984) discusses a case where subjects were asked to select either the word 'smug' or the word 'cosy' to complete sentences such as 'She looked . . . in her fur coat.' If primed with the word 'snug' such that the prime was uttered just above the audible limen, subjects invariably chose 'smug' as their sentence completion. But if the prime was uttered subliminally, the subjects chose 'cosy'. Such an experiment has two interesting consequences for our discussion. (1) While the liminal perception resulted in a response to structure, the subliminal one resulted in a response to *semantics*. Since the response to the subliminal presentation involved semantic processing, that presentation looks to have involved that aspectual nature consistent with being an intentional state. (2) Moreover, this case and the previous one of the polysemous words, like the blindsight cases, provide evidence that unconscious processing can be *different* from conscious processing: the different facilitation effects point to differences in processing.

In fact, it is difficult to know what Searle means when he claims that there can be unconscious intentionality only if the state is of a type that could become conscious. If he is talking about occurrent states, then one thing he might mean is that by an act of attention – or perhaps by some deeper method, such as psychoanalysis or the like – one could become conscious of what one was unconscious of. But, empirically, this claim just seems false for many of the relevant cases. Or Searle might mean that the sort of processing that takes place in the unconscious cases is the same as in conscious ones. But the blindsight and polysemous word cases raise reasonable doubts about this claim. And, surely, even if the processing were similar, given the clear existence of intentional states that are in no way in introspective awareness, the moral would be the *independence* of intentionality from consciousness, not the dependence. That these intentional states 'could' become the causes of introspective awareness seems completely extrinsic to their being *intentional* states. As Searle himself says, these states have their aspectual nature whether they are introspected or not. Finally, Searle might be thinking that only beings that have had consciously intentional states can have unconsciously intentional states. Even if this were true – and it is an empirical matter – there would still be no reason to think that intentional states, once existent, could not then have a life of their own, as it were, independent of consciousness. Indeed, the cases cited above are evidence of the independence of intentionality from introspective consciousness.

Finally, consider an everyday case, with normal subjects in normal circumstances, involving what might be called 'creativity'. When working on a problem, we often become bogged down in our thinking. Frustrated, we might just give it up – or at least take a break from it. Some time later, much to our surprise, we are suddenly introspectively aware of a way of dealing with the problem. Moreover, this 'answer' is not random. It has the appearance of being 'thought out'. Indeed, it is hard to understand how the answer could have come about unless it *was* thought out. And this very sophisticated sort of 'thinking out' surely requires intentionality, if conscious, introspectible thinking out does. There must be intentionality at the unconscious (not-introspectible) level. Intentionality itself does involve a kind of awareness, but not necessarily an introspectible awareness. And, once more, whether such reasoning processes as these are at all like introspectibly conscious ones is not at all obvious and is, surely, an empirical issue.

These cases – only a small selection of many that could be cited[10] – provide evidence that there are non-introspected and non-introspectible states that have intentionality, and the intentionality of such cases is quite independent of whether they involve representations that can cause introspective awareness.

Intentionality and Phenomenality

In more ways than one, C–I's commitment to the consciousness of intentionality underlies the claim that intentionality is essentially linked to consciousness. A second route is this. Intentionality involves awareness, and to be aware is to be conscious. But if intentionality is a conscious state, then, as Nagel (1974) made clear, there is something it is like to be in that state. That is, to have intentionality *feels* some way or other, because consciousness feels some way or other. And since to be in an intentional state feels like something, intentionality must be an essentially conscious state.

This argument, however, requires two assumptions, both of which are false: (a) there is only one sort of awareness, one sort of consciousness; and it involves what I have called introspective consciousness; (b) all awareness, all consciousness, *feels* some way or other. If my arguments in the previous section show that intentionality need not be introspectively conscious, then the above argument for the consciousness of intentionality and its assumption that there is only one kind of awareness, one kind of consciousness, must both be mistaken. Moreover, C–I is *also* mistaken about the second claim.

In a series of papers (1986, 1987a, b, 1989a, b, 1990), I have argued that it is a mistake to conflate the cognitive consciousness that makes us persons, the consciousness that is the focus of Searle's original paper (1980), with a phenomenal or phenomenological consciousness. My conclusion (1987b, 1989a, b, 1990) has been that these are *different* states evoking *different* criteria by which we separate ourselves from things like rocks. I have distinguished C2, the consciousness in which we are introspectively aware of our intentional states, from what I have variously called either 'Nagel-consciousness' (1987b) or 'CN' (1989a, b). And I have distinguished the awareness that is our first-order intentional state (C1) from either of these. When it comes to intentional states (C1 states) we are introspectively (C2) aware of, there is nothing it is like to be in either the introspective state or in the state introspected. CN states (phenomenal, or phenomenological, states) are not essential to C1 or C2 states, though CN states may (most) often *accompany* C2 states. Subjectivity and phenomenologicality (or phenomenality) are different states.

Here is a quite condensed version of one of my arguments. One can be in the same introspectible intentional state and have different phenomenal states, and one can have the same phenomenal state, but be in different introspectible intentional states; so introspectible intentional states and phenomenal states cannot be tied in essential ways.[11] Searle, surprisingly, accepts the truth of these facts and the force of this argument, but he then retreats to one of two positions, neither satisfactory.

The first retreat is to say that even though no particular phenomenal state is necessary for any particular kind of introspectible intentional state, some phenomenal state or other is necessary for every token of an introspectible intentional state (Searle, 1983, p. 90). The problem with this reply is that my previous papers give convincing cases of introspectible intentional states with no phenomenal states at all. If one really thinks about it, it is remarkable that anyone could think that intentionality – *meaning* objects – has anything to do with some phenomenal feeling, with some switch being turned on causing feelings to occur.

Perhaps even more surprisingly, Searle recognizes this objection as well, and he retreats to a second position: even if there are no phenomenal states underlying introspectible intentional states and consciousness, there are non-phenomenal but phenomenological states which are necessary. Having the thought-that-*p* just 'feels' some way or other, even if it does not feel some way or other. Such 'feelings', and all accompanying 'light-bulb' or 'switch' metaphors, sound to me like the last resort of a lost cause. A better recourse is to conclude that C2 and CN are two quite different consciousnesses.

Why would anyone think that intentionality must be felt (or 'felt')? I suspect the reason is the following. Through introspection (C2), we discover first-order intentionality (C1).[12] If asked how we know that the first-order intentional state is there, we meet this challenge by saying that there is something palpable about this introspective experience. We can just *feel* intentionality. But this use of 'feel' is similar to when we say 'It's going to rain tomorrow' and someone asks us why we think so. There are occasions where we might answer, 'I don't know. I just *feel* it.' This use of 'feel' does not describe any actual experiential feeling, but merely expresses our ignorance of our means of arriving at our belief. It is in this sense that we 'feel' first-order intentionality. We are aware of it and do not know how.

Undoubtedly, there are often phenomenal feelings that *accompany* our introspections of our intentional states. Aristotle probably felt these feelings in his heart; we, in our heads. The feelings *are not* the intentional states, and are not *required* (at least not conceptually) for such states. Descartes' (1642, pp. 50–1) discussion of our inability to image our distinction between a chiliagon and a 999-sided figure should have set this C–I confusion to rest a long time ago.

Whatever the correct explanation of why we are tempted to use 'feel' in these circumstances, our use is not grounded in any actual experiential feeling. Questions of intentionality and cognitive consciousness can – and should – be separated from questions of qualia or of phenomenology. So the second of C–I's reasons for tying intentionality to consciousness is also misbegotten, once more the result of confusing different concepts of 'consciousness'.

As the arguments of the last two sections have shown, intentionality need not be conscious in either an introspective or a phenomenal sense. C–I's claim that there is an essential link between intentionality and such sorts of consciousness is unjustified. And so is its claim that consciousness is unitary and indivisible. If we identify awareness with a sort of consciousness, then, of course, intentional states are conscious states – but not in a sense of 'consciousness' that will support C–I.

McGinn's Claim

I include McGinn among the defenders of C–I, but there are important differences between his view and those discussed above. For one thing, McGinn believes that there are intentional states that exist independently of consciousness and that their being intentional has nothing to do with their being able to cause consciousness (1988, p. 33). On the other hand, McGinn also believes that conscious states have intentionality in a special way and *that* intentionality is ultimately unanalysable for us and not able to be treated in the way other sorts of intentionality can be treated. This sort of intentionality is essentially linked to consciousness and can be fully understood only by understanding consciousness itself (1988, pp. 33–4). Since McGinn thinks consciousness is not understandable, given our possible conceptual schemes (1988, pp. 25–6; 1989), he thinks conscious intentionality will also never be fully understood.

What is it that McGinn means by 'consciousness'? My belief is that McGinn is thinking of consciousness as a phenomenal (and, perhaps, also phenomenological) state.[13] As I have argued elsewhere (1987b, 1989a, b), the only sense of a consciousness where there is something it is like to be in such a state – and McGinn accepts that description of consciousness – is that of phenomenal states. So the question is: do phenomenal states have a special sort of intentionality about them?

I think the answer is 'yes', but not in any sense that supports C–I. I argued (1989b) that it makes best sense of the clinical and experimental evidence to think that 'being phenomenal' is a property of all image-like representation, and image-like representation *is* different from other sorts of first-order (sentence-like) intentional states. However, there are two further points that keep me from joining the C–I camp, even that more interesting portion which McGinn occupies.

First, I argue that even if all image-like representation is phenomenal, we can separate out the *representational* nature of such states from the *phenomenal* nature. That this separation is both possible and worth while is seen from the fact that there is an alternative to my view, namely, that some image-like representational states are phenomenal and some are not. Although there are good theoretical reasons to reject this view, its possibility sheds some pertinent light on my own. I have shown that if the alternative were the case, then it would be reasonable to believe that the *representational* nature of those states that were phenomenal would be similar to that of those that were not. And so the representational nature even of the phenomenal states could not be *dependent* on their being phenomenal. Once one understands the representational nature of phenomenal states as separable from their phenomenal nature, then the problem of intentionality for those states becomes simply the (very difficult) problem of image-like representation. Kosslyn (1980, 1987), Cooper and Shepard (1984) and others are already giving us insight into the nature of such representation.

Second, I believe it is only because McGinn conflates phenomenal consciousness with introspective consciousness that he fails to see the above escape from his difficulty. But, as I have argued elsewhere (1989a, forthcoming), one can be in a phenomenal state without being introspectively aware that one is in that state. Once one understands the dissociation of phenomenal and introspective consciousnesses, phenomenality becomes less powerful seeming – and less interesting.[14]

Many people (for instance, Boghossian and Velleman, 1991) would argue that colour (hue) is a phenomenal property. I do not think it is (Nelkin, forthcoming); but if it is, then there are experiments that pretty clearly illustrate the dissociation of phenomenal states and introspection (Stoerig, 1987; Stoerig and Cowey, 1989). Blindsight patients have been shown to make colour discriminations based on presentations in their blind field, all the while denying that they see any colours in that field. Moreover, their discriminations are not crudely correlated to wave lengths but, instead, are strongly correlated to the sort of opponent-processing based discriminations made by normal colour observers. Ironically, these blindsight patients do not seem to be colourblind in any interesting theoretical sense.[15] So if colours are phenomenal, then Stoerig and Cowey's subjects are having phenomenal states that are not also introspectively conscious.

Afterword

As the first paragraph of this chapter indicated, a major consequence of tying intentionality, in an essential way, to consciousness was to be that functionalism about intentionality would necessarily be wrong. I am sure that that consequence is one of the features of C–I that attracted an entrenched anti-functionalist like Searle (1980) to it.

Searle, for instance, says that it is only the rarity and unfamiliarity of computers that lead us to think of computers as models of the mind, that once computers become as common as telephones we will see computers for what they are: mere mechanisms (1982, p. 6). But, as Donald Norman shrewdly points out (1986, p. 534), this kind of view involves a mistaken perspective on computers. It is not that we are enticed by the mystery of computers to take them as models of the mind. Computers, *unlike other machines*, were designed and built to work in the way the mind works. *That* is why we take them to resemble minds.

Nevertheless, the computer model should not blind us to the fact that, on reflection, intentionality is an enormously complicated topic. Whether intentionality can be captured by some sort of computer, symbolic or connectionist, remains an open question. But there is more reason to think that a functionalist account of intentionality *is* possible, once we realize that intentionality is independent of both phenomenal and introspective consciousnesses. For that matter, once we understand that there are at least three sorts of consciousness, and what the role of each is, there is nothing to prevent our expecting that a functionalist account of each type of consciousness is itself possible. Perhaps intentionality – and consciousness – will turn out to be like *life* after all.

Acknowledgement

I would like to thank Radu Bogdan, Bruce Brower, Graeme Forbes, Alan Soble, Jim Stone and, most especially, Carolyn Morillo (who read every draft of this chapter). They were individually and collectively responsible for the many redraftings of this chapter. Anthony Marcel made many valuable suggestions. Obviously, his own work also provided many of the cases referred to. Special thanks go to Ed Johnson and Martin Davies, who helped make this final version readable and focused. I would also like to thank the participants of the Tulane Seminar on Current Research (too many to mention individually) for the help they gave me on two earlier versions of this chapter.

Notes

1   'In this article I will argue that any intentional state is either actually or
potentially a conscious intentional state, and for this reason cognitive
science cannot avoid studying consciousness' (Searle, 1989, p. 194).
'A physical explanation of behavioral or functional states does not
explain the mental because it does not explain its subjective features:
what any conscious mental state is like for its possessor' (Nagel, 1979a,
p. 188).
'[I]ntentionality is a property precisely of conscious states, and arguably only of conscious states (at least originally). Moreover, the content
of an experience (say) and its subjective features are, on the face of it,
inseparable from each other' (McGinn, 1988, p. 24).

2   These are not meant to be synonyms exactly. I will bring out their purported differences in a later section ('Intentionality and Phenomenality').

3   For a view of consciousness that resembles what I call 'introspection',
see Rosenthal (1986, and chapter 10, this volume). Rosenthal himself
reserves the term 'introspection' for a use that does involve attention.
His use of 'consciousness' and my use of 'introspection' do have one
important difference: he says that to be conscious is also to be conscious
of a self that has the given experience. I make no such commitment.

4   By a low-level representation, I mean a representation in the sense in
which a reflection of a tree on a water surface is a representation of the
tree. Any case that is one of mere covariance, no matter how sophisticated, I mean to include under this heading. For instance, the grooves of
a record *represent* the music in this low-level sense; and a retinal image
represents an external object in this same sense.

5   Actually, McGinn (1988) is a partial exception here. He believes non-
conscious intentional states can be accounted for by such views, but not
conscious ones. Saying that McGinn distinguishes non-conscious intentional states from conscious ones may make it sound as if he thinks that
intentional states and conscious ones are not essentially linked. But his
division is not quite as clean as might be suggested, for he thinks that
the intentionality of conscious states is inseparable from their consciousness. For this reason, I include McGinn among the defenders of
C–I. And, I believe, his error lies in that same belief in the unitariness of
consciousness that Searle and Nagel adhere to (see the section below
'McGinn's Claim').

6   Searle (1990b, p. 635) claims to deny introspection altogether, but it is
important to see that what he is denying is a quasi-perceptual state. As
noted previously, I am not using 'introspection' as the name of such a
state. I am quite sure that Searle believes that when we have a visual
experience with the content, 'There is a brown dog in front of me', that
we are aware not only of the content but that it is a *visual* (as opposed
to auditory, tactile, etc.) experience we are having.

7 Searle might dislike my talking about 'low-level representations' *as representations* at all, but that disagreement would not be a substantive one.

8 I owe this way of putting this objection to a remark by my colleague, Jim Stone, though he might not recognize it in this form. For a similar objection to Searle, arrived at by different reasoning, see Bilgrami (1989).

9 Anthony Marcel (in conversation) presented this possibility to me. He is also responsible for the objection that led to the cautionary paragraphs on the hemi-neglect case, which is discussed below.

10 For a garden-variety specimen of this sort, see my discussion of the unconscious driving case (1987b). Many of the bibliographical references contain further cases.

11 Wittgenstein (1953) argued similarly.

12 I say 'first-order' because introspection itself involves a second-order intentional act of the mind whereby it is aware of C1 *as* C1.

13 Based on McGinn (1988, 1989), and on a paper he read at Tulane University in the spring of 1988.

14 For a view similar to mine, see Rosenthal (1986).

15 And, relevant to Searle, the normal colour channels seem to be obliterated in these patients: they seem to be using a 'back-up' system.

12
Sensational Sentences

GEORGES REY

I always think that when one feels one's been carrying a theory too far, then's the time to carry it a little further. A little? Good Heavens, man! Are you growing old?

(Max Beerbohm, quoted in Fodor, 1975)

The Language of Thought

The mind–body problem can be characterized as the problem of explaining how possibly any purely material process could give rise to the phenomena of mind. Significant advances have recently been made on this problem: functionalist and, in particular, computational theories provide just such possible accounts of how material processes could give rise to the phenomena of *thought*. However, they have seemed less successful in providing possible accounts of *feeling*. There are Locke's 'ideas of violet and marigold', Hume's 'taste of pineapple', Nagel's 'what it's like to be a bat' and, most recently, Frank Jackson's (1982, pp. 127–36) claims about what any physical–functional account of the mind–brain is bound to leave out, e.g. 'the hurtfulness of pains, the itchiness of itches'. Even many of those who find a 'language of thought' (LOT) hypothesis blindingly obvious as a theory of cognitive processing have been known to balk at it as a theory of qualitative states. In this chapter I do not want to so balk. In the spirit of Beerbohm and Fodor, I want unblinkingly to explore ways in which qualitative experience could be accommodated within the LOT hypothesis; how, to put the matter bluntly, sensations, like thoughts, could also be regarded as just more sentences in the head.[1]

Minimally, the language of thought hypothesis is the hypothesis that there is a formally specifiable language, an LOT, tokens of which are encoded in the nervous systems of intelligent creatures. These sentences have their meanings by virtue of either the role they play in that system, or the historical, co-variational and/or teleological role they play with respect to the external world.[2] Some of these tokens are triggered as a result of sensory transduction of stimuli, and form the input to a central cognitive system, which selects certain sentences from an initially pre-established set, tests their deductive consequences against this input for a 'best fit' and produces as output those sentences that pass that test above threshold. These latter sentences in turn are the input to a decision-making system, in which, on the basis of that input, and the creature's preferences and utility functions, a course of action is determined and caused to be executed.[3]

The above is, arguably, a minimal mind.[4] Human beings obviously have more complex psychologies, involving, for example fears, imagination, detestations, the understanding of a natural language, which this model does not address. The full CRTT (Computational Representational Theory of Thought) is the claim that all such further capacities could be captured essentially by supplementing the above with further specific computational capacities in such a way that any given propositional attitude, Φ, could be defined in terms of some computational operation, Ω_Φ, such that:

(CRTT) x Φ-s that p iff
$\quad$ ($\exists\sigma$) (σ is in x's LOT & $x\Omega_\Phi\sigma$ & (σ for x means [p]))

Thus, *Ann judges that snow is white* is analysed as the claim that Ann stands in a specific computational relation, Ω_{judge} to a sentence in her language of thought that means [snow is white]. Her thinking, hoping, imagining, expecting, desiring, preferring that snow is white might involve her standing in different such relations to that same representation; and her judging that snow is black would involve her standing in the same relation to a sentence that means [snow is black]. It will be useful to treat the computational relation, $x\Omega_\Phi\sigma$, independently of the full attitude, separating the computational (and/or syntactic) from the semantic issues raised by (CRTT)'s last clause, and so I will refer to the computational component of an attitude by prefixing 'comp-' to the ordinary word, thus speaking of 'comp-thinking', 'comp-hoping', 'comp-imagining' etc. In general, comp-ψ-ing is a relation merely between an agent and a sentence in abstraction from its semantic properties.

Three attitudes that will concern us here are those that underlie *judgement*, *preference* and *the disposition to verbal avowal*. We first consider *comp-judging* ('xJσ') as the relation to output from the sensory and belief fixation system and the input to the decision-making system; and *comp-preferring* ('xPσ') as the relation to sentences in the decision system that combine decision-theoretically with judgements in such a way as to determine basic act imperatives. For example, someone who decides to move her right leg might be someone for whom a certain sentence (e.g. 'There's a flower downhill, which I could get if I ran') was the output of her sensory–belief fixation system and the input to her decision system, wherein, as a result of a sentence ('I have that flower') comp-preferred there, a basic act imperative ('Move your right leg now') is produced, which in turn causes the corresponding basic act (the right leg moves). Given such functional characterizations of J and P, we may then define:

> x judges that p iff
> ($\exists\sigma$) (xJσ & σ for x means that [p])
> x prefers that p iff
> ($\exists\sigma$) (xPσ & σ for x means that [p])

Judgement and preference, on this view, correspond roughly to what other philosophers (for example, Alston, 1967; Goldman, 1970) have called 'occurrent' beliefs and preferences.

These states need not be available to the agent verbally or introspectively. Indeed, phenomena of akrasia, self-deception, as well as Nisbett and Wilson's (1977) cases of just plain self-ignorance and confabulation, all point to significant discrepancies between action and avowed thought: people act on preferences of which they are 'unaware', have beliefs that they deny, and often say things that do not express attitudes that otherwise enter into the production of their acts. Stich (1983, p. 231) sees such facts as occasions for thinking that the notion of belief irreparably breaks down. I have argued (Rey, 1988b) that they are better regarded as occasions for distinguishing two sorts of judgement, central (defined above) and 'avowed', such that:

> x avowedly judges that p iff
> ($\exists\sigma$) (xAσ & σ means that [p])

where 'xAσ' is 'x comp-avows σ', which can be regarded as a computational relation to a specific subset of the output of the perceptual, cognitive and decision-theoretic systems that is the input to a system for making assertions and self-reports. To borrow an analogy from Dennett (1978a, pp. 151–2), the avowals of a system stand to its central beliefs roughly as the claims of the White House press officer stand to the thoughts of the president. Avowals correspond to a familiar, weak notion of consciousness: reportability.[5] Distinguishing them from judgements and preferences permits us to separate issues of consciousness from the issues surrounding the role of judgements and preferences in standard cognitive explanations of behaviour.

A language of thought approach is attractive for a wide variety of reasons. Fodor (1975, ch. 2) emphasized the degree to which such a model is presupposed by contemporary hypotheses in cognitive psychology, in particular in theories of decision making, concept learning and perception. Elsewhere, he and others[6] have shown how the model helps capture the structure, systematicity, productivity and multiple roles of the attitudes; the rational, irrational, and purely causal relations among them; and how it permits a systematic treatment of the 'fine-grainedness' of the attitudes, or the phenomenon (revealed by such difficulties as 'the paradox of analysis', 'Mates' problem' and 'Kripke's puzzle')[7] in which apparently co-intentional expressions cannot be substituted *salva veritate*. Although many theories of mental states may be able to account for some of these features individually, (CRTT) arguably offers the best prospect for dealing with all of them in a unified fashion. It is this, what I take to be substantial independent plausibility of (CRTT), that provides my principal reason for attempting to apply it to the otherwise improbable case of sensory experience.

The issue of fine-grainedness bears particular emphasis for purposes of our discussion. As, for example, Kaplan (1978) and Perry (1979) have noted, standard theories of meaning seem to fail to capture all the distinctions between cognitive states that a reasonable psychology will need to draw. Intuitively speaking, there can be different ways of construing 'the same proposition': the proposition that a circle is a locus of co-planar point equidistant points is arguably the same proposition as that a circle is a circle; but obviously an agent could think it by the latter means without thinking it by the former. By supplementing a theory of meaning with (CRTT) we gain a graceful and intuitive means of capturing such further distinctions: for the two clauses of (CRTT) permit us to distinguish the *representations* (e.g. names, predicates, sentences) encoded in the agent's brain from the *concepts* or *propositions* that they might express. Different representations (such as 'circle' and 'locus of co-planar point equidistant points'; or 'London is beautiful' and 'Londres est belle') may play different roles in an agent's brain while still expressing the same concept or proposition (and, if Putnam's (1975b) 'twin earth' intuitions are correct, then two representations may play the same role but express different propositions). Thus, we might speak of a representation's 'role meaning' in contrast to its 'propositional meaning'. (Whether the 'role meaning' of a representation can *in general* be satisfactorily specified is not an issue that must be settled here. I will be considering only a few specific, probably very special cases.)

A particularly important example of the advantage of this way of characterizing the attitudes occurs in the case of 'indexical' thought. As Frege (1965), Casteneda (1968) and Perry (1979) have discussed, ordinarily only I can express the thought that GR is bored by saying, or thinking, 'I am bored'; you can't. You need to use some other sentence, such as 'GR is bored.' Indeed, I could *think* that I'm bored without thinking that GR is, even though the proposition expressed by 'I'm bored' and 'GR is bored' might be the same: in such a case my tokens of 'I am bored' would be tokens of a different representation than are my tokens of 'GR is bored', but they would arguably express the same proposition. How is this possible?

Exploiting the resources of (CRTT), we can suppose that, just as 'I' is a restricted singular term in English, there is presumably a similarly restricted singular term in the LOT. The restrictions govern its specific use: in English the speaker is supposed to use it only to refer to his or herself. In the LOT, the restriction will be something like: to refer only to the receiver of present inputs, the instigator of outputs, and the subject of intervening mental states. These restrictions need not be themselves *thought* by the agent; it is enough that they are causally realized: the effect of receiving sensory input, entering a mental state and deciding upon a course of action, involves comp-judging certain sentences containing this restricted singular term, whose content meaning is (the individual concept for) the actual agent, and whose role meaning is provided by its playing this specific causal role.[8] The following might be a rough characterization of the restrictions on such a 'first-person reflexive term' ('FPRT'):

> α is an FPRT for agent x iff:
>   (I-1)   Whenever an input Φ is received, x comp-judges $\ulcorner\Phi\alpha\urcorner$;
>   (I-2)   Whenever x is in a mental state M, x is disposed to comp-judge a predication $\ulcorner\Psi\alpha\urcorner$ that (ordinarily) gets released only when x is in M;
>   (I-3)   All preference states, and all basic action descriptions in x's decision system that cause action in some decision theoretic way are states and descriptions whose subject is α.[9]

Thus, an agent stimulated by red light might, by (I-1), come to comp-judge (the LOT for) 'I'm having a red sensation now', and by (I-2), 'I think there's now a fire nearby', which, in conjunction with a comp-preferring of 'I am not now near fires' would, by (I-3), cause her to comp-judge 'I should right now move *my* (=I) feet left', which in turn would directly (i.e. without further cognition) cause *her* feet to so move.[10]

Along the lines of (CRTT) above, we might characterize special 'first-person reflexive' thoughts thus:

> (LOT-I) x judges he* is F iff
> $(\exists\alpha)\ (\exists\Phi)\ \{\alpha$ is an FPRT for x & xJ$\ulcorner\Phi\alpha\urcorner$ & $\ulcorner\Phi\alpha\urcorner$ means [Fx]}

which is a special case, then, of making judgements about oneself at all:

> (LOT-II) x judges he is F iff {either x judges he* is F *or*
> $(\exists\alpha)\ (\exists\Phi)\ (\alpha$ denotes x & xJ$\ulcorner\Phi\alpha\urcorner$ & $\ulcorner\Phi\alpha\urcorner$ means [Fx]}

Thus it is that first-person reflexive thoughts exhibit a certain unanalysability and 'privacy': they cannot be analysed into other more 'objective' terms and, barring neurophysiological hook-ups that could cause a FPRT in one brain to play a similar role in another, it cannot happen that

> $(\exists\alpha)\ (FPRT(\alpha)\ \&\ xJ\ulcorner F(\alpha)\urcorner\ \&\ \ulcorner F(\alpha)\urcorner$ means [Fy], & x$\neq$y).

I cannot ordinarily think of Dr Lauben (the LOT for) 'I am wounded', nor he that of me, although of course we can each think of the other 'He is wounded.' It is this capacity of (CRTT) to capture such fine-grained perspectives on a proposition that I think provides the key to understanding the special features of qualitative experience, to an analogous account of which I now turn.

S-Restricted Predications

Let us suppose that, just as (I-1)–(I-3) provide restrictions on the entokenings of a specific singular term, there is another set of what I shall call 'S-restrictions' that constrain the entokenings of certain predicates. To be as ontologically neutral as possible, assume that these predicates standardly enter into 'object-less' predications, $\ulcorner s(\Phi)\urcorner$, read as $\ulcorner$It Φ-s$\urcorner$ on the model of the English 'It rains'.[11] The restrictions might be spelt out thus:

A sensory predication $s(\Phi)$ is S-res(tricted) for x iff it:

S-1: is comp-judged or comp-avowed by x normally *only* as a direct result of the output of sensory modules;

S-2: tokens cause characteristic processing $CP(\Phi)$ in x – e.g. comparisons with already stored Φ-representations, associations, and/ or preferences;

S-3: the functional role relating specific input to $CP(\Phi)$ provides the meaning of the predicate and the type-identity of the state.[12]

Given the general *comp-judging* ('xJσ') and *comp-avowing* ('xAσ') relations defined earlier, we now might define *sensing* as follows:

(S-DF) x *senses* F-ly iff
    $(\exists\Phi)$ (S-Res($\ulcorner s(\Phi)\urcorner$,x) & xJ$\ulcorner s(\Phi)\urcorner$ & xA$\ulcorner s(\Phi)\urcorner$ & CP(Φ) & Φ means [F])

That is: a sensory experience of type F consists of the characteristic processing peculiar to an S-restricted predicate, Φ, that means [F], a processing that is initiated by a comp-judgement and comp-avowal of the form [s(Φ)]. Thus, for example, a red sensory experience would involve comp-judging a restricted predication, 's(R)', as a result of the stimulation of predominantly L-wave sensitive cones, a comp-judgement that, by virtue of the predication's characteristic processing, produces further comp-judgements of 'warm', and 'advancing' predications.[13] It is by virtue of the processing initiated by such stimulation that the judgement has the content [It's looking red]. Similarly, a painful experience would involve a restricted predication occasioned by A- or C-fibre stimulation, as well as, standardly,[14] a preference that such stimulation cease.

(S-1)–(S-3) are the *defining* restrictions on S-predications. It is also worth remarking, however, that typically:[15]

(S-4) The predications are parameterized (i.e. are n-place) in specific ways peculiar to the sensory modality; e.g. the predication occasioned by L-wave stimulation might be something like 's(R(h,l,s,x,y))' involving specification of relative hue, lightness, saturation and position in a two-dimensional grid.[16]

(S-5)   The predications enter into some but not all logical combinations: something can look *red all over, red and blue, red in parts;* but
not *red or blue,* or *if red then blue.*

(S-6)   Comp-judged tokenings of these restricted predications provide
sufficient but *not necessary* evidential conditions for comp-judged
unrestricted observation predications, the LOT translations of such
predications as 'It's looking *red*', predications that, while they
are close to the output of sensory modules, are not subject to
these restrictions.

Clause (S-6) is important at least in the case of human beings who seem
to traffic in both restricted and unrestricted predications: people seem to be
able to conceive what they cannot sense, as well as sense what they cannot
otherwise conceive. An example of the former is the colour-blind; of the
latter, most of us who find experience a good deal richer than we ordinarily
find ourselves able to express.

On the present view, the difference between the colour-sighted and
the clever colour-blind, who detect colour differences by inference from
non-chromatic properties, is in the way their colour thoughts are represented. While they both can think the same proposition, [It's looking
red], one does it on the basis of a *restricted* predication that means [It's
looking red], whereas the other does it, for example, by an inference
from a restricted predication that means [It is reflecting to degree n].
Since hue and comparative reflectivity vary directly in most human environments, such a difference could go unnoticed behaviourally in those
environments.

Or suppose someone were to realize Paul Churchland's (1979, p. 28)
dream of a sound scientific education, and so think to herself (the LOT for)
'It seems to be selectively reflecting electromagnetic waves at 0.63×10^{-6} m'
whenever her retinas were so stimulated. Although this predication, too,
might be taken to mean [It's looking red], the judging of it would not constitute a red experience, since it is not suitably restricted (although someone
could probably get herself to leap to it whenever the restricted one occurred).

This latter possibility does raise, however, the interesting question of the
extent to which 'top-down' processing can sometimes interfere with and
seem to create sensory experiences that do not have their usual proximal
causes. It is well established that the nervous system frequently 'fills in' gaps
in retinal input, creating, for example, a homogenous colour field where
there are in fact demonstrable gaps (such as the optic disk, or 'blind spot'
where the optic nerve meets the retina). What is less well established, but
essential to sorting out the nature of sensations in such cases, is precisely
how such processing occurs. As Fodor (1983, pp. 76–7) points out with
respect to the similar phenomenon of 'phoneme restoration' observed in
word perception (Warren, 1970; Samuel, 1981), *some* 'top-down' processes
may be *internal* to a perceptual module, affecting the output of that module,

while others may be *external*, affecting not the output of the module but rather how that output is reported. Arguably, only the former sorts of processes would strictly affect the sensation itself, being further determinants of the comp-judging of restricted predications; the latter processes would affect only the transition from restricted to unrestricted predications, and so only the way in which the experience is conceived and then reported in unrestricted terms.

There are other ways that 'top-down' processing could affect people's experience. Certain forms of natural language processing seem to facilitate certain processes of thought. A good deal of at least anecdotal evidence suggests that having a natural language vocabulary for sensory experience – for example, for wine-tasting – can 'enrich' that experience. On the present view, this could happen in two ways: natural language processing could somehow directly cause changes in the processing of *restricted* predicates, producing more such predicates in a domain in which there had been fewer. Or, more plausibly, it could occasion more *un*-restricted predications for restricted predications that have been occurring all along but, for lack of the un-restricted ones, went 'unnoticed'. Wine-tasters in this latter way are not really tasting things differently, but are simply becoming, so to say, more sensitive to their own sensitivities.

A related question that is raised but need not be settled by this account is about the nature and extent of 'unconscious sensation' as in purported cases of hemianopia or blindsight in Weiskrantz et al. (1974), and of hypnotic analgesia in Hilgard (1977). Subjects in these experiments seem to be having some sort of *visual* experiences of which they are unaware. The above definition of 'sensing' in (S-DF) requires that the agent both (comp-)judge *and* (comp-)avow the restricted predication. But this allows the possibility of one occurring without the other: blindsight on this view could involve judging without avowing.[17] (Conversely, a limited sort of 'epiphenomenalism' could involve avowing without judging.)[18] I see it as an advantage of the proposed account that it leaves all of these possibilities open.

As I mentioned earlier, mental states divide into 'occurrent' as opposed to merely 'dispositional' states, a distinction that functionalist theories often do not bother to observe. Some of the implausibility of particularly functionalist theories of sensations has to do with conceiving them too dispositionally: a pain, after all, is not merely a disposition to enter certain further states, since pains could persist even when, for some extraneous reason, the actual disposition to cause further mental states were to be interrupted.[19] However, as their assimilation to the 'occurrent' processing state of comp-judging should already make clear, a sensory state on the proposed view is fully activated. Per restriction (S-2), such states involve some 'characteristic processing': they are best viewed not as single states but, along the lines of a proposal I have advanced elsewhere in regard to the emotions (Rey, 1980b, p. 188), as *processes* involving interactions among a variety of cognitive states.[20] A qualitative experience is presumably a process involving the comp-judging of a certain restricted predicate, a comparison of it with certain memories, involving restricted and unrestricted predicates and other associations, and the production in that and other ways of certain other restricted and unrestricted judgements.[21] Thus, red *experiences* are thought to be warmer, more advancing, and lighter than green ones (see Hardin, 1988, p. 129). Just how much of such a process counts as the having of a particular qualitative experience is a matter of empirical investigation.[22] All that is important for our purposes is that the experience not be metaphysically simple. This is, after all, what the dualist claims, and is all, in essence, that the 'materialist' (whatever her ontology) is committed to denying. What is epistemically brute – presented as simple in 'the order of knowing' – need not be metaphysically so – simple in the ultimate scheme of things.

The present proposal treats sensing as a species of propositional attitude and/or the processing of them. Such a treatment does require some account of our ordinary non-attitudinal ways of thinking about it. Much of our thought about sensations invites *reification*: it is *a pain, an itch, a sensation* that we experience. But this is an invitation that recent philosophy, if it has taught us anything, has surely taught us to resist.[23] At any rate, it has taught us this in the case of singular terms. Predicates are more problematic: 'what it's like to see red' can seem to involve knowledge of a real *property* that can only be appreciated 'from inside'. Knowledge of it can seem to be what distinguishes the colour-sighted from the colour-blind. In so far as the present account tries to capture this distinction as a distinction between judged predications, the invitation to qualitative properties can seem particularly natural. But I think it is worth resisting it here as well. Let us assume that it is at least logically possible that prodications might function in a language without there being a property corresponding to the predicate, and that the question of the existence of a property in addition to the predicate is settled by determining whether it is needed for any causal or explanatory work.[24] I submit that in the present case the restricted predicate, and the functional state in which it plays a role, are all we need.

Besides its interest as a *possible* account of qualitative experience, one positive argument for this account as an *actually* true one is that, by assimilating such experience to attitudes, we explain the essential *unity of the mind*, what it is that makes beliefs, desires, memories, hopes, fears *and* sensations all states of *the same sort of entity*. What are sometimes proposed as rival accounts seem to me to lack this unity. For example, biologistic[25] or dualistic accounts that regard qualia as biological or as entirely non-physical properties of a computationally organized brain have trouble explaining how a mind that thinks by computing manages to feel by being in some further *non*-computational relation to such further properties. The further properties seem gratuitous and accidental: unless they were somehow *represented* in that life, how could they be any more a part of a person's mental life than the colour of their brain? But then why should not the representations be enough, whether or not there are the corresponding properties?

The Standard Puzzles

Any such proposal about the nature of sensory experience is obliged to deal with some of the puzzling phenomena that such experiences notoriously seem to display. Sensory experience seems to be peculiarly 'private' to the subject of it, and to exhibit an unanalysability, 'lack of grain' and 'ineffability' that physical phenomena do not otherwise possess. Moreover, it seems to involve special, 'privileged' epistemic relations to these experiences, possibilities of publicly undetectable reversals among them, and a special epistemic state of 'knowing what it's like' to be in them. Aside from the unity it bestows upon the mind, much of the interest of the present account lies in its ability to explain these phenomena. I will deal with each in turn.

The special *privacy* of sensation is a consequence of these same peculiar restrictions, particularly (S-1) and (S-2). On the present theory, it is a deep nomological fact that one person comp-judges a restricted predication only when a sensory module is excited in a specific way. At least normally, no other condition is sufficient. In particular, I cannot comp-judge a restricted predication merely as a consequence of *your* sensory module being excited, nor you as a consequence of mine, although each of us could comp-judge the corresponding *un*-restricted predications under those circumstances. Nor do either of our own comp-judgements give rise to the characteristic processing in the other. I can think 'Things look red to you as they do to me', but not 'It's R-ing to you as it does to me.'[26] Of course, should two people become so computationally integrated that excitations from one of their modules causes entokenings in the other's central system, we *might* have some reason to think that they did in fact have the 'same sensation'. But this is not a possibility that will even be clearly definable for most pairs of brains, any more than for arbitrary pairs of computers.[27]

The 'unanalysability' of sensory experience is explained on this view in quite the same way as it is in the case of 'I' thoughts: just as no normal, unrestricted expression, or complex of expressions, can be substituted for 'I' in my first-person reflexive thoughts without changing the identity of those thoughts, so can no such expression replace the S-restricted predicates. Indeed, it is usually impossible to get someone to have a red experience merely by explaining it to them; as Ned Block (1978, p. 278) echoed Louis Armstrong, 'if you got to ask, you ain't never gonna get to know.'

Similarly, the 'lack of grain' to our sensational experience so often emphasized by, for example, Sellars (1956), may also be explained by the simplicity of the S-restricted predicates. When I have a pink-ice-cubish visual experience, there may not be any 'grain' or 'parts' to the seeming pink expanse, since the predications don't themselves indicate any parts, in the way that they may (in the case of vision) indicate hue, intensity, tone and relative position in a $2\frac{1}{2}$D grid. What you 'see' is simply what your restricted predicates represent, no more, no less.

The 'ineffability' of sensory experience is a consequence of the fact that no expressions in a natural language come close to playing the specific role that S-restricted predicates play in a system's internal language. Specifically, no predicates in a natural language are constrained by any restrictions analogous to (S-1) or (S-2), and it is quite unclear how they possibly could be. The situation here is rather different from that of FPRTs, where a convention in natural language for speaker self-reference can sufficiently mirror constraints (I-1)–(I-3). How might we mirror constraints (S-1)–(S-3) or (S-5)–(S-6)? What would it be like to create predications in a natural language that *as a matter of nomological fact* could be entokened *only* as a result of output from a sensory module, and that nomologically gave rise to a certain characteristic processing? Most of the constraints on tokenings of *natural language* predicates are *conventional* and pretty clearly not *nomologically* tied to any particular kind of situation (one can *token* any natural language expression pretty much at will). Of course, we might construct a system that was organized nomologically in this way. Computers may well afford the possibility of doing so. But then such computers may thereby afford the possibility of a machine having sensations (a possibility I worry about in Rey, 1983, 1988a).

The special privileges of knowing one's own state by and large fall out as features of a restricted predicate's characteristic processing. There are, of course, wide differences in the varieties of privileged access (Alston, 1971), but all of them involve some further, usually second-order cognitive state, or disposition to acquire such a state, being intimately tied to the sensational state itself: for example, if x is in pain then x believes/knows of herself that she is in pain, and/or conversely. Any such state may simply be *included* in the characteristic processing of the restricted predicate associated with the state: the experience of pain may well include the judgement and/or avowal that one is (and perhaps the distinct preference that one no longer be).[28]

Indeed, what has always seemed to me the strongest argument for some kind of functionalist story is that it provides the right and even an illuminating account of the usual first-person privileges. Any non-functionalist account – i.e. any account that makes the connection between a sensory state and a thought that one has it less tight, as in the biologistic and dualistic proposals mentioned earlier – risks what seems to me intolerable first-person scepticism.[29] If qualia are non-functionally defined objects, then their attachment to their role in my thought is accidental, and it would seem possible for me to think, clearly and otherwise normally, that I have one (of a certain kind) without it being of that kind, and for me to think that I have one (of a certain kind) without my actually having one (of that kind). For all I know now what seems to me clearly a green experience is actually a red one, what seems to me a sharp pain is actually a tickle, what seems to me to be the sound of a Beethoven quartet is actually the smell of skunk.[30] While there seems to me to be some room for error in our qualitative thoughts, if those errors cannot be cashed out in terms of further comparisons and judgements I would make, it is utterly mysterious what I should be taken to be mistaken about.

Scepticism about qualia, however, can arise in a special way in connection with the notorious problem of 'qualia reversals'. ('How do you know other people don't see red where you see green?') *Pace* much of twentieth century philosophy, I think this is a quite serious problem and won't attempt to do it justice here. Suffice it to say that the *usual* ways of raising the problem, as a problem for *behaviouristic* analyses of sensational states, obviously do not arise for a *functionalist* proposal of the sort I am proposing here. It is pretty easy to construct nomologically possible cases of reverse qualia involving *behaviourally equivalent* individuals; it is not nearly so easy to construct such cases involving *cognitively* and *computationally* equivalent ones.[31] Unlike the cases produced against behaviourism, the cases against functionalism require tampering with the internal organization of the agent, in which case, I submit, we are deprived of any confidence we might have in the privileged access of the agent to what she is experiencing, and so in the reality of the reversals she thinks she might have undergone. The same questions raised above, about how one knows in one's *own* case that one is correctly judging that one is seeing red or green, smelling skunk or hearing Beethoven, can be raised about such cases. If it is claimed that these properties transcend the patterns in our judgements, then it may well be wondered whether qualia had at such sceptical expense are really worth having, or are the object of anyone's genuine concern.

Lastly, there is the now well-worn problem of 'knowing what it's like'. As many writers have emphasized,[32] such 'knowledge' may be more a matter of an ability, e.g. *imagination* than of *cognition*. Comp-imagining, we surely have every reason to suppose, is a different relation than comp-judging: comp-judgements are the basis for action (the input to the decision system) where comp-imaginings presumably are not. Roughly, to com-imagine X-ing seems to involve being able to produce in certain addresses, protected from immediate consequences for action, many of the restricted predications that might result from actually X-ing. I can imagine what it's like to be on the coast at Big Sur, since I can comp-imagine many of the restricted predications that would be released by the sun, air, surf and cliffs were I actually there. This is made particularly easy for me since I can remember (and so comp-remember many of the predications caused by) being there. But memory doesn't seem to be essential. In *The Red Badge of Courage*, Stephen Crane provided what, according to veterans, were accurate depictions of what it was like to be in war, despite never having been in one, depictions that in turn seem to produce in readers similar comp-imaginings.

Thus, Nagel's and Jackson's problems of 'knowing what it's like to X' are the difficulties of being able to comp-imagine the restricted predications that are typically produced by X-ing. In so far as we don't share such predications with bats, we can't know what it's like for them. The inability is not a logical, but merely a computational one. Of course, the fact that we do not automatically enter such states as a result merely of learning an explanatory account of what goes on when one X-es is no argument against the truth or adequacy of that account. I don't need to have a heart attack in order to have a completely adequate account of heart attacks; nor do I have to be able to X (or be able to imagine, or 'know what it's like' to X) in order to have a completely adequate theory of X-ing.

Conclusion

It might be felt that this solution to the qualia problem is too glib, that I am just inventing *ad hoc* entities that are supposed to do the work of solving the qualia puzzles. And this would be true, were there no promise whatever of independent evidence for ascribing computational structures of the sort I have described. But I see no reason to be so pessimistic. Although it is by no means easy to see finally how to sort out the elaborate computational structure of the brain, we know we shall have to do this if we are to make sense of most contemporary information-processing models of cognition, that is, if we are to make sense of the combinatorial, deductive, inductive, abductive and decision-theoretic structures that many psychologists posit to explain standard regularities in peoples' behaviour.

Of course, it might also be felt that this solution to the qualia problem is simply *crazy*, that sensory experiences are *obviously* not sentences in the head. But any such objection needs to point to phenomena that the proposed account cannot explain. I have tried to show how it explains all the phenomena standardly thought perplexing about such experience (including why it doesn't introspectively *seem* to be correct). Perhaps there are defects in my accounts, or there are further phenomena that I have missed. The burden seems to me now clearly on the critic to cite them. But these defects or additional phenomena must, of course, be presented in terms that don't beg the question of whether such an account *could* be correct. Merely beating one's breast and saying that sensory experience simply doesn't *seem* sentential – as a surprising number of people have been inclined to do – obviously doesn't meet this requirement.[33]

If we are to take an explanatory view of the mind seriously, though, it might be wondered why S-restricted predications are needed. Perhaps positing them can explain some of the peculiarities associated with sensations, but one might well wonder why any system would have them, and in particular why just *those* restrictions. Although the need for evolutionary accounts of mental processes is often exaggerated, this much could be said: restricted predications are one very good way a cognitive system could keep track of 'the data', i.e. of the interactions with the external world that confirm, and so must not be determined by, the theories, desires, expectations that notoriously affect our un-restricted 'observation' judgements. Restricted predications are judgements that are normally made only as a conseqence of environmental interactions and in turn produce a stable characteristic effect upon us, independently of whatever else we might think or want. So the short answer might be: by specially marking the effects of our proximal interaction with the world, the S-restrictions help protect us from total 'top-down' delusions.

In talking as I have about sensations as sentences in the brain, it can appear as though I am making an appeal essentially to biology as the basis of phenomenology. However, as many functionalists have pointed out, although the biological brain may in fact be the medium in which certain functional and/or computational/representational properties are *realized*, it is by no means essential to that role; other substances (silicon, wires and glass, perhaps even beer cans) may do just as well. This point is often obscured in discussions that are otherwise laudable for the richness of the psychological details that they bring to bear upon the philosophical issues. For example, in his recent book on colour on which I have greatly relied, C. L. Hardin writes:

> the important point is that the characteristics and relationships of colors depend upon their biological substrate, and we delude ourselves if we suppose it possible systematically to understand the relations colors bear to each other in isolation from that substrate. (Hardin, 1988, p. 127)

But he then continues a few pages later: 'Why not regard the phenomenal domain as being in some fashion *constituted* by a subset of neural codes?' (p. 131). It is this last *non*-biological, essentially functionalist proposal that his own discussion, and mine here, has provided some reason to adopt; *nowhere* in his discussion, I submit, is there any essential appeal to biology *per se*. Sensations are constituted by a certain kind of *coding* process; so long as that process has a certain computational form, for example, the form set out by the S-restrictions, the *medium* of that process would seem to be entirely irrelevant. Indeed, how could it possibly be relevant? How could a mere physiological or other condition that was not represented in the coding of the mind possibly make a difference to how things feel? That is the question which I hope my account will at least have raised, and maybe have answered.

Acknowledgements

This chapter is a shorter and somewhat revised version of Rey (1991b) (the chief revision being an unburdening of the present account of extraneous semantic claims, the effects of which are noted in notes 2, 12, 15 and 24). I want to thank Jonathan Adler, Ned Block, Jennifer Church, Larry Hardin, Brian Loar, Joseph Levine, Bob Richardson and David Rosenthal for much good discussion and advice. Martin Davies also read the penultimate manuscript with great care, and made excellent editorial suggestions. Versions of the present work were delivered at the Washington DC Philosophy Club, the University of Cincinatti, SUNY Stony Brook, at the conference on 'Mind, Meaning, and Nature' at Wesleyan University in April 1989, and at Rutgers University and the University of Chicago. At the last, I was on a program with William Lycan, whose paper 'What is the "Subjectivity of the Mental"?' independently advances a view very like the one advanced here.

Notes

1   I should mention, however, that, *aficionado* though he is of a language of thought, Fodor himself (in conversation) has demurred from carrying the theory *this* far.
2   I don't mean to be glib here, only ecumenically to avoid all the issues about meaning that have dominated most recent discussions of CRTT, but which, I hope, don't bear crucially upon the issues to be discussed here. The various sorts of theories I have in mind here have been discussed by, for example, Stampe (1979), Loar (1981), Millikan (1984), Stalnaker (1984), Block (1986), Papineau (1987), Dretske (1988) and Fodor (1987, 1990a, 1990b).
3   Notice that this formulation is sufficiently abstract to allow for a still wide variety of, for example, serial and parallel architectures. Moreover, connectionist networks might be involved at any number of stages of the processes described.
4   In Rey (1991a, p. 75) I argue that all that is essential to a mind are such processes of perception, memory, reasoning and decision making. Thus, *pace* Lewis (1972, p. 212), it is this sort of theory, and not just any 'platitudes which are common knowledge among us', that on the present account is the basis for the Lewis–Ramsey-style definitions of mental terms.
5   I conceive this as 'reportability in principle', to avoid problems of aphasia and other linguistic inadequacies. More detailed knowledge of the computational architecture of the brain would doubtless provide us with a better criterion. For now we are in the position of someone characterizing a process not by a real criterion, but by merely a salient symptom of it. Note, though, that, for reasons I discuss in Rey (1983, 1988a), I doubt very much that such a computational story would capture what I think is our ordinary, much stronger notion of consciousness.
6   See Field (1978), Fodor (1981, 1987), Loewer and Rey (1991), Rey (1991b).
7   See, for example, Church (1946), Mates (1951), Burge (1978), Kripke (1979), Ackermann (1981) and Bealer (1982). Many of the problems raised by Schiffer (1987, ch. 3) seem to me of a piece with these problems, and amenable to similar treatment.
8   I have in mind a causal analogue to Kaplan's (1978) distinction between the 'content' and the 'character' of indexical terms. I leave it open whether it is the individual herself, or a function or concept that determines that individual, that is the ultimate constituent of the 'content'.
9   The echoes of Kant's 'Transcendental Synthetic Unity of Apperception' (1781, B131ff) are not coincidental. I present these conditions as *sufficient*

for a self-concept, in reply to, say, a certain sceptic who might claim that Kant's condition transcended the powers of any mere machine. I suspect that they are not necessary: the unity might be brought about less representationally. Perry (1986), for example, argues that in some cases no self-representation may be necessary for thoughts that nevertheless 'concern' oneself in so far as they simply get one's body moving appropriately.

10 I'm concerned here only with the FPRT. A related account would be needed for the other 'essential indexical' appearing here, 'now'.

11 I don't mean to suggest that people are in fact ontologically neutral. I suspect that they are not, but presume that this needn't be an issue here.

12 In response to some useful questions of Gary Gates, this clause is a modification of the content condition as it appears in Rey (1991b, pp. 91–2, see also note 16), where I essentially conflated the sort of semantics one might provide for 'looks red' with the sort that one ought to provide for 'is red'. The former, like the indexical (and other logical) terms with which it is being compared, arguably requires a internalist, e.g. conceptual role account; the latter, more of an externalist, e.g. co-variational account.

13 This is a gross over-simplification. A better candidate for the meaning of 'looks red' and of the corresponding restricted predicate would involve a more precise statement of the stimulation conditions and of the characteristic processing. Thus, Hardin (1988) writes: 'Given an object, an illumination configuration whereby a spot of light of a particular size and spectral content and intensity and duration falls on a given retinal area, a fully specified visual surround and an observer in a particular adaptive state, the result of the interaction is determinate by nature ...' (p. 76), proceeding later (pp. 129–38) to claim that some of that result – particularly standard associations and comparisons – is constitutive of the identity of a particular sort of experience.

14 There are by now well-known cases of lobotomized people, and people under various analgesiacs (e.g. nitrous oxide), who claim to be experiencing pains but 'no longer mind them'. Whether such experiences are still *painful* or not is, on the present account, an entirely verbal issue (concerning whether to include the standard preference (aversion) state as part of the characteristic processing of the state named by 'pain').

15 In Rey (1991b) these appeared, inappropriately, as defining conditions.

16 In Rey (1980a) I suggest that it is the mandatory assignment of two-dimensional position in the case of visual experience that accounts for the fact that (as Dennett, 1969, nicely put it) 'we are less tempted to strike up the band in the brain than we are to set up the movie screen.' I suspect it may also contribute to the inclination to posit properties corresponding to restricted predicates that I try to resist to in the next section.

17 But another possibility is that there are in such cases no restricted predications at all: vision becomes entirely unrestricted, in a way that

appears to be the case in proprioception, where one seems to know the position of one's limbs without there occurring any characteristic sensations.

18   Neurophysiological evidence for something along these latter lines has been advanced by Libet (1985) with regard to the phenomenology of choice.

19   The importance of this point emerged from conversations with Michael Antony, who in his (forthcoming) has raised a general argument against functionalism in this regard. See also Maudlin (1989) for a related discussion.

20   I, however, no longer subscribe to the 'physiofunctionalism' I endorsed there, according to which interactions with specific physical properties (e.g. of hormones and neuroregulators) are counted as partly constitutive of an emotional state. I discuss this issue further in Rey (1992).

21   Much of this is probably parallel processing.

22   As well as, to some extent, verbal decision, cf. note 14 above. An important empirical question that bears upon the philosophical worry about interpersonal commonalities of experience is the degree to which characteristic processing can be *localized*. The more global it is, of course, the less likely it is to be shared, which may provide some reason for making that, after all, community-wide decision in such a way as to restrict the amount of characteristic processing a sensation term is required to cover.

23   See Wittgenstein (1953, §§304–308), Quine (1953, ch. 1; 1960, ch. 5) and, for further discussion of the mental case, Dennett (1969) and Rey (1980a).

24   That is, whether it needs to be 'reckoned as the value of a variable' as in Quine (1953, ch. 1). Note that I shall presume that the semantics of expressions of the form $\ulcorner s(\Phi)\urcorner$ will be a *state* (of Φ-ing), about which it can at least be a logically open question, whether there is a real *property* corresponding to the predicate Φ. I take it that one natural way of expressing anti-realism about, for example, the apparent referents of moral as opposed to physical talk is to claim that moral predicates like 'x is good' do not, while physical predicates do, express genuine (e.g. causal) properties. But this is compatible with thinking, in a way that I shall adopt for the present discussion, that there is a *state* of something's, for example, 'being morally good' despite the lack of the corresponding property (thus, the state of something's being good might be claimed to consist not in the fact that it has a genuine property of goodness, but in the fact that people regard states of that kind in a certain way). Alternatively, but to my mind less transparently, one could claim that there is trivially a property for every predicate, and then express one's anti-realism by claiming that certain of those properties are not, for example, causal. And a rigorous nominalist might still have another way of expressing a similar distinction (say, between different sorts of predicates).

25   For example, Block's (1978), Searle's (1980), Shoemaker's (1984) and my

own (1980a) appeal to merely physiological states. See Rey (1992) for further discussion.

26 Of course, I can indirectly indicate that you might be doing so by thinking a mental representation of an English sentence, such as 'It's R-ing to you', which is meant to illustrate the limitation in question. The point here is that, strictly speaking, 'R' in 'It's R-ing to you' does not have the same role meaning of any mentalese restricted predication; rather 'R' simply stands in place of such a predicate to illustrate the specific *form* of the mentalese predication.

27 The one actual sort of case in which this *might* be thought to arise is that of Gazzaniga et al.'s (1962) 'split-brain patients'. For discussion that could, with the present claims, lead to conclusions about 'shared sensations' see Rey (1976), Nagel (1971) and Parfit (1984, §100). For reasons to be *very* cautious about conclusions in this regard see Rey (1992).

28 The extent to which such further states are in fact implicated in CP(Φ) is a question that does not need to be settled here. I only want to indicate the resources of the present theory to implicate them as need be.

29 Note that *behaviourist* and/or *expressive* views of first-person 'knowledge' such as one finds in Ryle and Wittgenstein can be regarded here as limiting cases of functional views, behaviourism being a functionalist theory with null intervening states.

30 Nelkin (1986) distinguishes between pain as what he calls 'an attitudinal' as opposed to a 'sensory' feeling, stressing the relative unimportance of the latter. While I agree with the distinction he is concerned to draw, on my account the 'sensory', in so far as it is a genuine state at all, is a special case of the more general attitudinal.

31 Ned Block (1990) has tried to produce such a case for specifically the kind of proposal advanced here. I reply to it more fully in Rey (1992). See also Shoemaker (1984) for excellent general discussion.

32 The *locus classicus* of this issue is Nagel (1974). Jackson (1982) presents a more specific form of it. This latter article, with replies of the sort I am pursuing here, particularly Levin (1986), Lewis (1988) and Nemirow (1990), are usefully gathered together in Lycan (1990b, pp. 478–518).

33 I am sympathetic, however, to those who may feel that such an account of our mental lives may not ground our *moral* intuitions. After all, it would be hard to *care* about the experiences of a computer programmed to process S-restricted predicates in merely the ways I have sketched (see my (1983, 1988a) for further discussion. But I see no reason to think that an explanatory psychology is obliged or even likely to justify what may in the end be arbitrary patterns in our personal and/or moral concerns for one another.

13
A Bat without Qualities?

KATHLEEN A. AKINS

The Bird's Eye View

The other day in a physiology seminar we were discussing the effect of retinal foveation on visual perception. The fovea is a small portion of the retina densely packed with receptor cells – a density that makes possible those visual tasks that require high spatial resolution, the identification of shape and texture, accurate depth perception and so on. The fovea, however, can 'see' only a small part of the entire visual field. So, much like directing a telescope across the night sky, foveated creatures move their eyes – shifting the 'interesting' parts of the scene in and out of the foveal area. This is why we, but not rabbits, move our eyes about.

Enter the eagle – or, rather, birds of prey in general. They too have foveated eyes, but eyes with even better spatial resolution than our own. The African vulture, for example, can discern live prey from dead at an elevation of 3,000–4,000 metres, an elevation at which it is difficult for us even to sight the bird (Duke–Elder, 1958). Eagles, too, have high resolution foveae. Because they dive for the ground at speeds greater than 200 mph, their eyes must be capable of extremely accurate depth perception. Indeed, given the broad range of visual information that an eagle makes use of in its behaviour, the evolutionary 'solution' was the development of *two* circular foveae connected together by a horizontal band of densely packed receptor cells (think here of the shape of a barbell). The horizontal band serves to scan the horizon. The central fovea, like those of most birds, looks to either side, each one (in the left and right eyes) taking in a different part of the world. Finally, the eagle has an extra pair of (temporal) foveae pointing forward, converging on a shared field – a foveal pair much the same as our own except with three times the density of receptor cells (Duke–Elder, 1958). It is this forward-looking foveal region that provides the high spatial resolution. Attending to the scene below via the temporal fovea, eagles spot their prey and dive at fantastic speeds, pulling up at exactly the right instant.

But therein lies a mystery, I thought, the mystery of the 'eagle's eye' view. Given two foveal areas and a horizontal band, how does an eagle 'attend to' a scene, look at the world? What does that mean and, more interestingly, what would that be like? Here, in my mind's eye, I imagined myself perched high in the top of a dead tree sporting a pair of very peculiar bifocal spectacles. More precisely, I pictured myself in a pair of quadra-focals, with different lenses corresponding to the horizontal band, foveal and peripheral regions of the eagle's eye. I wonder whether it is just like that, I thought, like peering successively through each lens, watching the world move in and out of focus depending upon where I look. First I stare through the horizontal section and scan the horizon for other predators; then I switch to my left central lens and make sure no one is approaching from behind; then I use the high-powered temporal lens to scrutinize the water below for the shadows of some dinner. Is that how the world looks to an eagle?, I wondered. Is that what it is like to have two foveae?

The Problem: Nagel's Claim and its Intuitive Basis

In 'What is it like to be a bat?' (1974), Thomas Nagel made the claim that science would not, and indeed, could not, give us an answer to these kinds of questions. When all of science is done and said – when a completed neuroscience has told us 'everything physical there is to tell' (Jackson, 1982, p. 127) – we will still not understand the experiences of an 'essentially alien' organism. It will not matter that we have in hand the finer and grosser details of neuroanatomy, neurophysiology and hence, the functional characterization of the system at various levels of complexity – nor will the 'completed' set of psychophysics provide us with the essential interpretative tool. For all of neuroscience, something would be missed – what it is like to be a particular creature, what it is like *for* the bat or the eagle.

There are many reasons, I think, both intuitive and theoretical, why Nagel's claims about the limits of scientific explanation have seemed so plausible. Nagel himself, for example, argued for this conclusion by appeal to a theoretic notion, that of a point of view. Phenomenal experience, he said, is necessarily an experience from a particular point of view, hence the facts of experience are essentially subjective in nature. On the other hand, the kinds of phenomena that science seeks to explain are essentially objective, or viewer independent – 'the kind [of facts] that can be observed and understood from many points of view and by individuals with differing perceptual systems' (Nagel, 1974, p. 145). So any attempt to understand the experience of an alien creature by appeal to scientific facts (facts about his behaviour and internal computational/physiological processes) will only serve to distance us from the very property we seek to explain: the subjectivity of phenomenal experience. Or so Nagel argued. Nagel's conclusion was that the only possible access one could have to the phenomenal experience of another organism is by means of a kind of empathetic projection – by extrapolation from one's case, we can ascribe similar experiences to other subjects. Needless to say, this is a process that will work well enough given a suitably 'like–minded' organism (such as another person) but which will be entirely inadequate for understanding the point of view of more alien creatures. Hence, given only empathetic means, said Nagel, we cannot know the nature of a bat's phenomenal experience.

Nagel's argument, like those of a number of other philosophers (for example, see McGinn, 1983), makes use of a variety of theoretic tenets – about the objectivity of scientific facts, the subjectivity of experience and about the nature of a point of view. In the usual case, such arguments hinge upon a claim that 'you can't get from there to here' – that there is no route from the objective to the subjective, from the non-intentional to the intentional, from the sub-personal to the personal, and so on – even given all of the resources of the natural sciences. These are views that must be addressed, I think, by argument, each in its own right or, better, met by a demonstration that the dichotomy at issue can in fact be bridged by scientific insight. Rather than address here these theoretic concerns, about subjectivity, point of view and so on, I want to look instead at the *intuitive* pull towards Nagel's conclusion – why most of us harbour that nagging suspicion that science must fail, that it cannot tell us what we want to know. This is the intuition that science will necessarily omit the one essential element of phenomenal experience, namely its very 'feel'.

The unfortunate fact of the matter, I think, is that these negative intuitions are well grounded in our everyday experiences. We have all faced the difficulty of trying to communicate the nature of a particular phenomenal experience, good or bad. 'It was awful, absolutely horrible!!' you might recount, speaking of a bad migraine headache – but, apart from a fellow migraine sufferer, no one seems the wiser for your description. Frustratingly, despite the listener's own extensive catalogue of aches and pains, any elaboration on the 'horribleness' of a migraine seems to do little good. 'Yes, it's a bit like that but . . . .' one will hedge, when asked how a migraine compares to an ordinary headache, one caused by tension or by sinus inflammation. Or is it like having a nasty hangover, a bad case of the flu, or like the stabbing pain one feels when the lights are suddenly switched on in a darkened room? 'It's sort of like that, except, only, um . . . well . . . much, much *worse!*' This is what a sufferer will typically reply, unsure, even in his own mind, what to make of such comparisons. (Does a migraine differ from a bad hangover only in intensity or is there in fact a difference in kind? Or does the difference in intensity *constitute* a difference in kind?) Ironically, the best descriptions one can give, the descriptions that elicit the most empathetic sounds and nods, are usually not descriptions of the pain at all, but of the beliefs and desires that go along with the migraine. 'If I knew the migraine wasn't going to end, I'd seriously wonder whether life was worth living' or 'the pain is so intense, you don't even want to roll over, to find a more comfortable position in which to lie' – it is such thoughts that make clear the severity of the experience. Describing the feelings *per se* just does not seem possible. You simply have to have a migraine.

Extend, then, this epistemic difficulty to the phenomenal experience of an alien creature. Suppose that an organism has sense organs of a completely unfamiliar kind and, further, that it processes the information gathered from these strange sense organs in a manner unique to its species (or at least, in a manner unknown to ours). This is an organism that, undoubtedly, will have experiences that we do not: some of its sensations will be nothing like our sensations. So if we think of an organism's phenomenological experience as constituted by the set of all those alien 'qualia', the problem of understanding seems insuperable. Given that we cannot comprehend by description the relatively familiar and circumscribed sensations of the migraine sufferer, what could we possibly know about an alien creature's point of view – about an entirely foreign phenomenological repertoire? If we can comprehend only those sensations that we have experienced, and if our own sensations are very unlike those of the bat, then we will be unable to understand a bat's phenomenology. This is the intuitive conclusion grounded in everyday experience.

The problem about the experience of bats, however, was, as Nagel described it, a problem about scientific description – whether science, not everyday conversation, could buy us any leverage on the bat's point of view. So what does common sense tell us here? The answer, I think, is that our conclusions about the ineffable nature of sensations fit hand in glove with another common feeling about the efficacy of science: to the average person, the suggestion that science might resolve these communicative difficulties seems quite strange, if not downright puzzling. How could science possibly help us in this respect?

Suppose, for example, that I am trying to describe to you a certain kind of feeling, say the pain of my broken toe. I might say something like this:

> Well, at first, when I tripped over the broom handle, there was a sharp, intense pain – a blinding flash of 'white' that occurred behind my eyes. Then the pain evened out to a dull throbbing in the toe – and, later, by that night, it had turned into what I think of as 'pain somewhere'. You know, that's the pain of a deep injury – when the pain is clearly where it should be, in this case, in the *toe*, but it's also nowhere in particular. Your whole body feels, well, dragged out.

If you have actually had a broken toe or another injury of this sort, these sensations might sound quite familiar. You know, for example, exactly what I mean by the phrase 'a blinding pain'. But if you have been fortunate enough to have avoided such traumas, certain parts of the description will seem quite peculiar. (A 'throbbing' pain you can understand, but what is it to have a pain that is 'blinding' or felt 'nowhere in particular'? Surely this is just a figure of speech?) One can, of course, on the basis of the description, obtain *some* understanding of the phenomenological properties at issue (after all, if asked about the pain of a broken toe, you could simply paraphrase the above description!). But it does little to help you understand how the pain actually *feels*. That is the part you cannot grasp given the description alone. Imagine, now, that you are given a completed model of human nociception, a model of all the neurophysiological/computational processess that underlie the production of pain, including, of course, the pain of a broken toe. That this model could in any way help seems entirely dubious. Why would you understand the *pain* of a broken toe any better if presented with a corpus of facts about C-fibres and A-fibres, conductance times, cortical and sub-cortical pathways, transmitter release, the function of endogenous opiates and so on? How could these statements about brain function possibly tell you about the *feeling* of a broken toe?

It is this intuitive sense of puzzlement, I think, that lies behind the more theoretical philosophical arguments of Nagel (1974), Block (1978), Jackson (1982), McGinn (1989) and Levine (chapter 6, this volume) – behind philosophical arguments that 'you can't get from here to there', that there is an unbridgeable explanatory gap between the facts of science and those of subjective experience. In this sophisticated guise, the puzzlement is not given a naive dualist expression: most philosophers do not hold that science must fail to explain phenomenological events because those events occur in a 'realm' beyond the physical world. Rather, the materialistic tenets are upheld: descriptions of neurological processes, it is generally agreed, are descriptions of inner sensations *in some sense of the phrase*. Moreover, given that sensations *are* brain processes, most Nagelians admit that science could not be entirely irrelevant to our understanding of an alien creature's experience. Neurophysiology, psychology and psychophysics will illuminate (no doubt) some aspects of an alien point of view. Still – and this is where the intuitive puzzlement resurfaces – no matter how much we come to understand about a brain's representational or computational capacities (the nature of its functional states at various levels of description, plus their structural and relational properties), the qualitative properties of that organism's point of view will still be missing. Again, it is the 'very feel' of the experience that science is said to leave out. But what exactly does this mean? What is given and what is not by science?

Think here of the difference between, say, a pristine page in a child's colouring book, with only the thick black outlines of the picture drawn in, and that same page alive with colour, the trees and flowers and birds given hue according to the whims and palette of a particular individual. In one we have the 'basic outline' of the image, the two-dimensional form; in the other, we have that outline plus the hues of the forms – colours that might have been different had the artist chosen otherwise. Now if we were given only the pristine page, various questions about the scene would remain unanswered. 'But is the sky blue or is it really grey?' 'Is the flower on the left yellow or is it actually white?' Without the completed picture, it is impossible to tell. It is questions analogous to these, then, that are allegedly left unanswered given only the neurological/computational facts about another organism's brain processes. Even if we knew the basic outline or, in Nagel's terms (1974, p. 179) the 'structural properties' of an alien creature's representational scheme, the very 'colour' of the experiences, the qualia, would still be missing. Like the missing colours of the outlined page, there are any number of ways, consistent with the structural properties of the representations, that those subjective experiences could be. What science can give us, at best, are boundaries on the space of possible qualia, on the pure 'colours' yet to be filled in. In this way, our everyday intuitions cast the problem of consciousness, both in its naive and philosophical forms, as largely a problem about the intrinsic or qualitative nature of sensations, about the 'greens, reds and blues' of phenomenal experience.

The Film

Imagine, then, that I, having dropped in from some future time towards the end of neuroscience, claim to have a film of 'what it is like'. I have, that is, a film of the phenomenology of the bat. While such a suggestion might at first seem unlikely, let me assure you that this film carries the stamp of approval of future science. For what science has found out, in the fullness of time, is that just as some people have suspected (Dawkins, 1986), the bat's sonar echo is used to solve the very same informational problems for which we humans use light. The bat uses the informational properties of sound to construct a representation of objects and their spatial relations. This is why the bat's experience can be presented on film to us, the human observers – why it has, I claim, a strangely 'visual' quality. Needless to say, this film was made in the appropriate Disney style: a 'cinerama' or 'sen-surround' film projected on a curved screen, 180 degrees around the theatre, presented to an audience outfitted in '3-D glasses', for the sake of stereo vision. And, of course, the film is in colour.

What, then, does the bat film look like? First, the plot is simple. It shows, from the bat's auditory viewpoint, a boring sort of chase scene: the bat, flying about, uses sonar signals to catch mealworms that have been thrown into the air by an experimenter. (Bats, of course, are not blind – they see as well as hear. For the purposes of this thought experiment, however, I am considering only their auditory sensations.) This feat is accomplished with a manoeuvre characteristic of the Little Brown bat. First the bat flaps around, emitting his Fm sonar signal (a cry that begins at about 60 khz and sweeps downward, through the intermediate frequencies, to a cry of about 20 khz) and waiting for something edible to appear; then when he sights a mealworm, he flies over and manoeuvres until he can swat the mealworm with his wing; performing a somersault, the bat then secures the prey in his tail pouch; finally, he reaches down to grab it, eating the mealworm from his pouch (figure 3). (Why bother with the pouch? As someone recently pointed out, 'Every good meal deserves to be eaten sitting down.'[1]) This is the basic

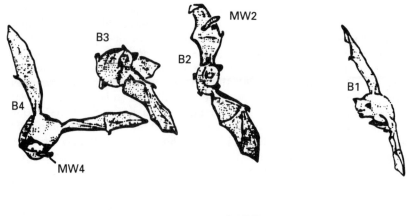

Figure 3   *A filmed sequence of a bat (*Myotis lucifugus*) capturing, by a somersault manoeuvre, a mealworm tossed into the air. Shown are the four sequential positions, beginning with the rightmost figure. In the first frame, the bat (B1) spots the mealworm (MW1), which is still rising from the toss. In the second frame, the bat uses its wing to deflect the worm downward. Next the bat catches the mealworm in a pouch between its tail and two legs. Finally, the bat ducks down to scoop out its meal. (Adapted from Webster and Griffln, 1962.)*

scenario, one that is repeated several times. Now, what the film actually shows to the human observer is a kaleidoscopic display of vibrant colour forms. Swirling and pulsating in three-dimensions, the coloured forms dance across the screen, colliding and dispersing, suddenly appearing or vanishing. That's all. That, I claim, is what it's like. It is not, of course, what we humans would see, if we were acting the part of the bat – if we, with our human visual systems, were trying to catch a mealworm (Nagel 1974). It is not 'visual' in the human sense. On the other hand, this is not a film from our point of view, but from the point of view of a bat.

As you, the reader, will no doubt object, something is clearly wrong with this story. That is, whether or not the film 'accurately depicts' some part of the bat's phenomenology – the sensory 'colours' – watching the swirling display seems to leave out much of what is surely important to the bat's point of view. First, unlike our experiences during a film of a roller-coaster ride or a hang-glider's flight, we do not feel any of the additional 'sympathetic' sensations appropriate to the moment. It does not seem to us that we are making any of the swooping and diving movements that are made by the bat. Nor do we understand the significance of the coloured images. Barring any sub-titles of the form 'now the somersault begins' or 'now you've got the mealworm in your pouch', you will not know what is happening – what you, as a bat, are doing. When the bright red image swirls across your left 'auditory' field, is something (the mealworm? a background object?) moving past you or are you moving relative to it (maybe this is a somersault?)? Then again, is anything even moving at all? Can you infer that the movement of the colours stands for movement in the world? Probably not. And what does the three-dimensional nature of the film buy you? What does it mean when one coloured patch appears behind or in front of another? Is this a spatial relation or . . . .? All in all, the coloured images hold little insight for the human observer.

As a first pass at explaining what is wrong with this story – why a cineramic film could not tell us what we want to know about the bat – note that, while not particularly helpful in this instance, such 'sen-surround' films are ex-tremely useful in understanding the human point of view. When we watch a film of, say, the hang-glider's flight, the pictures go proxy for the real world. The brain interprets the intensity, frequency and spatial cues of the film in much the same way as it would interpret these same properties of light, reflected by real objects in the three-dimensional world. Hence, we really do see (more or less) what is seen during a hang-glider's flight. Indeed, because the visual system informs both the vestibular and the sympathetic nervous systems, we even feel the non-visual sensations – the terror before the leap, the drop in the stomach that follows. Through watching the film, seeing from this novel perspective the world rush by and feeling the sympathetic sensations of movement, a good deal about the experience of hang-gliding is communicated. In other words, we can simulate another person's point of view just because (a) we share a similar visual system, and (b) we can artificially create the hang-glider's visual input.

Similarly, when we watch the film of the 'bat experience', we use the spectral cues in ways typical of human vision (what other choice could there be?). But what exactly does that mean? Unfortunately, we do not really know how colour vision works, in what 'typical' ways spectral cues are employed. What we do know is that the colours we see depend upon the current ambient light plus the profile of wavelengths that specific materials are disposed to reflect. Further, we suspect that spectral signals are involved in just those visual tasks for which intensity cues prove inadequate. For example, it is often postulated that such cues are used to define equi-luminescent borders, highlight the contrast between object and background, and to differentiate objects that are similar in all other respects (e.g. the ripe and unripe pear). (For a short explanation of colour pathways, see De Yoe and Van Essen, 1988; for a more thorough review of colour vision, see Gouras, 1984.) In other words, while we may think of the colour system as whatever neural machinery produces colour sensations, the colour system is more than that: it is that part(s) of the visual system that responds to, discriminates and utilizes spectral cues. It is this system, then, whatever it might be, that is activated when we see the film of the 'bat experience'.

Needless to say, a bat's colour sensations of acoustic stimuli would be quite another matter. Its sensations would not be tied to the ways in which external objects reflect ambient light nor would its sensations be a part of a system that uses the spectral composition of light for various information-processing tasks. The bat's colour sensations would be linked to properties of acoustic stimuli and to its auditory processes involved in spatial processing. As it turns out, although the bat film was presented as consisting of seemingly random coloured patches, I had in mind a specific process for the generation of those images. There was an informational relation between the properties of the visual image and those of the acoustic stimuli about which you, the 'viewer', were not told. That relation was as follows. First, the hue of the sensations (red, green, blue, etc.) encoded the frequency of the sound waves; second, the brightness of the colours gave the volume or intensity of the sound; and, third, the configuration of the patches showed, straightforwardly, the spatial properties of the sound waves. Finally, the film encoded the time delay of the echo or the bat's distance from surrounding objects. By making the coloured patches appear at different depths, spatial disparity mimicked a disparity in time – the amount of time it takes for the bat's outgoing cry to bounce off a distant object and return. The longer the delay between the cry and the echo, the further 'back' the coloured patches appeared in the 'visual' field. In this way, distance was represented by stereoscopic display.[2] Now, such an image of the sound field, in itself, would not buy the bat a sensory system for spatial perception. In order for the bat to perceive spatial relations in the world, something more would be needed: the visual images would have to be hooked up with various other neural processes 'further down the line' – with the bat's cortical pattern analysers that decode object shape, texture and identity, with the bat's vestibular and motor systems, and with, well, who knows what else? The fiction of the bat film, however, is that these colour sensations are what the bat experiences, *qualitatively* – a coloured image of the sound field, over time, as the bat pursues a mealworm.

One problem with the bat film now looks relatively clear: as a result of the differences between the human visual system and the bat auditory system, we cannot expect that by inducing colour sensations in ourselves we will understand the role that such sensations play in the bat's phenomenal world.[3] Because a 'sen-surround' film produces our visual experience through the usual means, we see the colours as we normally do, as the projection of moving coloured images upon a curved screen. Lacking the auditory/representational capacities of the bat, we do not experience the colours as does the bat, however that might be. All a film can show us are meaningless (albeit coloured!) visual events. Put another way, what the bat film seems to prove is that it is not for lack of the 'quality' of the bat's experience that his world eludes us. Even if, *ex hypothesi*, we were able to produce in ourselves the 'very feel' of the bat's experience, its 'qualitative' aspect, we would not understand the bat's point of view. Watching the swirl of colours, those sensations lack their proper representational content. We cannot expect to understand the bat's point of view, in other words, without access to both the representational and qualitative parts of its experience. And here we are given but one aspect, the phenomenological 'feel' of the bat's world.

Unfortunately, this way of putting things is not quite right, for it does not get to the root of the problem, does not fully explain why a film cannot give us the point of view of the bat. Let me try a different path. Both the description of the bat film as initially given and the conclusions drawn from it above presupposed that there could be a separation of the 'qualitative' and 'representational' aspects of phenomenal experience. 'What the bat hears is just like colour' the reader is told, 'except, of course, the colours mean something quite different. Imagine that!' This was how the thought experiment got off the ground. Yet sensible as that request might have seemed, we have no idea how to comply with it, what such a separation could be. As Daniel Dennett has often pointed out (see, for example, Dennett, 1988), what one is asked to imagine, what one can imagine and what one actually imagines are three distinct things. It is not clear that we do know how to separate our conscious experiences into two parts, the representational and qualitative aspects, or whether, indeed, this notion even makes sense. To illustrate this point, suppose that, instead of referring to the bat film, I had requested that you do the following:

> Open your eyes and look around your office (it's the end of term) – at the stacks of books and papers, at the piles of articles, unopened mail and ungraded papers. Note the way the scene looks to you, the inner phenomenology of the event. Now, a bat's consciousness is just like that – the feel of the scene is exactly the same – except, of course, all those visual sensations *mean* something very different to the bat. They represent quite different properties. Imagine that!

The problem is that you cannot imagine that, no matter how sincerely or hard you try. First, it would require that you 'strip away' the representational content of the entire office scene (say, by erasing the 'black lines' of the image, leaving only the 'crayoned' parts?). Then, by some other process, the intentional content of the bat's representations must be 'overlaid' upon the remaining bare sensory qualities (by a process akin to drawing in new lines or attaching new labels?). This, I contend, is not something we have any idea how to do: we do not know what the two 'parts' would be like, of and by themselves, so we have no inkling how to pull them apart or put them together. Our intuitions do not provide a concrete distinction between the qualitative and representational aspects of perceptions.

Still, you might well ask, why then, if there is no such distinction, did the bat example work at all? That is, in the bat film, we were asked to imagine meaningless coloured patches swirling across the screen – and we did. It also seemed perfectly reasonable to imagine that those colours played a representational role in the bat's experience, one that was different from the role they play in our conceptual scheme. But if there is no distinction between the qualitative and representational parts of experience, how could this be so? Certainly it seemed to us that we could imagine such a distinction.

The answer here is that the description of the film was intentionally misleading: it was designed to play upon a common experience, that of seeing images or pictures we can not identify. Staring at an abstract painting perplexedly, we scan the blobs of colour for form – what could that possibly be a picture of? – when, suddenly, the figure of a man emerges. The apparently meaningless blobs of paint are transformed into a comprehensible image. These are the cases in which we legitimately regard content and 'mere colour' as distinct: at first the canvas contains only formless coloured blobs; after the 'aha!' experience, the painting has meaning – and this despite the fact that the canvas remains physically unchanged. It was this kind of event that set the stage for the original bat film. Given our familiarity with pictures and drawings, we tried to imagine a similar kind of thing – a film of 'meaningless' coloured shapes, non–intentional and non-representational sensory qualities, such that, if only we knew the proper 'squint' of the bat, those images would have content for us as well. We imagined, or at least we thought we could imagine, an unchanging substrate of pure sensation – a substrate analogous to the physical paint upon the canvas – onto which the bat's meaning could be affixed. The problem, however, is that our experience of abstract art does not provide a genuine example of what we need, the separation of content from 'mere colour'. Viewing an abstract painting does not involve an experience of a 'meaningless' image in the proper sense, that is, because the sudden emergence of a form in an abstract artwork is not the experience of having sensory stimuli, devoid of content, instantaneously gain representational properties. Even if we do not initially see the coloured shapes as the ghostly portrait of a man, we do see the colours as something – as coloured shapes upon a canvas, external to us, 3 ft dead ahead. The same is true for the patches of colour in the bat film. Perceiving (or imagining) moving coloured patches on a screen is an intentional – or at least, quasi-intentional – event, an experience of coloured patches as coloured patches. So when we imagined the bat film, we did not thereby imagine pure sensory qualities, colour qualia devoid of content. Our understanding of abstract art forms was misleading because it fostered the illusion that we could imagine exactly that.

Where does this leave us with respect to Nagel's original question and its intuitive basis? In questioning whether we could ever understand an alien organism's point of view, we intuitively construe this problem as analogous to the everyday task of understanding the phenomenal experiences of each other. Here, because our own difficulties turn around individual sensations, around the 'feel' of sensory events – the pain of a migraine headache, the azure blue of the Mediterranean, the 'essence' of flamingo pink – we infer that the main stumbling block to understanding an alien creature must be the inaccessibility of those qualia. We treat a conscious experience, in other words, as a mere collection of qualia, as a bunch of individual sense data that have somehow come together to form a phenomenological whole. (Certainly, this is the route that most analytic philosophical debates have also taken. In the 'inverted spectrum' problem, for example, the question is asked whether it would be possible for two people to have exactly the same neural structures and functions and yet have their colour experiences be 'spectral inversions', one of the other. Could you, my neurological equivalent, see the sky as red even though I see it as blue? In the 'absent qualia' problem (Block, 1978), the question is whether an artificial system functionally identical to one's own brain could be entirely devoid of qualitative experience. If, given a Turing-machine table that described the functional states of my brain, the entire population of China could be talked into instantiating, for one hour, the state types specified by that table, would my aches, tickles and pains be somehow 'experienced' (collectively?) by all the citizens of China? These are the kinds of questions – questions phrased in terms of individual sensations – that are currently asked.)

What is overlooked by the intuitive construal of the problem are the following two points. First, because we are able to individuate, identify and catalogue some of our phenomenological experiences and to converse with other people about such perceptual experiences as 'that very colour' (referring, say, to the intense blue-green of the Mediterranean), it does not follow that these sensations come to exist *in vacuo*. This 'isolation' of those sensations (whether as a result of some internal process of individuation or merely in virtue of linguistic convention) does not thereby produce sensations that stand apart from our representational/conceptual schemes. What the intuitive view conflates, in other words, is an ability to refer to certain parts of conscious intentional experience with an ability to pick out its purely qualitative aspects. Isolation does not distil qualia from content. So, whatever the root of our everyday problems in communication, it is not the intrinsic nature of sensations *per se* that makes for trouble – or, rather, there is no reason to think that this is the case given our communicative problems. If our utterances do not refer to pure sensation, one sees that the problems of communicating our phenomenological experience are equally a problem about representational states.

Second, a point of view, as we know from our own – paradigmatic – case, is not a jumble of qualia. In the normal non-pathological subject, consciousness is systematic, representational and intentional (e.g. we represent objects as being a certain way or of a certain type). Moreover, such properties are not 'optional' parts of our conscious experience, merely accidental or inconsequential aspects, if they can be considered 'parts' at all. Rather, these properties are constitutive of a point of view. That we experience the world in any way at all – that it is like anything to be me – is made possible by exactly these properties. So, given that our own phenomenal experience is the starting point for an explanation of the very notion of a point of view, and that our own experience is not a mere collection of qualia, we must assume that the same holds for the bat. If there is anything it is like to be bat, we have no reason to think – indeed, there is no sense to the suggestion – that that bat's experience is but a collection of pure qualia.

The mistake of the intuitive view, then, was first to think that our problem of communication was one about pure qualitative states, and then, second, to import this interpretation of the problem into the task of understanding an alien point of view. If we construe our communicative failures to hinge upon pure qualitative states of which the speakers do not have a common experience, then what we face in understanding a foreign phenomenology is simply 'much more of the same' – for the bat will have more and more purely qualitative states of which we ourselves have had no experience. By misconstruing the nature of an interpersonal problem, the puzzle about another creature's point of view becomes a problem about pure qualia.

The upshot of the bat film, then, is this. Nagel has claimed that we will never understand the point of view of an alien creature. This is a claim that our intuitions support with a nod towards 'that something', pure phenomenal experience, which cannot be known merely by description, without personal experience. But if introspection does not yield any clear distinction between the representational and qualitative properties of experience, then we do not know, *a priori*, what insights or even what kinds of insights will result from empirical investigation. Certainly we cannot confidently declare that science must fail to unearth 'that something', for we have no clear idea to what this amounts; nor can one say what the scientific approach will necessarily leave out, if it must leave out anything at all. This gives us, I think, good reason to continue on with our empirical investigations of mental representation – to look towards the disciplines of neurophysiology, psychology and artificial intelligence – without undue pessimism about the relevance of their experimental results.

Ourselves as Subject

One consequence of tying together sensation and representational experience is that the nature of our own subjective experience is opened to investigation (Sellars, 1963; Dennett, 1978a; Churchland, 1983). It is as legitimate a subject of inquiry as the experience of other creatures. Because the questions about phenomenology are no longer focused on the intrinsic quality of particular sensations but on a phenomenology as a whole – complete with its representational/intentional nature – our ignorance extends to ourselves as well. We, as the 'owners' of our point of view, do not thereby understand its representational character. Hence, our study of representational systems is also an investigation into our own point of view.

This consequence is, I suspect, somewhat counter-intuitive. If anyone knows about my subjective experience, it is certainly me, or at least that is what we have always thought about the matter. By way of lending some small amount of plausibility to this result, then, I want to end this chapter by going back to the example at the beginning, that of the eagle. What did learning a simple anatomical fact about the eagle, about the foveation of the eye, tell us about that creature's experience? More importantly, how would a fact about an eagle nudge our sense of self, reflect upon the human experience?

In learning that the eye of the eagle has two separate foveal regions, it suddenly seemed clear that the experience of the eagle must be different from our own. On the other hand, when I tried to imagine *how* the experience of an eagle would differ from my own, I immediately adopted a hypothesis that incorporated my own visual system into the experience. I wondered, that is, whether being an eagle might not be akin to the experience I would have while wearing strange quadra-focals – whether it wouldn't be like shifting my own gaze from lens to lens sequentially. In essence, I incorporated my own foveal field into the experience of being an eagle. (This would give me, in effect, eight different levels of visual acuity: four lenses imposed upon my foveal and non-foveal regions.) Of course, nothing we know about the visual system of the bird of prey constrains its visual 'attention' in a similar way. Although my foveae must move from lens to lens sequentially, the bird need not have any analogous 'inner' eye that receives, serially, the information from the two foveae and the horizontal band. Because there are parallel lines from all regions of the retina, there is no reason why the brain must process the information sequentially – no reason why, say, the eagle must first attend to the left, then forward, then to the horizon just as I would. The eagle might 'attend' simultaneously to all this information at once, no matter how this might conflict with our intuitive notion of visual attention. This is a possibility that the anatomical data reveals.

Note that once we see how a notion of 'foveal' processing has been misapplied to the eagle's point of view, it is an interesting question whether or not we have also 'moved the eye inward' not merely in thinking about the eagle, but alas in thinking about ourselves. Here, I am referring to the many models of conscious attention that utilize, in one form or another, the 'spotlight' metaphor: the 'inner eye' of consciousness shifts like a searchlight from one neural event to another, successively attending to different mental events. This, too, is a 'foveal' theory of attention, not of another organism's consciousness but of our own. We apply the foveal metaphor to our conscious experience as a whole. Certainly, this is a model with intuitive plausibility. Something about it seems just right. The question that the eagle's eye raises, however, is about the basis of this appeal. Is it appealing because this is, in fact, how our inner experience is, or does it seem right just because the foveated nature of our visual experience colours our understanding of conscious attentive processes as a whole?

First, the former alternative could be true. The spotlight theory might seem plausible because, on looking inwardly at ourselves, we can see by introspection that our consciousness is sequentially focused on single events. That is, the introspective evidence coheres with the metaphor. But is this really so? Recall what it is like to struggle through a recalcitrant screen door weighed down by several bags of groceries. First, you juggle the groceries and grasp the door handle; then you feel a mosquito land on your ankle; then you hear the creaking door hinge and the rip of a paper bag; then the mosquito makes a stab with his proboscis; then you loose your grip on the handle; then the screen slams shut on your shin; then a tin can bounces off your thigh . . . Somehow, this strictly sequential narrative does not quite capture the experience, even if it does record the objective order of the external events. The very problem with such experiences is that 'everything happens at once'. In the midst of the calamity, what happens first – the bag ripping or the mosquito biting or the screen door slamming – is not always clear. On the basis of experience alone, there is no distinct ordering of all of the events, no clear sequence of this event, then this one, then this and finally that.

Perhaps, then, the explanation goes the other way about: perhaps the searchlight metaphor, combined with our story-telling practices and our understanding of the relevant causal chain of events, confer order upon the conscious events only in retrospect. What I am suggesting is that the spotlight metaphor may be adopted just because (a) we are foveated animals and (b) we do not actually perceive any firm order in the events (i.e. such events are not 'tagged' for time). Because we are such strongly visual organisms and because eye movements are required for our perception of the world, the metaphor seems plausible. Needing an explanation, we mistake our intuitive grasp of the visual perception of external events for an accurate description of internal attentional processes. We co-opt the visual notions of 'searching', 'focusing' and 'watching' and apply them to all of conscious experience. This, I think, is possible. What the eye of the eagle should make us wonder is whether our conception of ourselves might not be 'tainted' with the same foveal metaphors we naturally apply to other creatures.

The above example is not meant as a serious criticism of spotlight theories of conscious attention. Rather, it is given as a suggestive example of how it could come about that we are mistaken about our own inner events – how the way our own attentional mechanisms seem to us could diverge from how in fact they are. It offers a small glimpse of the ways a possible reconception of ourselves, and our point of view, could come about in the light of physiological/computational discoveries.

Still, the central idea of this chapter has been that we do not know what science will explain, just because we lack a firm grasp on the subject matter: the nature of conscious events. If so, we are in a funny position. We will know what science can tell us only after it has done so. Hence, only suggestive examples are now possible. What we can provide, however, are good reasons to wait – to see what science will do. In effect, this is what I have been attempting to show in this chapter.

Acknowledgements

This chapter began as an introduction to paper, 'What is it Like to be Boring and Myopic?' (Akins, 1993) where it served, in a much abbreviated form, to motivate the neuroscientific approach to the problem of consciousness used there. An earlier version appeared under the title 'Science and Our Inner

Lives: Birds of Prey, Bats and the Common (Featherless) Bi-ped' in a collection edited by Marc Beckoff and Dale Jamieson (1990). For their generous comments on and discussion of the manuscript, I would like to thank Marc Beckoff, Daniel C. Dennett, Dale Jamieson, Joseph Malpeli, Wright Neely, Brian C. Smith, Tony Stone, Tom Stoneham and Mary Windham. I would also like to thank Martin Davies for his extensive comments on the final draft.

Notes

1 That someone being Jeremy Butterfield.
2 This way of generating the film was given only for the sake of example, not because I think that this is what a bat's experience is really like. That is, assuming that a bat does have a point of view (and I doubt that it has), the film represents the properties of the sound field before the sound waves are transduced, processed and filtered by the basilar membrane, midbrain and auditory cortex of the bat. At the level of the auditory cortex (surely the first neural level at which conscious experience would be possible), the informational characteristics of the signal have been significantly changed.
3 It is an interesting question, however, whether, given the addition of dopplershift or velocity information to the visual display, our own visual systems could act as a spatial pattern analyser of some sort – that is, whether if we, given the intellectual knowledge of how the image is produced, were to look at the screen we could learn to use that information to guide our actions, say to walk around a room filled with objects.

References

Ackermann, F. 1981: The informativeness of philosophical analysis. In P. French, T. E. Uehling and H. Wettstein (eds), *Midwest Studies in Philosophy, Vol. 6: Foundations of Philosophy*, Minneapolis: University of Minnesota Press.

Adams, C. D. 1982: Variations in the sensitivity of instrumental responding to reinforcer devaluation. *Quarterly Journal of Experimental Psychology*, 34B, 77–98.

Adams, J. K. 1957: Laboratory studies of behavior without awareness. *Psychological Bulletin*, 54, 383–405.

Akins, K. A. 1993: What is it like to be boring and myopic? In B. Dahlbom (ed.) *Dennett and his Critics*, Oxford: Blackwell Publishers.

Allport, D. A. 1987: Selection for action: some behavioral and neurophysiological considerations of attention and action. In H. Heuer and A. F. Sanders (eds), *Perspectives on Perception and Action*, Hillsdale, NJ.: Lawrence Erlbaum Associates.

Alston, W. 1965: Expressing. In M. Black (ed.), *Philosophy in America*, Ithaca: Cornell University Press, 15–34.

Alston, W. 1967: Motives and motivation. In P. Edwards (ed.), *The Encyclopedia of Philosophy*, New York: Macmillan, 399–409.

Alston, W. 1971: Varieties of privileged access. *American Philosophical Quarterly*, 8, 223–41.

Amundson, R. 1986: The unknown epistemology of E. C. Tolman. *British Journal of Psychology*, 77, 525–31.

Anscombe, G. E. M. 1975: The first person. In S. Guttenplan (ed.), *Mind and Language*, Oxford: Oxford University Press, 45–65.

Anton, G. 1899: Ueber die Selbstwahrnemung der Herderkrankungen des Gehirns durch den Kranken bei Rindenblindheit und Rindentaubheit. *Archiv für Psychiatrie und Nervenkrankheiten*, 32, 86–127.

Antony, M. forthcoming: Against functionalist theories of consciousness.

Aristotle 1907: *De Anima*, with translation, introduction and notes by R. D. Hicks. Cambridge: Cambridge University Press.

Armstrong, D. M. 1968: *A Materialist Theory of the Mind*. New York: Humanities Press.

Armstrong, D. M. 1980: What is consciousness? In *The Nature of Mind*, Ithaca: Cornell University Press, 55–67.

Austin, J. L. 1946: Other minds. *Proceedings of the Aristotelian Society*, Suppl. 20, 148–87. Reprinted in J. L. Austin, *Philosophical Papers*, Oxford: Oxford University Press, 1961. Second edition 1970.

Austin, J. L. 1962: *How to Do Things with Words*. Cambridge, MA.: Harvard University Press. Second edition 1975.

Baars, B. J. 1988: *A Cognitive Theory of Consciousness*. Cambridge: Cambridge University Press.

Bach-y-Rita, P. 1984: The relationship between motor processes and cognition in tactile visual substitution. In W. Prinz and A. Sanders (eds), *Cognition and Motor Processes*, Berlin: Springer–Verlag, 149–60.

Baddeley, A. 1982: Domains of recollection. *Psychological Review*, 89, 708–29.

Baddeley, A. and Wilson, B. 1986: Amnesia, autobiographical memory, and confabulation. In D. C. Rubin (ed.), *Autobiographical Memory*, Cambridge: Cambridge University Press, 225–52.

Baldwin, J. M. 1906: *Mental Development in the Child and the Race*. New York: Macmillan.

Balota, D. A. 1983: Automatic semantic activation and episodic memory. *Journal of Verbal Learning and Verbal Behavior*, 22, 88–104.

Barbur, J. L., Forsyth, P. M. and Findlay, J. M. 1988: Human saccadic eye movements in the absence of the geniculo-calcarine projection. *Brain*, 111, 63–82.

Barbur, J. L., Ruddock, K. H. and Waterfield, V. A. 1980: Human visual responses in the absence of the geniculo-calcarine projection. *Brain*, 103, 905–28.

Bauer, R. M. 1984: Autonomic recognition of names and faces in prosopagnosia: a neuropsychological application of the guilty knowledge test. *Neuropsychologia*, 22, 457–69.

Bauer, R. M. 1986: The cognitive psychophysiology of prosopagnosia. In H. D. Ellis, M. A. Jeeves, F. Newcombe and A. Young (eds), *Aspects of Face Processing*, Dordrecht: Martinus Nijhoff, 253–67.

Bealer, G. 1982: *Quality and Concept*. Oxford: Oxford University Press.

Bechtel, W. 1985: Realism, instrumentalism, and the intentional stance. *Cognitive Science*, 9, 473–97.

Beckoff, M. and Jamieson, D. 1990: *Interpretation and Explanation in the Study of Animal Behavior. Vol. I: Interpretation, Intentionality, and Communication.* Boulder, Co.: Westview Press.

Bilgrami, A. 1989: Realism without internalism: a critique of Searle on intentionality. *Journal of Philosophy*, 86, 57–72.

Biro, J. I. 1985: Hume and cognitive science. *History of Philosophy Quarterly*, 2, 257–74.

Biro, J. I. 1991a: Consciousness and subjectivity. In Villaneuva, 1991, 113–33.

Biro, J. I. 1991b: Individualism and interpretation. *Acta Analytica* (Yugoslavia).

Biro, J. I. 1992: In defence of social content. *Philosophical Studies*, 67, 277–93.

Bisiach, E., Vallar, G., Perani, D., Papagno, C. and Berti, A. 1986: Unawareness of diease following lesions of the right hemisphere: anosognosia for hemiplegia and anosognosia for hemianopia. *Neuropsychologia*, 24, 471–82.

Black, M. 1954: Saying and disbelieving. In M. MacDonald (ed.), *Philosophy and Analysis*, Oxford: Basil Blackwell, 109–19.

Block, N. 1978: Troubles with functionalism. In C. Wade Savage (ed.), *Perception and Cognition: Issues in the Foundations of Psychology, Minnesota Studies in the Philosophy of Science, Vol. 9*, Minneapolis: University of Minnesota Press, 261–325. Reprinted in Block, 1980a, Vol. 1, 268–306. Excerpts reprinted in Lycan, 1990a and Rosenthal, 1991a.

Block, N. (ed.) 1980a: *Readings in the Philosophy of Psychology*. Cambridge, MA: Harvard University Press.

Block, N. 1980b: Are absent qualia impossible? *Philosophical Review*, 89, 257–74.

Block, N. 1986: Advertisement for a semantics for psychology. In P. A. French, T. E. Uehling, Jr and H. K. Wettstein (eds), *Midwest Studies in Philosophy, Vol. 10: Studies in the Philosophy of Mind*, Minneapolis: University of Minnesota Press, 615–78.

Block, N. 1990: Inverted Earth. In J. Tomberlin (ed.), *Philosophical Perspectives, Vol. 4: Action Theory and Philosophy of Mind*, Atascadero, CA: Ridgeview Publishing Company

Block, N. 1991: Evidence against epiphenomenalism. *Behavioral and Brain Sciences*, 14, 670–2.

Block, N. 1992: Begging the question against phenomenal consciousness. *Behavioral and Brain Sciences*, 15, 205–6.

Block, N. forthcoming: What neuropsychology tells us about the function of consciousness.

Block, N. and Fodor, J. A. 1972: What psychological states are not. *Philosophical Review*, 81, 159–81.

Bodamer, J. 1947: Die Prosop-Agnosie. *Archiv für Psychiatrie und Nervenkrankheiten*, 179, 6–53.

Boden, M. 1988: *Computer Models of the Mind*. Cambridge: Cambridge University Press.

Boër, S. E. and Lycan, W. G. 1980: Who me? *Philosophical Review*, 89, 427–66.

Boghossian, P. A. and Velleman, J. D. 1991: Physicalist theories of color. *Philosophical Review*, 100, 67–106.

Bonhoeffer, K. 1903: Casuistische Beiträge zur Aphasielehre. *Archiv für Psychiatrie und Nervenkrankheiten*, 37, 564–97.

Bonnano, G. A. and Stillings, N.A. 1986: Preference, familiarity, and recognition after repeated brief exposures to random geometric shapes. *American Journal of Psychology*, 99, 403–15.

Bowers, K. S. 1984: On being unconsciously influenced and informed. In

K. S. Bowers and D. Meichenbaum (eds), *The Unconscious Reconsidered*, New York: John Wiley, 227–73.

Brentano, F. 1973: *Psychology from an Empirical Standpoint*. Trans. by A. C. Rancurello, D. B. Terrell and L. L. McAlister, London: Routledge and Kegan Paul.

Brewer, W. F. 1988: Memory for randomly sampled autobiographical events. In U. Neisser and E. Winograd (eds), *Remembering Reconsidered: Ecological and Traditional Approaches to the Study of Memory*, New York: Cambridge University Press, 21–90.

Bruner, J. S. 1987: Life as a narrative. *Social Research*, 54, 11–32.

Bruner, J. S. and Postman, L. 1949: On the perception of incongruity: a paradigm. *Journal of Personality*, 18, 206–23.

Brunswik, E. 1956: *Perception and Representative Design of Psychological Experiments*. Berkeley, CA.: University of California Press.

Bruyer, R., Laterre, C., Seron, X., Feyereisen, P., Strypstein, E., Pierrard, E. and Rectem, D. 1983: A case of prosopagnosia with some preserved covert remembrance of familiar faces. *Brain and Cognition*, 2, 257–84.

Burge, T. 1978: Belief and synonymy. *Journal of Philosophy*, 75, 119–39.

Burge, T. 1986: Individualism and psychology. *Philosophical Review*, 95, 3–46.

Burnyeat, M. F. 1967–8: Belief in Speech. *Proceedings of the Aristotelian Society*, 68, 227–48.

Campion, J., Latto, R. and Smith, Y. M. 1983: Is blindsight an effect of scattered light, spared cortex, and near-threshold vision? *Behavioral and Brain Sciences*, 6, 423–86.

Castaneda, H-N. 1968: On the logic of attributions of self-knowledge to others. *Journal of Philosophy*, 65, 439–56.

Cheesman, J. and Merikle, P. M. 1984: Priming with and without awareness. *Perception and Psychophysics*, 36, 387–95.

Cheesman, J. and Merikle, P. M. 1985: Word recognition and consciousness. In D. Besner, T. G. Waller and G. E. Mackinnon (eds), *Reading Research: Advances in Theory and Practice, Vol. 5*, New York: Academic Press, 311–52.

Cheesman, J. and Merikle, P. M. 1986: Distinguishing conscious from unconscious perceptual processes. *Canadian Journal of Psychology*, 40, 343–67.

Chisholm, R. M. 1981: *The First Person*. Minneapolis: University of Minnesota Press.

Chomsky, N. 1980: *Rules and Representations*. Oxford: Basil Blackwell.

Chomsky, N. 1986: *Knowledge of Language*. New York: Praeger.

Chomsky, N. 1988: *Language and Problems of Knowledge*. Cambridge, Mass.: MIT Press.

Church, A. 1946: Review of Morton White's 'A note on the "paradox of analysis"', Max Black's ' "The paradox of analysis", again; a reply', Morton White's 'Analysis and identity: a rejoinder', and Max Black's 'How can analysis be informative?'. *Journal of Symbolic Logic*, 11, 132–3.

Churchland, P. M. 1979: *Scientific Realism and the Plasticity of Mind*. Cambridge: Cambridge University Press.

Churchland, P. M. 1985: Reduction, qualia and the direct introspection of brain states. *Journal of Philosophy*, 82, 8–28.

Churchland, P. S. 1983. Consciousness: the transmutation of a concept. *Pacific Philosophical Quarterly*, 64, 80–95.

Claparede, E. 1951: Recognition and 'me-ness'. In D. Rapaport (ed.), *Organization and Pathology of Thought*, New York: Columbia University Press, 58–75.

Cohen, N. J. and Squire, L. R. 1980: Preserved learning and retention of pattern analyzing skill in amnesia: dissociation of knowing how and knowing that. *Science*, 210, 207–9.

Colwill, R. M. and Rescorla, R. A. 1985: Instrumental responding remains sensitive to reinforcer devaluation after extensive training. *Journal of Experimental Psychology: Animal Behavior Processes*, 11, 520–36.

Conee, E. 1985: The possibility of absent qualia. *Philosophical Review*, 94, 345–66.

Cooper, L. A. and Shepard, R. N. 1984: Turning something over in the mind. *Scientific American*, 251, 106–14.

Cowey, A. 1985: Aspects of cortical organization related to selective attention and selective impairments of visual perception: a tutorial review. In M. I. Posner and O. S. M. Marin (eds), *Attention and Performance*, XI. Hillsdale, NJ: Lawrence Erlbaum Associates, 41–62.

Crick, F. and Koch, C. 1990: Towards a neurobiological theory of consciousness. *Seminars in the Neurosciences*, 2, 263–75.

Crowder, R. G. 1986: A history of subliminal perception in autobiograph. *Behavioral and Brain Sciences*, 9, 28–9.

Cummins, R. 1983: *The Nature of Psychological Explanation*. Cambridge, MA.: MIT Press.

Damasio, A. and Damasio H. 1983: The anatomic basis of pure alexia. *Neurology*, 33, 1573–83.

Damasio, A., Damasio, H. and van Hoesen, G. W. 1982: Prosopagnosia: anatomic basis and behavioral mechanisms. *Neurology*, 32, 331–41.

Damasio, A., Yamada, T., Damasio, H., Corbett, J. and McKee, J. 1980: Central achromatopsia: behavioral, anatomic, and physiologic aspects. *Neurology*, 30, 1064–71.

Davidson, D. 1980: The individuation of events. In *Essays on Actions and Events*, Oxford: Oxford University Press.

Dawkins, R. 1986: *The Blind Watchmaker*, London: Longman.

De Haan, E. H. F., Young, A. and Newcombe, F. 1987a: Faces interfere with name classification in a prosopagnosic patient. *Cortex*, 23, 309–16.

De Haan, E. H. F., Young, A. and Newcombe, F. 1987b: Face recognition without awareness. *Cognitive Neuropsychology*, 4, 385–415.

Dennett, D. C. 1969: *Content and Consciousness*. London: Routledge and Kegan Paul.

Dennett, D. C. 1976: Conditions of personhood. In A. O. Rorty (ed.), *The Identities of Persons*, Berkeley, CA.: University of California Press, 175–96.

Dennett, D. C. 1978a: *Brainstorms: Philosophical Essays on Mind and Psychology.* Cambridge, MA.: MIT Press.

Dennett, D. C. 1978b: Toward a cognitive theory of consciousness. In C. Wade Savage (ed.), *Minnesota Studies in the Philosophy of Science, Vol. 9,* Minneapolis: University of Minnesota Press, 201–28.

Dennett, D. C. 1983: Intentional systems in cognitive ethology: the 'Panglossian paradigm' defended. *Behaviorial and Brain Sciences,* 6, 343–90.

Dennett, D. C. 1987: *The Intentional Stance.* Cambridge, MA.: MIT Press.

Dennett, D. C. 1988: Quining qualia. In Marcel and Bisiach, 1988, 42–7. Reprinted in Lycan, 1990a, 519–48.

Dennett, D. C. 1991: *Consciousness Explained.* Boston: Little, Brown and Company .

Dennett, D. C. and Kinsbourne, M. 1992: Time and the observer: the where and when of consciousness in the brain. With open peer commentary and authors' response. *Behavioral and Brain Sciences,* 15, 183–247.

De Renzi, E. 1986: Current issues in prosopagnosia. In H. D. Ellis, M. A. Jeeves, F. Newcombe and A. Young (eds), *Aspects of Face Processing.* Dordrecht: Martinus Nijhoff, 243–52.

Descartes, R. 1642: *Meditations on First Philosophy.* In J. Cottingham (trans. and ed.), *René Descartes: Meditations on First Philosophy, With Selections from the Objections and Replies,* Cambridge: Cambridge University Press, 1986.

Descartes, R. 1964–76: *Oeuvres,* edited by C. Adam and P. Tannery, 11 vols. Paris: J. Vrin.

Descartes, R. 1984–91: *The Philosophical Writings of Descartes,* ed. John. Cottingham, Robert Stoothoff and Dugald Murdoch, 3 vols. Cambridge: Cambridge University Press.

Deutsch, F. 1957: A footnote to Freud's 'Fragment of an Analysis of a Case of Hysteria'. *Psychoanalytic Quarterly,* 26, 159–67.

Dewey, J. 1963: *Philosophy, Psychology, and Social Practice.* New York: Putnam.

De Yoe, E. A. and Van Essen, D. C. 1988: Concurrent processing streams in monkey visual cortex. *Trends in Neuroscience,* 11, 218–26.

Dickinson, A. 1989: Expectancy theory in animal conditioning. In S. B. Klein and R. R. Mowrer (eds), *Contemporary Learning Theories: Pavlovian Conditioning and the Status of Traditional Learning Theory,* Hillsdale, NJ.: Lawrence Erlbaum Associates, 279–308.

Dickinson, A. and Charnock, D. J. 1985: Contingency effects with maintained instrumental reinforcement. *Quarterly Journal of Experimental Psychology,* 37B, 397–416.

Dickinson, A. and Dawson, G. R. 1987a: The role of the instrumental contingency in the motivational control of performance. *Quarterly Journal of Experimental Psychology,* 39B, 77–93.

Dickinson, A. and Dawson, G. R. 1987b: Pavlovian processes in the motivational control of instrumental performance. *Quarterly Journal of Experimental Psychology,* 39B, 201–13.

Dickinson, A. and Dawson, G. R. 1988: Motivational control of instrumental performance: the role of prior experience of the reinforcer. *Quarterly Journal of Experimental Psychology*, 40B, 113–34.

Dickinson, A. and Dawson, G. R. 1989: Incentive learning and the motivational control of instrumental performance. *Quarterly Journal of Experimental Psychology*, 41B, 99–112.

Dickinson, A. and Shanks, D. R. 1985: Animal conditioning and human causality judgment. In L.-G. Nilsson and T. Archer (eds), *Perspectives on Learning and Memory, Hillsdale*, NJ.: Lawrence Erlbaum Associates, 167–96.

Dixon, N. F. 1971: *Subliminal Perception: The Nature of a Controversy*. New York: McGraw Hill.

Dixon, N. F. 1981: *Preconscious Processing*. New York: Wiley.

Dixon, N. F. 1984: Subliminal perception. In R. L. Gregory (ed.), *The Oxford Companion to the Mind*, Oxford: Oxford University Press, 752–55.

Donnellan, K. 1966: Reference and definite descriptions. *Philosophical Review*, 75, 281–304.

Dretske, F. 1988: *Explaining Behavior: Reasons in a World of Causes*. Cambridge, MA.: MIT Press.

Duke-Elder, S. 1958: *System of Ophthalmology: The Eye in Evolution (Vol. I)*. St Louis: Mosby

Duncan, J. 1985: Two techniques for investigating perception without awareness. *Perception and Psychophysics*, 38, 296–8.

Ellenberger, H. F. 1970: *The Discovery of the Unconscious*. New York: Basic Books.

Erdelyi, M. H. 1985: *Psychoanalysis: Freud's Cognitive Psychology*. New York: Freeman.

Erdelyi, M. H. 1986: Experimental indeterminacies in the dissociation paradigm. *Behavioral and Brain Sciences*, 9, 30–1.

Eriksen, C. W. 1960: Discrimination and learning without awareness: a methodological survey and evaluation. *Psychological Review*, 67, 279–30.

Field, H. 1978: Mental representation. *Erkenntnis*, 13, 9–61. Reprinted in Block, 1980a, 78–114.

Field, H. 1980: *Science without Numbers*. Oxford: Basil Blackwell.

Flanagan, O. 1989: *The Science of Mind*, second edn. Cambridge, MA.: MIT Press.

Flanagan, O. 1992: *Consciousness Reconsidered*. Cambridge, MA.: MIT Press.

Flavell, J. H. and Wellman, H. M. 1977: Metamemory. In R. V. Kail, Jr and J. W. Hagen (eds), *Perspectives on the Development of Memory and Cognition*. Hillsdale, NJ.: Lawrence Erlbaum Associates, 3–33.

Flohr, H. 1991: Brain processes and consciousness: a new and specific hypothesis. *Theory and Psychology*, 1, 245–62.

Fodor, J. A. 1975: *The Language of Thought*. New York: Crowell.

Fodor, J. A. 1981: *Representations*. Cambridge, MA.: MIT Press.

Fodor, J. A. 1983: *The Modularity of Mind*. Cambridge MA.: MIT Press.

Fodor, J. A. 1987: *Psychosemantics: The Problem of Meaning in the Philosophy of Mind*. Cambridge, MA.: MIT Press.

Fodor, J. A. 1990a: *A Theory of Content*. Cambridge, MA.: MIT Press.

Fodor, J. A. 1990b: Psychosemantics. In Lycan, 1990a, 312–38.

Forrester, J. 1984: Freud, Dora and the untold pleasures of psychoanalysis. In L. Appignanesi (ed.), *Desire*, London: Institute of Contemporary Arts, 4–9.

Foss, J. 1989: On the logic of what it is like to be a conscious subject. *Australasian Journal of Philosophy*, 67, 205–20.

Fowler, C. A., Wolford, G., Slade, R. and Tassinary, L. 1981: Lexical access with and without awareness. *Journal of Experimental Psychology: General*, 110, 341–62.

Frege, G. 1965: The thought: a logical inquiry (trans. by A. M. and Marcelle Quinton). *Mind*, 65, 289–311. Reprinted in P. F. Strawson (ed.), *Philosophical Logic*, Oxford: Oxford University Press, 1967, 17–38.

French, P., Uehling, T. and Wettstein, H. (eds) 1979: *Contemporary Perspectives in the Philosophy of Language*. Minneapolis: University of Minnesota Press.

Freud, S. 1953a: The Interpretations of Dreams (Part 1). In J. Strachey (ed. and trans.), *Standard Edition of the Complete Psychological Works of Sigmund Freud, Vol. 4*. London: Hogarth Press. (Original work published 1900.)

Freud, S. 1953b: The Psychopathology of Everyday Life. In J. Strachey (ed. and trans.), *Standard Edition of the Complete Psychological Works of Sigmund Freud, Vol. 6*. London: Hogarth Press. (Original work published 1901.)

Freud, S. 1953c: Fragment of an Analysis of a Case of Hysteria ('Dora'). In J. Strachey (ed. and trans.), *Standard Edition of the Complete Psychological Works of Sigmund Freud, Vol. 7*. London: Hogarth Press, 1–122. (Original work published 1905.)

Freud, S. 1958a: Recommendations for Physicians on the Psychoanalytic Method of Treatment. In J. Strachey (ed. and trans.), *Standard Edition of the Complete Psychological Works of Sigmund Freud, Vol. 12*. London: Hogarth Press, 107–20. (Original work published 1912.)

Freud, S. 1958b: On Beginning Treatment. In J. Strachey (ed. and trans.), *Standard Edition of the Complete Psychological Works of Sigmund Freud, Vol. 12*. London: Hogarth Press, 121–44. (Original work published 1912.)

Freud, S. 1963: Introductory Lectures on Psychoanalysis (Part 3). In J. Strachey (ed. and trans.), *Standard Edition of the Complete Psychological Works of Sigmund Freud, Vol. 16*. London: Hogarth Press. (Original work published 1916–17.)

Freud, S. 1964: New Introductory Lectures on Psychoanalysis. In J. Strachey (ed. and trans.), *Standard Edition of the Complete Psychological Works of Sigmund Freud, Vol. 22*. London: Hogarth Press. (Original work published 1933.)

Freud, S. 1985: *The Complete Letters of Sigmund Freud to Wilheim Fliess, 1887–1904*. J. M. Masson (ed. and trans.). Cambridge: Cambridge University Press.

Freud, S. and Breuer, J. 1955: Studies on Hysteria. In J. Strachey and A. Strachey (eds and trans.), *Standard Edition of the Complete Psycholotical Works of Sigmund Freud, Vol.* 2. London: Hogarth Press. (Original work published 1895.)

Gallup, J. 1982: *Feminism and Psychoanalysis: The Daughter's Seduction.* London: Macmillan.

Gay, P. 1988: *Freud: A Life for Our Time.* London: Dent.

Gazzaniga, M., Bogen, J. E. and Sperry, R. W. 1962: Some functional effects of sectioning the cerebral commisures in man. *Proceedings of the National Academy of Sciences,* 48, 1765.

Gelman, D., Rosenberg, D., Kandell, P. and Crandall, R. 1992: Is the mind an illusion? *Newsweek,* 20 April 1992, 71–2.

Gillan, D. J., Premack, D. and Woodruff, G. 1981: Reasoning in the Chimpanzee: I. Analogical reasoning. *Journal of Experimental Psychology: Animal Behavior Processes,* 7, 1–17.

Goldman, A. 1970: *A Theory of Human Action.* Englewood Cliffs, NJ.: Prentice Hall.

Gould, S. and Lewontin, R. 1979: The sprandels of San Marco and the Panglossian paradigm: a critique of the adaptionist paradigm. *Proceedings of the Royal Society,* B205, 581–98.

Gouras, P. 1984: Colour vision. In N. Osborn and J. Chader (eds), *Progress in Retinal Research, Vol. 3,* Oxford: Pergamon Press, 227–61.

Graf, P., Mandler, G. and Haden, P. 1982: Simulating amnesic symptoms in normal subjects. *Science,* 218, 1243–4.

Gregory, R. L. (ed.) 1987: *The Oxford Companion to the Mind.* Oxford: Oxford University Press.

Grice, H. P. 1957: Meaning. *Philosophical Review,* 66, 377–88.

Griffin, D. R. 1984: *Animal Thinking.* Cambridge, MA.: Harvard University Press.

Grünbaum, A. 1984: *The Foundations of Psychoanalysis: A Philosophical Critique.* Berkeley, CA.: University of California Press.

Grünbaum, A. 1986: Precis of *The Foundations of Psychoanalysis: A Philosophical Critique. Behavioral and Brain Sciences,* 9, 217–84.

Gunderson, K. 1971: *Mentality and Machines.* New York: Doubleday-Anchor.

Hammond, L. J. 1980: The effect of contingency upon appetitive free-operant behavior. *Journal of the Experimental Analysis of Behavior,* 34, 297–304.

Hampshire, S. 1971: Feeling and expression. In *Freedom of Mind.* Princeton, NJ.: Princeton University Press, 143–59.

Hardin, C. L. 1988: *Color for Philosophers.* Indianapolis: Hackett.

Hare, R. M. 1988: Replies. In D. Seanor and N. Fotion (eds), *In Hare and his Critics,* Oxford: Oxford University Press.

Harman, G. 1973: *Thought.* Princeton, NJ.: Princeton University Press.

Hécaen, H. and Angelergues R. 1962: Agnosia for faces (prosopagnosia). *Archives of Neurology,* 7, 92–100.

Heilman, K. M. 1979: Neglect and related disorders. In K. M. Heilman and E. Valenstein (eds), *Clinical Neuropsychology,* New York: Oxford University Press, 268–307.

Helmholtz, H. 1968: Concerning the perceptions in general. In W. Warren and R. Warren (eds), *Helmholtz on Perception: Its Physiology and Development*, New York: Wiley, 171–203.

Hempel, C. G. 1965: *Aspects of Scientific Explanation*. New York: The Free Press.

Hénley, S. H. A. 1984: Unconscious perception re-revisited: a comment on Merikle's (1982) paper. *Bulletin of the Psychonomic Society*, 22, 121–4.

Hershberger, W. A. 1986: An approach through the looking-glass. *Animal Learning and Behavior*, 14, 443–51.

Hertel, P. in press: Remembering with and without awareness in a depressed mood: evidence of deficits in initiative. *Journal of Experimental Psychology: General*.

Hilgard, E. 1977: *Divided Consciousness: Multiple Controls in Human Thought and Action*. New York: Wiley.

Holender, D. 1986: Semantic activation without conscious identification in dichotic listening, parafoveal vision, and visual masking: a survey and appraisal. *Behavioral and Brain Sciences*, 9, 1–66.

Holland, P. C. 1979: Differential effects of omission contingencies on various components of Pavlovian appetitive conditioning. *Journal of Experimental Psychology: Animal Behavior Processes*, 5, 178–93.

Horgan, T. 1984a: Jackson on physical information and qualia. *Philosophical Quarterly*, 34, 147–52.

Horgan, T. 1984b: Functionalism, qualia, and the inverted spectrum. *Philosophy and Phenomenological Research*, 44, 453–69.

Jackson, F. 1982: Epiphenomenal qualia. *Philosophical Quarterly*, 32, 127–36. Reprinted in Lycan, 1990a, 469–77.

Jackson, F. 1986: What Mary didn't know. *Journal of Philosophy*, 83, 291–95. Reprinted in Rosenthal, 1991a, 392–4.

Jacoby, L. L. 1984: Incidental versus intentional retrieval: remembering and awareness as separate issues. In L. R. Squire and N. Butters (eds), *Neuropsychology of Memory*, New York: Guilford Press, 145–55.

Jacoby, L. L., Allan, L. G., Collins, J. C. and Larwill, L. K. 1988: Memory influences subjective experience: noise judgments. *Journal of Experimental Psychology: Learning, Memory and Cognition*, 14, 240–7.

Jacoby, L. L. and Brooks, L. R. 1984: Nonanalytic cognition: memory, perception and concept learning. In G. H. Bower (ed.), *The Psychology of Learning and Motivation: Advances in Research and Theory (Vol. 18)*, New York: Academic Press, 1–47.

Jacoby, L. L. and Dallas, M. 1981: On the relationship between autobiographical memory and perceptual learning. *Journal of Experimental Psychology: General*, 3, 306–40.

Jacoby, L. L. and Kelley, C. M. 1987: Unconscious influences of memory for a prior event. *Personality and Social Psychology Bulletin*, 13, 314–36.

Jacoby, L. L., Kelley, C. M. and Dywan, J. 1989a: Memory attributions. In H. L. Roediger, III and F. I. M. Craik (eds), *Varieties of Memory and Consciousness: Essays in Honour of Endel Tulving*, Hillsdale, NJ.: Lawrence Erlbaum Associates.

Jacoby, L. L. and Whitehouse, K. 1989: An illusion of memory: false recognition influenced by unconscious perception. *Journal of Experimental Psychology: General*, 118, 126–35.

Jacoby, L. L. and Witherspoon, D. 1982: Remembering without awareness. *Canadian Journal of Psychology*, 36, 300–24.

Jacoby, L. L., Woloshyn, V. and Kelley, C. M. 1989b: Becoming famous without being recognized: unconscious influences of memory dividing attention. *Journal of Experimental Psychology: General*, 118, 115–25.

James, W. 1890: *The Principles of Psychology*. New York: Henry Holt and Company.

Johansson, G. 1973: Visual perception of biological motion and a model for its analysis. *Perception and Psychophysics*, 14, 201–11.

Johnson, M. K. 1988: Reality monitoring: an experimental phenomenological approach. *Journal of Experimental Psychology: General*, 117, 390–4.

Johnson, M. K., Foley, M. A., Suengas, A. G. and Raye, C. L. 1989: Phenomenal characteristics of memories for perceived and imagined autobiographical events. *Journal of Experimental Psychology*: General, 117, 371–6.

Johnson, M. K. and Hasher, L. 1987: Human learning and memory. *Annual Review of Psychology*, 38, 631–68.

Johnson, M. K. and Raye, C. L. 1981: Reality monitoring. *Psychological Review*, 88, 67–85.

Johnson-Laird, P. N. 1983: *Mental Models*. Cambridge: Cambridge University Press.

Johnson-Laird, P. N. 1988: A computational analysis of consciousness. In Marcel and Bisiach, 1988, 357–68.

Johnston, W. A., Dark, V. and Jacoby, L. L. 1985: Perceptual fluency and recognition judgments. *Journal of Experimental Psychology: Learning, Memory, and Cognition*, 11, 3–11.

Kant, I. 1781: *Critique of Pure Reason*. Second edition 1787. Translated by N. Kemp Smith. New York: St Martin's Press, 1929.

Kaplan, D. 1978: On the logic of demonstratives. In French et al. , 1979, 401–12.

Kardiner, A. 1977: *My Analysis with Freud: Reminiscences*. New York: Norton.

Karnath, H-O. 1988: Deficits of attention in acute and recovered visual hemineglect. *Neuropsychologia*, 26, 27–43.

Karnath, H-O. and Hartje, W. 1987: Residual information processing in the neglected visual half-field. *Journal of Neurology*, 234, 180–4.

Kelley, C. M., Jacoby, L. L and Hollingshead, A. 1989: Direct versus indirect tests of memory for source: judgments of modality. *Journal of Experimental Psychology: Learning, Memory, and Cognition*, 15, 1101–8.

Kelley, C. M., Lindsay, D. S. and Holland, S. forthcoming: Ease of generation and the phenomenology of memory.

Kolers, P. A. 1976: Reading a year later. *Journal of Experimental Psychology: Human Learning and Memory*, 2, 554–65.

Kosslyn, S. M. 1980: *Image and Mind*. Cambridge, MA.: Harvard University Press.

Kosslyn, S. M. 1987: Seeing and imaging in the cerebral hemispheres: a computational approach. *Psychological Review*, 94, 148–75.

Kripke, S. 1979: A puzzle about belief. In A. Margalit (ed.), *Meaning and Use*, Dordrecht: Reidel, 239–83.

Kripke, S. 1980: *Naming and Necessity*. Oxford: Blackwell.

Kunst-Wilson, W. R. and Zajonc, R. B. 1980: Affective discrimination of stimuli that cannot be becognized. *Science*, 207, 557–8.

Lacan, J. 1982: Intervention on transference (trans. J. Rose). In J. Mitchell and J. Rose (eds), *Feminine Sexuality: Jacques Lacan and the Ecole Freudienne*, London: Macmillan, 61–73. (Original work published 1952.)

Lambert, M. J., Shapiro, D. A. and Bergin, A. E. 1986: The effectiveness of psychotherapy. In S. L. Garfield and A. E. Bergin (eds), *Handbook of Psychotherapy and Behavior Change: An Empirical Analysis (3rd edn)*, New York: Wiley, 157–211.

Landis, T. , Cummings, J. L. , Christen, L. , Bogen, J. E. and Imhof, H-G. 1986: Are unilateral right posterior cerebral lesions sufficient to cause prosopagnosia? Clinical and radiological findings in six additional patients. *Cortex*, 22, 243–52.

Landis, T. , Regard, M. and Serrat, A. 1980: Iconic reading in a case of alexia without agraphia caused by a brain tumour: a tachistoscopic study. *Brain and Language*, 11, 45–53.

Laplanche, J. and Pontalis, J-B. 1980: *The Language of Psychoanalysis* (trans. D. Nicholson-Smith). London: Hogarth Press.

Leahey, T. H. 1987: *A History of Psychology: Main Currents in Psychological Thought*. Englewood Cliffs, NJ.: Prentice Hall.

Leibniz, G. W. 1714: *Principles of Nature and Grace, Based on Reason*. Reprinted in R. Ariew and D. Garber (eds and trans.), *G. W. Leibniz: Philosophical Essays*. Indianapolis: Hackett, 1989.

Levin, J. 1986: Could love be like a heatwave? Physicalism and the subjective character of experience. *Philosophical Studies*, 49, 245–61. Reprinted in Lycan, 1990a, 478–90.

Levine, J. 1983: Materialism and qualia: the explanatory gap. *Pacific Philosophical Quarterly*, 64, 354–61.

Levine, J. 1989: Absent and inverted qualia revisited. *Mind & Language*, 3, 271–87.

Levine, J. 1991: Cool red. *Philosophical Psychology*, 4, 27–40.

Lewis, D. 1966: An argument for the identity theory. *Journal of Philosophy*, 63, 17–25. Reprinted in D. Lewis, *Philosophical Papers, Vol. 1*, Oxford: Oxford University Press, 99–107, 1983.

Lewis, D. 1972: Psychophysical and theoretical identifications. *Australasian Journal of Philosophy*, 50, 249–58. Reprinted in Block, 1980a, 207–15, and Rosenthal, 1991a, 204–10.

Lewis, D. 1979: Attitudes *de dicto* and *de se*. *Philosophical Review*, 88, 513–43.

Lewis, D. 1983: Postscript to 'Mad Pain and Martian Pain'. In D. Lewis, *Philosophical Papers, Vol. 1*, Oxford University Press: Oxford, 130–32.

Lewis, D. 1986: *On the Plurality of Worlds*. Oxford: Basil Blackwell.

Lewis, D. 1988: What experience teaches. In Lycan, 1990a, 499–519.

Libet, B. 1985: Unconscious cerebral initiative and the role of conscious will in voluntary action. *Behavioral and Brain Sciences*, 8, 529–66.

Loar, B. 1981: *Mind and Meaning*. Cambridge: Cambridge University Press.

Loar, B. 1989: Social content and psychological content. In R. Grimm and D. Merrill (eds), *Contents of Thought*, Tucson: University of Arizona Press, 99–110.

Loar, B. 1990: Phenomenal properties. In *Philosophical Perspectives, Vol. 4, Action Theory and Philosophy of Mind*, Atascadero, CA.: Ridgeview, 81–108.

Locke, J. 1700: *An Essay Concerning Human Understanding*, 4th edn, ed. Peter H. Nidditch. Oxford: Oxford University Press, 1975.

Lockery, S. 1989: Representation, functionalism and simple living systems. In A. Montefiore and D. Noble (eds), *Goals, No-goals and Own Goals*, London: Unwin Hyman, 117–58.

Lockhart, R. S. 1984: What do infants remember? In M. Moscovitch (ed.), *Infant Memory*, New York: Plenum, 131–43.

Loewer, B. and Rey, G. 1991: *Meaning in Mind: Fodor and his Critics*. Oxford: Blackwell.

Loftus, E. 1979: *Eyewitness Testimony*. Cambridge, MA.: Harvard University Press.

Logan, G. D. 1988: Toward an instance theory of automatization. *Psychological Review*, 95, 492–527.

Lorenz, K. 1973: *Behind the Mirror*. New York: Harcourt Brace Jovanich.

Luborsky, L., Crits-Christoph, P. and Mellon, J. 1986: Advent of objective measures of the transference concept. *Journal of Clinical and Consulting Psychology*, 54, 39–47.

Lycan, W. G. 1987: *Consciousness*. Cambridge, MA.: MIT Press.

Lycan, W. G. (ed.) 1990a: *Mind and Cognition: A Reader*. Oxford: Basil Blackwell.

Lycan, W. G. 1990b: What is the subjectivity of the mental? In J. E. Tomberlin (ed.), *Philosophical Perspectives, Vol. 4, Action Theory and Philosophy of Mind*, Atascadero, CA.: Ridgeview, 109–30.

McGinn, C. 1982: *The Character of Mind*. Oxford: Oxford University Press.

McGinn, C. 1983: *The Subjective View*. Oxford: Oxford University Press.

McGinn, C. 1988: Consciousness and content. *Proceedings of the British Academy*, 74, 219–39. Reprinted in McGinn, 1991, 23–43.

McGinn, C. 1989: Can we solve the mind–body problem? *Mind*, 98, 349–66. Reprinted in McGinn, 1991, 1–22.

McGinn, C. 1991: *The Problem of Consciousness*. Oxford: Basil Blackwell.

McGlynn, S. and Schacter, D. L. 1989: Unawareness of deficits in neuropsychological syndromes. *Journal of Clinical and Experimental Neuropsychology*, 11, 143–205.

Macmillan, N. A. 1986: The psychophysics of subliminal perception. *Behavioral and Brain Sciences*, 9, 38–9.

Malcolm, N. 1963a: Knowledge of other minds. In *Knowledge and Certainty*, Englewood Cliffs, NJ.: Prentice-Hall, 130–40.

Malcolm, N. 1963b: Wittgenstein's *Philosophical Investigations*. In *Knowledge and Certainty*, Englewood Cliffs, NJ.: Prentice-Hall, 96–129.

Malcolm, N. 1977: Thoughtless brutes. In *Thought and Knowledge*, Ithaca: Cornell University Press, 40–57.

Maloney, C. 1985: About being a bat. *Australasian Journal of Philosophy*, 63, 26–49.

Mandler, G. 1989: Memory: conscious and unconscious. In P. Solomon, G. Goethals, C. Kelley and B. Stephens (eds), *Memory: Interdisciplinary Approaches*, New York: Springer-Verlag.

Mandler, G. and Nakamura, Y. 1987: Aspects of consciousness. *Personality and Social Psychology Bulletin*, 13, 299–313.

Mandler, G., Nakamura, Y. and van Zandt, B. J. S. 1987: Nonspecific effects of exposure on stimuli that cannot be recognized. *Journal of Experimental Psychology: Learning, Memory, and Cognition*, 13, 646–8.

Marcel, A. J. 1974: Perception with and without awareness. Paper presented at the Meeting of the Experimental Psychology Society, Stirling, Scotland.

Marcel, A. J. 1980: Conscious and preconscious recognition of polysemous words: locating the selective effects of prior verbal context. In R. S. Nickerson (ed.), *Attention and Performance VIII*, Hillsdale, NJ.: Lawrence Erlbaum Associates, 435–57.

Marcel, A. J. 1983a: Conscious and unconscious perception: experiments on visual masking and word recognition. *Cognitive Psychology*, 15, 197–237.

Marcel, A. J. 1983b: Conscious and unconscious perception: an approach to the relations between phenomenal experience and perceptual processes. *Cognitive Psychology*, 15, 238–300.

Marcel, A. J. 1988: Phenomenal experience and functionalism. In Marcel and Bisiach, 1988, 121–58.

Marcel, A. J. and Bisiach E. (eds) 1988: *Consciousness in Contemporary Science*. Oxford: Oxford University Press.

Marcus, S. 1974: Freud and Dora: story, history, case history. *Partisan Review*, Winter 1974.

Marr, D. 1982: *Vision*. San Francisco: Freeman.

Marshall, J. C. and Halligan, P. W. 1988: Blindsight and insight in visuo-spatial neglect. *Nature*, 336, 766–7.

Masson, J. M. 1984: *Freud: The Assault on Truth*. London: Faber.

Mates, B. 1951: Synonymity. *University of California Publications in Philosophy*, 25, 201–26. Reprinted in L. Linsky (ed.), *Semantics and the Philosophy of Language*, Chicago: University of Chicago Press, 1952.

Maudlin, T. 1989: Computation and consciousness. *Journal of Philosophy*, 86, 407–32.

Meadows, J. C. 1974: The anatomical basis of prosopagnosia. *Journal of Neurology, Neurosurgery, and Psychiatry*, 37, 489–501.

Mellor, D. H. 1977–8: Conscious belief. *Proceedings of the Aristotelian Society*, 78, 87–101.

Mellor, D. H. 1980: Consciousness and degrees of belief. In D. H. Mellor (ed.), *Prospects for Pragmatism*, Cambridge: Cambridge University Press, 139–73.

Mellor, D. H. 1984: What is computational psychology? *Proceedings of the Aristotelian Society, Supplementary Volume* 58, 37–53.

Merikle, P. M. 1982: Unconscious perception revisited. *Perception and Psychophysics*, 31, 298–301.

Merikle, P. M. 1984: Toward a definition of awareness. *Bulletin of the Psychonomic Society*, 22, 449–50.

Merikle, P. M. and Reingold, E. M. 1990: Recognition and lexical decisions without detection; unconscious perception? *Journal of Experimental Psychology: Human Perception and Performance*, 16, 574–83.

Merikle, P. M. and Reingold, E. M. 1991: Comparing direct (explicit) and indirect (implicit) measures to study unconscious memory. *Journal of Experimental Psychology: Learning, Memory, and Cognition*, 17, 224–33.

Meyer, N. 1975: *The Seven Percent Solution.* London: Hodder and Stoughton.

Miller, G. A. 1966: *Psychology: The Science of Mental Life.* Harmondsworth: Pelican.

Miller, J. G. 1939: Discrimination without awareness. *American Journal of Psychology*, 52, 562–78.

Millikan, R. 1984: *Language, Thought, and Other Biological Categories.* Cambridge, MA.: MIT Press.

Montefiore, A. 1989: Intentions and causes. In A. Montefiore and D. Noble (eds), *Goals, No-goals and Own Goals*, London: Unwin-Hyman, 58–80.

Moore, G. E. 1942: A reply to my critics. In P. A. Schilpp (ed.), *The Philosophy of G. E. Moore*, New York: Tudor Publishing Company, 533–677. Second edition 1952.

Moore, G. E. 1944: Russell's 'Theory of Descriptions'. In P. A. Schilpp (ed.), *The Philosophy of Bertrand Russell*, New York: Tudor Publishing Company, 175–226.

Moore, G. E. 1959: Is existence a predicate? In *Philosophical Papers*, London: George Allen and Unwin Ltd, 114–25.

Moscovitch, M. 1984: The sufficient conditions for demonstrating preserved memory in amnesia: a task analysis. In L. R. Squire and N. Butter (eds), *Neuropsychology of Memory*, New York: Guilford Press, 104–14.

Nagel, T. 1971: Brain bisection and the unity of consciousness. *Synthese*, 22, 396–413. Reprinted in J. Glover (ed.), *The Philosophy of Mind*, Oxford: Oxford University Press, 1976, 111–25.

Nagel, T. 1974: What is it like to be a bat?, *Philosophical Review*, 83, 435–50. Reprinted in T. Nagel, *Mortal Questions*, Cambridge: Cambridge University Press, 1979, 165–180. Also reprinted in Rosenthal, 1991a, 422–8.

Nagel, T. 1979a: Panpsychism. In *Mortal Questions*, Cambridge: Cambridge University Press, 181–95.

Nagel, T. 1979b: Subjective and objective. In *Mortal Questions*, Cambridge: Cambridge University Press, 196–213.

Nagel, T. 1986: *The View from Nowhere.* Oxford: Oxford University Press.

Navon, D. 1986: On determining what is unconscious and what is perception. *Behavioral and Brain Sciences*, 9, 44–5.

Neisser, U. 1963: The imitation of man by machine. *Science*, 139, 193–7.

Nelkin, N. 1986: Pains and pain sensations. *Journal of Philosophy*, 83, 129–48.

Nelkin, N. 1987a: How sensations get their names. *Philosophical Studies*, 51, 325–39.

Nelkin, N. 1987b: What is it like to be a person? *Mind & Language*, 2, 220–41.

Nelkin, N. 1989a: Propositional attitudes and consciousness. *Philosophy and Phenomenological Research*, 49, 413–30.

Nelkin, N. 1989b: Unconscious sensations. *Philosophical Psychology*, 2, 129–41.

Nelkin, N. 1990: What is consciousness? Paper presented to the Society for Philosophy and Psychology, University of Maryland, June 1990.

Nelkin, N. forthcoming: Phenomena and representation. *British Journal for the Philosophy of Science*.

Nemirow, L. 1980: Review of T. Nagel, 'Mortal Questions' *Philosophical Review*, 475–6.

Nemirow, L. 1990: Physicalism and the cognitive role of acquaintance. In Lycan, 1990a, 490–9.

Newcombe, F. , Young, A. and de Haan, E. H. F. 1989: Prosopagnosia and object agnosia without covert recognition. *Neuropsychologia*, 27, 179–91.

Nisbett, R. E. and Wilson, T. D. 1977: Telling more than we can know: verbal reports on mental processes. *Psychological Review*, 84, 231–59.

Nolan, K. A. and Caramazza, A. 1982: Unconscious perception of meaning: a failure to replicate. *Bulletin of the Psychonomic Society*, 20, 23–6.

Norman, D. A. 1986: Reflections on cognition and parallel distributed processing. In D. E. Rumelhart, J. L. McClelland and the PDP Research Group (eds), *Parallel Distributed Processing; Explorations in the Microstructure of Cognition*, Cambridge, MA.: MIT Press, 531–46.

Norman, D. A. and Shallice, T. 1986: Attention to action: willed and automatic control of behavior. In J. R. Davidson, G. E. Schwartz and D. Shapiro (eds), *Consciousness and Self-regulation*, New York: Plenum Press.

Oatley, K. 1987: Experiments and experience: usefulness and insight in psychology. In H. Beloff and A. M. Colman (eds), *Psychology Survey, Vol. 6*, Leicester: British Psychological Society, 1–27.

Papineau, D. 1987: *Reality and Representation*. Oxford: Basil Blackwell.

Parfit, D. 1984: *Reasons and Persons*. Oxford: Oxford University Press.

Parisi, T. 1987: Why Freud failed: some implications for neurophysiology and sociobiology. *American Psychologist*, 42, 235–45.

Peacocke, C. 1992: *A Study of Concepts*. Cambridge, MA.: MIT Press.

Pepperberg, I. 1987: Acquisition of the same/different concept by an African Grey Parrot (Psittacus erithacus): learning with respect to categories of color, shape, and material. *Animal Learning and Behavior*, 15, 423–32.

Perenin, M. T. and Jeannerod, M. 1975: Residual vision in cortically blind hemifields. *Neuropsychologia*, 13, 1–7.

Perry, J. 1979: The problem of the essential indexical. *Nous*, 13, 3–21.

Perry, J. 1986: Thought without representation. *Proceedings of the Aristotelian Society*, Suppl. 60, 137–51. Reprinted in J. Perry, *The Problem of the Essential Indexical and Other Essays*, Oxford: Oxford University Press, 1992.

Piaget, J. and Inhelder, B. 1956: *The Child's Conception of Space*. London: Routledge and Kegan Paul.

Pöppel, E. 1983: Residual vision is an answer to what? *Behavioral and Brain Sciences*, 3, 459–60.

Pöppel, E. , Held, R. and Frost, D. 1973: Residual visual function after brain wounds involving the central visual pathways in man. *Nature*, 243, 295–6.

Popper, K. and Eccles, J. 1977: *The Self and its Brain*. Berlin, Heidelberg, London, New York: Springer International.

Purcell, D. G., Stewart, A. L. and Stanovich, K. E. 1983: Another look at semantic priming without awareness. *Perception and Psychophysics*, 34, 65–71.

Putnam, H. 1975a: The nature of mental states. In *Mind, Language and Reality*. Cambridge: Cambridge University Press.

Putnam, H. 1975b: The meaning of meaning. In K. Gunderson (ed.), *Language, Mind, and Knowledge*, Minneapolis: University of Minnesota Press, 131–93.

Pylyshyn, Z. 1984: *Computation and Cognition*. Cambridge, MA.: MIT Press.

Quine, W. 1953: *From a Logical Point of View and Other Essays*. New York: Harper and Row.

Quine, W. 1960: *Word and Object*. Cambridge, MA.: MIT Press.

Raney, A. A. and Nielsen, J. M. 1942: Denial of blindness (Anton's symptom). *Bulletin of Los Angeles Neurological Society*, 7, 150–1.

Reason, J. T. 1979: Actions not as planned. In G. Underwood and R. Stevens (eds), *Aspects of Consciousness, Vol. 1*, London: Academic Press.

Redlich, F. C. and Dorsey, J. F. 1945: Denial of blindness by patients with cerebral disease. *Archives of Neurology and Psychiatry*, 53, 401–17.

Reingold, E. M. and Merikle, P. M. 1988: Using direct and indirect measures to study perception without awareness. *Perception and Psychophysics*, 44, 563–75.

Renault, B., Signoret, J. L., DeBruille, B., Breton, F. and Bolgert, F. 1989: Brain potentials reveal covert facial recognition in prosopagnosia. *Neuropsychologia*, 27, 905–12.

Rescorla, R. A. and Skucy, J. C. 1969: Effect of response-independent reinforcers during extinction. *Journal of Comparative and Physiological Psychology*, 67, 381–9.

Rey, G. 1976: Survival. In A. Rorty (ed.), *The Identities of Persons*, Berkeley, CA.: University of California Press.

Rey, G. 1980a: What are mental images? In N. Block, 1980a, 117–27.

Rey, G. 1980b: Functionalism, and the emotions. In A. Rorty (ed.), *Explaining Emotions*, Berkeley, CA.: University of California Press, 163–95.

Rey, G. 1983: A reason for doubting the existence of consciousness. In R. Davidson, G. Schwartz and D. Shapiro (eds), *Consciousness and Self-Regulation, Vol. 3*, New York: Plenum, 1–39.

Rey, G. 1986: What's really going on in Searle's 'Chinese Room'. *Philosophical Studies*, 50, 169–85.

Rey, G. 1988a: A question about consciousness. In H. Otto and J. Tuedio (eds), *Perspectives on Mind*, Dordrecht: Reidel.

Rey, G. 1988b: Toward a computational account of *akrasia* and self-deception. In B. McLaughlin and A. Rorty (eds), *Perspectives on Self-Deception*, Berkeley, CA.: University of California Press, 264–96.

Rey, G. 1991a: An explanatory budget for connectionism and eliminativism. In T. Horgan and G. Graham (eds), *Connectionism and the Philosophy of Mind*, Dordrecht: Kluwer.

Rey, G. 1991b: Sensations in a language of thought. In Villanueva, 1991, 73–112.

Rey, G. 1992: Sensational sentences switched. *Philosophical Studies*, 67, 73–103.

Richardson-Klavehn, A. and Bjork, R. A. 1988: Measures of memory. *Annual Review of Psychology*, 39, 475–543.

Rizzo, M. , Hurtig, R. and Damasio, A. R. 1987: The role of scanpaths in facial recognition and learning. *Annals of Neurology*, 22, 41–5.

Rosenberg, J. F. 1977: Speaking lions. *Canadian Journal of Philosophy*, 7, 155–60.

Rosenthal, D. M. 1985: Intentionality. *Midwest Studies in Philosophy*, 10, 151–84. Reprinted with postscript in S. Silvers (ed.), *Rereresentation: Readings in the Philosophy of Mental Representation*, Dordecht: D. Reidel, 1989, 311–39, postscript 341–4.

Rosenthal, D. M. 1986: Two concepts of consciousness. *Philosophical Studies*, 49, 329–59.

Rosenthal, D. M. 1990a: A theory of consciousness. Report No. 40, Center for Interdisciplinary Research (ZiF), Research Group on Mind and Brain, University of Bielefeld.

Rosenthal, D. M. 1990b: The colors and shapes of visual experiences. Report No. 28, Center for Interdisciplinary Research (ZiF), Research Group on Mind and Brain, University of Bielefield.

Rosenthal, D. M. 1990c: Why are verbally expressed thoughts conscious? Report No. 32, Center for Interdisciplinary Research (ZiF), Research Group on Mind and Brain, University of Bielefeld.

Rosenthal, D. M. (ed.) 1991a: *The Nature of Mind*. Oxford: Oxford University Press.

Rosenthal, D. M. 1991b: Consciousness and speech. Unpublished typescript.

Ross, J. R. 1970: On declarative sentences. In R. A. Jacobs and P. S. Rosenbaum (eds), *Readings in English Transformational Grammar*, Waltham: Ginn and Co, 222–72.

Ross, M. 1989: Relation of implicit theories to the construction of personal histories. *Psychological Review*, 96, 341–57.

Rovee-Collier, C. 1989: The joy of kicking: memories, motives, and mobiles. In P. R. Solomon, G. R. Goethals, C. M. Kelley and B. R. Stephens (eds), *Memory: Interdisciplinary Approaches*, New York: Springer-Verlag, 151–80.

Runeson, S. and Frykholm, G. 1983: Kinematic specification of dynamics as an informational basis for person-and-action perception: expectation, gender recognition, and deceptive intention. *Journal of Experimental Psychology: General*, 112, 585–615.

Russow, L-M. 1982: It's not like that to be a bat. *Behaviorism*, 10, 55–63.

Ryle, G. 1949: *The Concept of Mind*. London: Hutchinson.

Sacks, O. 1984: *A Leg to Stand On*. Summit Books: New York.

Samuel, A. 1981: Phoneme restoration: insights from a new methodology. *Journal of Experimental Psychology: General*, 110, 474–94.

Schacter, D. L. 1987: Implicit memory: history and current status. *Journal of Experimental Psychology: Learning, Memory and Cognition*, 13, 501–18.

Schacter, D. L., McAndrews, M. P. and Moscovitch, M. 1988: Access to consciousness: dissociations between implicit and explicit knowledge in neuropsychological syndromes. In L. Weiskrantz (ed.), *Thought Without Language*, Oxford: Oxford University Press, 242–78.

Schank, R. C. and Abelson, R. P. 1977: *Scripts, Goals, Plans and Understanding*, Hillsdale, NJ.: Lawrence Erlbaum Associates.

Schiffer, S. 1987: *Remnants of Meaning*. Cambridge, MA.: MIT Press.

Schooler, J. W., Gerhard, D. and Loftus, E. F. 1986: Qualities of the unreal. *Journal of Experimental Psychology: Learning, Memory, and Cognition*, 12, 171–81.

Seamon, J. G., Marsh, R. L. and Brody, N. 1984: Critical importance of exposure duration for affective discrimination of stimuli that are not recognized. *Journal of Experimental Psychology: Learning, Memory, and Cognition*, 10, 465–9.

Seanor, D. and Fotion, N. (eds) 1988: *Hare and his Critics*. Oxford: Oxford University Press.

Searle, J. 1980: Minds, brains, and programs. *Behavioral and Brain Sciences*, 3, 417–57.

Searle, J. 1982: The myth of computers. *New York Review*, 29 April, 3–6.

Searle, J. 1983: *Intentionality: An Essay in the Philosophy of Mind*. Cambridge: Cambridge University Press.

Searle, J. 1988: The realistic stance. *Behavioral and Brain Sciences*, 11, 527–9.

Searle, J. 1989: Consciousness, unconsciousness, and intentionality. *Philosophical Topics*, 17, 193–209. Reprinted in Villanueva, 1991, 45–66.

Searle, J. 1990a: Is the brain a digital computer? *Proceedings of the American Philosophical Association*, 64(3), 21–37.

Searle, J. 1990b: Consciousness, explanatory inversion, and cognitive science. *Behavioral and Brain Sciences*, 13, 585–642.

Searle, J. 1992: *The Rediscovery of Mind*. Cambridge, MA.: MIT Press.

Sellars, W. 1956: Empiricism and the philosophy of mind. In H. Feigl and M. Scriven (eds), *Minnesota Studies in the Philosophy of Science, Vol. 1*, Minneapolis: University of Minnesota Press. Reprinted in Sellars, 1963, 127–96.

Sellars, W. 1963: *Science, Perception and Reality*. London: Routledge and Kegan Paul.

Sellars, W. 1964: Notices on intentionality. *Journal of Philosophy*, 61, 655–65.

Shakespeare, W. 1951: *Macbeth* (ed. J. D. Wilson). Cambridge: Cambridge University Press. (Original work published 1623.)

Shallice, T. 1972: Dual functions of consciousness. *Psychological Review*, 79, 383–93.

Shallice, T. 1988: *From Neuropsychology to Mental Structure*. Cambridge: Cambridge University Press.

Shallice, T. and Saffran, E. 1986: Lexical processing in the absence of explicit word identification: evidence from a letter-by-letter reader. *Cognitive Neuropsychology*, 3, 429–58.

Shanks, D. R. 1987: Acquisition functions in contingency judgment. *Learning and Motivation*, 18, 147–66.

Shanks, D. R. 1989: Selectional processes in causality judgment. *Memory and Cognition*, 17, 27–34.

Shanks, D. R. , Pearson, S. M. and Dickinson, A. 1989: Temporal contiguity and the judgement of causality by human subjects. *Quarterly Journal of Experimental Psychology*, 41B, 139–59.

Shevrin, H. and Dickman, S. 1980: The psychological unconscious: a necessary assumption for all psychological theory? *American Psychologist*, 35, 421–34.

Shimamura, A. P. 1986: Priming effects in amnesia: evidence for a dissociable memory function. *Quarterly Journal of Experimental Psychology*, 38A, 619–44.

Shoemaker, S. 1975: Functionalism and qualia. *Philosophical Studies*, 27, 291–315.

Shoemaker, S. 1981a: The inverted spectrum. *Journal of Philosophy*, 74, 357–81.

Shoemaker, S. 1981b: Absent qualia are impossible – a reply to Block. *Philosophical Review*, 90, 581–99.

Shoemaker, S. 1984: *Identity, Cause, and Mind*. Cambridge: Cambridge University Press.

Sidelle, A. 1989: *Necessity, Essence, and Individuation: A Defense of Conventionalism*. Ithaca: Cornell University Press.

Sidis, B. 1898: *The Psychology of Suggestion*. New York: Appleton. Reprinted edn, 1973, Arno Press.

Smart, J. J. C. 1959: Sensations and brain processes. *Philosophical Review*, 68, 141–56. Reprinted in V. C. Chappell (ed.), *The Philosophy of Mind*, Englewood Cliffs, NJ.: Prentice-Hall, 1962, 160–72.

Smith, M. L., Glass, G. V. and Miller, T. I. 1980: *The Benefits of Psychotherapy*. Baltimore: Johns Hopkins University Press.

Stampe, D. 1979: Towards a causal theory of linguistic representation. In French et al., 1979, 81–102.

Stalnaker, R. 1984: *Inquiry*. Cambridge, MA.: MIT.

Stich, S. 1978: Beliefs and subdoxastic states. *Philosophy of Science*, 45, 499–518.

Stich, S. 1983: *From Folk Psychology to Cognitive Science: The Case Against Belief*. Cambridge, MA.: MIT Press.

Stoerig, P. 1987: Chromaticity and achromaticity: evidence for a functional differentation in visual field defects. *Brain*, 110, 869–86.

Stoerig, P. and Cowey, A. 1989: Wavelength sensitivity in blindsight. *Nature*, 342, 916–18.

Strawson, G. 1987: *Freedom and Belief*. Oxford: Oxford University Press.

Strawson, P. F. 1959: *Individuals*. London: Methuen.

Stroh, M. A. , Shaw, M. and Washburn, M. F. 1908: A study of guessing. *American Journal of Psychology*, 19, 243–5.

Stuss, D. T. and Benson, D. F. 1986: *The Frontal Lobes*. New York: Raven Press.

Sulloway, F. J. 1979: *Freud, Biologist of the Mind: Beyond the Pschyoanalytic Legend*. New York: Basic Books.

Sutherland, N. S. 1989: *Macmillan Dictionary of Psychology*. London: Macmillan.

Sutton, R. S. and Barto, A. G. 1981: An adaptive network that constructs and uses an internal model of its world. *Cognition and Brain Theory*, 4, 217–46.

Swinney, D. 1979: Lexical access during sentence comprehension: (Re)consideration of context effects. *Journal of Verbal Learning and Verbal Behaviour*, 18, 645–59.

Talland, G. A. 1968: *Disorders of Memory and Learning*. Harmondsworth, Middlesex: Penguin.

Thomson, D. M. 1986: Face recognition: more than a feeling of familiarity? In H. D. Ellis, M. A. Jeeves, F. Newcombe and A. Young (eds), *Aspects of Face Processing*, Dordrecht: Martinus Nijhoff, 118–22.

Tolman, E. C. 1932: *Purposive Behaviour in Animals and Man*. New York: Appleton–Century–Crofts.

Tranel, D. and Damasio, A. R. 1985: Knowledge without awareness: an autonomic index of facial recognition by prosopagnosics. *Science*, 228, 1453–4.

Tranel, D. and Damasio, A. R. 1988: Non-conscious face recognition in patients with face agnosia. *Behavioural Brain Research*, 30, 235–49.

Tulving, E. 1983: *Elements of Episodic Memory*. New York: Oxford University Press.

Tulving, E. 1985: Memory and consciousness. *Canadian Psychology*, 26, 1–12.

Tulving, E., Schacter, D. L. and Stark, H. A. 1982: Priming effects in word-fragment completion are independent of recognition memory. *Journal of Experimental Psychology: Learning, Memory, and Cognition*, 8, 336–42.

Tye, M. 1986: The subjectivity of experience. *Mind*, 95, 1–17.

Ungerleider, L. G. and Mishkin, M. 1982: Two cortical visual systems. In D. J. Ingle, M. A. Goodale and R. J. W. Mansfield (eds), *Analysis of Visual Behavior*, Cambridge, MA.: MIT Press, 549–86.

Van Gulick, R. 1985: Physicalism and the subjectivity of the mental. *Philosophical Topics*, 13, 51–70.

Van Gulick, R. 1988a: A functionalist plea for self-consciousness. *Philosophical Review*, 97, 149–81.

Van Gulick, R. 1988b: Consciousness, intrinsic intentionality and self-understanding machines. In Marcel and Bisiach, 1988, 78–100.

Van Gulick, R. 1989: What difference does consciousness make? *Philosophical Topics*, 17, 211–30.

Vendler, Z. 1972: *Res Cogitans*. Ithaca: Cornell University Press.

Vendler, Z. 1984: *The Matter of Minds*. Oxford: Oxford University Press.

Vendler, Z. 1988: Changing places? In D. Seanor and N. Fotion (eds), *Hare and his Critics*, Oxford: Oxford University Press.

Villanueva, E. 1991: *Philosophical Issues 1: Consciousness*. Atascadero, CA: Ridgeview Publishing Company.

Volpe, B. T. , Ledoux, J. E. and Gazzaniga, M. S. 1979: Information processing of visual stimuli in an 'extinguished' field. *Nature*, 282, 722–4.

Von Monakow, C. 1885: Experimentelle und pathologisch-anatomische Untersuchungen über die Beziehungen der sogenannten Sehsphäre zu den infracorticalen Opticuscentren und zum N. opticus. *Archiv für Psychiatrie und Nervenkrankheiten*, 16, 151–99.

Warren, R. 1970: Perceptual restoration of missing speech sounds. *Science*, 167, 392–3.

Warrington, E. K. and Weiskrantz, L. 1968: New method of testing long-term retention with special reference to amnesic patients. *Nature*, 217, 972–4.

Warrington, E. K. and Weiskrantz, L. 1970: Amnesia: consolidation or retrieval? *Nature*, 228, 628–30.

Warrington, E. K. and Weiskrantz, L. 1974: The effect on prior learning on subsequent retention in amnesic patients. *Neuropsychologia*, 12, 419–28.

Warrington, E. K. and Weiskrantz, L. 1982: Amnesia: a disconnection syndrome? *Neuropsychologia*, 20, 233–48.

Wason, P. C. and Evans, J. St B. T. 1974: Dual processes in reasoning? *Cognition*, 3, 141–54.

Weber, M. 1968: *Economy and Society* (eds G. Roth and C. Wittich). New York: Bedminster Press. (Original work published 1922.)

Webster, F. A. and Griffin, D. R. 1962: The role of the flight membranes in insect capture in bats. *Animal Behavior*, 10, 332–40.

Wegman, C. 1985: *Psychoanalysis and Cognitive Psychology: A Formulation of Freud's Earliest Theory*. London: Academic Press.

Weiskrantz, L. 1977: Trying to bridge some neuropsychological gaps between monkey and man. *British Journal of Psychology*, 68, 431–45.

Weiskrantz, L. 1980: Varieties of residual experience. *Quarterly Journal of Experimental Psychology*, 32, 365–86.

Weiskrantz, L. 1986: *Blindsight: A Case Study and Implications*. Oxford: Oxford University Press.

Weiskrantz, L. 1987: Residual vision in a scotoma: a follow-up study of 'form' discrimination. *Brain*, 110, 77–92.

Weiskrantz, L. 1988: Some contributions of neuropsychology of vision and memory to the problem of consciousness. In Marcel and Bisiach, 1988, 183–99.

Weiskrantz, L., Warrington, E. K., Saunders, M. D. and Marshall, J. 1974: Visual capacity in the hemianopic field following a restricted occipital ablation. *Brain*, 97, 709–28.

White, S. L. 1986: Curse of the qualia. *Synthese*, 68. Reprinted in S. L. White, *The Unity of the Self*, Cambridge, MA.: MIT Press, 75–101.

Whiten, A. and Byrne, R. W. 1987: Tactical deception in primates. *Behavioral and Brain Sciences*, 11, 231–73.

Wilensky, R. 1978: *Understanding Goal Based Stories*. Research Report 140. New Haven, CT: Yale University Department of Computer Science.

Williams, A. C. 1938: Perception of subliminal visual stimuli. *Journal of Psychology*, 6, 187–99.

Williams, B. A. 1976: The effects of unsignalled delayed reinforcement. *Journal of the Experimental Analysis of Behavior*, 26, 441–9.

Williams, M. D. 1976: Retrieval from very long-term memory. Unpublished doctoral dissertation. University of California, San Diego.

Witherspoon, D. and Allan, L. G. 1985: The effect of a prior presentation on temporal judgments in a perceptual identification task. *Memory and Cognition*, 13, 101–11.

Wittgenstein, L. 1921: *Tractatus Logical-Philosophicus*. Translated by D. F. Pears and B. F. McGuinness. London: Routledge and Kegan Paul, 1961.

Wittgenstein, L. 1953: *Philosophical Investigations*. Translated by G. E. M. Anscombe. Oxford: Blackwell.

Young, A. W. 1988: Functional organization of visual recognition. In L. Weiskrantz (ed.), *Thought Without Language*, Oxford: Oxford University Press, 78–107.

Young A. W. and de Haan, E. H. F. 1988: Boundaries of covert recognition in prosopagnosia. *Cognitive Neuropsychology*, 5, 317–36.

Young, A. W., de Haan, E. H. F. and Newcombe, F. 1990: Unawareness of impaired face recognition. *Brain and Cognition*, 14, 1–18.

Young, A. W. and Ellis, H. D. 1989: Childhood prosopagnosia. *Brain and Cognition*, 9, 16–47.

Young, A. W., Ellis, A. W., Flude, B. M., McWeeny, K. H. and Hay, D. C. 1986: Face-name interference. *Journal of Experimental Psychology: Human Perception and Performance*, 12, 466–75.

Young, A. W., Hay, D. C. and Ellis, A. W. 1985: The faces that launched a thousand slips: everyday difficulties and errors in recognizing people. *British Journal of Psychology*, 76, 495–523.

Young, A. W., Hellawell, D. and de Haan, E. H. F. 1988: Cross-domain semantic priming in normal subjects and a prosopagnosic patient. *Quarterly Journal of Experimental Psychology*, 40A, 561–80.

Zihl, J. 1980: 'Blindsight': improvement of visually guided eye movements by systematic practice in patients with cerebral blindness. *Neuropsychologia*, 18, 71–7.

Zihl, J. 1981: Recovery of visual functions in patients with cerebral blindness: effect of specific practice with saccadic localization. *Experimental Brain Research*, 44, 159–69.

Zihl, J. and von Cramon, D. 1979: Restitution of visual function in patients with cerebral blindness. *Journal of Neurology, Neurosurgery, and Psychiatry*, 42, 312–22.

Zihl, J. and von Cramon, D. 1985: Visual field recovery from scotoma in patients with postgeniculate damage. *Brain*, 108, 335–65.

Zihl, J., von Cramon, D. and Mai, N. 1983: Selective disturbance of movement vision after bilateral brain damage. *Brain*, 106, 313–40.

Zihl, J. and Werth, R. 1984: Contributions to the study of 'blindsight' – II. The role of specific practice for saccadic localization in patients with postgeniculate visual field defects. *Neuropsychologia,* 22, 13–22.

Zukav, G. 1979: *The Dancing Wu Li Masters: An Overview of the New Physics.* London: Bantam Books.

Index of Names

Index of Subjects

absent qualia (Block), 17–18, 20, 36, 123, 126–7, 129, 137, 145–7, 269
abstract emergentism, 164–8
access, notion of, 10–11, 125
access consciousness, 3, 10–13, 240–57
access to consciousness, failures of, 71–2
accessibility, possibility and objectivity, 186–7
action
    intentional account of, 106–20
    theory of the control of, 2–3
'action slips', 2, 3, 8
adaptation
    to environment, role of consciousness, 7, 74–89
    to omission schedules, 109–10, 113
akrasia, 242
Alice's Adventures in Wonderland, 43, 56, 108
amnesia, 48, 68, 70, 75–6, 82–3, 83, 147, 148, 153
analgesia, 247, 255n.
analogy, and indirect description, 187–9
animals
    intentionality of action in, 9, 105–20

intuitive ascription of phenomenal consciousness to, 25
see also bat; rats
anosognosia, 69–71
anthropomorphism, 112
Anton's syndrome, 69
appearance/reality distinction (Kripke), 122–4, 134, 136n.
attention
    'foveal' theory of, 271–2
    limitations of human mechanisms for, 271–2
attribution theory of remembering, 77, 79–82, 84–6
autobiographical memory *see* memory

bat
    film of, 263–70
    sonar echo, 263–6
    what it is like to be a, 15–16, 178–96, 259–70
be, something that it is like to, see phenomenal consciousness
behaviour
    ambiguous between intended and unintended, 92–104
    belief and desire criteria in intentional, 105–20

memory in the control of, 84
qualitative difference between
conscious and unconscious,
6–7, 41, 44, 55–6
behaviourism, 1–2, 115–16, 251,
257n.
belief criterion in intentional action,
106, 108–10, 118–20
beliefs, 9–10, 40
distinguished from subdoxastic
states, 11–13
false, 112–13
biologism, 248, 250, 253
bird's eye view, 258–9
blindness
cortical, 48
denial of *see* Anton's syndrome
partial *see* hemianopia
blindsight, 6–7, 38, 48, 59–63, 70,
73, 89, 147, 227, 228–9, 247
colour discriminations in
patients, 236–7
body–mind problem *see* mind–body
problem
brain
and consciousness, 155–77
limitations of power, 171–4
location of executive functions in,
83
brain injury, and visual
impairments, 58–73
brain-headed systems, 18, 20–1

'Cartesian Theatre', 31–2
case studies
blindsight in DB, 59–63
cognitive psychology of intention
in Dora, 90–104
prosopagnosia in PH, 65–7, 72
of psychoanalytic inference from
Miss Lucy R, 98–9, 102
unilateral neglect in PS, 68
word recognition impairment in
ML, 63
causal judgement, and intentional
action, 117–18

central state materialism, 18, 20
closed mindedness, 40
cognitive psychology
of intention (Freud), 90–104
as natural science and human
science, 90–1, 97–100, 104
colour, 35, 124–5, 138–42
discriminations in blindsight
patients, 236–7
qualia *see* redness
spectrum inversion 143–5, 269;
see also knowledge argument
(Jackson)
workings of vision, 265–6
colour-blindness, 246
communication, problems of,
269–70
computational model narratives,
and psychoanalysis, 8, 90–104
Computational Representational
Theory of Thought, 241–8
computational theory of mind,
166–7, 176n., 237
conceivability arguments, 35, 121–4,
126, 127–8, 130
concepts, narrow and broad
content, 132–4
confabulation, 77, 78
conflict of intentions, 95–7, 104
conscious awareness
indicators in the study of
unconscious perception, 44–7
measurement of, 44–56
theoretical constructs versus
empirical measures, 41–3
conscious recollection 7–8
as prerequisite for intentional
action, 74–89
see also memory
consciousness
attempts to define, 1
causal status of, 88–9
and cosmology, 155–77
different kinds of 3; *see also*
access consciousness;
phenomenal consciousness